THE FOUNDATIONS OF ADULT EDUCATION IN CANADA
Second Edition

DEDICATIONS

To Mary
 Gordon Selman

To all the members of the Canadian Association for Adult Education—past, present and future—for your vision, your commitment and your leadership
 Michael Cooke

To Jan
 Mark Selman

To my companion learners—Paige, Kimberly and Lesley
 Paul Dampier

The Foundations of Adult Education in Canada

Second Edition

GORDON SELMAN
Professor Emeritus
University of British Columbia

MICHAEL COOKE
George Brown College of Applied
Arts and Technology

MARK SELMAN
Simon Fraser University

PAUL DAMPIER
Northern Lights College

THOMPSON EDUCATIONAL PUBLISHING, INC.
Toronto

Canadian Cataloguing in Publication Data

Main entry under title:

The foundations of adult education in Canada.

First ed. written by Gordon Selman and Paul Dampier.
Includes index.
ISBN 1-55077-083-7
1. Adult education—Canada—History. I. Selman, Gordon R., 1927-

LC5254.S425   1997   374.971'09   C97-930493-8

ISBN 1-55077-083-7
Printed in Canada.

Table of Contents

Study groups at Morrell, PEI, with Catherine Mary ("Tat") Sears of Antigonish, taken at the time of the filming of *The Rising Tide*. Courtesy of Archives, St. Francis Xavier University. Original source unknown.

Preface

There is considerable concern in the field of adult education today that a tradition is being lost. Adult educators are generally aware that a field which at one time had its own vision of the kind of society it was helping to define and to bring about is increasingly losing its philosophical roots. Adult education is becoming a service industry instead of having its own philosophical foundation. Along with the advantages that flow from the professionalization and institutionalization of the field in recent decades, there has been a loss of a sense of direction and a sense of common purpose. It is not within the powers of the authors to persuade the field that it should be something other than it is, but part of the function of examining the foundations of adult education, which is our focus, is to describe and interpret what the field has been and to consider options as to where it may choose to go in the future. In fact, it is argued here that adult education is increasingly not one enterprise, but several, and that the lines between the different sectors are being increasingly clearly drawn.

A recent commentary about the state of Canada in the present decade makes the point that certain forces are causing the sense of common interest and common goals in Canadian society to be "hollowed out." It is being consciously hollowed out so that those promoting changes of a certain kind will find it easier to lead the country in other directions. If Canadians have no strong sense of what it is they stand for, it will be correspondingly easier to lead them away from previously established values and to change them into something else.

Could adult education be going through this same experience? Is the field, which has had a strong tradition of being part of a movement to make Canadian society a more caring, democratic and equitable one, being "denatured" as a result of forces that are tying adult education predominantly to vocational and technical matters and requiring it to be a slave to the cash register? Is the field, which has in the past been allied with the struggle for social betterment, now being forced to behave in such a way that it reinforces rather than ameliorates the gaps between the "haves" and the "have-nots" in Canadian society? Is this enterprise, which at one time established an impressive international reputation for educational programs related to what has been termed "the imaginative training for citizenship," lost the sense of challenge inherent in such a goal?

The casual observer might be forgiven for wondering why a book on the "foundations" of adult education—or of anything, for that matter—requires revision after less than a decade. Surely the foundations remain more or less the same, even if current events necessitate some altered responses. There are two main reasons why such a view is not satisfactory, at least not in the present instance. The first and more fundamental one is that the foundations of adult education include not only the history and nature of the field as it has developed over time, but also the nature of the society of which it is a part and which it is serving. If we know anything about contemporary society, it is that it is in a state of constant change, and at an ever accelerating rate. The experience of the 1990s has confirmed this fact once again, perhaps to an extent equaled by no other decade. The other reason why revisions are called for at this time arises from the changes which have taken place in the practice of adult education in these few years. Two phrases, "new communications technologies" and "the budget crunch," will serve to suggest some dimensions of these changes. To these factors must be added a third, less majestic one— one that in some respects the authors were aware of when the first edition went to press (and in others respects have been brought to their attention in the interim)—the book had gaps in its coverage and areas which could stand more satisfactory treatment. So when the publisher came to the point of needing to reprint the book, the authors readily agreed that some revisions would be useful.

Adult educators are extremely conscious of change. We are constantly speaking of change as a reason why we and our fellow citizens must continue to learn throughout our lives. We might even be seen to be among the "ambulance chasers" of change, attempting to be on hand whenever men and women are faced with change and needing to respond to it through learning. The marketing approach to our work, which has been forced ever more stringently upon so many practitioners in recent years, has perhaps accentuated that situation. Financial restrictions are forcing the field ever more exclusively to follow in the wake of public demand. For all the Club of Rome's urging us to go beyond "crisis learning" to "maintenance learning," by and large we operate in a responsive rather than a preventive mode.

Most adult educators are particularly aware at the present time of how change is affecting their work. Institutional roles are shifting, boundaries between the public and private sectors do not stay the same for long, financial pressures on their activity that seemed severe enough have become even more extreme in the 1990s, and the impact of changes in the technology of communication—all these constantly present new challenges.

The field of adult education has taken on a greater significance since the publication of the first edition of this book. This has flowed from the increased recognition in modern society of the necessity of lifelong learning, of which the adult education sector is a part, and perhaps the part which is most in need of expansion. At the beginning of the 1990s, there was evidence that policy makers and educational officials were accepting the concept of lifelong learning and paying more attention to the provision of learning opportunities for adults. This was particularly true in the case of the upgrading of the Canadian work force. What has taken place during the 1990s is a dramatically more widespread acceptance of the importance of lifelong learning on the part of many outside the education and vocational training sectors. Those involved in many other fields—organizational development, management training, social psychology, political science and citizenship, to name but a few examples—have now taken up the theme of lifelong learning and have elaborated its implications for their fields. In many of these other areas, though the term which is used is lifelong learning, its application is mainly in the field of adult learning.

The widening of interest in adult and lifelong learning has important implications for the field of adult education. In the main, the most visible and well known "adult educators," as the term has traditionally been understood, have generally been located in educational institutions and in the educational or training units of other organizations. As the implications or applications of adult learning are perceived in many other areas of society, the professional functions of the adult educator are required in other settings. This has led to two major changes in the field, and will likely lead to a third.

In the first instance, educational institutions have been doing a great deal of work under contract for other organizations. (This has been particularly welcome in a period of financial stringency in that it brings additional income into the institution.) The second noticeable trend has been the number of adult education professionals who have gone into the consulting business rather than work for educational institutions. As private entrepreneurs, usually without the overhead costs and policy encumbrances of the large institutions, such persons have frequently found ample opportunity for successful practice. The third trend which will presumably follow will be the increased tendency for governments and institutions outside of the education sector to employ (or train for themselves) specialists in adult education.

This second edition of *The Foundations of Adult Education in Canada* has been prepared by a somewhat altered team of editors. Although a great deal of his work continues to appear in the book, Paul Dampier, who wrote approximately half of the first edition, was not able to take part in the revision process. Taking his place along with Gordon and Mark Selman is Michael Cooke, known to many in the field as the former Executive Director of the

Canadian Association for Adult Education and current Dean of the Faculty of Community Services and Health Services at George Brown College of Applied Arts and Technology in Toronto. His experience in education, both in Canada and internationally, his knowledge of French, and his relationships with adult educators in Quebec bring new strengths to the team.

When the first edition of this book was published in early 1991, the authors and publisher hoped that it would at least in part meet the long-felt need for a Canadian text on the foundations of adult education. Here we were, in a country which had made many significant contributions to the field of adult education and had gained an outstanding international reputation in the field, having to rely on texts that were published in other countries and which made little, if any, reference to the Canadian experience. Further, such foreign texts had nothing to say about the socio-political setting in which adult education had developed in this country and which had in many respects influenced the nature of the field. The authors have been pleased that the first edition of this book has been widely read and has been adopted for use in a number of professional training programs in colleges and universities across the country.

In preparing this second edition we have considered carefully the reactions and suggestions we have received from others in the field, and to the extent we felt ready to do so, have responded accordingly. Any treatment of the foundations of our field calls for judgments based on authors' social and political views. Every effort has been made to provide a balanced and reasonably comprehensive view of the field, but we recognize that our interpretations of the Canadian adult education experience, and of the work of those who have played a part in it, may well differ from those of others.

The greatest single regret of the original authors was their inability to include in the book a major section on adult education in Quebec. Apart from reference to some individual programs in Quebec and a brief section on the development of public policy towards adult education in that province, the story of the field in French-speaking Canada was not dealt with. This gap was explicitly recognized in the first edition. We are very happy that, as a result of the work of Vince Greason, this edition gives a much more comprehensive treatment to the field in Quebec. Currently, Vince is a staff person for the Mouvement d'éducation et d'action communautaire du Québec (MEPACQ), a provincial organization representing popular education groups throughout Quebec. During the 1970s he worked with several local popular education groups in Quebec City and in the 1980s with the South African Congress of Trade Unions Solidarity Committee and the Metro Labour Education Centre in Toronto.

Two other significant gaps in the first edition have been accorded more extended treatment this time, thanks to experts in those areas. The first is that of women and adult education. It is clear that women have provided remarkable leadership throughout the history of adult education. They have been particularly influential in the voluntary sector and in the administration of adult education programs. However, their story and their perspective is notably absent in much of the literature. With this in mind, the authors sought assistance from women who are knowledgeable about the field and were especially pleased that Dr. Shauna Butterwick and Dr. Tammy Dewar agreed to contribute to this volume. Shauna Butterwick has written a general appraisal of women's contributions to adult education in Canada and has reflected on their experience (see Chapter 4). She is an Assistant Professor in the Adult Education Program in the Department of Educational Studies at the University of British Columbia and an active member of a variety of feminist and advocacy organizations, including the Canadian Congress for Learning Opportunities for Women (CCLOW), the Women's Employment and Training Council (WETC), as well as the British Columbia Chapter of the Canadian Centre for Policy Alternatives (CCPA). Tammy Dewar holds an M.Ed. and Ph.D. in adult education. She has experience in training instruction and design, workplace learning distance/on-line instruction, women's issues in adult education and postmodern approaches to research. Currently, she is based in Calgary and is working as a consultant in adult education. Her contribution to this volume appears as Chapter 11 and provides a postmodern perspective and critique.

The second area referred to is that of education in the labour movement. We are delighted to include three pieces on the subject in Chapters 2, 6 and 12 respectively written by D'Arcy Martin. For the past seventeen years, D'Arcy has been a leading educator in the Canadian labour movement, first with the Steelworkers, then the Communications Workers, and until recently with the Communications, Energy and Paperworkers Union of Canada. He is also a founding member of the Mayworks Festival of Working People and the Arts and the Ontario Workers Arts and Heritage Centre. We were also pleased to be able to enlist the assistance of Bill Fallis, a Professor at George Brown College, in connection with our examination of the impact of technological developments on the delivery of instruction.

The roles of the four authors whose names appear on the title page have been varied. Paul Dampier who was engaged in another project when this one came along, reluctantly decided not to take part. A great deal of his earlier work, most notably in Chapters 5 to 8, is retained in this second edition.

Michael Cooke, who is Dean of the Faculty of Community Services and Health Sciences at George Brown College in Toronto, assisted with the review of the entire first edition, suggesting necessary changes and updating. In addition, he updated Chapter 8 on public policy in the various jurisdictions of Canada with extensive help from a team of informants from across the country, many of them long-standing members and friends of the Canadian Association for Adult Education. They included John Fisher and June Morgan in Alberta, Kathryn Barker, Elayne Harris and Ron Faris in British Columbia, Louise Gordon, Carolyn Hole, Robin Millar and Deo Poonwassie in Manitoba, Patrick Flanagan and John Morris in New Brunswick, Barb Case in Newfoundland, Teresa MacNeil in Nova Scotia, Diane Laberge, Terry Anne Boyle, and Alan Thomas in Ontario, Barbara McNutt and Don Glendenning in Prince Edward Island, Wendy Wright and Richard Bonokoski in Saskatchewan, Sally Ross and Aron Senkpiel in the Yukon, and Mark Cleveland in the Northwest Territories. Michael also co-ordinated Vince Greason's work on Chapter 3 on Quebec, D'Arcy Martin's sections on the labour movement and Bill Fallis's piece on technology which is included in Chapter 12.

Mark Selman took part in general discussions about the second edition, reviewed and commented on much of the manuscript and revised his chapter on philosophical considerations. Mark is Associate Dean of Continuing Studies at Simon Fraser University and an Associate Professor in the Humanities at the same university. He is a past president of the Canadian Association for the Study of Adult Education.

Gordon Selman, who is a Professor Emeritus of the University of British Columbia, co-ordinated the entire project. In particular, he wrote the new final chapter, updated the rest of the book, and liaised with Shauna Butterwick and Tammy Dewar on their chapters on women and adult education.

From the beginning, those involved in this book have been aware that, in a sense, they have limited their approach to the "foundations" of the field. It is possible to argue that we have included little, for instance, on the psychological foundations of the field. This has been a conscious choice, based on the view that other sources exist, both Canadian and foreign, which provide such information. We have concentrated on those aspects of the foundations that are more country-specific—the nature of the field in Canada and the political, social and cultural milieu in which adult education in this country has functioned. This is not to say that the topics on which we have chosen to concentrate are more important. Rather we have tried to focus on what we see to be the most crucial gaps in the literature that is otherwise available. We rejoice in the fact that scholarly work in Canada is providing us with an ever-richer sense of the context of our work in this country. We hope that this second edition is a significant further contribution to that effort.

Complementary Texts

This book is published along with two recommended companion volumes: (1) *Learning for Life: Canadian Readings in Adult Education* (edited by Sue M. Scott, Bruce Spencer and Alan Thomas) and (2) *The Purposes of Adult Education: A Guide for Students* (by Bruce Spencer). The latter is intended as a companion both to this volume and to *Learning for Life*.

1

Terms and Functions

It is important to any field of practice, and certainly to any field of study, to be able to identify the essential characteristics of the enterprise. These matters are far from settled in the field of adult education. Or perhaps it is more accurate to say that they have been settled repeatedly to the satisfaction of particular scholars or practitioners, but have not remained settled. It is small comfort that many other fields are in the same situation at the present time.

The matter is complicated by the fact that, as Knowles has pointed out,[1] the single phrase "adult education" is used to refer to at least three different phenomena. It refers, first of all, to a set of activities. The sum total of all acts of participation by individuals, and programs offered by a vast range of institutions, provides us with an overall picture of adult education as an activity in our society. Secondly, the term is used to refer to the intellectual process by means of which adults seek, or are assisted, to learn things. This comes close to what might be termed the discipline of adult education. And thirdly, the phrase is used to refer to the social system which is made up of individuals and organizations concerned with the education of adults. This field, or "movement," as it has frequently been termed, has worked towards the increased recognition by our society of the importance of adult education and has tried to gain greater resources and policy support for the work. Adult education is dealt with in all three of these dimensions in this volume. Fascinatingly complex, it is; tidy, it isn't. An insistence on orderliness, precision and tight typologies may just be a distinct liability in coming to a full appreciation of the nature of adult education.

In this chapter, the term adult education will be examined and defined, with some attention to its historical evolution. This is followed by the description of two other sets of terms, the first group which are frequently used synonymously with adult education and a second group which are related to, but quite distinctly different from, adult education. Next, some general methodo-

---

[1] M.S. Knowles, *A History of the Adult Education Movement in the United States* (Huntington, N.Y.: Krieger, 1977) p.viii.

logical terms will be described and distinguished, as will their implications for the relationship of the learner to educational resources. Finally, there is a section on the functions of adult education.

Naming the Enterprise

It is a standing joke in adult education circles that there is such a lack of agreement about some basic terminology in the field. The problem—to the extent that it is one—is not just that practitioners are unclear what the terms mean as they use them; it is that, there being no agreed upon set of terms in the field, people use different terms for the same thing. Adult educators, depending on their institutional setting, may refer to their work as community education, continuing education, further education, adult training, continuing studies, extension—or even adult education. There is no standardized lexicon of terms in the field, though Verner[2] and others, from time to time, have suggested terminological schemes. Perhaps the field is too diverse, too subject to regional and occupational idiosyncrasies and developing too rapidly to make the prospect of standardized terminology a realistic one.

There has come to be a significant difference in meaning between the two terms, "the education of adults" and "adult education." The education of adults is used as a more inclusive term and refers to all purposeful efforts by which adults seek to learn, or are assisted to learn. The term adult education, though somewhat fluid in meaning, tends to refer to a narrower spectrum of such activities, ones which are designed especially for adults and usually are part-time or, if full-time, of relatively short duration. For instance, adults who decide to return to college or university on a full-time basis are certainly adults engaged in education, but would not normally be included in the statistics of adult education activities.

In this and related cases, adult education can be seen to be an administrative category. Under one set of circumstances, the adults may be considered "regular" students; under another, "adult education" students. If the persons referred to above studied the very same subject, but did so on a part-time, evening course basis, they might well be counted as adult education students. If they attended full time, they would not.

In many of its settings, be it school board night classes or company training programs, for instance, adult education has developed historically as an "added on" and often secondary or marginal activity for the sponsoring organization. And for the vast majority of adult learners, participation in educa-

---

[2] C. Verner, *A Conceptual Scheme for the Identification and Classification of Processes* (Chicago: Adult Education Association of the USA, 1962); C. Verner, "Definition of Terms" in G. Jensen, A.A. Liveright & W. Hallenbeck, *Adult Education: Outlines of an Emerging Field of University Study* (Washington: Adult Education Association of the USA, 1964).

tional activities is a part-time, or if full-time, a short duration, activity. As a result many definitions of the term adult education which were developed in the early years of the movement included the idea of its part-time nature. One definition, for instance, is that provided by Bryson in what is generally considered the earliest text book for the field. He defined adult education as "all activities with an educational purpose that are carried on by people engaged in the ordinary business of life."[3] Other definitions of this type referred in some way to the part-time or short-term nature of adult education activities.

Although it is clearly the case that most adult learners pursue their further education on a part-time basis, most definitions of adult education no longer include such a reference. In what is considered the starting point of many modern developments in adult education, *The 1919 Report* to the British Ministry of Reconstruction by its Committee on Adult Education defined adult education as follows:

> ... all the deliberate efforts by which men and women attempt to satisfy their thirst for knowledge, to equip themselves for their responsibilities as citizens and members of society or to find opportunities for self expression.[4]

The perspective represented in this definition was that of the adult learner and emphasized the purposes for which the adult engaged in this activity. In his well-known work *The Design of Education*, Houle reflected this and added to it. Adult education is the process by which men and women

> ... seek to improve themselves or their society by increasing their skill, knowledge or sensitivities; or it is any process by which individuals, groups or institutions try to help men and women improve in these ways.[5]

Houle concluded by placing emphasis on the process by means of which the providers of adult education relate to the adult. It was this element on which Verner chose to concentrate:

> Adult education is the action of an external agent in purposefully ordering behaviour into planned systematic experiences that can result in learning for those for whom such activity is supplemental to their primary role in society, and which involves some continuity in an exchange relationship between the agent and the learner so that the educational process is under constant supervision and direction.[6]

These two elements are combined in what is currently perhaps the most frequently cited definition of adult education, one contained in the Recommendation on the Development of Adult Education, which was prepared by

---

[3] L. Bryson, *Adult Education* (New York: American Book Co., 1936) p.3.

[4] *The 1919 Report*, Report of the Adult Education Committee to the United Kingdom, Ministry of Reconstruction (Nottingham: University of Nottingham, 1980 [1919]) p.34.

[5] C.O. Houle, *The Design of Education* (San Francisco: Jossey-Bass, 1972) p.32.

[6] C. Verner, *A Conceptual Scheme*, p.2-3.

the United Nations Educational, Scientific and Cultural Organization (UNESCO) at the request of member states and formally approved in 1976. It defined adult education as:

> ... the entire body of organized educational processes, whatever the content, level and method, whether formal or otherwise, whether they prolong or replace initial education in schools, colleges and universities as well as in apprenticeship, whereby persons regarded as adult by the society to which they belong develop their abilities, enrich their knowledge, improve their technical or professional qualifications or turn them in a new direction and bring about changes in their attitudes or behaviour in the twofold perspective of full personal development and participation in balanced and independent social, economic and cultural development ...[7]

This somewhat cumbersome, but inclusive definition acknowledges the awkward issue of how to define adult. Even within any one society, it is not a simple matter to deal with this question. Age is certainly the key factor, but status of adulthood is variously defined in various social roles, such as in the courts, the right to drive a motor vehicle, to get married, or to vote. The framers of the UNESCO Recommendation, faced with the problem of relating to all countries in the world, acknowledged the necessity of defining adulthood but termed it, "persons regarded as adult by the societies to which they belong."

It is important to make the distinction between adult education and adult learning. Learning is the intended end-product of education. Much, if not most, of adult learning in our society takes place outside of our educational institutions and the programs which they offer. As Thomas has put it, "education floats in a sea of learning."[8]

The creation of educational programs comes about when the learning of certain things in our society is seen by constituted authorities as desirable or necessary, or when opportunities to learn are so consistently in demand by individual adults that there is clearly merit—or profit—in providing the services. If the society decides that certain kinds of vocational or technical training for adults is necessary in order to make possible the economic advancement of the country as a whole, then educational programs are created, or purchased, to meet that need. Similarly, if it is realized that a lack of basic education or that a lack of working knowledge of the language of the country on the part of adult immigrants is limiting to both the individuals and the community, services are put in place to correct the situation. From the adults' point of view, if they cannot speak the language used around them, or

---

[7] UNESCO, *Recommendation on the Development of Adult Education*, published in Canada (Ottawa: Canadian Commission for UNESCO, 1980 [1976]) p.3.

[8] A.M. Thomas, "Government and Adult Learning," in F. Cassidy & R. Faris (Eds.), *Choosing Our Future* (Toronto: OISE, 1987) p.109.

if, in view of technological change, they now need to become computer literate, for instance, then they will in many cases go seeking the opportunity to learn these things and there will be a response in the form of educational programs—from the public or the private sectors.

Parallel or Overlapping Terms

There are several terms related to adult education, some used synonymously with it, which are commonly encountered in the field.

Andragogy. This term is frequently heard in connection with adult education. The word is in a sense a contrasting term to "pedagogy." The dictionary defines the latter as "the science or art of teaching," but the Greek root of the word contains a reference to "boy" or "child." The word andragogy makes use of a different Greek root, and was invented to refer specifically to the "science or art of teaching adults." The term was first used in Europe but was given greater prominence when it was adopted by Malcolm Knowles and featured in his widely used text book for the field, *The Modern Practice of Adult Education*, which was first published in the early 1970s.[9] The term has since come into wide use, particularly in academic circles. It is, for instance, used in the official name of the academic program on adult education of the Université de Montréal.

Continuing Education. This term is used by many as synonymous with adult education. In a number of institutional settings, however, there is the connotation of furthering one's education beyond a significant level which has already been achieved. Universities, for instance, tend to be comfortable with the term on the assumption that it implies the subsequent education of their graduates, or at least educational activities at a reasonably advanced level. There is a relatively recent movement in the field to broaden the meaning of the term by extending it to cover any situation where the person is "moving on," particularly within the more formal, credential-related aspects of education.[10] The term "further education" is sometimes used with a similar meaning (though in Britain it tends to be vocational in emphasis).

Extension. The term extension has had two main uses in North America. The first is often referred to as "agricultural extension" and relates to educational services provided particularly to those who live in rural and small town settings, and is often vocational in emphasis. There is a long tradition of such work in North America, where governments, universities and other agencies have provided a wide variety of vocational, social and cultural programs for rural people.[11] There has also been a strong tradition in North America of

---

[9] M.S. Knowles, *The Modern Practice of Adult Education* (Chicago: Association Press/Follett Publishing, 1980).

[10] A.M. Thomas, "Government and Adult Learning," p.106.

universities referring to most or all their adult education activities as university extension. The term was borrowed initially from Great Britain, and in the early decades involved universities mainly in providing, in another place or at another hour of the day, a version of many of the same kinds of teaching (usually without written assignments) which they delivered to their "regular" students on campus. In the early years of this century, a new, more varied and broadly based type of university extension service was developed in North America and it generally retained the use of the term extension. In recent decades, however, the term extension has been seen by some in the universities as reflecting a concept of the institution's role which is too broad in character and a number of universities have changed the name of their "extension" units to such terms as continuing education, continuing studies or some variation on the theme.

Community Education. This term is used by some synonymously with adult education. This is true particularly of those working at a local or community level. The adult education unit of a local school board, for instance, is frequently called by such a name. But in many instances there is also a significant philosophical or value-related dimension to the use of this term which sets it apart from the field of adult education as a whole. For many practitioners of "community education" there is a wish and intention that what they are doing should have a vital connection with the character of community life in the region they are serving. Rather than simply respond to the expressed needs of individuals for educational services, they wish to relate their programs to forces working for change and improvement in community life. They wish to make a difference to the quality of life in their communities.[12] Such a point of view goes back in Canada at least as far as the "lighted schoolhouse" movement of the 1920s,[13] the folk school movement of the 1930s and later[14] and the community school movement of more recent decades.[15]

Related Terms

There are a number of terms which are a step further removed from adult education than the ones dealt with in the previous section but which are closely related or overlapping in some respects.

---

[11] D.J. Blackburn (Ed.), *Extension Handbook* (Guelph: University of Guelph, 1984).

[12] S. Brookfield, *Adult Learners, Adult Education and the Community* (New York: Teachers College Press, 1984).

[13] R. England, *Living, Learning, Remembering* (Vancouver: University of British Columbia, Center for Continuing Education, 1980).

[14] J.R. Kidd (Ed.), *Adult Education in Canada* (Toronto: Canadian Association for Adult Education, 1950).

[15] P.F. Prout, *Community Schools in Canada* (Toronto: Canadian Education Association, 1977).

Lifelong Education and Lifelong Learning. Perhaps because adult educators have been among those who have promoted the concept of lifelong education in recent decades, and of course because lifelong education does include the adult years, there has been a tendency in some quarters to confuse—or use interchangeably—the terms adult education and lifelong education. In fact they are quite different: lifelong education refers to educational influences on the person over the entire life span—during childhood and youth, as well as the adult years—and adult education refers only to the latter. The confusion of the two terms was reinforced by the classic report of the Adult Education Committee of the U.K. Ministry of Reconstruction in 1919, which stated that adult education should be a "permanent national necessity, an inseparable aspect of citizenship, and therefore should be both universal and lifelong."[16] In more recent decades, the concept of lifelong education is one which has been developed in the work of UNESCO, since approximately 1960. The idea was given great impetus by the report of UNESCO's International Commission on the Development of Education (the Faure Commission) and its report *Learning to Be*,[17] which appeared in 1972. In this report and several publications which have subsequently been produced by the UNESCO Institute on Education (Hamburg), the idea of lifelong education and of "the learning society" have been further developed.[18] Within such a framework, the society's formal educational institutions (schools, colleges, universities, and so on) are seen to be only part of the resources in society for the education of the individual; the home, the workplace, one's social and recreational activities and other aspects of life are all seen to be the settings for educational activities in "the learning society." Canadians played a significant part in developing the concept of lifelong education. Dr. J. Roby Kidd explored the territory in two books[19] before the term gained wide currency and Dr. Alan Thomas published several papers during the 1960s which analyzed the implications of the concept.[20]

From one point of view, lifelong learning can simply be recognized as a fact. It is clear that individuals, some perhaps more actively than others, do go on learning throughout their whole life span—from the cradle to the grave. The desirability of lifelong learning has been expressed in the literature of

---

[16] *The 1919 Report*, p.5.

[17] UNESCO, *Learning To Be* (Paris: UNESCO, 1972).

[18] R.H. Dave (Ed.), *Foundations of Lifelong Education* (Oxford: Pergamon, 1976); A.J. Cropley (Ed.), *Towards a System of Lifelong Education* (Oxford: Pergamon, 1980); C.K. Knapper & A.J. Cropley, *Lifelong Learning and Higher Education* (London: Croom Helm, 1985).

[19] J.R. Kidd, *How Adults Learn* (New York: Association Press, 1959); and J.R. Kidd, *The Implications of Continuous Learning* (Toronto: W.J. Gage, 1966).

[20] A.M. Thomas, "The Learning Society" in CAAE/ICEA, *National Conference on Adult Education* (Toronto/Montreal: CAAE/ICEA, 1961); and CAAE, *A White Paper on the Education of Adults in Canada* (Toronto: CAAE, n.d. [1966]).

societies since ancient times, but has received more focussed attention, in tandem with lifelong education, in the last few decades. Although lifelong learning may be associated with learning for any purpose, there has been a strong, perhaps dominant, philosophical thrust which associates it with liberal-democratic values, "education for liberation" and "self-fulfilment."[21] The writings of Paul Lengrand[22] in the late 1960s and the UNESCO report *Learning to Be* of 1972 helped to establish this philosophical direction, and this has been developed further in the work of UNESCO's Institute of Education at Hamburg. The terms lifelong education and lifelong learning have now become coin of the realm in educational discussion, embracing but going far beyond the field of adult education.

Open Learning. The term open learning has emerged in the last few decades. It is related to the idea of "the learning society," which is in turn associated with lifelong learning. The terminology was borrowed in part from the British institution, the Open University, which began operation in 1971.[23] Open learning, like many educational terms, is rather variously defined, but the connotation is that of open accessibility to and utilization of resources for the assistance of learning. Rather than be limited to particular curricula, places or times for study, the learner has access to a wide range of resources which may be utilized when and as the learner sees fit. The emphasis is on giving learners the optimum degree of control over their own learning, and in such a situation the teacher, if there is one present (often the expert is present in the form of books, programmed or modularized instructional units, and so on), is seen as a facilitator or advisor, rather than as a content expert who directs the educational process. The term open learning is used in various ways. One emphasizes that all learners have access to instructional resources, rather than only those who have certain levels of formal education or certification. Another use of the term refers to a local learning centre—in an industry, for instance—where the employee has access to a range of educational resources and may utilize these as they are relevant to his or her needs, and at a time and pace which are convenient.

Recurrent Education. Although the term recurrent education is used rather loosely in the field, it is appropriately restricted to forms of organization of the world of work and the world of education in such a way that the individual may move back and forth between the two during the adult working years.[24]

---

[21] C.K Knapper & A.J. Cropley, *Lifelong Learning and Higher Education*, p.19.

[22] P. Lengrand, *An Introduction to Lifelong Education* (Paris: UNESCO, 1970).

[23] N. MacKenzie, N. Postgate & J. Scupham (Eds.), *Open Learning* (Paris: UNESCO, 1975); W. Perry, *The Open University* (San Francisco: Jossey-Bass, 1977); E. Stabler, *Founders* (Edmonton: University of Alberta, 1986).

[24] OECD, *Recurrent Education: Trends and Issues* (Paris: OECD/Center for Educational Research and Innovation, 1975).

The concept was developed in Sweden in the 1960s and introduced by that country to the Organization for Economic Co-operation and Development (OECD), where it relatively rapidly gained acceptance among some of the more industrialized countries. The key to a system of recurrent education is paid educational leave, which makes it possible for employees to take time off from their working careers in order to return to full-time or part-time education and not suffer undue disadvantage in either setting—work or education. Legislation in support of various forms of recurrent education has existed in Europe since the late 1960s.[25] Recurrent education should not be understood only as a way for workers to keep up to date with their vocations. The originators of the concept saw various social benefits as well. Youth who were restless in school could go into the world of work at the end of Grade 10, with opportunities provided for them to return to education when they had a clearer sense of what they wanted to do. In conditions of high rates of unemployment, many persons could be productively employed in furthering their education. And older workers, who may have received relatively limited formal education in their youth, could return to education. Recurrent education as a formal or comprehensive policy has received some study in North America and has found its way into some settings (often through union or other agreements) but has yet to be widely adopted on this continent.

Community Development. Community development is an educational and social process which has been closely associated with adult education—and vice versa. There have been adult education specialists who have claimed that community development is a sub-division of their field,[26] but that is not the general view. Community development is usually seen as a process by which members of a community, however defined, determine to take stock of their community, set goals for desirable change and work towards those goals. It is clear that in the process of community development there is need for a great deal of learning on the part of those involved—about the state of their community, the goals which can be agreed upon, the resources available to assist the community in its actions, the range of options available and the management of the group processes involved in all these efforts. As set forth so effectively by Lovett[27] and Brookfield,[28] the community development process, far from being contained within the field of adult education, properly requires the leadership of a range of professionals—in such fields as social work,

---

[25] C. Titmus, *Strategies for Adult Education* (Chicago: Follett, 1981).

[26] C. Verner & A. Booth, *Adult Education* (New York: Center for Applied Research in Education, 1964).

[27] T. Lovett, *Adult Education, Community Development and the Working Class* (London: Ward Lock Educational, 1975).

[28] S. Brookfield, *Adult Learners, Adult Education and the Community.*

community planning and public administration—as well as a range of content experts, selected in accordance with the goals identified by the community. Canada has a rich experience in many aspects of community development, as revealed in Draper's volume, *Citizen Participation: Canada*, and other sources.[29]

Some General Methodological Distinctions

It may also be helpful at the outset to describe some broad categories related to the methodology or organization of content in the field. They help us to think in a more systematic way about the multiplicity of methods and approaches which are employed.

Social Organization of the Learner. The popular image of adult education activity is that of the class being taught by an expert or teacher who knows more about the subject than do the students and who sets about teaching it to them. Indeed a vast amount of adult education follows that pattern. The instructional techniques utilized by the teacher may vary, according to what is being taught—be it Greek history, how to manage your investments, how to repair your outboard motor, how to perform certain technical tasks on the job, how to bake bread or how to draw the human figure—but the basic relationship of student to teacher may be essentially the same. There are other kinds of group activities, however, where there is no acknowledged expert present. These may be discussion groups where those present are sharing their experience and knowledge. They may be groups in which the members take turns studying up on topics and presenting information about them to their colleagues. It may be a case of a group of citizens discussing a subject for the purpose of making a decision about future action. Another variation of such "peer" groups consists of the members all having shared some experience—reading a book, seeing a play, hearing a record or listening to or watching a broadcast and then engaging in a discussion of the topic or the experience. Some such peer groups have designated discussion leaders and some do not.

The other setting in which the learner may be situated is to be alone. Considerable research has been carried out in recent years, by Tough[30] and many others, into what Tough has termed the self-directed learner. This refers to individuals who set about to learn something but who do not go to a class or in any other way put themselves under the tutelage of a teacher or agency, and who remain in control of the educational process themselves. The re-

---

[29] J. Draper (Ed.), *Citizen Participation: Canada* (Toronto: New Press, 1971); Department of Adult Education, Ontario Institute for Studies in Education, *Second National Workshop on Community Development* (Toronto: Dept. of Adult Education, OISE, 1969); J. Lotz, *Understanding Canada* (Toronto: NC Press, 1977).

[30] A. Tough, *The Adult's Learning Projects* (Toronto: OISE, 1971).

search into this phenomenon indicates that almost everyone engages in such self-directed education. In many cases, however, the learner is studying or learning alone but is under the direction of some other agency. Study in such a setting is a rapidly growing phenomenon in our society, a development which is spurred on by technological change, most notably in the use of the computer. The traditional form of such education was the correspondence or guided reading course. The student was directed to read certain texts or carry out certain work and then submit an assignment for marking to a tutor or sponsoring agency. The course often concluded with an examination. This method relied on the printed or written word and usually involved mailing assignments back and forth. What was at one time called correspondence education has in recent years become distance education (that is, the teacher or agency is at a distance removed from the student). Whereas instruction and response traditionally involved only the mails, now there is considerable reliance on the telephone, audio and video tapes, broadcasts to augment other materials and, in some cases, local study and tutoring centres where students can seek needed assistance or contact with other students. Another major form of study by oneself is modularized instruction, sometimes computer-based. The student is "led through" a course of instruction, asked to respond frequently in order to demonstrate whether the material has been learned, and then given further instruction, depending on the success of the feedback. A third type of setting for the individual learner consists of the local resource or open learning centre. In this case the student is provided with a range of learning aids—books, tapes, programmed instruction, manuals—and is able to utilize these resources at the time and to the extent he or she wishes.

In addition to the group settings and individualized settings illustrated above, it may be appropriate to refer to community settings. These are group situations as well but may be distinguishable on the basis of their focus of interest. Gatherings which are part of the community development process, for instance, may be organized in order to take stock of community opinion or to come to a conclusion about choices to be made. There may be a substantial element of education or learning as part of the occasion, but the ultimate focus may not be on the learning so much as on securing satisfactory community representation and making decisions.

Organization of Content. Current thinking about the way in which education, including adult education, is organized in terms of the content and the relationship between the learner and the sponsor of the activity divides the field into three main approaches: formal, non-formal and informal education. Such terminology is in use among educational planners at the national and international levels,[31] and has readily been adopted by adult education in that

---

[31] P.H. Coombs, *The World Crisis in Education: The View from the Eighties* (New York: Oxford,

it fits well with the large variety of approaches utilized in that field. Formal education is the type of program format associated with full-time study in traditional educational institutions. It usually involves comprehensive curricula, is staged or graded into multi-year levels and is linked to a graduated system of certification or accreditation. It has been described by Coombs as "institution bound" or "time bound," in that normally students are required to move at a certain pace through the system.

Non-formal education comprises all other organized, systematic educational activity which is carried out in society, whether offered by educational institutions or any other agency. It is aimed at facilitating selected types of learning on the part of particular sub-groups in the population. It may, for instance, take the form of a one-week short course, a one-day conference, a series of evening classes, a correspondence course, or some other form of instruction, the essential characteristic being that the event has been consciously planned as an educational experience. Non-formal education may include such activities as a literacy class, a short course for up-dating a professional person, an agricultural extension course for farmers or rural women, a short course for the training of volunteers, community programs in the field of health, nutrition, family planning or co-operatives or a class in music appreciation. This approach is well suited to many learning needs, and to societies in various stages of development. Similar activities have in some circles traditionally been called non-credit courses, but that term does involve another set of issues.

The third type of educational approach, informal education, is frequently unorganized, unsystematic, and at times perhaps even unintentional. Coombs states that this third type "accounts for the bulk of any person's total lifetime learning" and he defines it as "the lifelong process by which every person acquires and accumulates knowledge, skills, attitudes and insights from daily experiences and exposure to the environment—at home, at work, at play."[32] International planners in the field of education such as Coombs and Lowe suggest that in considering the educational system and resources of any society, it is appropriate to consider not only the formal educational systems in operation but also the network of non-formal and informal educational capabilities as well.[33]

1985); J. Lowe, *The Education of Adults: A World Perspective* (Toronto: OISE, 1982).

[32] P.H. Coombs, *The World Crisis in Education*, p.24.

[33] P.H. Coombs, *The World Crisis in Education*; J. Lowe, *The Education of Adults*.

The Relationship of the Learner to Educational Resources

While this topic overlaps in some respects with ones covered elsewhere in this section, it is of major relevance to adult education practice and deserves separate mention. It has to do with the accessibility of instructional resources in the variety of educational settings among which the adult moves, and may make choices. At one end of the spectrum, perhaps, is the case of an institution or set of institutions which has the exclusive right to grant certain credentials and which prescribes the means by which these credentials may be earned. An example might be a medical or other professional faculty at a university, which limits its intake, prescribes the program and means of study and constitutes the only means of gaining entry to professional practice. A further step along the continuum may be represented by a college which controls certain certification (a degree, diploma, certificate) but where entry into the program is reasonably open and the courses are available by full or part-time study, and perhaps by distance education delivery, as well as face to face.

Another type of situation may be represented by a proprietary secretarial school. Entry may be open to anyone who is reasonably competent in the basics, intake may be on a continuous basis and instruction may be individualized and self-paced, utilizing instructional materials which are available to students and non-students alike. Further, the skills being learned may be achievable by other means and the opportunity for gaining employment based on those skills may not be limited on the basis of how they were achieved. (Employers may be quite accustomed to doing their own testing of prospective employees for their competence in office or technical skills, but they are frequently prepared to take some other institution's word for the knowledge or skills acquired in a university, an accountancy program, or in some other educational program.)

Another step along the continuum may be represented by the distance education student; for instance, someone taking a correspondence course. Having enrolled, the student typically acquires instructional resources in the form of a manual of instruction and text books. The student is then free to proceed at whatever pace he or she chooses (usually within certain limits), calling on the resources provided and any others available. But if the course is for some form of credit, there will be restrictions in terms of what assignments should be written, and there will likely be examinations to be completed. The student is working "on his own" but subject to some conditions imposed by the accrediting institution. A further stage in the direction of self, as distinct from institutional control of the conditions of learning, is represented by the individual's use of a local learning centre, for example a learning centre in a factory or a storefront drop-in learning centre for adult basic education. Here the flexibility in terms of the time, duration and form of study undertaken may be very great, limited by the materials and experts available on which the student may call. Perhaps the "learner autonomy" end of the spectrum is appropriately represented by the "self-directed" learner. In this case the person may decide what to learn, may start (and stop) at any point, adjust the learning goals at any time, choose the style or educational process or resources which will be called upon, consult any persons or other resources available and have control over the costs to be incurred. There are many hazards in the path of self-directed learners, as there are for full-time study in a professional university program, but they are very different ones. The former maximizes independence and flexibility, but also the hazards which accompany lack of structure and imposed discipline. The full-time institutional student faces—willingly in most instances—quite the reverse.

It is perhaps appropriate in this section on the relationship between the learner and educational resources to mention two terms of growing importance in the field, "prior learning assessment and recognition" and "learning outcomes." Prior learning assessment and recognition (PLAR) is the practice whereby an educational institution grants entry to its programs, or advance standing towards one of its credentials, to a learner who may not have the formal educational certification normally expected but who is judged to have the necessary knowledge or background, often achieved through their work, non-formal courses or some other type of experience. This practice has been in effect for a very long time in certain quarters, but has more often than not been carried out as a privately handled arrangement for particular individuals, rather than as a matter of publicly announced policy and therefore available to all prospective students. An exception to this, perhaps, has been the "mature-student clause," which has been in effect in many universities and under which admission or advance standing has been granted to certain adults at the discretion of university officials.

There are two essential elements of a system of prior learning assessment and recognition: that educational institutions are required to be more precise than they have been in the past concerning the state of knowledge and/or skills they require of entering students; and that prospective students seeking such placement must somehow document or demonstrate, in a way acceptable to the institution, that they possess such knowledge and skills. A basic distinction must be made in this connection; what is involved here is not "credit for experience," but rather credit for the learning that may have resulted from experience.[34] Prospective students who are seeking recognition in this connection are usually required to demonstrate their prior learning by one of two methods, either by taking exams that involve the knowledge which is re-

---

[34] S. Simosko & Associates, *Assessing Learning: A CAEL Handbook for Faculty* (Columbia, Maryland: Council for Adult and Experiential Learning, 1988).

quired, or by preparing what is usually called a "portfolio," which documents the means by which they have acquired the prior knowledge they are claiming. The preparation of the examinations and the vetting of the student portfolios are carried out by experts in the subject areas concerned.

The practice of prior learning assessment and recognition and the advance placement of students based on the student's prior knowledge require a well-documented awareness of the skills and knowledge involved in all courses and programs. For this reason an increased emphasis on learning outcomes has accompanied systems of PLAR. Institutions have needed to state clearly and in some detail what the outcomes of their various offerings are expected to be if they are to be able to measure prospective students against such criteria.

Government's increased acceptance of the concept of lifelong learning (especially as it relates to vocational qualifications) and its increased insistence on efficiencies within educational systems have combined to give added prominence in public policy to PLAR and the learning outcomes approach to curriculum development. The government of Quebec was the first into the field in Canada, with indications of interest appearing as early as 1982 and budgetary provision following two years later.[35] A number of other provinces have since adopted similar policies and federal work force development practices have also emphasized such approaches.[36]

The Functions of Adult Education

What is adult education for? Such a question can be answered at several levels, and from different perspectives. At the most profound level, the answer leads us to an examination of the ideas of philosophers who have had something to say about education and human development. At a more applied or policy related level, the matter is often approached by examining the "functions" of adult education, seeing them from the point of view of both the individual and the society as a whole.

Perhaps the most common typology of functions, as seen from the individual's point of view, comprises four categories:

1. Vocational—this has to do particularly with the knowledge and skills required to perform a job.

2. Social—this relates to the individual's social roles in life as family member (parent, child, and so on), as a member or leader of social

---

[35] R. Isabelle & F. Landry, "Prior Learning Assessment in Quebec Colleges," in S. Simosko & Associates, *Assessing Learning: A CAEL Handbook for Faculty.*

[36] A.M. Thomas, "The Utilization of Prior Learning Assessment in Canada," *Canadian Journal for University Continuing Education, 18,* 1, 7-26.

groups and organizations (at work, in community life, and so on) and as a citizen (a voter, volunteer, community worker, and so on).

3. Recreational—this relates to the individual's recreational activities, be it playing a game, appreciating or performing in the arts or keeping up to date on a field of interest.

4. Self-development—this is a rather amorphous category, and to varying degrees may overlap with the other three. It may be seen to relate to the sorts of goals we associate with liberal education—learning how to think critically, express oneself, broaden one's horizons. Feelings about oneself, others and the ultimate values in life may be said to fall into this category as well.

The foregoing kind of formulation was fairly common in the literature of the field some decades ago and is based on the roles or "fields of action" of the individual.[37] Other formulations put forward in the 1960s, when adult education as a field of study was under active development, put more focus on the functions as they related to intellectual functioning. In his chapter in the American *Handbook*, which appeared in 1960, Hallenbeck made reference to such terms as remedial, assimilative and compensatory.[38] In the text book by Verner and Booth, which appeared four years later, the terms used were expansional (the acquiring of new knowledge and skills), participational (citizenship), integrational (combining knowledge with experience) and personal (the development and maturing of the individual).[39]

Sir Josiah Stamp, nineteenth-century British economist and industrialist, described the functions of adult education as assisting the adult "to earn a living, to live a life and to mould a world."[40] In a somewhat similar vein, Thomas Kelly, in presenting an historical overview of adult education in Great Britain in recent centuries, has used the following terms: education for salvation, for vocation, for civilization, for participation and for recreation.[41] In a rather sweeping and colourful attempt to present all this more simply, Dwyer, in his *Ivory Towers in the Marketplace*, suggested that for the individual, the essential functions of adult education were two: to increase the "life

[37] See for instance A.A. Liveright, *A Study of Adult Education in the United States* (Boston: Centre for the Study of Liberal Education for Adults, 1968).

[38] W. Hallenbeck, "The Function and Place of Adult Education in American Society," in M.S. Knowles (Ed.), *Handbook of Adult Education in the United States* (Chicago: Adult Education Association of the USA, 1960) pp.29-38.

[39] C. Verner & A. Booth, *Adult Education* (New York: Centre for Applied Research in Education, 1964).

[40] Cited in G. Selman, in *Adult Education in Canada: Historical Essays* (Toronto: Thompson Educational, 1995) p.284.

[41] T. Kelly, "The Historical Evolution of Adult Education in Great Britain," in M. Tight (Ed.), *Education for Adults*, vol.2 (London: Croom Helm, 1983) pp.3-19.

chance" and the "life space" of the person.[42] The first term refers to basic education, vocational training and personal development which permitted the person to get ahead in terms of the kind of career or life situation that the person wanted. Life space refers to broadening the horizons of the person's life, in terms of interests and the capacity for enjoyment and appreciation.

Three examples will be presented of the functions as seen from the social or community view. The first is from Hallenbeck again, in which he uses the more personally related headings which were common at the time, but describes these consistently in terms of how the individual will use these powers (communications skills, improved human relations, expediting personal growth and facilitating participation) in the community setting.[43] In his international review of the field, Lowe approached the description of functions largely from the point of view of nations and governments. He saw occupational training as the most widely accepted function. He felt there was support for two other functions in the less-developed countries: inculcating a sense of national identity and helping to overcome poverty (economic development). Other functions for adult education included "helping societies adjust to the interaction of social and technological change," fostering social justice (by enabling more people to gain the benefits of economic development) and "reducing conflict in the political and employment spheres."[44]

The most recent of these social views of adult education to be cited comes from Peter Jarvis. He lists the functions as follows:

- Maintenance of the social system and reproduction of existing social relations.
- Transmission of knowledge and the reproduction of culture.
- Individual advancement and selection.
- Leisure time pursuit and institutional expansion.
- Development and liberation.[45]

In their textbook for the field, which appeared in 1982, Darkenwald and Merriam attempted to combine the personal and social functions. They stated the functions of the field as follows:

- Cultivation of the intellect.
- Individual self-actualization.
- Personal and social improvement.

---

[42] J. Dwyer, *Ivory Towers in the Market Place* (New York: Bobbs-Merrill, 1956).

[43] W. Hallenbeck, "The Function and Place of Adult Education in American Society."

[44] J. Lowe, *The Education of Adults: A World Perspective*, pp.33-35.

[45] P. Jarvis, *The Sociology of Adult and Continuing Education* (London: Croom Helm, 1985) pp.133-50.

- Social transformation.
- Organizational effectiveness.[46]

Such formulations of the functions of the field are cast in general enough terms to have application to Canada, and perhaps most if not all other societies. They would not all be embraced with equal enthusiasm by a totalitarian regime, or for that matter, as Lowe has pointed out, by any government.[47] From a Canadian point of view, all of the functions described are familiar. It is not surprising that in a country which has been so pre-occupied at times with the socialization of immigrants and with developing a sense of national identity, many of the most noteworthy achievements in the field have been related to citizenship and social development functions of the field. The other point which should be made is that the community, through government, although it may realize the value of all the functions of adult education, may not regard all functions as equally deserving of public financial support. There may be a willingness to spend public funds for vocational or academic training, for instance (in the belief that these are crucial to the economic development of the nation) but an insistence that recreational types of learning should be fully paid for by the "consumer." A fuller elaboration of this matter is to be found in the chapters on public policy further on in this book.

---

[46] G. Darkenwald & S. Merriam, *Adult Education: Foundations of Practice* (New York: Harper & Row, 1982) pp.43-64.

[47] J. Lowe, *The Education of Adults: A World Perspective.*

2

Adult Education in English-Speaking Canada

The enterprise of adult education, like any field of social practice, responds to the nature of the society within which it is functioning. One would expect, therefore, to find that the field of adult education in Canada reflects many features of our history as a people and our present social context. That this is the case can be amply demonstrated. Indeed, some features of the history of the field would be difficult to understand without some knowledge of the history and nature of the society that produced them. It is the purpose of this chapter to examine some of these features and relate them to developments in the field of adult education.

It may justifiably be said that, in large measure, adult education does not have an agenda of its own, but rather relates itself to the interests of others. Exceptions will be noted in the account which follows, but adult education tends to be the servant of the purposes of other elements in the society. This fact is caused, or at least reinforced, by the fact that in the vast majority of cases, adult education is a marginal enterprise sponsored by organizations whose chief aims and objectives lie elsewhere. In most of its settings, the education of adults is seen to be a means to an end rather than as an end in itself. The goal is most frequently not more fully functioning people, as such, but more productive workers, more expert practitioners, more informed citizens—and perhaps more institutional clients.

Because adult education, in most of its settings, is a servant of interests other than its own, it is not surprising that it reflects in its nature the characteristics of the society within which it operates. Canada is a nation which has continuously throughout its history received large numbers of immigrants, and it is to be expected that citizenship education in its various dimensions, and carried out by various means, should be a prominent feature of the adult education scene. In fact a case can be made for citizenship education being

the area in which Canadian adult education has made many of its most significant contributions to the field. To take another example, with education having
been assigned under the constitution of Canada as a provincial responsibility
and economic development patterns having been very unequal from region to
region, one would expect very great differences in the nature and extent of
adult education development from one region to another. Indeed this is a
prominent feature of the field in Canada. To move to a more negative example, the relative difficulty (some would say failure) in Canadian society to
build effective understanding between English- and French-speaking regions
of the country is all too evident in adult education, just as it is in society as a
whole. It appears to be justified to state that adult education in Canada reveals,
illustrates or reflects many of the characteristics of the society of which it is a
part.

External Influences

Although it is clear that many of the most outstanding projects in Canadian
adult education were distinctively Canadian in origin and character, we have
as well borrowed many institutional forms from elsewhere. The two most
obvious sources have been Great Britain and the United States, but other
countries have contributed as well. In the most recent decades particularly,
Canadian adult education has drawn heavily on ideas about the field which
have come from the international community.

British Influences

It was only natural—and to be expected—that as large numbers of immigrants came to Canada from Great Britain, they would bring with them the
knowledge of certain educational programs and institutions with which they
had been familiar in their former homes. In addition, there was a great deal of
travel back and forth between the two countries and many British newspapers
and other publications were read by Canadians. In view of this, it is not
surprising that English-speaking Canadians adopted a number of British institutional forms in the field of adult education, as they did in other areas of life.
Five examples, spread over some 150 years, will be described: the mechanics'
institutes, the Y.M.C.A., university extension, the Workers' Educational Association and the Open University.

Mechanics' institutes were created in Great Britain as a means of providing
scientific and technical information for workers, especially skilled workers, or
"mechanics." These tradesmen knew how to carry out the procedures of their
trades, but frequently had not had an opportunity to learn the scientific background or the "why" of those procedures. Started with a mixture of self-help
and philanthropic motivation, mechanics' institutes were experimented with as
early as 1800 in Edinburgh, but the movement did not begin in earnest until

the foundation of the London Mechanics' Institution early in the 1820s.[1] Within twenty years there were more than three hundred institutes in Britain. (In subsequent years most institutes in Britain strayed from their original purpose and became general cultural organizations for their communities.) In the meantime, the movement had come to Canada—or more accurately, to the Canadian colonies. In late 1830, an institute was established in Toronto. The following year the first was established in Halifax and, at about the same time, in Montreal.[2] Institutes were established in British Columbia as well, but not until the early 1860s.[3] Ontario was where the institutes were most fully developed, there being 311 of them by 1895. The Department of Education in Ontario for a period even saw the institutes as the chief agency through which "the upgrading of workers in the technical arts could be achieved."[4] In Canada, as in Britain, the mechanics' institute movement was almost entirely gone by the end of the century. Many of the organizations turned their libraries over to the municipality, to be used as the nucleus of, or as an addition to, the municipal library services.

A somewhat similar process can be seen in the case of the Young Men's Christian Association (Y.M.C.A.), except in this case, the institution took root in Canadian soil and continues to be active. The Y.M.C.A. was established in London in 1844 and was originally intended as a place where young men who had come to the city from the rural and small town areas could go to find healthy, constructive social activities. Within fifty years there were 651 Y.M.C.A.'s in Britain alone and the movement had spread around the world. In 1853, nine years after the first branch had been founded in Britain, a Y.M.C.A. was established in Toronto, which soon began to offer evening classes and other educational activities.[5] The organization soon spread across Canada, first to the larger centres and then to many smaller towns as well, frequently providing evening classes of various kinds before the public educational authorities took up the task.

University extension activity (although there were precursors of various kinds) is generally thought to have begun at Cambridge University in 1873, at the instigation of James Stuart.[6] Oxford University soon took part as well. The

---

[1] T. Kelly, *A History of Adult Education in Great Britain* (Liverpool: Liverpool University, 1962); J.F.C. Harrison, *Learning and Living 1790-1960* (London: Routledge and Kegan Paul, 1961).

[2] C.B. Fergusson, *Mechanics' Institutes in Nova Scotia* (Halifax: Public Archives of Nova Scotia, 1960); F. Vernon, *The Development of Adult Education in Ontario 1790-1900* (Unpublished Ed.D. Thesis, University of Toronto, 1969).

[3] G. Selman, in *Adult Education in Canada: Historical Essays* (Toronto: Thompson Educational, 1995) p.402.

[4] F. Vernon, *The Development of Adult Education in Ontario* (Unpublished Ph.D. Thesis, University of Toronto, 1969).

[5] M. Ross, *The Y.M.C.A. in Canada* (Toronto: Ryerson, 1951).

[6] T. Kelly, *A History of Adult Education in Great Britain.*

early work consisted of the production of syllabuses and the delivery of series of lectures in the cities of Britain, delivered in the main by university faculty. It tended to consist of the same kind of lecturing which was performed at the university, followed by oral or written questions. (Written work came later.) By 1890, extension centres had been established in 250 communities. Between 1885 and 1905, Oxford alone had arranged for 32,146 extension lectures in 577 centres, for 424,000 students.[7] University extension came to both the United States and Canada during the 1890s. This lecture type of extension work was apparently not well suited to North American society, however. A number of American institutions, in at least 28 states, got into the field, but by the end of the century, such work had declined almost to the vanishing point. A new, North American model of university extension was to emerge soon. In the meantime, Canadian universities entered the field. Although in both cases some earlier experiments can be identified, Queen's University and the University of Toronto were the first universities to enter the field on a regular basis, Queen's in 1888 and Toronto three years later.[8] A Canadian Association for the Extension of University Teaching, based on this early British model of extension work, was formed at a founding conference in Toronto in 1891, but it appears to have died within a year.[9]

A fourth institutional form of adult education which was "imported" from Great Britain is the Workers' Educational Association (WEA). Founded in Britain in 1903, the WEA represented a partnership among the working class, the co-operative movement and the universities, the latter delivering the instruction and the former two, the students.[10] The working class in Britain was generally denied access to higher education at the time and the WEA provided a means to deliver instruction of a university level to working-class leaders. Albert Mansbridge, the founder and director of the association, made a tour of Canada and other "Dominions" in 1917. Out of his visit to Canada came a WEA organization, founded in Toronto the following year.[11] This organization has had a continuous history in Ontario since that time, but its existence elsewhere in Canada was short-lived.[12]

---

[7] J. Creese, *The Extension of University Teaching* (New York: American Association for Adult Education, 1941).

[8] G. Selman, *A History of The Extension and Adult Education Services of the University of British Columbia 1915 to 1955* (Unpublished M.A. Thesis, University of British Columbia, 1963); J.A. Blyth, *A Foundling at Varsity* (Toronto: University of Toronto/School of Continuing Studies, 1976).

[9] E.A. Corbett in J.R. Kidd, *Adult Education in Canada* (Toronto: Canadian Association for Adult Education, 1950).

[10] T. Kelly, *A History of Adult Education in Great Britain.*

[11] Workers' Educational Association of Canada, *Workers' Educational Association 1903-1953* (Toronto: W.E.A., 1953).

[12] See for instance, G. Selman, *A History of ...Adult Education Services.*

The final example which will be mentioned is that of the Open University. This institution was formally established in 1969 and began instruction two years later.[13] The Open University had the effect of modernizing and revitalizing the approach to distance education, with its combination of correspondence instruction, supplementary broadcasting and publishing, residential short courses and support services at the local and regional levels. This example has inspired significant new developments in the field of distance education in Canada, most notably, perhaps, in Athabasca University in Alberta and the Open Learning Agency of British Columbia.

American Influences

While it is true that many immigrants have come to Canada from the United States, as was the case with Britain, perhaps a stronger reason in the American case for the influence of American educational ideas was the fact that the two North American countries were faced with similar kinds of nation-building tasks. In both cases, these were "immigrant societies." Newly arrived residents needed to learn about their new homelands and its ways, and in many cases learn a new vocation. Both nations were faced with the challenges and opportunities of establishing their cultural identities, and of developing their far-flung national territories. And both developed federal government structures and had to work out systems for dividing responsibilities and delivering government services through a network of national, provincial/state and local authorities. There have been profound differences in the approach of the two nations to these tasks, but many of the challenges have been essentially the same and it is not surprising that many similar approaches have been adopted. In the selective list of examples which follows, brief reference will be made to five institutions or program models: agricultural extension, Chautauqua and correspondence education, the North American model of university extension, school board and college approaches to adult education and human relations training.

The field of agricultural extension is perhaps a classic case of a challenge faced by the peoples of both countries, which they set about addressing in similar ways. Clearly in both Canada and the United States, the opportunities for agricultural development in their huge territories were enormous and basic. Ways had to be found to provide information, education and other forms of assistance to those who moved into the field of agriculture, which for many was an entirely new occupation. Faced with a similar task, the two countries followed distinctive courses of action. From small beginnings, often on a very

---

[13] N. MacKenzie, R. Postgate & J. Scupham (Eds.), *Open Learning* (Paris: UNESCO, 1975); W. Perry, *The Open University* (San Francisco: Jossey-Bass, 1977); E. Stabler, *Founders* (Edmonton: University of Alberta, 1987).

localized basis, agricultural activities began in both countries. Agricultural extension was carried out by three main types of organizations: voluntary associations of producers such as farm organizations and commodity groups, government and other public agencies, and the private sector—fertilizer companies, financial institutions or other proprietary firms.[14] In the case of agricultural extension, Canadians developed many ideas of their own. The scale of the American agricultural economy and of their government initiatives in the field, however, were bound to have an influence on Canada. As well, many leaders and public officials in Canadian agriculture had received their advanced training in the United States and became aware of American methods. Voluntary organizations of farm people—the Grange, the Farmers' Union and the American Farm Bureau Federation—had branches or stimulated similar organizations in Canada, such as the Farmers' Institutes.

In the area of public policy, the American Morrill Act of 1862 was of basic importance in setting the goals for agricultural extension and creating the Land-Grant colleges in each state, which were to serve as the base of operations for much extension work. The institutional framework was further developed with the passage of the Smith-Lever Act in 1914, which created the Co-operative Extension Service, a co-operative venture of the state and federal governments.[15] In Canada, agriculture was designated as a shared federal and provincial responsibility and each jurisdiction has developed its own approach. The federal government has exercised a strong influence on this work, however, through cost-sharing provision for particular activities, research activity and "information and the direct provision of service through demonstration and research facilities and personnel in the regions."[16] "Extension agents" or "agricultural representatives" have been widely used in Canada, as in the United States, but here they have been employed on the whole by provincial departments of agriculture rather than by the extension service, as in the United States. It is fair to say that both countries have learned from the experience of the other in this field, but it is clear that the American example has had a strong influence on Canadian practice in various ways.

A second area in which American experience had an influence on developments in Canada combines two related features of the American scene, the Chautauqua Institution and a methodology which it pioneered, correspondence instruction. What started out as a residential summer training program for Sunday school teachers in 1874 at Chautauqua in up-state New York developed over the years into a flourishing institution with widespread influ-

[14] D.J. Blackburn (Ed.), *Extension Handbook* (Guelph: Ontario, University of Guelph, 1984).

[15] M.S. Knowles, *A History of the Adult Education Movement in the United States* (Huntington: New York, Robert Krieger, 1977).

[16] D.J. Blackburn (Ed.), *Extension Handbook*, p.7.

ence and many imitators.[17] Chautauqua was a pioneer in many areas of education—methods of foreign language teaching, the Literary and Scientific Study Circle movement, and correspondence education being among the best known. Its work in correspondence education had important influence on the development of that methodology in subsequent years in university and other circles, and throughout North America.[18] Quite separate from the original Chautauqua Institution, companies of travelling "Chautauquas" sprang up in the United States, taking education and entertainment to towns throughout the country, typically in the familiar Chautauqua tents. Sheila Jameson has told the story of the operation of some of these Chautauqua circuits in Canada in the period from shortly after the World War I until the 1930s.[19]

We have seen that university extension on the British model had influence in Canada late in the nineteenth century, but that an effort to build a national movement and organization on that basis had foundered in Canada, as it did in the United States. In 1907, the University of Wisconsin began the development of a new type of university work, one which took as its starting point, not the kind of teaching and subject matter which had been traditional university fare, but rather the educational needs of the people to be served.[20] Instead of relying on the traditional lecture method and restricting itself to the usual academic content, the university devised other ways of serving the educational needs of adult citizens—correspondence instruction, audio-visual devices of various kinds, short courses and workshops, information pamphlets, travelling "field men" who were expert in the practical application of their fields of knowledge and scientific and consulting support services. The "Wisconsin idea" hit a responsive chord elsewhere in North America and was perhaps the dominant thrust of such work at the time of the creation of the National University Extension Association in 1915.[21] In the meantime, the University of Saskatchewan had begun agricultural extension work (1910) and the University of Alberta had created an Extension Department (1912) very much on the Wisconsin model.[22] Other Canadian universities were to do the same.[23]

---

[17] T. Morrison, *Chautauqua* (Chicago: University of Chicago, 1974).

[18] M.S. Knowles, *A History of the Adult Education Movement*; J.R. Kidd, *Adult Education in Canada*.

[19] S. Jameson, *Chautauqua in Canada* (Calgary: Glenbow-Alberta Institute, 1979).

[20] F.M. Rosentreter, *The Boundaries of the Campus* (Madison: University of Wisconsin, 1957); M.S. Knowles, *A History of the Adult Education Movement*; T.J. Shannon & C.A. Schoenfeld, *University Extension* (New York: The Centre for Applied Research in Education, 1965).

[21] M.S. Knowles, *A History of the Adult Education Movement*.

[22] P.J. Blenkinsop, *A History of Adult Education on the Prairies: Learning to Live in Agrarian Saskatchewan 1870-1944* (Unpublished Ph.D. Thesis, University of Toronto, 1979); R.J. Clark, *A History of the Department of Extension at the University of Alberta 1912-1956* (Unpublished Ph.D. Thesis, University of Toronto, 1985).

[23] F. Peers in J.R. Kidd, *Adult Education in Canada*; J.R. Kidd, *Adult Education in the Canadian*

Two other institutional forms were to have a strong influence on Canadian practice in adult education as well—the school board-sponsored "night class" program and the community college. In both Canada and the United States, ways had to be developed in their vast territories to create educational authorities at the local or municipal level which would share responsibility with provincial/state governments in the delivery of appropriate education for children. In the case of both countries, this was accomplished through the creation of a system of elected school boards at the local level.[24] Beginning in the 1830s and expanding rapidly in subsequent decades, adult education services were provided as well by school boards in many of the American states.[25] Although the story is not known in detail as yet, school board night classes appear to have begun in Canada in the 1850s, although their development—and even their existence—was somewhat sporadic for some time after that.[26] While clear evidence of the American model having influenced Canada in this case is difficult to document, it seems obvious given the sequence of events. It is certainly the case that when Canadian governments were examining the alternatives before them in the 1960s with respect to the development of college systems, the varied American models were carefully studied, and in some instances, emulated.[27]

Finally, reference will be made to human relations training. In its contemporary forms, the human relations and leadership training movement arose in large measure from the research of Kurt Lewin and the pioneering work of the National Training Laboratory in Group Development which began operation in 1947 in Bethel, Maine.[28] This work had a direct influence on Canada as Canadians took part in programs in the United States and brought the techniques back for application in their home areas. This aspect of adult education has not been well documented in Canada, but it is clear that subsequent work in this field in Vancouver, Fort Qu'Appelle and other centres was directly influenced by the American experience.

University (Toronto: Canadian Association for Adult Education, 1956).

[24] L.A. Cremin, *American Education: The Colonial Experience 1607-1783* (New York: Harper and Row, 1970); J.D. Wilson, R.M. Stamp & L-P Audet (Eds.), *Canadian Education: A History* (Scarborough, Ontario: Prentice-Hall Canada, 1970).

[25] M.S. Knowles, *A History of the Adult Education Movement*.

[26] J.R. Kidd, *Adult Education in Canada*; J.R. Kidd, *18 to 80: Continuing Education in Metropolitan Toronto* (Toronto: Board of Education, 1961).

[27] J. Dennison & P. Gallagher, *Canada's Community Colleges* (Vancouver: University of British Columbia, 1986).

[28] L.P. Bradford in M.S. Knowles (Ed.), *Handbook of Adult Education in the United States* (Chicago: Adult Education Association of the USA, 1960).

Other Countries

It is possible to trace the influence in Canada of adult education experience in a number of other countries, especially in the current period. One example will be provided from the earlier years, that of the influence of the folk school. Established first in Denmark in the 1840s and stimulated by the ideas of N.S.F. Grundtvig, the Danish Folk High School movement soon became famous and for at least a hundred years provided an inspiration for adult educators and others in many countries.[29] A number of well-known leaders in Canadian adult education, among them key figures in the formation of the Canadian Association for Adult Education in the 1930s, made pilgrimages to Denmark. There was as well a lively folk school movement in Canada, especially in Ontario and the West. Its history in Canada is not well documented, and the boundary line between what may appropriately be called folk schools and other types of residential education is vague. However, it may be stated that the period from the late 1930s to the late 1950s was the high point of the folk school movement in Canada.[30]

The influence from other countries in the most recent period has been more in the form of ideas than in institutional structures. The first example to be cited is that of recurrent education. This concept was described in the first chapter. It was created in Sweden in the late 1960s and soon gained widespread acceptance in Western Europe and the Organization for Economic Co-operation and Development (OECD).[31] Canada, which is a member of OECD, has taken an interest in the idea and the federal government has conducted two substantial studies of its application to Canada.[32] The second example is that of lifelong education and lifelong learning. Some early developmental work on the idea was carried out in Canada, but the chief impetus to the idea as far as the international community was concerned has come from reports produced by UNESCO and by its Institute on Education in Hamburg. The terminology surrounding the concepts has become coin of the realm in the field of adult education in Canada and featured prominently in two well-known provincial royal commissions on education which reported in 1972, the Worth Commission in Alberta and the Wright Commission in Ontario. A third example of such influences has been the impact on thinking in Canada

---

[29] E. Stabler, *Founders: Innovators in Education—1830-1980* (Edmonton: University of Alberta, 1987).

[30] J.K. Friesen in J.R. Kidd, *Adult Education in Canada*; J.K. Friesen & J.M. Parsey, *Manitoba Folk Schools* (Winnipeg: Manitoba Co-operative Services Branch, 1951); E. Loosley, *Residential Adult Education: A Canadian View* (Toronto: Canadian Association for Adult Education, 1960).

[31] C. Titmus, *Strategies for Adult Education* (Chicago: Follett, 1981).

[32] Commission on Educational Leave and Productivity, *Education and Working Canadians* (Ottawa: Labour Canada, 1979); National Advisory Panel on Skill Development Leave, *Learning For Life* (Ottawa: Department of Employment and Immigration, 1984).

of the concept of development as it has been conceived in the international community, and more particularly the prominence given to the significance of non-formal and informal adult education in this context.[33] Finally, reference should be made to the work of several "radical" writers in the last few decades whose ideas have encouraged Canadian adult educators to consider the social and political implications of their work. Three examples which might be mentioned, among many, are Tom Lovett, Ivan Illich and Paulo Freire.[34] The work—and personal visits—of these and other adult educators have had major impact on the thinking of many Canadian adult educators, encouraging them to re-examine their liberal and "service ethic" approach to the field and to consider the relevance of the field as a factor in social change.

Canadian Responses to the Canadian Context

Canadian adult education has a high reputation in the international community of adult educators. Studies of the field which take a world view of its history and characteristics consistently cite Canada's contributions, frequently mentioning such projects as the Antigonish Movement, National Farm Radio Forum, the Women's Institutes, Frontier College, the National Film Board and the work of outstanding Canadian individuals, most notably J.R. Kidd and Allen Tough.[35] Canadians are widely considered to have responded to their challenges as a people by devising educational responses which not only successfully meet their own needs, but in many instances have useful application elsewhere.

There are a number of features of the Canadian experience in the northern portion of the North American continent which may be seen to have had an impact on aspects of Canadian adult education. As well, they may be seen as forces which elicited from Canadians who were involved in the provision of adult education the particular institutional forms, selection of goals and content and educational procedures which have been developed here.

---

[33] P. Coombs, *The World Crisis in Education: The View from the Eighties* (New York: Oxford University, 1985); B. Hall & J.R. Kidd (Eds.), *Adult Learning: A Design for Action* (Oxford: Pergamon, 1978).

[34] P. Freire, *Pedagogy of the Oppressed* (New York: Herder & Herder, 1970); P. Freire, *The Politics of Education* (Massachusetts: Bergin & Garvey, 1985); I. Illich, *Deschooling Society* (New York: Harper and Row, 1970); T. Lovett, *Adult Education, Community Development and the Working Class* (London: Ward Lock Educational, 1975); T. Lovett, C. Clarke & A. Kilmurray, *Adult Education and Community Action* (London: Cromm Helm, 1983).

[35] A.S.M. Hely, *New Trends in Adult Education* (Paris: UNESCO, 1962); J. Lowe, *The Education of Adults: A World Perspective* (Paris: UNESCO, 1982); T. Lovett et al., *Adult Education and Community Action*.

Citizenship in an Immigrant Nation

First, and perhaps most obvious, Canada is a nation of immigrants. Except for First Nations people (who may themselves have been immigrants to this land in the distant reaches of unrecorded history), Canadians—the present generation or their ancestors—have come as immigrants from other lands. The two "founding races" of Canada are seen to be the immigrants who came in such large numbers in the colonial period from Great Britain and from France. Since that time, immigrants have come from many lands. This unique ethnic or racial mix has led to the present Canadian social and cultural policy of "bilingualism and multiculturalism." Canadians are fond of comparing their own social policy of "the Canadian mosaic" with the policy adopted in the United States, which is often referred to as "the melting pot."

The essential point is that Canada has throughout its history received relatively large numbers of immigrants, and one of its most essential tasks has been to provide educational opportunities for many of these newcomers. Beyond the immediate requirements of the immigrants, however, there has been an ongoing pre-occupation in Canada with "the Canadian identity." What should be the essential characteristics and goals of this collection of people who make up the Canadian nation? It is significant that the landmark Royal Commission on National Development in the Arts, Letters and Sciences, which reported to the Canadian people in 1951 and which has been the most profound study of Canadian cultural policy ever carried out, introduced their report with the following quotation from St. Augustine:

> A nation is an association of reasonable beings united in a peaceful sharing of the things they cherish; therefore to determine the quality of a nation, you must consider what those things are.[36]

Canadians have been struggling with that question throughout their history as a people, in the light of both the changing ethnic and cultural mix resulting from continuous immigration, and also the concern on the part of many Canadians over the influence on Canadian development of its large and dynamic neighbour to the south, the United States of America.

The education of immigrants has been a constant pre-occupation of Canadian society, including adult education. This has taken the form of both language and citizenship education. The federal government has for many decades assumed the cost of language instruction (English or French) for recent immigrants and has shared the cost of such work beyond the initial period. This language instruction was carried out by a variety of agencies, mostly local educational institutions or voluntary agencies. The senior level of

---

[36] Royal Commission on National Development in the Arts, Letters and Sciences, *Report* (Ottawa: King's Printer, 1951) p.xxiii.

government established a Citizenship Branch in the federal administration in the late 1940s which fostered in a variety of ways the assimilation of new-comers to Canada and effective communication between the ethnic communities and the Canadian mainstream. The federal government undertook much of this work on its own, but also co-operated closely with other bodies, most notably the Canadian Citizenship Council, and for a time beginning in the 1950s, a series of local citizenship councils across the country which were formed as a result of Citizenship Branch initiatives and supported in their activities by both the Branch and local leadership.

With respect to the broader field of citizenship education, it may justifiably be claimed that this is the main thrust of many of the best-known Canadian contributions to the field of adult education. Defining the term "citizenship education" presents a problem. A narrower or "civics" approach might include only a knowledge of the structure and processes of government and a knowledge of particular issues on which decisions must be made by the community. A more comprehensive definition—the one that is being used in the present case—ranges much more widely and has as well to do with the various ways in which citizens play a role in determining the nature of the society of which they are a part, and also their attitudes and disposition towards such participation.

The importance of citizenship education in this broad sense in the Canadian adult education tradition has been noted by various observers. The opinion which is perhaps most valuable in this regard is that of Gordon Hawkins, who was Associate Director of the Canadian Association for Adult Education for several years during the 1950s and who was well informed about adult education in both Canada and Britain. In an article written in 1954 and intended for publication first in Britain, Hawkins pointed out that whereas adult education in Britain had a tradition of academic study and tutorial work, the situation in Canada was very different. In Canada

> the concern is more with what one might call the "community" aspects of adult education. Partly this is a consequence of geography and time. With newly formed and changing communities, with immigrant groups, with the awful challenge of distance, methods and aims are bound to be different. But there is also a newer, consciously evolved philosophy of adult education. It stems from a deep concern with the processes of democracy—with *how* the individual and the group and the community work, as much as with *what* they set out to achieve. Hence the emphasis in their scheme of things on group work, community organization, discussion methods and techniques, leadership courses and so on, and, as a background to all that, on the use of mass media to spread a common basis of information for their discussion and their social actions.[37]

---

[37] G. Hawkins, "As Others See Us," *Food for Thought, 14*, 8 (1954) p.2.

A number of Canadian adult education projects which have made a contribution to the field of citizenship education, broadly conceived, will be briefly described.

Perhaps the most famous adult education project in Canada and the best-known outside our borders is the "Antigonish Movement"—the extension work in co-operative education of St. Francis Xavier University in Antigonish, Nova Scotia. It is also the best-documented of adult education projects in Canada.[38] St. Francis Xavier University, a Roman Catholic institution, under the leadership of the Rev. James Tompkins and the Rev. Moses Coady, decided to devote effort to the economic improvement of the fishermen, farmers and industrial workers of its economically depressed region. The work began officially in 1928 and the major strategies adopted were that of community development and the creation of co-operative and credit union organizations. Remarkable results were achieved and the Antigonish Movement soon became well known internationally. The methods used for social and economic development were soon seen to have application in the emerging societies of the Third World, and over the years hundreds of persons from other nations came to Antigonish to study the extension methods being employed. The university constructed special facilities to house such visitors, and as well has sent teams of instructors abroad to train leaders in other regions.

The co-operative movement is based on the idea that the membership of the organization should participate actively in management decisions. Because this participation needs to be conducted on the basis of appropriate information and understanding, most co-operatives are actively involved in educational activity. As Ian MacPherson, the historian of the co-operative movement in Canada, has put it, "co-operators most caught up in their movement have been essentially adult educators."[39] Educational activities sponsored by the co-operative movement in Canada have been traced back to the early years of this century. An educational institute for the co-operative movement in the West was formed in 1951, and a Western Co-operative College established in 1959 (a building of its own becoming available three years later).[40] A somewhat parallel movement took place in French-speaking Canada, with a training institution eventually being established at Levis, Quebec.

---

[38] G. Boyle, *Father Tompkins of Nova Scotia* (New York: Kenedy & Sons, 1953); M.M. Coady, *Masters of Their Own Destiny* (New York: Harper & Bros., 1939); I. Delaney, *By Their Own Hands* (Hantsport, Nova Scotia: Lancelot Press, 1985); A.F. Laidlaw, *The Campus and the Community* (Montreal: Harvest House, 1961); A.F. Laidlaw (Ed.), *The Man from Margaree* (Toronto: McLelland & Stewart, 1971); M. McClelland, *Coady Remembered* (Antigonish, Nova Scotia: St. Francis Xavier Press, 1985); P. Milner (Ed.), *Human Development through Social Change* (Antigonish, Nova Scotia: Formac Publishing, 1979); E. Stabler, *Founders*.

[39] I. MacPherson, in F. Cassidy & R. Faris (Eds.), *Choosing Our Future* (Toronto: OISE, 1987).

[40] I. MacPherson, in M.R. Welton (Ed.), *Knowledge for the People* (Toronto: OISE, 1987).

A second major sector of citizenship education in Canada is represented by the two crown corporations, the Canadian Broadcasting Corporation and the National Film Board of Canada. Both were created in the 1930s and both were given the mandate, among others, to educate Canadians about their country, their fellow citizens and the issues facing Canadian society.[41] Canadians have from the very beginning of their national experience looked upon government as a constructive instrument for social development. Various writers have contrasted the attitudes in this respect in Canada and in the United States. The Canadian attitude towards the role of government has been described as "constructive socialism."[42] Richard Gwyn has stated that it is taken for granted in Canada that "the state, for all its periodic inefficiencies, will cause the society to progress for the benefit of all the individuals in it."[43] Canadians, in the words of E.H. Carr, have accepted the idea of "the strong state exercising remedial and constructive functions."[44] Part of the reason for this may be that Canada has had a relatively small population, considering the size of its territory, and in many instances, if socially important functions were to be performed, only government had the resources to make it happen. Canadians were willing to see enormous quantities of public resources go into the construction of the first transcontinental railway and to see the subsequent national railway and our first national airlines created by crown corporations. These are just a few examples of the great reliance Canadians have placed on the public sector. There has been, of course, a considerable shift in such attitudes in the most recent decades.

The Canadian Broadcasting Corporation was created in 1936, a successor to the Canadian Radio Broadcasting Commission, which had existed since 1932.[45] It was to provide education as well as entertainment for the people of Canada. In the early decades of its existence, the Corporation was especially anxious to establish co-operative working relationships with other educational organizations. Its involvement with the Canadian Association for Adult Education and the Canadian Federation of Agriculture in National Farm Radio Forum, with the former in Citizens' Forum, and with the Canadian Institute on Public Affairs on the Couchiching conferences are outstanding examples.

The National Film Board of Canada (NFB) was created in 1939, the successor organization to the Government Motion Picture Bureau, which had functioned since 1923.[46] Its mandate was in large measure to inform Canadi-

[41] G. Evans, *John Grierson and the National Film Board* (Toronto: University of Toronto, 1984); F.W. Peers, *The Politics of Canadian Broadcasting 1920-1951* (Toronto: University of Toronto, 1969).

[42] C. Berger, *The Writing of Canadian History* (Toronto: Oxford, 1976).

[43] R. Gwyn, *The 49th Paradox* (Toronto: Totem, 1985) p.160.

[44] E.H. Carr, *The New Society* (Boston: Beacon Press, 1951) p.78.

[45] F. Peers, *The Politics of Canadian Broadcasting*.

ans about their country. It, like the Canadian Broadcasting Corporation, was part of a nation-building strategy. The first director of the NFB was a charismatic and controversial figure, John Grierson, who was a genius in the genre of the documentary film.[47] The NFB from its earliest existence displayed a capacity to create world-class documentary films. That level of excellence has been maintained over the years. No sooner was the NFB created (in 1939) than Canada was plunged into World War II. Canada did not enter that conflict wholeheartedly united about the issues involved and so, for the first few years of the NFB's existence, the Board was serving at least two causes—the original one in its mandate, to strengthen the Canadian identity and sense of common cause, and as well the task of rallying the Canadian people behind the war effort. Propaganda thus became a major function of the Film Board from the beginning, a role with which Grierson was perfectly comfortable. As he frequently put it, "Art is not a mirror, but a hammer."[48] Grierson stayed with the NFB for only six years, but he left his stamp on the organization.

It is one thing to make marvellous documentary films; it is another to get people to watch them. During World War II and immediately thereafter, the Film Board tackled that challenge, and with brilliant success.[49] Through the activities of its field staff across the country and with the co-operation of agencies in each province (frequently the extension department of the provincial university), the NFB took the leadership in establishing "film councils" in hundreds of cities and towns across Canada and established support services for these organizations. Film depositories were established in each province or region and "film circuits" were created. This involved providing a variety of films for each community for a period of time, at the end of which those films would be sent on to the next town on the circuit, and the first community would receive a fresh collection. The local film council had the responsibility of finding audiences to see the films in their care. This was done by various means, largely by arranging for other community organizations which were interested in the content of particular films to show them at their meetings, but also through regular "film nights" organized by the film council itself. By these and other means, the Film Board was successful in having its films seen by a remarkably large audience across the country. Evans states that at the end of the war, there was an average monthly attendance of 465,000 at Board films. Rural circuits alone were reaching a quarter of a million viewers a month.[50] The Board also made high-quality "instructional" films, which were

---

[46] G. Evans, *John Grierson and the NFB*.

[47] Ibid.

[48] D.B. Jones, *Movies and Memoranda* (Ottawa: Canadian Film Institute, 1981) p.6.

[49] G. Evans, *John Grierson and the NFB*; C.W. Gray, *Movies for the People* (Montreal: National Film Board, 1976).

widely used by educators in various settings across the country. The film circuit system was maintained until the 1950s, when the advent of television and other factors brought it to an end, at least in its original form.

Another aspect of the NFB's work which is of interest, and has been highly regarded internationally, is its role in placing film-making (and later videotape) facilities in the hands of those involved in the community development process. The activity was one element of what was termed "Challenge for Change," a project which was launched in 1966. The first experiment with this technique was conducted on Fogo Island, Newfoundland, in a project conducted in co-operation with the Extension Department of Memorial University and the local people. Part of the community development process involves the community in assessing itself. Film-making equipment was placed in the hands of the local people, to be used as a tool in creating a film or films which reflected, to the satisfaction of those involved in the process, the thinking of the community about its present state and its aspirations. The films also became a powerful instrument for conveying the community's wishes to agencies such as departments of government which had resources or powers at their disposal on which the local community wished to call. Fogo Island and other early experiments with this technique were eagerly seized upon by planners, especially in the developing countries, and the key actors—in the Film Board and Memorial University—were soon in great demand to advise on similar projects. A second element of the Challenge for Change project was a series of short films which were designed as discussion starters for courses or community meetings about matters related to citizenship, dealing with the bureaucracy and so on. Not officially part of Challenge for Change, but similarly closely related to action for social change are special units, such as the Women's unit of NFB, which have produced important films about issues in Canadian society.

The Canadian Association for Adult Education (CAAE), under the leadership of its first director, E.A. Corbett, took the initiative in the creation of two important educational projects involving print, broadcasting and local study groups, National Farm Radio Forum and Citizens' Forum. The former, being the original venture, gained a world-wide reputation and has been adapted for use in many other countries.

It has already been pointed out that one of the major tasks facing Canadian society was to extend education to the rural parts of the population. This had to do with the vocational and technical aspects of agricultural pursuits, but also with building a society in Canada which included rural people in a meaningful way. E.A. Corbett had formerly been involved for many years in university extension work in Alberta and had a keen sense of what was most

---

[50] G. Evans, *John Grierson and the NFB*.

needed in rural Canada. The CAAE, in co-operation with the Canadian Federation of Agriculture and building on earlier experiments in Ontario, approached the CBC about a proposed national educational program, which was to become National Farm Radio Forum.[51] Farm Forum was a program which involved four principal elements: the local listening and discussion group; a printed pamphlet on each week's topic; a weekly radio broadcast, also on the topic for the week; and feedback to the program organizers concerning the group's opinions on the topics discussed (and also feedback to all listening groups on what opinions had been throughout their region on the previous week's topic). The CAAE, through its provincial allies (often the university extension departments), organized the groups and produced and mailed the pamphlets. (The Federation of Agriculture assisted in these tasks.) The CBC produced the broadcasts. The listening groups, having read the pamphlet and having met to listen to the broadcast, then turned off the radio and went on to discuss the subject, afterwards conveying their opinions or consensus to a "provincial secretary," who went on the air at the end of each broadcast in order to report back to all groups on reactions to the previous week's topic. By these means, rural listeners in all parts of Canada were engaged over a twenty-six-week season in the consideration of a range of topics generally related to the interests of rural people—topics on agricultural policy, international trade, community and family life, or other public affairs topics. The program went on from 1941 until 1965 and over that period involved persons from all parts of Canada in the consideration of significant questions affecting their lives and the welfare of their communities. Benefits were seen for the individuals involved, but there was also an intent to contribute to the sense of common interest among Canadians. It was part of a strategy on the part of Corbett and other leaders of the enterprise to play a part in building the Canadian national community.[52] Development planners from other countries saw potential in the Farm Forum approach for their own development plans. UNESCO requested that the CAAE prepare a study of the project through which its methods could be made known to the international community. This was carried out by Alex Sim, one of the pioneers of Farm Forum, and was published in 1954 by UNESCO.[53] It has been stated that over forty countries subsequently made use of some form of the project.[54]

---

[51] R. Faris, *The Passionate Educators* (Toronto: Peter Martin, 1975); R.A. Sim, *Canada's Farm Radio Forum* (Paris: UNESCO, 1954).

[52] E.A. Corbett, *We Have With Us Tonight* (Toronto: Ryerson, 1957); R. MacKenzie in J.R. Kidd, *Adult Education in Canada*; R. Faris, *The Passionate Educators*.

[53] R. Sim, *Canada's Farm Radio Forum*.

[54] J.R. Kidd, *Learning and Society* (Toronto: Canadian Association for Adult Education, 1963).

In the period of reconstruction thinking during and immediately after World War II, it was decided to develop a program which utilized the methods of Farm Forum but which would be aimed at a more general, perhaps mainly urban, listening audience and would focus on general citizenship and public affairs topics. Thus was created Citizens' Forum, a joint project of the CAAE and the CBC, which began on the national network in 1943 and continued for twenty years.[55] It is clear that this program arose from a conscious feeling on the part of many adult educators that the movement should contribute to the "reconstruction" of Canadian and international society, following a decade of depression and world war.[56] This project represents a further major contribution of the instigator E.A. Corbett to the development of the Canadian nation. Corbett has been seen by observers outside the field of adult education as "a leader of the intellectual mafia" who were "promoters of a Canadian national consciousness."[57]

Another important and distinctive Canadian contribution to education in the field of citizenship, social and cultural development was the Joint Planning Commission (JPC). Created in 1947 at the instigation of E.A. Corbett, this "organization" brought together, usually three times a year, the representatives of many national agencies—departments of government, voluntary agencies, churches, labour and business groups—a wide range of groups actively involved in the educational, social and cultural development of Canada.[58] The word "organization" is put in quotation marks because there was no such thing as membership, in the usual sense. The CAAE provided the secretariat and called the parties together for the regular meetings, but the participating organizations sent representatives only because the meetings continued to be useful to them, not because of a membership commitment. Indeed it likely would not have been possible to maintain the useful mix of organizational representation—the private and public sectors together—if a formal membership had been required. Emphasis was placed on exchange of information about the activities, plans and concerns of the various bodies. Laidlaw indicates that during the program year 1954-55, for instance, participants in the JPC included 114 organizations: 49 voluntary organizations, 18 government departments and agencies, 17 university extension departments, 15 business and professional groups, 6 provincial departments of education, 5 church

---

[55] R. Faris, *The Passionate Educators*; I. Wilson in J.R. Kidd, *Adult Education in Canada*; I. Wilson, *Citizens' Forum: Canada's National Platform* (Toronto: OISE, 1980).

[56] I. Wilson in J.R. Kidd, *Adult Education in Canada*; I. Wilson, *Citizens' Forum*.

[57] W.R. Young, *Making The Truth Graphic: The Canadian Government's Home Front Information Structure and Programs during World War II* (Unpublished Ph.D. Thesis, University of British Columbia, 1978) p.22-23.

[58] C. Clark, *The Joint Planning Commission* (Toronto: Canadian Association for Adult Education, 1954).

organizations and 4 labour organizations.[59] There were valuable exchanges of information and views about matters of mutual interest, and programs which informed the participants about important national issues such as broadcasting policy, national royal commissions and other significant government actions, the educational potential of television and similar topics. The JPC continued in operation until 1968, reaching one high point in 1964, when the Prime Minister, L.B. Pearson, addressed the group (on International Co-operation Year).[60] The organization had been the object of study by many visitors from other countries over the years. The maintenance of such clearing house or co-ordinating bodies in adult education had proven to be a very difficult achievement and many came to study this success story in Canada.

The final example of citizenship education—the Women's Institutes organization—is of a distinctly different type. It may be said that the Women's Institutes, now a world-wide movement, were a Canadian "invention." The first local institute was founded in Ontario in 1897 at the instigation of Adelaide Hoodless, an active leader in women's organizations. The aims of the W.I.s as they have subsequently developed have generally to do with citizenship and with the quality of life for rural and small town women. They contribute to community betterment, are advocates to government and others concerning the welfare of children, women and the family, and sponsor a wide range of educational activities on household arts and related matters for their own membership and other interested persons.[61]

The Challenge of Distance and Regionalism

The Canadian story has to a very large extent been one of coping with the hugeness of scale of the country, especially in view of the relatively small population. One of the major schools of interpretation of Canadian history has seen the St. Lawrence waterway and the extension of its influence westwards by means of modern transport and communications as the key to Canadian survival and development.[62] In the early decades of Canadian nationhood, there was an awareness of the fragility of the country and a realization that the nation must be bound together East to West (to some extent in defiance of the North-South geographical regions which linked parts of Canada more naturally with American territory than with the rest of Canada) by such means as

[59] A.F. Laidlaw, *The Campus and the Community.*

[60] G. Selman, "Alan Thomas and the Canadian Association for Adult Education 1961-1970" in *Adult Education in Canada: Historical Essays.*

[61] E. Chapman in J.R. Kidd, *Adult Education in Canada*; R. Collins in J.R. Kidd, *Learning and Society* (Toronto: Canadian Association for Adult Education, 1963); E. Rand, *Federated Women's Institutes of Canada: A History 1919-1960* (Ottawa: F.W.I.C., 1961).

[62] C. Berger, *The Writing of Canadian History.*

the railways and the telegraph, and when it became available, by broadcasting. In more recent decades there has also been an awareness on the part of many of a threat of cultural rather than physical domination from the United States, and conscious efforts have been made to strengthen the quality of communications and cultural development within Canada.

The educational activities of the Canadian Broadcasting Corporation and the National Film Board, some of which have already been referred to, are clearly a part of the Canadian nation's deliberate efforts to combat the distances that are a fact of life in Canada. Similarly, National Farm Radio Forum and Citizens' Forum may be seen as projects which attempted to offset the problems of distance—by means of the mails and radio broadcasting—in order to engage Canadians in all parts of the country in an informed consideration of issues in which Canadians have a common interest.

There have been other significant adult education projects in Canada which may be seen in the same context. One is the co-operation of the CBC and a voluntary agency, the Canadian Institute on Public Affairs, in the organization and broadcasting of major conferences on public affairs topics—summer meetings at the Lake Couchiching conference centre of the Y.M.C.A. and winter conferences held in Toronto.[63] Several national organizations in Canada which focus on national and international affairs have developed strong programs over the decades by means of establishing local branches or chapters in the main population centres and servicing these by means of print—newsletters and other publications—and by sending speakers on tours or circuits so they could speak to many of the branches. Canadian organizations which flourished by these means have included the Men's and Women's Canadian Clubs, the Canadian Institute on International Affairs, and the League of Nations Society and its successor, the United Nations Association.

It has been pointed out that, in a variety of ways, some successful adult education projects have involved means of coping with the geographical separation of the far-flung regions of the country. The other side of the coin is the tendency in Canada towards regionalism or sectionalism. The outstanding cultural critic, Northrop Frye, termed it a "garrison mentality" and characterized the regions of the country as "solitudes touching other solitudes."[64] The most obvious feature of this phenomenon in Canadian life is the gulf which exists between the French-speaking Canadians in the Province of Quebec and the rest of English-speaking Canada. Here the facts of geography are reinforced by differences in language, culture and provincial rights. Significant contributions to adult education within Quebec are hardly known to the

[63] F. Peers in I. Wilson et al., *Education in Public Affairs by Radio* (Toronto: Canadian Association for Adult Education, 1954).

[64] N. Frye, *Divisions on a Ground* (Toronto: Anansi, 1982) p.59.

rest of the country. And because education is a provincial responsibility under the Constitution, the pace and character of adult education services also varies greatly from one province to the next.

There have been important regional developments in adult education in Canada. Three examples will be cited. The Antigonish Movement has already been described briefly. What might be noted in addition at this time is the fact that, not only did St. Francis Xavier University serve its own immediate region with its co-operative education program, but it also inspired similar (though less lasting) programs of much the same kind in the neighbouring provinces of New Brunswick and Prince Edward Island.

There was a provincial and regional concept behind the Banff School of Fine Arts (as it was originally called) in Alberta from the very beginning. Founded in the depths of the Great Depression, the school was from the outset seen as a resource for people throughout Alberta and beyond who were interested in the arts but did not have available at the local level the expertise of instruction and other resources which would enable them to advance their skills to the higher level which they sought.[65] Under the leadership of Donald Cameron, the Banff institution grew from its small beginnings to a large residential and educational facility which operates on a year-round basis and in a wide range of subject matter. It operates many programs under its own auspices and acts as a hotel or residential educational facility for many other groups as well.

There has always been a "sense of partnership" between librarians and adult educators. Indeed, in the years before the emergence of a self-conscious adult education movement in Canada, librarians were among the most forceful advocates of the need for adult education services. The importance of library services as a resource for adult education activity is obvious. In the early decades of the development of library services in Canada, they tended to be highly local in character. The Public Library Commission in British Columbia launched an experiment in the late 1920s which helped to set a new course for library development in that province, and elsewhere in Canada and the world.[66] It involved creating a library organization which would serve a whole region (the Lower Fraser Valley in British Columbia), some twenty-four municipalities, and moving the holdings around the region, as required, to meet local needs and requests. This experiment was financed initially by the Carnegie Corporation of New York and it was a manifestation of its success that when that grant ran out, in the depth of the Depression (1932),

---

[65] D. Cameron, *Campus in the Clouds* (Toronto: McClelland & Stewart, 1956); and D. Cameron, *The Impossible Dream* (Privately printed, 1977).

[66] M.C. Holmes, *Library Service in British Columbia* (Victoria: Public Library Commission of B.C., 1959); M. Gilroy & S. Rothstein (Eds.), *As We Remember It* (Vancouver: University of British Columbia/School of Librarianship, 1970).

twenty-two of the twenty-four municipalities involved voted to continue the service as a charge against local taxation. Helen Stewart, who had headed up the project, subsequently received many invitations from other countries to consult about the establishment of similar systems elsewhere.[67]

Another dimension of the effects of the size of Canada on the development of adult education has been that of the "frontier." The consciousness of a frontier has been a continuing phenomenon in the life of Canada from its earliest days. In the early years, this was thought of mainly in terms of "the West." More recently the focus has been on the northern parts of Canadian territory. Our most famous historian, H.A. Innis, has pointed out that by contrast with the United States, Canada has had a "hard" frontier. Many of Canada's resources are hard to get at; the climate in much of the country is inhospitable, and many of the resources are hidden in the earth's crust and difficult to extract and move to market. As S.D. Clark has put it, "What was called for in the opening up of this northern half of the continent were massive accumulations of capital, large scale forms of economic organization, long lines of communication and transportation, and extensive state support."[68]

It was against this background that another unique Canadian adult education institution, Frontier College, did its work.[69] Founded in 1899 as the Canadian Reading Camps Association, the work of the College has for most of its history concentrated on English language instruction (most of the students were recent immigrants) and what today we would term adult basic education. Frontier College arranged with the employer in the camp to provide a regular job for a worker to be supplied by the College. The latter then recruited persons, usually from the universities, who agreed to perform such jobs and also, in the evenings and on weekends, to organize educational activities for any of the workmen who would be interested in such activity. The "worker-teacher" earned his wage from the employer for his regular daytime duties, and received little or no pay for his role as educator. This project went on quietly for many decades, largely unnoticed even in the world of adult education. But when, in the 1960s, Canada began to take note of the extent of illiteracy and under-education in the country and began to mount substantial programs in those areas, it was "discovered" that Frontier College had extensive experience in adult basic education and was a valuable resource in helping Canadians prepare themselves for this work.[70] Frontier College

---

[67] M. Gilroy & S. Rothstein, *As We Remember It*.

[68] S.D. Clark, *Canadian Society in Historical Perspective* (Toronto: McGraw-Hill, 1976) p.55.

[69] A. Fitzpatrick, *The University in Overalls* (Toronto: Hunter-Rose, 1920); G.L.Cook in M. Welton, *Knowledge for the People*.

[70] I. Morrison in M. Brooke (Ed.), *Adult Basic Education* (Toronto: New Press, 1972).

subsequently became involved in community development programs as well, and has in more recent decades concentrated on inner-city projects and on programs for farm workers. It has been a model for serving frontier camps or communities and has been studied by persons from various other countries. It has received international awards for its contributions to literacy education. Frontier College is a clear example of how an institutional form and a methodology were developed in response to the social and economic circumstances pertaining in the areas to be served.

The Federal-Provincial Context

Under the Canadian Constitution, education is assigned as a provincial responsibility. Each of the ten provinces has in many respects gone its own way in this field, and institutional arrangements vary markedly from one province to another, especially (though not only) at the post-secondary level. The federal government has certain tasks assigned to it in the field of education—education in the Northern Territories, of Native people, those in the armed forces (and their dependents), and those in federal penal institutions. In addition, by agreement with the provinces, the federal government has played a role in several other areas of education, such as language and citizenship training for immigrants; bilingualism education for civil servants and others; citizenship education and the promotion of inter-ethnic communication and understanding; grants to the provinces to share in financing post-secondary education; support of museums; rehabilitation of disabled persons; and in recent decades, direct assistance to various local groups (older persons, for instance). The federal government has also rendered direct assistance to educational activity within the labour movement by providing supporting grants for such work to national labour bodies.

The outstanding further example of how the federal government has "cooperated" with the provinces in the field of adult education is that of adult occupational training.[71] A detailed account of federal-provincial relations in this field is provided in a subsequent chapter. It is simply noted here that up until the late 1960s, the federal authorities sought to encourage the provinces to be more active in this area by indirect means—by providing funds which could be drawn upon by the provinces on a matching basis. With new legislation in 1967, the federal government assumed a more direct role in the provision of such training.

---

[71] J.D. Wilson et al., *Canadian Education: A History*; J.S. Dupre et al., *Federalism and Policy Development: The Case of Adult Occupational Training in Ontario* (Toronto: University of Toronto, 1973); J.W.G. Ivany & M.E. Manley-Casimir (Eds.), *Federal-Provincial Relations: Education Canada* (Toronto: OISE, 1981).

An important "side effect" of the legislation of the 1960s and beyond may be seen in the field of Adult Basic Education (ABE)—literacy to high school completion and English (or French) as a second language (ESL) training. When, as a result of the funds made available by legislation of 1960, greatly expanded facilities and programs for vocational training began to become available, it was revealed just how many people in Canada were not able to cope with the programs offered because of lack of basic education and/or lack of knowledge of the language. The federal authorities were therefore drawn into having to finance ABE and ESL activity on a very large scale. The Canadian government's "War on Poverty" measures which were launched in the mid-1960s added emphasis to such work. The new legislation in 1967, the Occupational Training Act, made more direct and adequate provision for such work. Six out of the ten provinces took up the federal offer to wholly fund provincial "NewStart" corporations, which were designed to provide leadership in ABE activities in the regions.

Such federal initiatives had the effect of revealing the extent of the need for ABE and ESL in Canada and of beginning to meet the need. However, when austerity budgets in the early 1970s forced the federal authorities to cut back on its work in ABE and ESL, the task fell into the hands of the provinces. Nothing was more obviously a provincial responsibility, after all, than basic education. The provinces responded very unevenly to this challenge—as they have to all aspects of adult education—but for better or for worse, the ball was largely back in their court. The 1960s had been a period of strong federal government leadership in adult education. But as in the case of Canadian federation as a whole, the late 1960s and the subsequent decades brought strong decentralizing tendencies.[72] In this latter case, one can see a further demonstration of how trends and developments in the broader context of national life were reflected in the field of adult education.

Community and Communitarianism

During the great debate over the Free Trade Agreement with the United States which took place during the federal election campaign of 1988, there was a great deal of attention focussed by those opposed to the Agreement on distinctive features of Canadian culture and society which might be endangered by the creation of a "level playing field" between the two countries.[73] Perhaps the most prominent aspects of Canadian life which were identified in

---

[72] R. Bothwell, I. Drummond & J. English, *Canada Since 1945* (Toronto: University of Toronto, 1981); J.M.S. Careless, *Canada: A Story of Challenge* (Toronto: MacMillan, 1970); M.S. Cross & G.S. Keeley (Eds.), *Modern Canada: 1930-1980s* (Toronto: McClelland & Stewart, 1984); D.V. Smiley, *Canada in Question: Federalism in the Seventies* (Toronto: McGraw Hill, 1972).

[73] E. Finn (Ed.), *Canada: Don't Trade It Away* (Ottawa: Canadian Union of Public Employees, 1978).

that connection were Canadians' greater confidence in government as an instrument of public benefaction, and the greater tendency in Canada to care for each other's welfare, or as Robin Matthews and others have termed it, "the communitarian tradition in Canada."[74]

Reference has already been made to the tendency in Canada (usually seen in contrast to American views) to rely on government as an instrument to facilitate social well-being and progress. Our leading historiographer has termed it "constructive socialism"[75] and another historian, "the social service state."[76] In a landmark sociological study of Canadian society published in 1961, Kaspar Naegele pointed out that Canadians were more ready to trust government than were Americans.[77] We have seen earlier how the crown corporation, be it in the form of a national railway or airlines, broadcasting network or film production organization, has been used repeatedly in Canada as a means of serving the economic, social and cultural strengthening of the nation. One of our leading historians, A.R.M. Lower, has put it this way: "At every critical juncture of our national life, when we have been faced with a choice between individualism and socialization, we have chosen socialization."[78] This may help to explain also why in Canada there has been such a heavy emphasis on public educational institutions—schools, colleges, universities—as the means of delivering adult education services.

It has been stated by Leslie Armour, a contemporary Canadian philosopher, that "communitarianism and its outcomes" is one of the sets of ideas which has most strongly shaped Canadian life.[79] He has placed a great deal of stress on the community as the source of Canadians' identity. Our most prominent cultural historian and critic, Northrop Frye, frequently stressed the tendency of Canadians to draw strength—and in the case of our artists, vision—from the local community.[80] Perhaps in the ideas of such writers it is possible to see the reason why community education and community development have found such fertile ground in Canada.

Community development has been at the heart of a number of significant and well-known adult education projects in Canada. National Farm Radio Forum led to many community improvement projects at the local level. The Joint Planning Commission, which has already been described, may be seen

---

[74] R. Matthews, *Canadian Identity* (Ottawa: Steel Rail, 1988).

[75] C. Berger, *The Writing of Canadian History*, p.200.

[76] R. Bothwell et al., *Canada Since 1945*, p.311.

[77] K.D. Naegele in B.R. Blishen et al. (Eds.), *Canadian Society: Social Perspectives* (Toronto: MacMillan, 1961) p.27.

[78] Cited in B. Ostry, *The Cultural Connection* (Toronto: McClelland & Stewart, 1978) p.55.

[79] L. Armour, *The Idea of Canada* (Ottawa: Steel Rail, 1981) p.109.

[80] See for instance, N. Frye, *Divisions on a Ground*.

as having made an important contribution to the social and cultural development of the Canadian community and sense of identity for two decades in the post-World War II period. The Antigonish Movement in Nova Scotia proceeded largely by means of community development methods. Mention has also been made of the important contribution of the National Film Board to community development methodology through its Challenge for Change project.

Canadian communities were the site of many other community development projects. Examples of community development activity abound in the Canadian story. Robert England has described how he and his wife developed the prairie "lighted schoolhouse" into an instrument of community development in the early 1920s. His work and that of his staff in the ethnic communities along the Canadian National Railways route across the prairies (under the sponsorship of the railway) deserves to be better known than it is.[81] Mr. and Mrs. Harry Avison conducted a community development project at The Pas, Manitoba, under the auspices of the Canadian Association for Adult Education in the late 1930s.[82] Florence O'Neill's memorable articles on the work she carried out in the small towns of Newfoundland during the early 1940s represent an important stage in this work as well.[83] The Royal Commission on Agriculture and Rural Life, which carried out its work in Saskatchewan from 1952 to 1956, was an important pioneer in the use of a public inquiry and its related research activity as an instrument of community development. Shortly thereafter the Government of Manitoba decided to launch "one of the first official community development programs in Canada,"[84] a program among Metis people of that province.[85] It is clear that the Quiet Revolution in Quebec during the 1960s and thereafter involved several forms of community development work, as did aspects of the federal government's War on Poverty measures of the latter half of the decade. The latter included, for instance, community development activities under the Agricultural Reconstruction and Development Act, and community development projects carried out under the Company of Young Canadians, Opportunities for Youth and the Local Improvement Projects. Mention should be made as well of a series of projects carried out in the early 1970s in Eastern Ontario under the sponsorship of Algonquin College in Ottawa.[86] In the very early 1970s the federal govern-

---

[81] R. England, *Living, Learning, Remembering* (Vancouver: Centre for Continuing Education, University of British Columbia, 1980).

[82] M.R. Welton, "'A Most Insistent Demand': The Pas Experiment in Community Education," *Canadian Journal for the Study of Adult Education*, 1, 2 (1987) pp.1-22.

[83] F. O'Neill in J. Draper (Ed.), *Citizen Participation: Canada* (Toronto: New Press, 1971).

[84] J. Draper, *Citizen Participation: Canada*, p.246.

[85] J. Legasse in J. Draper, *Citizen Participation: Canada*.

[86] A. Stinson in J. Draper, *Citizen Participation: Canada*.

ment entered into a series of agreements with groups of First Nations people in Canada to provide community development services.[87] At about this same time, the National Film Board was getting into its Challenge for Change project, which has already been described. As well, Frontier College, which had mainly concentrated on its worker-teacher activities, began in the early 1970s to enter into contracts with provincial governments under which the College provided personnel to conduct community development projects in designated towns.[88]

The early and mid-1970s brought a wave of fiscal austerity in Canada and, in some quarters, a turning to more conservative government philosophies. The years of flourishing community development activities were over. Once again, the linkage between events in the broader Canadian society and those in adult education were obvious. Trends begun in the 1970s have become even more pronounced since that time.

The Impact of General History on the Development of Adult Education

While many more detailed examples could be given to illustrate further the clear connection between the general history of Canada and that of adult education—and the necessity of having knowledge of the broader history in order to fully understand developments in adult education—two examples will be provided in greater detail.

The first is that of "The 1943 Manifesto," which was approved and published in that year by the Canadian Association for Adult Education (CAAE). The Manifesto was a declaration of principles endorsed (unanimously) by a national conference of the organization. It was a brief statement containing a general introduction and a statement of seven principles. It refers to the need for "a new Canadian and world society" and invites interested individuals and groups to join in the "urgent educational task" of working towards that end.[89] It declares that "academic aloofness and neutrality are not enough" and declares itself in support of certain principles. Among these, for instance, is the assertion that "social controls and planning are necessary" and that it is "probable that the area of public ownership and control should be extended ... " This declaration, it is fair to say, had little practical effect on the program of the Association[90] and was replaced three years later by another declaration. However, it earned the CAAE a reputation for being anti-free enterprise,

---

[87] J. Lotz in J. Draper, *Citizen Participation: Canada.*

[88] See for instance F. & N. McLeod in J. Draper, *Citizen Participation: Canada.*

[89] Full text in J.R. Kidd, *Learning and Society,* pp.108-109.

[90] G. Selman, "The Canadian Association for Adult Education in the Corbett Years: A Re-evaluation" in *Adult Education in Canada: Historical Essays.*

gained it some enemies, and colours some public attitudes towards the organization to this day. When one comes to examine this incident closely, in terms of what was going on in the rest of society at that time, the action, while perhaps politically unwise in some ways, was hardly surprising. The depression had left a legacy of doubt about the future of Canadian society and some elements of socialist thinking had become quite broadly accepted.[91] There was great concern—in the armed forces and at home—that the end of the war would bring a return to economic problems and unemployment. At this time in the war, much attention was being given to the problems of reconstruction, and ideas for reform were in the air. Indeed the following year the Liberal government brought in several significant welfare measures. Faris has shown that there were ideological and social forces which converged at this time in the CAAE and which help to explain the concurrence on such a manifesto.[92] There may be many questions still to be considered in providing a full and satisfactory explanation as to why such a manifesto was passed, but it is clear that any attempt to explain it only in terms of the views of a few key leaders or relationships internal to the CAAE would fall far short of the mark. There were forces at work in the broader Canadian society which were clearly powerful in explaining the action that was taken in this adult education organization.

A second such example has to do with the emergence, mainly during the 1960s and early 1970s, of provincial organizations of adult educators, and of their relationship with the national organization, the Canadian Association for Adult Education. The CAAE was formed in 1935 and, except for a few short-lived regional bodies which came and went from time to time, by 1950 it was still the only organization of adult educators, at least in English-speaking Canada.[93] During the 1950s, provincial organizations emerged in two provinces, Saskatchewan and British Columbia. In 1961, after a review of its operations, the B.C. body decided to alter its nature and asked the national organization, the CAAE, to change its constitution in order to create "divisions," provincially-based bodies which would be integral parts of the CAAE, and not just affiliates. This change was made and, during the course of the 1960s, adult educators in six provinces created divisions of the CAAE. But as the 1960s progressed, regionalism and the decentralization of initiative within Canadian confederation as a whole greatly increased,[94] and populist ideas

---

[91] D. Creighton, *The Forked Road: Canada 1939-1957* (Toronto: McClelland & Stewart, 1976).

[92] R. Faris, *The Passionate Educators*.

[93] G. Selman, "Specialization or Balkanization: Organizations of Adult Educators," in *Adult Education in Canada: Historical Essays*.

[94] R. Bothwell et al., *Canada Since 1945*; J.M.S. Careless, *Canada: A Story of Challenge*; D.V. Smiley, *Canada in Question*.

were strengthening in various aspects of Canadian life. When, in 1967, educators in Alberta came to form a provincial body, they decided that it would remain an autonomous organization rather than be a division of the national one. Pressures began to increase within the CAAE of a populist and provincially based nature to abandon the tightly integrated form of national organization and to enable the provincial bodies to become autonomous (but affiliated) organizations. This was brought about in the early 1970s. The point which needs to be stressed is that an awareness of what was going on in the broader society—the turbulent populist movements and the basic shifts in power and initiative within confederation—places the developments within the adult education movement in an entirely different light. There were forces within the field of adult education which provide some explanation for these developments,[95] but an awareness of the broader picture can make clear some of the connections between a particular field—adult education—and the society of which it is a part.

Aside from the two specific examples just described, there have been many instances of how developments in the field of adult education have reflected other events. The two world wars are particularly obvious examples. These traumatic crises in the life of the nation catapulted enormous numbers of persons into unaccustomed roles—men and women in the armed forces, many into new or expanded wartime industries, many women into the work force for the first time which required them to learn many things, and quickly. The Great Depression of the 1930s placed many persons into altered circumstances, requiring major adjustments on their part, and also elicited from governments a wide range of new policies and provisions in adult education.[96] A combination of forces in the late 1950s—economic recession, high rates of unemployment, and the "shock" which came with recognition of Soviet leadership in space technology—combined to produce a large scale attempt to upgrade the competence of the Canadian work force (The Technical and Vocational Training Assistance Act of 1960). The "War on Poverty" policy of the federal government, announced in 1965, resulted in various pieces of legislation which profoundly altered government policies towards adult education. Many of the social movements which emerged in the 1960s and 1970s, such as the women's movement, the environmental movements, disarmament groups and the like, have added important new dimensions to the adult education enterprise in Canada. The neo-conservative policies of federal and many provincial governments in the late 1980s and since brought a shift in adult education to a greater concentration on vocational or occupational training,

---

[95] G. Selman, "Alan Thomas and the CAAE 1961-1970."

[96] G. Selman, "Adult Education in British Columbia during the Depression" in *Adult Education in Canada: Historical Essays*.

and a shift of a major portion of such work from the public to the private sectors.

It is clear that adult education is predominantly a "reactive" enterprise in our society. It responds to the circumstances and the "agenda" of the community within which it functions. Whereas back in the 1930s and 1940s, the field could be said to have been a social movement, with goals of its own and with a vision of what kind of society it wished to help to create, the field has changed profoundly since that time. While there are still sectors of the field which are inspired by those kinds of goals, adult education today is over-whelmingly dominated by what has been termed the "service ethic."[97] With increased professionalization and institutionalization of the field, adult educa-tion is seen increasingly as a service to individuals rather than as a force to shape the nature of the community. Such changes are lamented by some adult educators, but most appear to welcome the professionalization of the field and see no necessary philosophical implications in their calling. They are content to leave decisions about how knowledge will be used to the individual learner. Many social movements in Canada, however, such as the labour movement, the women's and environmental movements, co-operative and many church-related groups, have a different view, and may be the basis of an emerging "popular education" movement in this country.

Stages in the Development of Adult Education in Canada

In the brief account which follows, the history of adult education in this country is divided into six periods.[98] Such time frames are artificial creations, but they are sometimes helpful in identifying significant trends and notable milestones.

Before 1867

This was largely a period of scattered, informal beginnings, under private and voluntary auspices. It was a time of book clubs, literary and scientific societies, music, handicraft and art associations. It was also a time of heavy reliance on institutional forms which were imported from elsewhere—a kind of adult education colonialism. This included mechanics' institutes, the Y.M.C.A. and voluntary organizations of agricultural producers, for instance. Certain cultural organizations which were to have a long history, the Institut canadien of Montreal (1844) and the Royal Canadian Institute of Toronto (1849), were established in this period. There appears to have been little in the

---

[97] See K. Rockhill in R. Taylor, K. Rockhill & R. Fieldhouse, *University Adult Education in England and the USA* (London: Croom Helm, 1985).

[98] For a more detailed account, see G. Selman, "Stages in the Development of Canadian Adult Education," *Canadian Journal of University Continuing Education*, *10*, 1 (1984) pp.7-16.

way of publicly financed adult education, though public libraries began to appear in some areas, the government of Upper Canada began to subsidize the mechanics' institutes, and the Toronto School Board offered night school classes for a few years beginning in 1855.

1867-1914

Adult education was still largely under private auspices in this period, but important steps were taken which laid the groundwork for the expansion of the public sector.

As the population increased and settlement pushed West and North, there was a continuation of the phenomenon of study groups, institutes and associations devoted to educational and cultural matters. Mechanics' institutes, Y.M.C.A.s and, after 1868, Y.W.C.A.s were formed in increasing numbers. Representative of the wide range of other voluntary organizations which became active in the field are the National Council of Women (founded in 1893) and the forerunner of the home and school movement founded in Beddeck, Nova Scotia, two years later.

Agricultural extension, under both private and public auspices, came into its own in this period. The Grange (the first in 1872), Farmers' Institutes (the first in 1894) and other agricultural societies flourished. The C.P.R. and the federal government operated experimental farms beginning in the mid-1880s. After the turn of the century, the federal and some provincial departments of agriculture became engaged on a large scale in educational activities. Co-operative education in relation to agriculture was under way early in the new century. In 1913 the federal parliament passed the Agricultural Instruction Act, which made federal funds available for use by the provinces for agricultural extension work, an important step in itself, but also significant in that it pioneered the means subsequently to be used by Ottawa to fund other types of vocational education. Other departments of government, for instance, Marine and Fisheries and the Geological Survey, began to offer educational services in this period.

Public educational institutions began in greater numbers to get into the field. The Toronto School Board reinstituted its night classes in 1880 on a permanent basis. Night classes in technical subjects were greatly expanded at the turn of the century. Queen's University became the first university in Canada to begin extension work on a permanent basis in 1889, and Toronto and McGill soon followed suit. After the turn of the century, with the creation of provincial universities in Saskatchewan and Alberta, these two adopted the more broadly based approach to university extension which had been pioneered at the University of Wisconsin.

Three other important organizations had their origins in this period. The first Women's Institute was founded in Stoney Creek, Ontario, in 1897. An organization devoted to the education of rural women and to improving the quality of rural life, the women's institute movement subsequently spread quickly and became world wide. The Canadian Reading Camp Association began its activity in 1899 and has continued its work in frontier camps and communities until very recent times, changing its name in 1919 to Frontier College. The origins of co-operative education in Canada are obscure, but the founding of the Caisse Populaire in 1900 should be noted in that connection.

1915-1939

A traumatic period in the life of the country, these twenty-five years also witnessed the beginning of a conscious adult education movement in Canada and the creation of a number of noteworthy projects. The best-known program during World War I was Khaki College, which provided educational services to servicemen in Britain and Europe. The counterpart in World War II was the Canadian Legion Educational Service, which served both overseas and Canadian-based troops.

A number of important adult education institutions were created in Canada during these years. University extension was begun at many universities, the best-known project being the co-operative education project of St. Francis Xavier University in Nova Scotia, often referred to as the Antigonish Movement. The Workers' Educational Association was established in several centres in Canada in 1918, but was short-lived everywhere but in Ontario. Sir George Williams University, long an evening college and an important source of part-time degree study, was founded in Montreal in 1926. The Banff Centre, originally the Banff School of Fine Arts, was founded under University of Alberta auspices in 1933. And in the late 1930s, two of our most important national institutions were created, the Canadian Broadcasting Corporation and the National Film Board of Canada.

A sign of the growing maturity of the field of adult education was the creation in 1935 of the Canadian Association for Adult Education. Organizational meetings the previous year had laid the groundwork for this step and had commissioned the first national survey of adult education activities.[99] Founded largely by university and government people, the CAAE was originally intended to be a clearing house and information centre for adult education in Canada, but under the dynamic leadership of E.A. Corbett, and influenced by the crisis presented by the world war, the organization was transformed into a direct programming agency, largely in the field of citizenship education.

---

[99] P. Sandiford, *Adult Education in Canada: A Survey* (Toronto: University of Toronto, 1935).

Certain government services developed extensively during this period. In 1919, with the passage of the Technical Education Act, the federal government provided funds for use by the provinces in vocational training, the same device, essentially, which continued to be used until the mid-1960s. Important measures were enacted both federally and provincially as a response to the Great Depression of the 1930s, aimed at providing training and work, but also at improving the morale of the people.

The crisis of the depression and the deep concern about the future of Canadian (and the world) society produced many efforts during the 1930s to study and rethink the basic elements of the citizen's relationship to fellow citizens, and the nature and role of government. A great deal of this effort was directly related to politics and produced several political movements. But much of such study activity was carried out under other sponsorship, for instance, groups under United Church auspices which prepared and issued a major proposal, "Christianity and the Social Order," and other policy statements. The Social Gospel movement was very lively in those desperate days, as were many forms of radical political advocacy.

1940-1959

This was a vibrant time in the life of Canada, in war and peace, and also in the field of adult education. Many of the best-known accomplishments in Canadian adult education were created or gained prominence during these years and there was considerable expansion of provision in this area by public authorities.

The wartime period mobilized Canadians to unaccustomed tasks on an unprecedented scale. Whether in the armed forces, wartime industries or the vast network of civilian and voluntary support services, Canadian men and women responded—and learned—as never before. Canada emerged from the war with an expanded economy and a new sense of identity as a nation. The educational efforts of the Wartime Information Board and of many other organizations during the war years contributed to these changes.[100]

The CAAE, under the leadership of Corbett and Kidd, made remarkable contributions in these two decades. Foremost among these were the three projects in the field of citizenship education, Farm and Citizens' Forum and the Joint Planning Commission, which have been described earlier in this chapter. The post-war period was one of continuing large scale immigration to Canada and both government, through the newly-formed Citizenship Branch, and the voluntary sector, with the effective leadership of the Canadian Citizenship Council, provided many services to "New Canadians."

---

[100] W.R. Young, *Making the Truth Graphic*.

Cold War tensions and Canada's active role as a leading middle power on the world scene at this time encouraged the activities of several important organizations concerned with education about international affairs, including the United Nations Association, the Canadian Institute on Public Affairs and the Canadian Institute on International Affairs. Canadian adult educators, most notably J. Roby Kidd, also began to play an important role at UNESCO and elsewhere in the international adult education movement.

Local and provincial governments in many parts of Canada became involved more actively in the field. The community centre movement swept the country, creating new means of making educational and recreational services accessible at the neighbourhood level. School board adult education programs began to expand rapidly in some areas, most notably in British Columbia. Whereas in 1945 only one province in Canada had a formally constituted adult education section within its department of education, by 1957 seven provinces had taken that step, and by 1961 they all had done so. In Manitoba, the provincial government launched an important community development project among the Metis people. The federal government also began to expand its educational work with First Nations people.

The National Film Board gained world recognition in this period for the excellence of its productions. In order to carry out its mandate of interpreting Canada to Canadians, it devised an outstandingly successful domestic distribution system, which has already been described and which resulted in the Board's productions being seen by a remarkable percentage of the Canadian population.

This was a period, especially in the 1950s, in which a sense of professionalism was emerging in adult education (see Chapter 9). Organizations of adult educators began to appear in some provinces and the CAAE inaugurated series of regional conferences in both the Maritimes and the West. Several universities offered credit courses on the subject of adult education for the first time in the 1950s, and in 1957, the University of British Columbia introduced the first full degree (Masters) program in Canada in this field.

1960-1979

In these two decades enormous strides were made in the field of adult education and this account can at best mention only some highlights. Developments such as the expansion of national investment in vocational and technical training, the "War on Poverty" which began in the mid-1960s, the political strains within Canadian confederation, the emergence of a series of important new social movements, the development of a whole new system of educational institutions (the community colleges) and the gradual acceptance of the fact that education must be seen not as "preparation for life" but as an ongoing part of life—these and other significant changes led to the increased acceptance and vast expansion of adult education within a concept of lifelong learning.

In very broad terms, the 1960s may be seen as a period of important federal initiatives and the 1970s as one in which the provinces began to play a more prominent role. Canada's international stature in the field was demonstrated in 1960, when UNESCO's Second World Conference on Adult Education was held in Montreal and J. Roby Kidd of Canada was elected conference president. The conference is generally seen to have articulated for the field the conviction that adult education had passed the stage of being seen largely as a remedial activity, something one engaged in to make up for what had been missed earlier, and instead should be seen as part of a normal pattern of adult life.

The federal government made enormous contributions to adult education in these years. The character of technical and vocational education was transformed by a great infusion of federal funds, as well as by the decision taken in the mid-1960s by the federal authorities to move into the direct provision of vocational and technical training, rather than leaving it to the initiative of the provinces. Related to the expansion of vocational education was the federal role in the development of adult basic education and English and French as a second language instruction. In both areas federal efforts accelerated educational provision and resulted in pressure being placed on the provinces to increase their efforts as well. Another important area of federal contribution flowed from the "War on Poverty" approach begun in 1965, which spawned a great range of community development, local initiative and social development activities. The bilingualism and multiculturalism policies endorsed by the federal government in this period spurred much educational activity. Lastly, in this highly selective list of federal initiatives, reference should be made to Ottawa's annual grants, which began in the early 1970s, in support of the educational activities carried out by organized labour in Canada.

Developments at the provincial level in this period were, as usual, extremely varied, and a description of them will be left largely to Chapter 8, which deals with policies within each jurisdiction. In some provinces particularly, new policies were increasingly based on a concept of lifelong learning. In the year 1972, the UNESCO report entitled *Learning To Be* was issued, endorsing a lifelong learning strategy and calling for increased attention to adult education as a matter of priority. In the same year, two influential provincial studies in Canada, the Worth Commission in Alberta and the Wright Commission in Ontario, made ambitious proposals explicitly based on the same concept.[101] The Alberta government also instituted its important

---

[101] See UNESCO, *Learning To Be* (Paris: UNESCO, 1972); *A Choice of Futures*, Report of the Commission on Educational Planning (Edmonton: Queen's Printer Province of Alberta, 1972); *The*

Further Education Council policy in the 1970s, which is widely recognized as having greatly strengthened adult education in that province.[102] Reference has already been made to the creation of a whole new system of post-secondary institutions, beginning in the 1960s—the community colleges and institutes. This generally had the effect of making opportunities for continuing education, in academic, vocational and general education areas, more readily available to adults at the local and regional level.[103]

The increasingly obvious fact that adult education was a growing enterprise in Canadian society at this time was confirmed by statistical reports (see Chapter 5 for details). According to Statistics Canada figures, in slightly over twenty years, from 1960 to 1983, the percentage of Canadian adults who were registered each year in some form of adult education increased from approximately 4 percent to approximately 20 percent.[104]

1980-The Present

This period has been increasingly dominated by neo-conservative public policies, including fiscal restraint and the downsizing of both the role and the size of government and of some public institutions. In summarizing the trends of the period, Peter Newman has observed that during these years there was a "power shift from community to self" and that Canadians got the message "that the social contract was no longer valid and that everyone was on their own."[105] This period experienced the passage of the Charter of Rights and Freedoms; two referenda in Quebec and the failure of the Meech Lake and the Charlottetown Accords; the passage of both the Free Trade Agreement and subsequently the North American Free Trade Agreement; and the rise of the Reform Party and the Bloc Québécois. The Mulroney government in Ottawa is associated in the public mind with many of these developments, but it was the Chretien government's budget of early 1995 that was the defining act in signalling the dramatic decentralization of power to the provinces and the erosion of the welfare "provider state."[106]

Learning Society, Report of the Commission on Post-Secondary Education in Ontario (Toronto: Ontario Ministry of Public Services, 1972).

[102] D.E. Berghofer & A.S. Vladicka, *Access to Opportunity 1905-80* (Edmonton: Alberta Advanced Education & Manpower, 1980); *Further Education: Policies, Guidelines, Procedures* (Edmonton: Advanced Education, 1975).

[103] J.D. Dennison & P. Gallagher, *Canada's Community Colleges* (Vancouver: University of British Columbia Press, 1986).

[104] Dominion Bureau of Statistics, *Survey of Adult Education 1960-61* (Ottawa: Queen's Printer, 1964); Secretary of State/Statistics Canada, *One in Every Five: A Survey of Adult Education in Canada* (Ottawa: Sec. State/Statistics Canada, 1984).

[105] P.C. Newman, *The Canadian Revolution 1985-1995* (Toronto: Viking [Penguin], 1995) pp.70-71.

[106] R. Gwyn, *Nationalism without Walls* (Toronto: McClelland & Stewart, 1995); P. Newman, *The Canadian Revolution.*

In one sector of adult education, that of vocational and technical training, the federal authorities provided significant leadership in this period. The National Training Act of 1982 signalled the beginning of a policy of "privatizing" a major portion of such training and in recent years, with the development of the Labour Force Development Boards (federal and provincial), much power was transferred to the provinces and to management and organized labour within the various jurisdictions. The subsequent abandonment of the Development Boards in some provinces has introduced some uncertainty into the situation. In the context of vocational and technical training, the federal authorities have given public endorsation to a policy of lifelong learning and have given support to the prior learning assessment and recognition movement, as part of the labour-force development strategy.

The impact of some of these federal policies on the provision of adult education in Canada has been profound. Public educational institutions have been severely affected by fiscal restraint and, as a result, financial pressure has been placed on all their activities. Particularly hard hit have been low priority activities, such as adult and continuing education services, which have been required to become more self-supporting—in many cases, profit making. In the case of the community colleges, much dislocation has been caused by government's diversion of a major portion of work force development programs, including adult basic education and second language learning, to the private sector. In non-vocational areas, the general result has been the great reduction—in some cases the abandonment—of adult education activities which are least able to be self-supporting, including many services to the most disadvantaged citizens. In general, it can be said that the "haves" in society have continued to be well served; the "have-nots" have fared less well. This has been particularly noticeable at the post-secondary level. At the same time, there has been a flowering of educational entrepreneurs in the private sector, taking advantage of federal vocational and technical training policies favouring the purchase of training from private sector organizations.

Provincial policies have generally fallen in line with those of the federal government. Some provincial governments have been more extreme in their treatment of social services, including adult education, than others, but fiscal austerity has been the situation everywhere. In some cases, there has simply been a shortage of funds; in others, provincial governments have also been following an active policy of downsizing the public sector. At the time of writing, for instance, the Alberta government has for all practical purposes given away its educational communications network, ACCESS, and the Ontario government has announced that it is considering privatizing TV Ontario. The Labour Force Development Boards, which were created in very recent years to oversee the use of public funds in vocational and technical education, are already being disbanded in some provinces. At the program level, there is a general trend that involves the continuation of those aspects of the field which are best able to pay their way financially and the reduction or elimination of those sectors which cannot.

Technological developments in the period have had a profound effect on the nature of programming for adult learners. Distance education, which had been on the increase since the inauguration of the British Open University at the beginning of the 1970s, has been further influenced by the expansion of educational broadcasting and by the increasingly widespread availability of the personal computer. Distance education has been transformed from a mainly print-based methodology to one which is increasingly delivered "on-line" by means of the computer. While computer-based instruction may on the one hand contribute to the physical isolation of the learner at the cost of the social dimension of the educational experience, the methodology has capacity as well to facilitate an increased level of communication for the distance education student between student and teacher and among students. Adult education programming about the use of computers has become a major industry in adult education in these two decades, and the utilization of the computer as a means of delivering educational services has made profound changes in the methodologies of the field.

Changes that have taken place in Canadian society, some of which are noted above, and resultant changes in the practices of many of the public educational institutions, have combined to encourage the growth of the popular education movement in Canada. A wide variety of voluntary organizations, the social movements, the churches and many other community groups have been encouraged to become more active in adult education programming as part of their means of dealing with a society increasingly dominated by the neo-conservative, big-business agenda. This has been an observable trend in the past in times of trouble in society, dating from the emergence of the adult education movement in Britain in the late decades of the eighteenth century, and amply demonstrated again in Canada in the Great Depression of the 1930s.[107] Several forces combined since the 1980s in Canada to encourage a popular education resurgence. These include: the "rights conscious" atmosphere which has followed the enactment of the Charter of Rights and Freedoms in 1982; the cutbacks in the adult education activities by the public educational institutions; the activities of the "New Social Movements" which have emerged since the 1960s (the women's movement, peace and disarmament groups, environmental concern groups, and groups working on behalf of various disadvantaged groups in society, including First Nations people, seniors, low income groups); and groups whose interests or welfare have been

---

[107] T. Kelly, *Adult Education in Great Britain;* G. Selman, "Adult Education in British Columbia during the Depression."

damaged as a result of cuts in the social safety net. The scale and implications of this undoubted expansion of the popular education sector of adult education in Canada have yet to be documented, but it is clear that they are substantial. It remains to be seen what the consequences will be of the accelerated growth of a major segment of the field which tends to be adversarial to prevailing public policies.

The extent of adult education activity in Canada, which as indicated above expanded enormously in the previous period, has continued to grow at a rapid rate. Statistics Canada reports on the field, albeit sporadic, continue to document this growth. From a participation rate of 4 percent of Canadian adults per year in 1960 and just under 20 percent in 1983, the rate had increased to 33 percent by 1992.[108] When we take into account the significant growth in the Canadian population overall in those decades, this represents a truly impressive increase in the size of the adult education enterprise in the country.

The Case of Education in the Labour Movement: Pre-1970

By D'Arcy Martin[109]

Far too many Canadians, including many union members, assume that the labour movement consists of a few men with flashy suits and big salaries, sitting behind desks in sumptuous offices. Certainly many unions now have a sizable full-time staff, but a few highly publicized leaders—villains like Hal Banks or heroes like Bob White—overshadow the small army of committed men and women who have taken time out after work to keep their unions going, without any expectation of material reward for themselves.[110]

The nerve and voluntary effort of working people, so essential in building their labour movement, have long been nurtured by adult education, both informal and non-formal. Today, courses run by unions are the most significant non-vocational adult education to which working people have access, involving directly over 100,000 Canadians a year.[111] Often both the instructor and the participant are donating their time and, in most instances, their only material reward is a couple of meals while using a paid leave from regular employment in order to learn together. And unions are vital partners in work-

---

[108] Statistics Canada, *Adult Education and Training Survey* (Ottawa: Statistics Canada, 1993).

[109] The material in this section was prepared for this book by D'Arcy Martin, a leading educator in the Canadian labour movement. The principal authors are grateful for his contribution.

[110] Craig Heron, *The Canadian Labour Movement: A Short History,* 2nd ed. (Toronto: James Lorimer and Company, 1996) p.x.

[111] Bruce Spencer, "Educating Union Canada." *Canadian Journal for the Study of Adult Education, 8,* 2 (1994) pp.45-64.

place and community education initiatives on issues such as occupational health and safety, literacy, violence against women, anti-racism and the arts.

It is testament to the strength of anti-union views in our society that many otherwise-informed adult educators know little about the scope and richness of this work. On any weekend, there are literally dozens of courses underway in union halls, community centres and hotel rooms. The walls are covered with flip chart paper, videos are playing, role plays are moving from heated argument into laughter, instructors are steering the group back into the session objectives ... in short, lively, practical and innovative adult education is happening. Yet this activity is usually invisible to the educators in the community-based literacy centre around the corner, and even more so to the electronics teacher at the local college, or the professor of accounting in the nearby university extension program.

Nonetheless, the educators hired with the dues of unionized workers have become increasingly effective in producing original videos,[112] in contributing to policy debates on issues such as Prior Learning Assessment and Recognition,[113] and in adapting to their culture the tools developed elsewhere in the field, from role plays to on-line Internet courses.[114] To look at labour education in Canada is to open a vibrant, volatile and significant chapter of adult education history.

The Development of Adult Education in Canada's Labour Movement

The lessons of collective action by workers have traditionally been learned on the job and in the streets. By contesting management rights in the workplace, by withdrawing labour power in a strike, by joining allies in political action, union activists continue to develop their knowledge, confidence and skills. Any non-formal, structured education programs remain, even today, secondary to the learning that members gain through voluntary engagement in action. Struggle is a teacher, working in the head, heart and feet of workers who have decided to stand up for themselves. Thus, it is no accident that a gripping account of a fishermen's strike in Nova Scotia is entitled *The Education of Everett Richardson*[115] and traces the changes in consciousness of a

---

[112] Some of these are produced internally, as with "It's Not a Game," a collective bargaining tape done by the Canadian Labour Congress. Others are done in co-operation with outside producers, such as "Who Wants Unions?" a documentary on union-busting consultants co-produced by the CLC with the National Film Board.

[113] Unions participated actively in the process leading to the Canadian Labour Force Development Board. (1997), *Prior Learning Assessment and Recognition*. Ottawa: CLFDB.

[114] For example, the Labour College correspondence course is now conducted by Athabasca University on a distance education basis, including telephone coaching. During the fall of 1996, Jeff Taylor and Bruce Spencer from Athabasca University led a course over the Internet entitled "Labour Education and the Internet."

[115] Silver Donald Cameron, *The Education of Everett Richardson: The Nova Scotia Fishermen's Strike,*

worker, the spiral of action-reflection-action which renews social movements from the grassroots up.

At times dramatically public, and at other times masked by the daily routines of work, this action can be traced far back in Canadian history. Contemporary Aboriginal leaders have emphasized the differences between union practice and their own approaches to decision making. Yet certainly early producers of fish and fur, both Aboriginal and colonial, faced issues of work and learning about work. By the early 1800s, associations of workers in the canals, crafts people in the print shops and workshops, took on cultural and educational roles with their members as well as public advocacy. Public campaigns like the Nine-Hour Day Movement of the early 1870s were led by printers, whose work required both literacy and mobility, two keys to spreading the word of unionism.[116] Labour councils, even before being legalized, ran reading rooms for workers. Later, broad public mobilizations like the Winnipeg General Strike of 1919 drew upon the organizational and writing skills picked up by organizers in the increasingly broad public school system. Yet formal courses run by unions were yet to come. Indeed, they required some sustained mobilization of a type difficult to find in early Canadian labour.

> This was, for long periods of our history, an inert culture. For all of the cultural inertia of the working class, however, its apparent fragmentation, acquiescence and accommodation could change with the drop of a hat or, more precisely, the drop of a wage, the demise of a skill, or the restructuring of a job.[117]

During the 1920s and 1930s, the Workers Educational Association (WEA) was a major source of knowledge for union activists. In its heyday, the WEA organized a wide range of inexpensive, non-credit night classes for workers, taught by university professors. By the late 1930s, led by Drummond Wren, it had grown to twenty-four associations in Ontario, fifteen in the rest of the country, and was reaching out to thousands of farmers as well as the urban working class. Typical of its stance was a commitment to social and collective action, tempered by academic caution and a desire to maintain broad support from the government and the public.[118] Meanwhile, the social movements of the 1930s and the industrial organizing drives of the 1940s relied on links between labour activists and their community and political counterparts.

1970-71 (Toronto: McClelland and Stewart, 1977).

[116] Rob Kristofferson, "The Downtown Tour," first of three walking tours, *The Workers City* (Hamilton, Ontario: Ontario Workers Arts and Heritage Centre, 1995) pp.2-8.

[117] Bryan D. Palmer, *Working Class Experience: Re-thinking the History of Canadian Labour, 1800-1991* (Toronto: McClelland and Stewart, 1992) p.21.

[118] Ian Radforth and Joan Sangster, "'A Link Between Labour and Learning': The Workers Educational Association in Ontario, 1917-1951" *Labour/Le Travailleur*, No.8/9 (Autumn/Spring, 1981-82) pp.41-78.

While pushed back during the Cold War, these links were often strengthened in study groups and cultural activities.[119]

In the mid-1950s, the Canadian Association for Adult Education pulled together a meeting with the Canadian Labour Congress (CLC) to develop a basis of co-operation between educators inside the labour movement and those outside, particularly in universities.[120] By this time, the growing industrial unions had developed an internal capacity to do much of the basic training of union representatives. People like Howard Conquergood and Gower Markle had come from the Y.M.C.A. into full-time positions as labour educators, while people like Max Swerdlow and Bert Hepworth moved into similar jobs from a background of internal union action. Hence the unions had either taken educators and turned them into unionists, or vice versa. Either way, there was a nucleus of increasingly experienced and knowledgeable adult education practitioners in the unions who operated independent of the formal adult education institutions.[121]

The independent capacity of labour to teach its own activists was reaffirmed at a 1975 conference which drew nearly 150 delegates from the labour movement, educational institutions and government.[122] The keynote speech was given by Roby Kidd, then Secretary-General of the International Council for Adult Education, and the policy statement at the end called on governments to balance their contributions to management education with financing for labour education. This was in tune with the interest in policy circles in "tripartism," an approach to developing public policy by direct involvement of business and labour in the government process. Union leaders simply said that they didn't have the internal capacity to staff such processes, and required public subsidy to develop it—particularly since unionists paid far more in taxes than was ever recompensed by their participation in publicly funded adult education programs. Shortly afterwards, Labour Canada set up a program to provide direct funding to labour centrals and independent unions, co-ordinated by the former Steelworkers education director, Gower Markle.

---

[119] See, for example, the stories in Susan Meurer and Charlie Angus eds., *Carved from the Rock: Stories from our Union's Past*. Toronto: Miners' History Project, National Office, United Steelworkers of America, 1995.

[120] Canadian Labour Congress—Canadian Association for Adult Education, *Conference Report: Labour University Co-operation on Education* (Ottawa: Canadian Labour Congress, 1956) p.11.

[121] For this and other parts of the story, I draw on years of conversation with Alan Thomas, one of the very few professional adult educators in Canada who was known and trusted by union educators in those years. See Alan Thomas, "How Labour Education Developed in English Canada," unpublished presentation to the Labour Education course, Adult Education Department, OISE, March 6, 1997.

[122] Brian Pearl (Ed.), *Labour Education in Canada: Report of the National Conference on Labour Education* (Ottawa: Labour Canada, 1975) pp.3-17.

This grant was used mostly to develop formalized instructor manuals for the courses being taught across the country, to establish an audio-visual production arm for the unions, and to provide scholarships so that smaller affiliates could participate fully in the available courses.[123] Discussions about use of the funds became a fixture on the agenda of education committee meetings in the central labour bodies, the provincial federations of labour and the Canadian Labour Congress. There, they jostled for space with items like job training, labour history in the school system, and sharing of content and method to improve the weekend and week-long courses that are the bread and butter (also the bread and roses) of union education. For nearly two decades, with the steady and committed work of CLC staff such as Larry Wagg, Jean Bezusky and Danny Mallett, this funding was used to support innovation and build capacity within labour education. When it was cut in the mid-1990s, most unions returned to their core programs, funded from dues or from funding negotiated from the employers in some form of Paid Educational Leave program. Of these, by far the most developed is that of the Canadian Auto Workers, whose Family Education Centre in Port Elgin, Ontario, is one of the finest adult education facilities in the country.

The history of labour education in Canada, then, is entwined with the social action current of adult education. The bias towards action, the impatience with academic theory, the resistance to professionalism, the shortage of resources—these are characteristic of other parts of the field such as literacy and human rights education. Yet there is a particular feel to education within the labour movement, a union culture, which is distinct.[124] Those seeking written reference material will be drawn to the broader literature of Canadian labour history to tease out the learning dimension from the experiences of telecommunications work, industrial work, union history and working class communities.[125] However, understanding will emerge best in conversation with those who teach and learn in this largely oral part of Canada's adult education tradition.

---

[123] Alan Thomas, David Beatty, and Dorothy MacKeracher, *Labour Canada's Labour Education Program: The First Four Years* (Ottawa: Labour Canada, 1982) pp.182-237.

[124] D'Arcy Martin, *Street Smart: Learning in the 'Union Culture'*. Unpublished Ed.D. Thesis, Department of Adult Education, OISE, pp.22-52.

[125] Joan Newman Kuyek, *The Phone Book: Working at the Bell* (Toronto/Kitchener: Between the Lines, 1979); David Sobel and Susan Meurer, *Working at Inglis: The Life and Death of a Canadian Factory* (Toronto: James Lorimer and Company, 1994); Sam Gindin, *The Canadian Auto Workers: The Birth and Transformation of a Union* (Toronto: James Lorimer and Company, 1995); Franca Iacovetta, *Such Hardworking People: Italian Immigrants in Postwar Toronto* (Montreal and Kingston: McGill-Queen's University Press, 1993).

The Face of Canadian Unionism

Many Canadians picture unions as narrow, mechanistic, shrinking and somehow anachronistic. For adult educators outside the unions, it is important to understand how misleading these stereotypes are, and how deeply they are resented by those whose passionate personal convictions build and sustain the movement.

The involvement of labour in social coalitions, around human rights, gender equity and economic development, is in fact very broad. It starts from the community level, as with the Days of Action that mobilized hundreds of thousands of people into the streets of London, Hamilton, Peterborough, Kitchener and Toronto in 1995-96. And it reaches the national level, in structures like the Action Canada Network and the Women's March for Jobs and Justice.

The creative activity of unions, in defence of Canadian culture and in celebration of working-class culture, is extending through music and visual arts, reflected in events like the annual Mayworks Festival of Workers and the Arts.[126] Such initiatives, while valuable, do little to stem the tide of negative imagery from the mass media, both in Canada and the United States. Most union activists spend more time watching American television than thinking about unionism or fine arts. The resulting media invisibility today is a form of disenfranchisement, the modern equivalent of lacking the right to vote.[127]

American television has played a central role in undermining the personal and collective confidence of Canadian workers and replacing it with an envy whose base is in class and nation. When the Machinists union in the United States monitored prime-time television, they discovered that workers in unionized occupations are portrayed as clumsy, uneducated fools who drink, smoke and have no leadership ability. Unions themselves are almost invisible on television, and when they appear, it is as a violent, degrading and obstructive presence. The majority of workers in unionized occupations are the "nameless, personality-less people who take orders, do their jobs and disappear."[128]

Because the economic and political control "the tube" exercises is so enormous, television is the main long-range target for labour arts work. Yet the financial cost of entering this level of competing imagery is beyond the reach

---

[126] See Carole Conde and Karl Beveridge, *First Contract: Women and the Fight to Unionize* (Toronto: Between the Lines Publishing, 1986).

[127] Carole Corbeil, in "Documenting Dangers on the Job Not a Time to Pull Artistic Punches," her review of the first Mayworks Festival, *The Globe and Mail*, May 1, 1986.

[128] Summarized in Catherine Macleod, "How Television Portrays Workers," one in a series of handouts called "Decoding the Media," used in the course manual *Labour's Access to the Media* (Toronto: Canadian Labour Congress, 1985).

of most unions. Working in a smaller scale, arts-positive unionists have come to rely on two sets of claims—access to cultural resources and dignity in representing workers and their organizations.[129]

The issue of access is clear enough. Most public arts funds and practically all commercial investments in the arts and media are channeled to production in which workers have no stake. Securing a share of resources to portray labour's own realities makes sense both in terms of the taxes workers pay and the market share they represent.

The issue of representation is more subtle. Workers and their organizations are practically invisible in mainstream media, and when they do appear it is not usually in positive roles. Over time, however, unions have come to realize that glamourizing workers and unions has its own set of problems. For labour to challenge its negative public image, unions are beginning to develop an arts theory that respects workers' experience.[130] The development of this "labour aesthetic" can unearth and display the jewels of creativity, talent and will in the working class.

The movement in Canada is not only creative; it is gaining in strength. A generation ago, about 30 percent of workers belonged to unions in both the United States and Canada. By the early 1990s, the proportion in the United States was down below 15 per cent, while in Canada it was over 35 per cent. In other words, Canadian labour has twice the depth and presence of American labour, which is reflected in our political culture by gains such as Medicare, and the commitment to preserving those gains in the face of government cuts and employer pressure to privatize. With a recent change in leadership at the AFL-CIO, American labour, too, seems to be reversing its decline and moving to a more activist stance, an "organizing model" rather than a "service model." This should help create a more receptive climate across North America to unions.

Far from being outmoded, unions are rising to the challenge of economic restructuring and cuts to social programs in an open-minded and skillful way. This includes approaching progressive employers with an offer of intelligent co-operation, a value added to their mission, while using on arrogant employers the tactics of union judo—taking their momentum in order to bring them

---

[129] A labour critique of class bias in the arts is "expressed in terms of the twin measures of accessibility (or the democratic right of workers to participate in activities which they pay for as taxpayers) and portrayal (or the right of working people to see themselves reflected and respected in the media)." Susan Crean, "Labour Working With Art," *Fuse Magazine*, No.44 (1987) p.30.

[130] The "labour aesthetic" raises the possibility of actually shifting taste, intervening directly in the process by which the arts evolve. This is the scale of thinking engaged in by the protagonists of Serge Guilbaut's book, *How New York Stole the Idea of Modern Art* (Chicago: University of Chicago Press, 1983). Those people actually developed an aesthetic, abstract expressionism, coded it into arts criticism and linked it to an institutional base (in the Guggenheim Museum), a shift in the art market and an intervention in politics.

down to a level of equality. In celebrating and struggling, Canadian unions are more inclusive and dynamic than at any time since the 1930s.[131]

This is not to suggest that labour educators are working in a perfect world. There are tensions and setbacks, a frustrating distance between rhetoric and the reality of internal practices, a pattern of internal rivalries that is wasteful and weakening. Yet the potential is great for participatory process, socially critical content and increased dynamism among working-class learners. This potential was recognized by the 450 labour educators who assembled in Toronto for an "Educ-Action" conference in early April, 1997. While a third of the participants came from the United States and Latin America, the majority were practitioners within Canada, either directly employed by unions or working in allied organizations such as associations of homeworkers, or workers information and action centres.

The goal of such educators is to equip workers to meet employers, allies and adversaries with creativity and skill. Courses can be broadly classified in the following three categories: (a) skills courses like grievance handling, designed to give members the tools they need to do their work as union activists; (b) issues courses like human rights, designed to keep members current on issues affecting the workplace and labour-management relations; and (c) labour studies courses like labour economics, designed to help members understand the rich history and complex social and political dynamics of the labour movement in Canada and internationally.[132] In each, the issues of democracy and effectiveness are worked through by the educators who work within the movement, and their allies in the adult education field.

Some of these allies are to be found in the universities, but less so than in countries like Britain[133] or the United States.[134] While sympathetic individuals in the university have been drawn into labour courses, from Rick Williams in Halifax to Kate Braid in Vancouver, the major organic link in Canada is the protocol between Quebec unions and the universities, especially the Université du Québec à Montréal. Informal links in English-speaking Canada are

---

[131] Mary Cornish and Lynn Spink, *Organizing Unions* (Toronto: Second Story Press, 1994); Julie White, *Sisters and Solidarity: Women and Unions in Canada* (Toronto: Thompson Educational Publishing, 1993).

[132] Bruce Spencer, "Labour Education for 2001." Paper prepared for Proceedings of the 37th Annual Adult Education Research Conference, University of South Florida, 1996, 288-294. Posted as a core reading in the Solinet Web Site, as part of the course "Labour Education on the Internet," Athabasca University, 1996, p.4.

[133] John Field, "Labour Education in Canada" Northern College, Barnsley, South Yorkshire: Report on a British Council Study Tour, 1983.

[134] In the United States, major universities established Labor Studies Programs with active union involvement, and often drew union activists there even for basic "tools" courses. Hence, the University and College Labor Educators Association has been a dynamic force for many years, and continues to publish regularly the *Labor Studies Journal*.

maintained through the Learned Societies, including since 1995 the Canadian Labour Education and Research Association.

The face of Canadian labour education then, is rarely to be found in prime-time television or in university departments. It is more likely to shine in a modest social action project, when a socially committed adult educator connects in some way with a labour activist as both try to put into practice a genuine pedagogy of the oppressed.[135]

The Function and Culture of Adult Education in the Labour Movement

"No training—no strength."[136] In a unionized workplace, employees have a right to representation. They may want support in an individual clash with management or effectiveness in asserting a collective need such as vacations, job training or workplace health. To exercise their right effectively will involve learning, either by themselves or by fellow workers.

In a healthy union, they will be encouraged to take a course themselves or to select the fellow worker whom they most respect, with confidence that the union will enhance that person's knowledge, confidence and skill as needed. Their representative will be entitled to time off the job to learn, will have any lost wages replaced, and will attend a two-to-five-day session with ten or twenty other people whose learning needs are similar. On returning to the workplace, the representatives will apply what they have learned, and many will have had their appetite whetted for other adult learning.

Implied in this general sketch is a whole culture of adult education. Labour education is based more on collective than on individual rights, more on social dedication than on professional credentials, more on advocacy than on implementation, more on political vision than on measurable competencies. For these reasons, it may seem strange at first to those steeped in the professional, institution-based side of adult education practice.[137]

These are the dynamics of adult education within a social movement. While unions here are considered as educational agents for their members, they are primarily representative and advocacy organizations, engaged in collective bargaining and in mobilization for social change. Any educational programming takes place within this context, and must create an environment

---

[135] Paulo Freire, *Pedagogy of the Oppressed* (New York: Herder and Herder, 1971).

[136] A worker in a paint factory, discussing the courses offered by his union. See Peter Sawchuk, "Report on Learning to Local 200-O of the Communications, Energy and Paperworkers Union of Canada." Occasional Paper of the Working Class Learning Strategies Project, directed by David Livingstone, OISE, 1996.

[137] See Mechthild U. Hart, *Working and Educating for Life: Feminist and International Perspectives on Adult Education* (London: Routledge, 1992).

for learning by adults who usually have had little luck with the formal educational system.

Union courses can be initiated and sponsored at different levels of a central labour body (organized geographically at the municipal, provincial and federal level to bring together workers with a common experience of region regardless of the work they do) and at different levels of an "affiliate" (organized sectorally, to bring together workers with some common experience in the workplace regardless of geography).

Within an "affiliate" union, such as the United Food and Commercial Workers or the Canadian Union of Public Employees, there are essentially three levels of decision making, the local, the region or district, and the national (perhaps in consultation with an international headquarters). At the local level, participants for courses are selected, and the costs of participation covered. At the region or district level, requests for courses are handled by staff, who in turn are often assigned to teach. At the national level, courses are designed, videos are produced, and scheduling is co-ordinated. While this pattern differs among unions, in all there is some form of consensus required before courses really get off the ground.

Some affiliates are too small, or too scattered, to handle educational needs internally. And larger affiliates have found it valuable to have their members mix with others and to join forces for more specialized courses. For this reason, courses are often put on at a municipal level by labour councils, at a provincial level by Federations of Labour, and on a national level by the Canadian Labour Congress.

Two points might be noted here about the work of the labour centrals, the education that links up affiliates. The Quebec labour movement, for over a decade, has handled its financing and organization of courses independently, including use of federal and provincial grants. In effect, there is a form of "sovereignty-association" already operating within labour education. Secondly, while the affiliates have often protected their turf by keeping the central labour bodies relatively weak and underfunded, public funding has sustained their capacity to do innovative and substantial work nonetheless. Hence we find workplace literacy, health and safety, pay equity, anti-racism, tech change, skills training and adjustment addressed educationally by the labour councils, provincial federations and the Canadian Labour Congress. As education providers, the central labour bodies play a significant role, but those familiar with unions in other countries may overestimate the role, not realizing how the relative weakness of central labour bodies in Canada is also a product of Canada's geographical dispersion and history. As Craig Heron has said:

> We have never really had a single national labour movement that grew steadily from humble origins in the nineteenth century to its current healthy size ... Rather, a long series of often independent, locally or regionally based move-

ments rose and declined, depending on the opportunities for organizing that were created within the economy, class relations and the state.[138]

For those readers interested in following up this discussion, a wealth of material is available, on top of sources already mentioned.[139]

* * *

This chapter has been concerned with describing the connection between Canada's historical experience as a nation and the form and content of the adult education enterprise which has been developed. In addition to borrowing various institutional forms from other countries, Canadian adult educators have responded in outstandingly creative and innovative ways to conditions in our own society. Many of these Canadian programs and projects, developed to meet Canadian circumstances, have been judged by authorities in other lands to be of value to them, and have been studied and adapted for use elsewhere. It is likely true to say that no other aspect of education in Canada has had as much impact outside our borders than the field of adult education.

---

[138] Heron, *The Canadian Labour Movement*, p.16.

[139] Of particular interest are a collection of essays on feminism and unionism by Linda Briskin and Patricia McDermott, *Women Challenging Unions: Feminism, Democracy and Militancy* (Toronto: University of Toronto Press, 1993); a study of young workers by Thomas W. Dunk, *It's a Working Man's Town: Male Working-Class Culture in Northwestern Ontario* (Montreal and Kingston: McGill-Queen's University Press, 1991); and an interpretation of the effects of "re-structuring" in two Ontario communities by Jamie Swift, *Wheel of Fortune: Work and Life in the Age of Falling Expectations* (Toronto: Between the Lines, 1995).

Popular education uses many innovative techniques, such as theatre, to assist in learning.
Assemblée générale du Mouvement d'éducation populaire et d'action communautaire du Québec, April 1985.
Courtesy of the author.

3

Adult Education in Quebec

By Vincent Greason

Many of the issues confronting adult educators and learners in Quebec are similar to those experienced by their colleagues in the rest of Canada. As these issues have been dealt with elsewhere, this section mainly focuses on issues which take on a unique perspective in Quebec.

Several of the transformations presented in this chapter have occurred largely unnoticed, as adult education has not tended to be a focal point for educational debate. However, some of them have an undeniable impact on the very nature of the field. Developments such as rapid identification of adult education with employment and economic concerns, for example, or the increasing tendency to force adults into upgrading or retraining as a condition for receiving welfare or unemployment benefits, touch at the heart of an educational philosophy based upon a holistic voluntary approach to the adult educational act. Yet, these developments have never really been submitted to a public debate.

This chapter is a brief overview of francophone adult education in Quebec. It does not pretend to be exhaustive or to present the situation of Quebec anglophone adult education, nor does it deal with adult education for francophones outside of Quebec.

Overview of Adult Education in Quebec

Some of the most remarkable educational developments in Canada during the modern period have occurred in Quebec. Prior to the start of the "Quiet Revolution," as signalled by the election of the Liberals under Jean Lesage in 1960, control over most aspects of Quebec education was maintained by the all-powerful and all-pervasive Roman Catholic Church. Prior to the 1960s, Quebec's educational system was geared to the training of an elite.

One fundamental change brought about by the Quiet Revolution was the setting up of "public" education. A Royal Commission on Education, chaired by respected Laval University professor Alphonse-Marie Parent, was established in 1961 and issued its five-volume report in increments between 1963 and 1966.[1] One of the Parent Commission's first recommendations was the establishment of a Ministry of Education, a recommendation that was acted upon in 1964.[2] The Parent Commission is generally credited with setting the philosophical orientations for Quebec public education until the mid-1990s.

Adult education first appears in Quebec in the early industrial period. As early as 1889, the Quebec government under Mercier created night schools in Montreal and Quebec City in order to permit labourers to complete their basic education. Numbers were so great that many workers had to be turned away.[3]

In the first half of the twentieth century, the co-operative credit union movement, under the leadership of Alphonse Desjardins, marked Quebec, as the network of Caisses Populaires was organized. One of the important tools used by Desjardins to build the Quebec co-op movement was adult education. During the 1920s and 1930s, Catholic Action, a church-based lay movement, formed many of the future leaders of the Quiet Revolution through its program of social analysis based on the "See-Judge-Act" model. Rural networks, including among others the Association féminine de l'éducation et d'action sociale (AFÉAS), organized different initiatives for adults ranging from radio shows to extension courses, union education and public lectures. In spite of these scattered initiatives, it was the arrival of the Quiet Revolution which really permitted a flowering of adult education in francophone Quebec.

With the Quiet Revolution, as previously mentioned, came the Parent Commission. One of the three working committees set up by Parent was on adult education and was chaired by Claude Ryan.[4] Many of Ryan's recommendations were retained by the Parent Commission, and an adult education bureaucracy, the Direction générale de l'éducation des adultes (DGÉA), was integrated into the new MÉQ.

The new DGÉA had an enormous task. Prior to the Quiet Revolution, only one in two Quebecers between five and sixteen years of age was in school; only 16 percent of students went beyond high school (equivalent to Grade 11). In the early 1960s, an estimated 80,000 adults were registered in adult educa-

---

[1] Quebec, *Report of the Royal Commission of Inquiry on Education in the Province of Quebec* (Quebec: Les Presses Des Marais, 1963).

[2] The Ministère de l'éducation du Québec will hereafter be referred to as the MÉQ.

[3] Centrale de l'enseignement du Québec, Confédération des syndicats nationaux, *Histoire du mouvement ouvrier au Québec* (Montréal, 1984) p.34.

[4] Ryan later became well known as the editor of the influential newspaper, *Le Devoir*. After a short stint as leader of the Quebec Liberal Party, he became Minister of Education in Robert Bourassa's government in the 1980s.

tion courses offered by institutions. In the period following the Quiet Revolution, adult education was marked by two major reforms: (1) the broadening of adult access to educational services; and (2) an emphasis on permitting adults to upgrade or complete their formal schooling.[5] By the end of the 1970s, accessibility of the system was such that seventy-nine school boards offered formal adult education services, with more than 410,000 registrants. A further 56,000 adult registrants attended formal adult education programs which were offered by forty-six different CEGEPs.[6]

Apart from these initiatives in the formal education sector, adult education in the informal sector also blossomed following the reforms instituted during the Quiet Revolution. In fact, the 1971 decision of the MÉQ to fund a program for popular education enhanced educational opportunities for thousands of adults within trade unions, co-operatives, and in particular within the voluntary sector, where hundreds of community based groups, many still thriving today, took root in small communities, rural areas, and working class neighbourhoods of major urban centres.

Other initiatives in non-institutional adult education sprang up as well during this period. In 1972, Télé-Université, part of Université du Québec network was created; Radio-Québec (today Télé-Québec) was established, in 1973, with a broad educational mandate.

In 1980, the Parti Québécois government followed through on a commitment to study various aspects of education, including adult education, and appointed a Commission d'étude sur la formation des adultes, with Michèle Jean as its president. The Jean Commission was given a broad mandate to investigate both vocational and socio-cultural aspects of adult education and to frame a comprehensive adult education policy for Quebec.

The Jean Report[7] proposed organizing the entire education system around the principle of lifelong education. It made recommendations for greater government co-ordination and leadership in the broad area of adult education. Finally, and perhaps most controversially, the Jean Report argued for the universal entitlement for all citizens to fifteen years of full-time subsidized education.

Unfortunately, the Jean Commission submitted its report as Quebec entered into a period of severe economic and post-Referendum depression. Many of its proposals were deemed unrealistic, and in 1984 the Quebec government

---

[5] Conseil supérieur de l'éducation (CSÉ), *Pour un accès réel des adultes à la formation continue* (Québec, 1996), p.1.

[6] Institut canadien de l'éducation des adultes (ICÉA), *Apprendre a l'âge adulte* (Montréal, 1994) p.36. The specificity of CEGEPs will be discussed later in this chapter. CEGEP means Collège d'enseignement général et d'enseignment professionnel.

[7] Commission d'étude sur la formation des adultes, *Apprendre: une action volontaire et responsable* (Québec, 1982).

issued a policy statement and action plan for adult education. Entitled *Continuing Education Program, Policy Statement and Plan of Action*, the statement retained only a few of Jean's minor proposals. In fact, this statement indicated for the first time that government policy towards adult education would be dictated more by economic than educational concerns.

In 1994, with the Parti Québécois back in power, an eighteen-month process of public consultation on the state of the education system in Quebec was convoked by Education Minister Jean Garon. Called the Estates General on Education, this process was seen as the first holistic attempt to review Quebec's education system since the time of the Parent Commission some thirty years earlier. Three reports were produced during the life of the Estates General.[8]

Adult education occupied an important place during the life of this consultation. The nomination of Robert Bisaillon, former head of the Conseil supérieur de l'éducation, as co-president, certainly raised the profile of adult education within the Commission itself.[9] Under his direction, the principle of lifelong learning made great leaps, as can be seen in the final report:

> Adult education has a long history in Quebec. It has been marked not only by successful and innovative initiatives but also by setbacks. After 30 years, we now have a clearer picture of what we can and must do. In our opinion, this would be an opportune time for Quebec to draft a *lifelong education policy*, given that major guiding principles must be defined for the education system and that, clearly, lifelong learning must be one of these principles. Although we hesitated to call for such a policy during the first stage of the Estates General, we now believe that one must be formulated. A consensus has been reached on the main objectives that might be included in this policy: it could foster more coherent actions and organization of services and reflect the recognition of people's right to lifelong education.[10]

This historic call by the Estates General for a clear government policy on lifelong learning marked the fruitful culmination of years of pressure mounted by the Institut canadien de l'éducation des adultes (ICÉA).

Founded in 1946, the Institut has been, from the very beginning, the catalyst for serious reflection and analysis of the trends marking the development of adult education in francophone Canada, especially Quebec. The francophone equivalent of the Canadian association for adult education, the ICÉA is

---

[8] Cf. Commission des États généraux sur l'éducation, *The State of Education in Quebec* (Quebec, 1996) (report of the first phase); *A Summary of the Regional Conferences* (Quebec, 1996) (report of the second phase); *Renewing Our Education System: Ten Priority Actions* (Quebec, 1996) (final report).

[9] Under Bisaillon's leadership, the CSE consistently pushed the Quebec government to strengthen its commitment to adult education. His appointment as co-president of the Estates General was generally well received by the adult education community.

[10] Commission des États généraux, *Renewing Our Education System*, p.36.

a coalition of union, institutional and non-formal education partners dedicated to advancing and defending adult education in all of its diversity.

Like the CAAE, the Institut saw its federal funding cut in 1995, a decision which has had a major impact on the organization and on its independent research capacities. With fewer researchers, the Institut has been forced to cut back many of its activities, notably in the areas of popular education, media analysis and new technologies. On the other hand, it completed, in 1995, a major survey of Quebec's needs in adult education.[11]

Selected Issues Relating to Adult Education in Quebec

Four major issues will have an impact on adult education over the coming years in Quebec. While many of these same issues have been dealt with elsewhere in this book, this section will attempt to situate them in terms of their specificity for Quebec.

Poverty and Unemployment

The Quebec bishops reported in 1994 that 18 percent of Quebec's population lived below the poverty line.[12] In the same year, Statistics Canada, using 1990 census data, reported that

- 14.5 percent of Quebec families lived below the poverty line;
- one in four Quebec families were single-parent; nine times out of ten, a woman headed the single-parent family; 55 percent of single-parent families lived on social assistance.[13]

Experts agree that long-term chronic (under)employment, officially at more than 11 percent for more than twenty years, is the largest single factor explaining Quebec's high poverty level.[14] While these and similar statistics are neither new nor unreported, it was the women's movement which managed to bring the issue of Quebec poverty onto the political agenda. Through the Bread and Roses march of the spring of 1995, and the subsequent use of public forums such as the 1996 Social and Economic Summits, the women's movement, led by the Federation of Quebec Women,[15] made the issue of poverty, and in particular female poverty, unavoidable when attempting to understand modern Quebec society.

---

[11] For more history, consult the brochure: ICÉA, *Repères pour une mémoire collective, 1946-1996* (Montréal, 1996) 12 pages.

[12] Assemblée des évêques du Québec, *Sortons le Québec de l'appauvrissement* (Montréal, mars 1994).

[13] CSÉ, *Pour un accès réel*, pp.9-10.

[14] Ibid., p.15. The Conseil notes further that a difference of up to 6 percent exists between the real and official levels of unemployment.

[15] An accredited popular education group.

In its attempt to combat unemployment and poverty, the Quebec government has invested massive amounts of educational resources into adjustment and retraining programs. At the same time, it has devised a multitude of programs aimed at raising the employability levels of the so-called apt (employable) portion of the inactive population, notably welfare recipients.[16]

Changing World of Work

The internationalization of markets, creation of large trading blocks and arrival of Free Trade has changed Quebec's economic base. A shift from mass-production to value-added production has resulted in a concurrent shift in Quebec's employment opportunities from the primary and secondary sectors to the tertiary or service sector. In 1996, manufacturing accounted for less than 25 percent of Quebec's employment, and only 4 percent of jobs were to be found in the primary and agricultural sectors.[17]

In a service-based economy, the transformation of raw materials is no longer the primary source of wealth creation; wealth is increasingly created by the production of knowledge and applied knowledge especially through industries dependent upon research and development. New information and communications technologies have led to the development of important new industries related to the generation, acquisition and transmission of knowledge. Quebec is in the forefront of these developments, particularly in the area of software development, production and marketing. At the same time, technological change has created an urgent need to update the skills of the present work force in order to keep pace with the rapidly changing needs of the modern workplace. Finally it must be noted that in Quebec, as elsewhere, technological change also means the "creation" of job loss as the introduction of new technologies is often accompanied by falling employment and the decline of more traditional industries.

For all of these reasons, the arrival of new technologies draws the world of science and industry much closer to the educational system. Rapid and major changes in industry have forced the public educational system to adapt, improvise and innovate in the areas of skills training and research and development.

For francophone Quebec, the predominance of the English language in a twenty-first century world redefined by new technologies presents its own series of challenges. From navigating the Internet to training on the latest numerically controlled equipment; from reading computer manuals for the

---

[16] See, for example, Ministère de la Sécurité du revenu, *Un Parcours vers l'insertion, la formation et l'emploi: la réforme de la sécurité du revenu* (Québec, 1996).

[17] See Pierre Fréchette, "Croissance et changements structurels de l'économie" in Gérard Daigle *Le Québec en jeu* (Montréal: Les Presses de l'Université de Montréal, 1992) p.31.

latest version of *Windows* to publishing research in learned journals, the hegemony of English at the end of the twentieth century contributes to Quebecers' fears for the health of French as a living language in North America.

Francophone adult educators and learners face similar hurdles as they attempt to overcome the challenges raised in the new domain of technological illiteracy, which the Council of Europe warns is the next threat in the process of social dualization. Not long ago, literacy was a term reserved for the acquisition of basic reading writing and numeracy skills, but there is a definite tendency to broaden the definition. In the eyes of some, the world of the twenty-first century will be increasingly divided along the lines of those who will master new technologies and those who will be left behind.[18]

Changing Demographics

The nature of Quebec society has dramatically changed over the past thirty years. As has just been noted, it is poorer, but it is also older, more urbanized and more diverse.

Aging. With its birth rate in decline, Quebec is faced with a steadily aging population. A study undertaken by the *Conseil supérieur de l'éducation* shows that nearly three-quarters of what will be the active population of the first years of the next decade is already active in the late 1990s. This fact, along with a decline in the number of young people arriving on the job market in the next decade, means that employers will be forced to maintain and retrain an aging work force. It is in this context that the educational issue of labour adjustment and retraining must be seen.[19]

Immigration. Most of Quebec's immigrant population is concentrated in the Montreal metropolitan area. Since the 1970s, an increasing percentage of this population has arrived from south-east Asia, Africa and Latin America, replacing in numbers the traditional European immigrant.

This immigration pattern, along with Quebecers' rejection of the Trudeau era policies of multi-culturalism in favour of a policy of integrating immigrants into a francophone common public culture, has led to some tension between the francophone majority and some immigrant communities. In this context, schools, inter-community dialogue and other issues related to the socialization of immigrant populations into the dominant community will continue to be issues which adult educators will need to address, in the classroom and in society, over the coming years.

Urban-regional tensions. Quebec's development over the past few decades is similar to that of the rest of the country in that its population has become

---

[18] See CSÉ, *Pour un accès réel*, p.5. See also, Claudie Solar, "Nouvelles tendances en education des adultes," p.452.

[19] Ibid., p.13.

highly concentrated around several urban areas. This developmental pattern has had drastic consequences on several peripheral regions. The disappearance of basic services such as post offices, railways and schools has irreparably damaged the social fabric of many small communities, exacerbating at the same time regional disparities. The loss of basic services leads in turn to a diminishing population base as people leave the regions.[20]

With their very survival at stake, several regions, notably the Gaspé, the North Shore and Abitibi, are fighting back. Highly organized, they are demanding control over their own regional development, insisting upon a devolution of powers in order to have local control over resource development and employment strategies. Some see adult education as an important element in an overall strategy to assist local or regional communities in taking control over their own development.[21]

Changing Nature of the State

As elsewhere in the Western world, the Quebec state is in the transitional phase from a Keyesian to a post-Keyesian form of organization and the characteristics of the new state are well known: reduced government expenditures in the name of debt and deficit reduction, the slashing of social programs including public expenditures on education, the shrinking of the size and scope of government itself and so on. Because the state has played such a critical role in Quebec's recent period of self-affirmation, the stakes involved in this change are very high.[22]

A key element in Quebec's downsizing strategy has been the attempt to reduce the part of the population that will continue to receive direct government aid. An analysis of recent developments in the field of training and retraining highlights quite clearly this pruning tendency. New programs, destined for the so-called inactive part of the population, have as their primary objective the removal of very clear sectors of the population from welfare rolls: able-bodied welfare recipients, single-mothers with young children, the cyclically unemployed. These groups are forced into training, at the cost of seeing their benefits slashed, if not totally cut.

---

[20] ICÉA, *Apprendre à l'âge adulte*, p.22. Interestingly, a 1994 study prepared by the Institut québécois de recherche sur la culture concluded that the lack of social, recreational and cultural resources, and not the lack of employment opportunities, were the principal reasons that young people were leaving Quebec's regions.

[21] CSÉ, *Pour un accès réel*, p.9.

[22] Literature abounds on the importance and role of the state for Quebec's development. See for example: Jeanne Kirk-Laux and Maureen Molot, *State Capitalism: Public Enterprise in Canada* (Ithaca: Cornell University Press, 1988); Dale Postgate and Kennetih McRoberts, *Quebec: Social Change and Political Crisis* (Toronto: McClelland and Stewart, 1976).

The privatization of formerly public services is another key element in the state's effort to reduce its size and the scope of its intervention. Privatization has its specific expression in the field of education where increasingly skills training is moving into private hands. It also finds expression in the increased corporate sponsorship of post-secondary programs in the universities and Collège d'enseignement général et professionnel (CEGEPs) as well as in the private sponsorship of university research.

Actors and Issues in Quebec Adult Education

Labour Adjustment, Training and Retraining

Two reasons motivate beginning this section on actors in Quebec adult education with a discussion of labour adjustment, training and retraining. First, control over labour adjustment and training initiatives is a politically contentious issue in Quebec, as one of Quebec's historical demands has been the withdrawal of the federal government from any role in this sector. Second, as the Institut canadien de l'éducation des adultes points out, if in fact governments claim that they are spending more money than ever on adult education, it is largely as a result of their expenditures in the area of labour adjustment and retraining.[23]

However, though beginning this section with a discussion of training issues, it is important to draw attention to a pointed warning from the Estates General:

> … it must be clear that *adult education is not limited to job-related training and retraining* … Cultural enrichment, civic education and language training needs must also be met.[24]

Since 1967, when the Adult Occupational Training Act opened the door for the federal government to assume full control over a jurisdiction which had previously been provincial, Quebec has demanded full control over powers related to employment and training. For Quebec, employment policy, training and adult education are all intimately inter-related and must cease to be an area of shared jurisdiction.

Jurisdictional issues aside, and in spite of the duplication of services offered by the two levels of government, there is little to distinguish federal from Quebec training and retraining programs over the past decade. Following the lead of the Organization for Economic Development and Co-operation (OEDC), both governments have adopted the idea that a restructured economy needs to reflect the new context of international competitiveness. The policy

---

[23] ICÉA, *Apprendre à l'âge adulte*, p.49.

[24] Commission des États généraux, *Renewing Our Education System*, p.35.

of both governments has been to adjust labour on the supply side to the needs of the market. Adjusting the worker has become more important than adjusting the economy.

In 1986, the federal government introduced, through the Canadian Jobs Strategy, programs which were designed to match available skills with labour shortages in certain areas, and to improve the overall employability of the work force. In 1987, it signed an agreement with the Quebec government, whereby Quebec would gain control over training programs offered in educational institutions. Responsibility for training in industrial settings was not touched by this agreement. The impact of this agreement was unexpected and quite far reaching. Since the main thrust of the Canadian Jobs Strategy involved workplace training and retraining, nearly 40 percent of Quebec's educational training budget was spent outside of educational institutions and devoted to customer-driven training (la formation sur mesure).

In 1989, the federal government introduced major reforms to unemployment insurance, withdrawing federal participation from the program and using hundreds of millions of insurance dollars for retraining purposes. This reform clearly marked Ottawa's desire to withdraw from its social responsibility to provide an "insurance program" to protect against unemployment. Similar tendencies were reinforced in 1993-94 with a further gutting of the unemployment insurance program.

In Quebec, the same tendencies were at work. In 1991, the Liberal government of Robert Bourassa issued its "Enoncé de politique sur le développement de la main-d'ouevre" with a key proposal being the decentralization of training initiatives through the setting up of the Société québecoise pour le développement de la main d'oeuvre (SQDM). Similar to initiatives in other provinces, the SQDM, a multi-party organization with regional satellites, was responsible for developing a single model of labour-adjustment program delivery.[25]

Issues in Adjustment and Training

Duplication of services. With the incursion of the federal government into the field of training and retraining, two levels of government developed a myriad of duplicate and sometimes conflicting initiatives. The setting up of the SQDM did not yield a streamlining effect and the duplication of services continued well into the 1990s.

---

[25] In June 1997, the Quebec government announced the dismantling of the SQDM. It will be replaced in January 1998 by a new agency, Emploi Québec. This, coupled with the announcement from Ottawa that the Federal government intends to withdraw from the field of training, indicates the highly volatile nature of this field in the late 1990s.

Apart from the Ottawa-Quebec duplication, serious duplication exists within the Quebec government itself due to overlapping jurisdictions between the MÉQ, the Ministry of Employment and the Ministry of Income Security and Skills Training. This confusion led to such a proliferation and overlapping of programs that at the end of 1996 there were, in Quebec alone, literally hundreds of different training programs dependent upon and competing for government funding.

Law 90—The Training Law. Complicating even more the duplication experienced in the field of labour adjustment and retraining are the provisions of Law 90 (1995) which ensures that by 1999 all Quebec employers, with a payroll of more than $250,000, must spend 1 percent of the amount paid on wages on employee upgrading or retraining.

At best, this law is ambiguous from the point of view of adult education. On the one hand, it indicates a serious effort by the Quebec government to foster a "training culture," which has been sorely lacking in the small- and medium-size business sector, the backbone of Quebec's economy. On the other hand, it seems to undermine initiatives within the "public" domain of adult education. Already the law is having a tremendous impact on public education in that most adult education programs and initiatives are now planned and controlled by ministries responsible for employment in either the Quebec or the federal governments. Governments, not educational institutions and educators, are determining the priorities, schedules, types of training, and the entrance requirements for adult trainees. At the same time, for the educational institutions which offer these programs, the "clients" are more often businesses than individual adults. The training offered is job-oriented, short-term, and heavily weighted to performance.

Privatization. At the end of the 1990s, a "training industry" is beginning to make its mark in Quebec, where it often assumes the form of the "training business." Increasingly, since the Canadian Jobs Strategy (1986), responsibility for both the content and the delivery of training has shifted to the hands of private enterprises, as the post-Keyesian state divests itself of the responsibility in this field. The so-called "welfare state" has given way to the "midwife state," facilitating private enterprise and the marketplace to take advantage of locally depressed labour markets. As elsewhere in Canada, many public training dollars are being diverted from public educational institutions and are flowing into the hands of private trainers and consultants.

Adult Education within the Formal Education System

When Quebec's school system was set up thirty years ago, its objective was to permit young people to gain the skills necessary to move into the modern industrial era. As previously mentioned, the main objective of adult education when the system was set up was to allow those adults who "missed out" the first time around to either complete their initial education or make up missing skills in such a way as to permit their participation in the job market or in society.

Since the 1960s, great strides have been made in democratizing the Quebec education system, making it accessible to all parts of the population. Nevertheless, in spite of this progress, one in five Quebec adults (1996 statistic) will not complete the equivalent to third-year high school (Grade 11). Considering this to be the minimum level necessary for a basic education, the Conseil supérieur de l'éducation advances this figure as the number of Quebec adults who will be unable to keep up in an ever-changing society.[26] Other studies by the Conseil confirm that fully 35.3 percent of Quebecers presently in high school will drop out before completing their high school education.[27]

With the Policy Statement (1984) and according to the Public Instruction Law, adult education should be fully integrated into the priorities of the Quebec educational system. Indeed, in a historic first, ministry regulations specifically dedicated to adult education came into effect in 1994.

However, formal adult education in Quebec has steadily lost ground since the Jean Commission. A partial explanation for this can be found because much public, journalistic, and governmental attention has been focussed on the staggering high-school drop-out rates of the young people just referred to. Anguish has also been expressed concerning the difficulties experienced by the Quebec school system in preparing its graduates to meet the requirements of the rapidly changing job market. In this context, adult education has been largely ignored.

Issues in Formal Adult Education

Secondary School Graduation Diploma (Adult). Two different classes of Secondary School diploma are offered in Quebec. On the one hand, students who successfully complete the equivalent of eleven years of formal schooling graduate with either a Secondary School Diploma or a Vocational Secondary School Diploma. However, adults who return to the formal school system after having previously left it and who successfully complete a different set of requirements graduate with an Adult High School Diploma. Courses leading to the Adult High School Diploma, recognized by the Ministry of Education, are offered through the Adult Education Services of local school boards or directly through the Ministry.

---

[26] CSÉ, *Pour un accès réel*, p.11. The actual figure is 20.6 percent according to 1991 census data. The similar figure in the rest of the country is 11.9 percent. ICÉA concludes that 40 percent of the adult population in Quebec has not completed their basic high school diploma. Voir ICÉA, *Libérer les forces créatrices et productives, Brief to the Estates General on Education*, 1995,p.7.

[27] CSÉ, *Vers un modèle de financement en éducation des adultes* (Québec, 1994) p.51.

At the Estates General, the issue of the value and recognition of diplomas obtained in adult education was raised. Secondary school diplomas issued by the adult education sector are not recognized by the CEGEP and universities.[28] Secondary-level courses offered by the adult sector are not always equivalent to those offered in the youth sector. To remedy this situation, many adult learners and adult educators suggested that students in the adult sector be subject to the same ministry prepared examinations and graduation requirements as students in the youth sector.

Users of Adult Services. From 1990 to 1994, approximately 130,000 adults were registered in school board general-level adult education services.[29] During this period, two of every five registrations were for part-time studies. Generally speaking, the registrants in general-level adult education programs were young people, with nearly two out of every three registrants being under thirty years of age in 1993-94. This same age category represented 45 percent of school board literacy registrants as well.

At the Estates General hearings, several issues were raised relative to the young users of adult education services. First, there was almost unanimous agreement that adult education services are overrun by young people. Consequently, "real" adults have less access to these services, where places are already limited by fixed budgets. Secondly, young people can, and do, enroll in secondary-level general education courses in the adult sector when they are sixteen years of age. Consequently, adult educators complained that young people, lacking in autonomy and presenting frequent behavioural problems, actually compromise the application of androgogical approaches which are so important in real adult education.[30] Finally, the Estates General established a broad consensus that adult education must not constitute an alternative for young people who want to avoid meeting initial education requirements.[31]

Role of the CEGEP. Out of the Parent Commission recommendations came the CEGEP, a specifically Québécois form of post-secondary educational institution. CEGEPs offer programs to young adults, generally between seventeen and twenty years of age, for either university entry or occupational or vocational preparation.

Historically, CEGEPs have offered a certain number of adults an occasion to continue or upgrade their formal education. In fact CEGEPs are increasingly being used as a conduit by different levels of government who purchase training or retraining seats which they then make available to the unemployed

---

[28] Commission des États généraux, *State of Education*, p.88.

[29] CSÉ, *Pour un accès réel*, p.26.

[30] Commission des États généraux, *State of Education*, p.84.

[31] Ibid., p.91.

or to those on welfare. About 100,000 adults, many of them young, frequented Quebec CEGEPs in this way in 1990.

Increasingly, like community colleges elsewhere in the country, the CEGEPs are using government-sponsored training programs as a way to solving their own financial crisis brought about by reduced government funding from the MÉQ. They are designing programs to respond to the "needs" of a paying clientele, whether this be government-sponsored individuals or businesses being forced to comply with the provisions of Law 90.[32]

This situation compromises seriously the "voluntary" nature of the traditional adult student. Such a change in the nature of the adult student attending CEGEP was noted during the Estates General as several deputations from the college sector observed that the notion of "adult" seems to have been eliminated in the 1994 College Education regulations, as have all references to adult needs and particular learning rates.[33]

Prior Learning Assessment.[34] One of the biggest   obstacles confronting adults wishing to complete or upgrade their formal education is gaining recognition for their prior learning experiences. Lack of recognition for these experiences can actually be a barrier to upgrading. Unfortunately, while Quebec was one of the leaders in this emerging field in the 1980s, it fell far behind several other provinces in the 1990s.[35]

While retained as a major concern in the 1984 Policy Statement, the reality of Prior Learning Assessment in the 1990s is one of confusion.[36] During the Estates General, adults recounted their difficulties in receiving recognition for their academic efforts from one institution to another. They also expressed difficulty in receiving recognition for their non-academic life experiences. Spokespeople for immigrant communities pointed out that the influx of immigrant populations has had, and will continue to have, an impact in the delivery of adult educational services. The host society must recognize that immigrants arrive in Quebec already possessing skills and credentials.[37]

The Estates General noted a widespread agreement within the educational community as to the desirability of Prior Learning Assessment, particularly for women wishing to return to school or to the work force, for newly arrived

---

[32] CSÉ, *Accroître l'accessibilité et garantir l'adaptation* (Québec, 1992) pp.36-37.

[33] Commission des États généraux, *State of Education*, p.85.

[34] This section deals with Prior Learning Assessment as it relates to educational institutions. There is an equivalent policy at the SQDM where a non-MÉQ accredited system of competency recognition is being developed. Called UEC (unités d'éducation continue), the proposal, if implemented, would require industries or businesses offering training to grant certain credits based, for example, on prior workplace experience.

[35] Commission des États généraux, *State of Education*, p.84.

[36] CSÉ, *Pour un accès réel*, p.19.

[37] Ibid., p.13.

immigrants, or for older workers who are hit by plant closures and need retraining. All of these adults need prior learning recognition so as not to be forced to re-learn what they already know or to be penalized before entering the job market.

With widespread acceptance of the principle of Prior Learning Assessment, and given Quebec's former leadership role, it is difficult to understand the institutional confusion which characterizes the field. But confusion there is.

At the secondary school level, the principle of prior learning recognition for both academic and experiential credit is enshrined in the Public Instruction Law (Article 250).[38] Prior-learning criteria are established centrally by the MÉQ through a process described by the Conseil supérieur de l'éducation as bureaucratized and lacking in flexibility.[39] The application of these criteria are left to individual school boards, but not all school boards have developed a prior learning assessment service. Roughly 8,000 requests are handled annually by Quebec school boards to establish academic equivalencies.

At the college level, each CEGEP is responsible for developing its own Prior Learning Assessment, which generally is composed of five steps. Some CEGEPs have systematically developed this service, while many deal with requests on an ad-hoc basis. Only in Montreal-area CEGEPs has any sensitivity to the specific needs of the immigrant communities been developed. Fewer than five hundred adults per year use the Prior Learning Assessment services offered by Quebec CEGEPs.[40]

Non-Institutional Initiatives in Adult Education

Popular Education

For twenty-five years the popular education movement (éducation populaire autonome—ÉPA) in Quebec has been at the forefront of the struggle for social justice.[41] More than 1,000 popular education groups are currently accredited by the MÉQ, working in sixteen different sectors including welfare and tenant rights organizations, injured workers groups, women's centres and shelters, organizations of the unemployed, popular literacy groups. Adults participating in this form of non-formal education tend generally to be from socially and economically disadvantaged sectors of the population, are often

---

[38] Ibid., p.21.

[39] Ibid., pp.24-25.

[40] Ibid., p.21.

[41] In English, see Adèle Chené and Michael Chervin, *Popular Education in Quebec: Strengthening Social Movements* (American Association for Adult and Continuing Education, 1991). This study is a bit dated but gives a good overview of the phenomenon as it was in the 1980s. The Conseil supérieur de l'éducation sees the formation of voluntary popular education groups in the flurry of initiatives following the Rapport Parent. Cf. CSÉ, *Pour un accès réel*, p.1.

not highly educated, and are generally not reached by the formal educational services offered by school boards or other institutions. Thousands of adults avail themselves of activities organized by popular education organizations every year to learn about their rights and to participate actively in the social and political debates of the day.

Largely inspired by the thinking and praxis of Paulo Friere, on the one hand, and Collette Humbart and the group from l'Institut oecuménique pour le développmement des peuples (INODEP) in France on the other, popular education in Quebec today continues to be an important alternative educational resource. The Estates General recognized this importance:

> if we admit that people must be able to satisfy their training needs on a lifelong basis in order to take charge of their personal and community life, we must also acknowledge that these needs sometimes require solutions other than courses or the type of expertise schools can offer. In our opinion, it is high time these popular education agencies were recognized and their role and relationship with the education system clarified.[42]

In 1978, the Mouvement d'éducation populaire et d'action communautaire du Québec (MÉPACQ)[43] voted the following definition of "éducation populaire autonome" which is still in use today:

> *Éducation populaire autonome* covers a variety of learning activities and critical reflections by which citizens collectively take action. These activities further lead citizens, individually and collectively, to a "prise de conscience" [heightened understanding] of their working or living conditions, which they will use to effect short and long term social, economic, cultural and political changes in their milieu.[44]

Issues Confronting Popular Education

Struggle for a legal status. Despite almost three decades of funding by the MÉQ, the popular education program remains discretionary. Ministry support for this form of adult education is not enshrined in any law, and the Ministry of Education Act, which defines the responsibilities of the minister, does not include popular education among the fields of responsibility of the minister.

The issue of legal status became extremely important following the decision of the Liberal government of Daniel Johnson to dismantle the program in

---

[42] Commission des États généraux, *Renewing Our Education System*, p.34.

[43] The MÉPACQ and two other allied organizations, the Table des fédérations et organismes nationaux en ÉPA and the Regroupement des groupes populaires en alphabétisation (RGPAQ) represent about 600 local, regional and national popular education groups. The Regroupement des organismes volontaires d'éducation populaire (ROVEP), which split from the MÉPACQ in 1987, represents another 30 organizations.

[44] Mouvement d'éducation populaire et d'action communautaire du Québec et al., *Pour une reconnaissance et un financement accru de l'éducation populaire autonome* (Montréal, 1992). See also another definition in CSÉ, *Vers un modèle de financement*, p.29.

1994. With the arrival of the Parti Québécois to power in 1995, the dismantling process was brought to a halt as one of the election promises of the new
government was to give legal recognition to popular education in its first
mandate. At the end of 1996, steps in this direction were announced as a
follow-up to the Estates General.

Funding. Underfunding represents a second main issue confronting popular education groups. Though funded since 1971, little or no correlation exists
between the work done by popular education groups and the funding they
receive from the MÉQ. Two distinct programs, with a combined 1996-97
budget of $15 million, are dedicated to popular education: the Program de
soutien à l'éducation populaire autonome (PSÉPA) and the Program de soutien à l'alphabétisation populaire autonome (PSAPA). Under the PSÉPA,
which supports non-literacy initiatives, the MÉQ funding covers only educational activities and does not include core funding. Consequently, an average
popular education group receives less than $10,000 per year for its educa-
tional work. While some groups are funded by other ministries, the MÉPACQ
estimates that 25 percent of the groups it represents survive on PSÉPA funding alone. The Estates General on Education called on the MÉQ to make the
funding of popular education groups one of its priorities, a historical first.

Independence. The struggle for autonomy is a third perennial issue confronting popular education organizations. Representing a unique form of direct democracy, popular education groups are controlled by their General
Assembly, composed of all the members. Popular education groups in Quebec
are called les groupes d'éducation populaire autonome, and "autonome" is
more than just a word: popular education groups are not controlled by public
institutions (such as school boards or CLSCs[45]), government bodies (such as
local Canada Employment Centres or Centres Travail-Québec), nor by unions,
churches or businesses. Popular education groups belong to and are controlled
by their members. On the other hand, popular education groups find themselves under constant pressure to define themselves in terms of the formal
education system. Both the MÉQ, and the main teachers union[46] insist upon
seeing popular education as complementary to the educational system. Even
the Estates General, while calling for its formal recognition, called also for
clarification as to the relationship of popular education to the formal system.

---

[45] Centre local des services communautaires, community-based, government-financed, public health
clinics.

[46] A ministry working paper, produced in 1995 and rejected by representatives of the popular education movement, placed popular education as "complementary" to the school system. The Centrale
de l'enseignement du Québec (CEQ), in its recent *Relever le défi de l'éducation tout au long de la
vie*, (1996) repeats this complementary vision.

Literacy

A 1989 Statistics Canada study revealed that nearly one in five adult Quebecers had severely limited reading and writing skills, and that a further 24 percent were able to read only the simplest of texts. This study concluded that fully 46 percent of the adult population experienced some reading or writing difficulty in performing tasks encountered in their daily lives.[47]

These all too eloquent statistics indicate that a large number of Quebecers have difficulty fully participating in all aspects of their private and civil lives. As the Estates General noted:

> The statistics in this area are appalling. A study by Statscan in 1991 revealed that the reading skills of nearly 900,000 adult Quebecers were too limited to allow them to read everyday documents. Over one-third of students enrolled in literacy programs were young people under thirty years of age. These statistics are even more preoccupying when viewed in relation to the fact that labour-market requirements are now higher. The endemic nature of the literacy problem, despite efforts to raise Quebecers' level of schooling, is also a source of concern. An in-depth study should be undertaken and more aggressive measures implemented to eliminate illiteracy.[48]

Two kinds of literacy programs are presently offered in Quebec. School boards, through their adult education sector, offer literacy classes in a formal setting; popular education groups offer literacy training in an informal setting. Unlike in the rest of the country, neither private enterprise nor public libraries offer literacy services within francophone Quebec. More importantly, one-on-one tutoring is rarely, if ever, the model used for literacy training.

Over one-third of students presently registered in literacy programs offered by school boards are under the age of thirty.[49] Literacy courses offered through the school boards are credit courses and participants in these programs are generally attempting to obtain their high school diploma. While some administrators believe that school boards should assume full responsibility for literacy training, thereby reducing popular education groups to a recruiting and transitional role, such a view is not widely held. Indeed, in the context of broader funding cutbacks, some school boards even chose to reduce their literacy programs in the mid-1990s.

On the other hand, popular education literacy groups offer non-formal literacy programs to learners, often economically disadvantaged, who do not wish a "school" environment. Literacy done in a popular education setting offers an integrated learning approach using original teaching methods. It is non-credit and provides learners with the skills they need to become full-

---

[47] CSÉ, *Pour un accès réel*, p.11.

[48] Commission des États généraux, *The State of Education*, p.90.

[49] Ibid., p.84.

fledged members of society. Popular literacy groups, under the PSAPA program, receive a minimum core funding of $25,000 per year. At the Estates General, representatives from the school boards, popular literacy groups, learners and educators all agreed that the illiteracy problem in Quebec is big enough, and the needs diverse enough, to leave room for both the school board and popular education approach to literacy.[50]

Media and Distance Education

Another form of non-formal adult education active in Quebec may be found in the media and distance education. As mentioned in the historical section of this chapter, Télé-Québec, founded as Radio-Québec in 1973, has had from its very foundation an educational mandate. This network produces and broadcasts annually original educational programming on issues ranging from the environment to current affairs.

Distance education is another form of non-formal adult education which provides adults across the province with improved access to educational services. Distance education represents a vehicle for adults to obtain credit courses at all levels.

Télé-Université, a division of the Université du Québec network, offers baccalaureate programs in administration, communications and industrial relations. More than 200,000 persons register annually with Télé-Université.[51] The Quebec universities have also jointly offered, since 1984, 121 hours weekly of credit courses through CANAL, a UHF television station.

CEGEP level distance education, while limited in scope, is offered primarily by the Rosemont CEGEP in Montreal. In 1986, this CEGEP offered sixteen courses in French, administration, history, economics, psychology and philosophy. Other CEGEP offer distance education in agriculture and administration.

Finally, high school distance education is offered through the Direction des cours par correspondance of the MÉQ. Some 150 different courses are annually offered to more than 30,000 registrants.

During the Estates General, many participants expressed the belief that distance education is about to undergo spectacular development as a result of new information and communications technologies.[52]

---

[50] Ibid., p.85.

[51] ICÉA, *Apprendre à l'âge adulte*, p.115.

[52] Commission des États généraux, *State of Education*, p.84.

Conclusion

As is the case elsewhere in Canada, adult education in Quebec is at a crossroads. On the one hand, the notion of lifelong learning is being taken more seriously than ever before. Governments, industry and educators all agree that learning must continue long after an individual has completed his or her initial formal schooling. However, whereas historically schools and school boards have offered a wide variety of non-credit, public-interest adult night courses, in the Quebec of the late 1990s, most adult education offered by public institutions is either required by an adult to complete his or her adult secondary school diploma (necessary for getting most jobs) or has been purchased by government for training or retraining.

A similar tendency may be seen on the non-institutional front as well, where a new form of adult education is taking shape. Training, retraining, skills development; on-the job, off-the-job, no-job-at-all—the field of employability has become a new panacea in Quebec. For private enterprise, consultants and community-based organizations training has become a veritable industry. The question of "training for what" remains largely unanswered as no long-term solutions for the unemployed have yet been proposed.

This, then, is the context in which interest in adult education has been growing in Quebec. Seen in this light, adult education risks being limited to a "make-up" function, aimed at helping individuals complete their formal education or improve their job possibilities. Unfortunately, other more traditional aspects of adult education—such as learning for the sake of learning or learning to think critically and collectively—seem to be shunted to the side.

4

Lest We Forget: Uncovering Women's Leadership in Adult Education

By Shauna Butterwick

Selective and partial vision will doubtless always be part of the historical enterprise, but perhaps by taking thought we can at least reduce its incidence. What are the characteristics of the things we are able to perceive? What makes other things invisible to scholars? And what must happen to bring some hitherto unseen part of past reality into visibility?—Anne Firor Scott[1]

The purpose of this chapter is to draw attention to the contributions of women's organizations and women's leadership to the field of adult education in Canada. Women are and have been contributing in significant ways as players in the familiar historical movements of adult education, for instance in the Antigonish Movement and in Citizens' Forums. They have also been leaders and creators of alternative organizations where the principles of learner-centered adult education have been both applied and further developed. Today, as in the past, women work as scholars researching and writing about learning and teaching, as educators and practitioners working in diverse contexts to deliver adult education programs, and as learners exploring ways to break out of poverty, to break out of violent relationships, to learn new technologies, and to develop skills and knowledge to create safe and caring communities.

---

[1] Anne Firor Scott, "On Seeing and Not Seeing: A Case of Historical Invisibility," *The Journal of American History 71*, 1 (June 1984) p.7.

The goal of this chapter is to highlight some particular activities of women and women's organizations in the "foundations" of adult education in Canada. This chapter is not a comprehensive overview. This would require more than one chapter of a book; indeed, to do such a topic justice, multiple studies are needed, the results of which would fill many bookshelves. Just as the opening quote argues, this chapter is therefore selective and partial.[2] But before moving to discuss women's organizations and women leaders in the field of adult education, I want to begin with some cautionary notes about the problems of attempting such a discussion. I include these comments here to remind readers that to address the substantive issues touched upon in any discussion about reconstructing adult education's history means that we not only "add women in" but we also examine and ultimately change those practices of knowledge/history/story construction. One can do justice to projects that seek to include stories that have been marginalized or invisible only if one also undertakes to alter the "social organization of knowledge."

Under Construction

Inserting a chapter on women's contribution is problematic, not only because more research needs to be done in this area but also because the notion of "women's contribution" must be tempered with a recognition of the diversity of women's experience and of how that experience is also about race, class, sexual orientation, ablebodiness, and age.[3] Just as male leaders and scholars in the field have been challenged for their narrow vision, feminist scholars must acknowledge how their social locations influence what stories are told.[4] Any attempt to create an account of the "foundations" of adult education must continue to ask "who's here and who's not here" and to acknowledge our limitations and work toward creating a more inclusive discussion about the history, field and practice of adult education.

As has been mentioned elsewhere in this book (see chapter by Tammy Dewar) and in other materials, the marginalization and invisibility of women—their contributions and experiences as organizers, leaders, educators and learners/participants—has unfortunately been evident in the foundational

---

[2] Library research for this article was greatly supported by Susan Diane, master's student in the Adult Education program in the Department of Educational Studies at the University of British Columbia.

[3] See, for example: Linda Nicholson, "Interpreting Gender," *Signs 20*, 1 (1994) pp.79-105; Audre Lorde, "Age, Race, Class and Sex," in Candace West & Sarah Fenstermaker, *Sister Outsider* (Freedom, Ca: The Crossing Press, 1984); and "Doing Difference," *Gender & Society 9*, (1995) pp.8-37.

[4] My approach to writing this chapter is influenced by my experiences as an active member of several local and national Anglophone feminist organizations since the early 1980s. As a middle-aged woman, I am continually struck by the contradictory aspect of my identity/location, one which simultaneously positions me as an insider with respect to the dominant and privileged culture in Canadian society by virtue of my age, European heritage, middle-class life, ablebodiness and sexual orientation, and as an outsider in patriarchal relations of ruling.

literature of adult education.[5] Others in the field have commented on this shortcoming and on the significance of professionalization, institutionalization, linguistic conventions, and male bias as key factors in omission of women in the history of adult education. Yet, the lack of information is not surprising if one takes the position that knowledge construction is far from neutral,[6] but a political process embedded with issues of power and authority. As Dorothy Smith notes:

> Our relation to others in our society and beyond it is mediated by the social organization of its ruling. Our "knowledge" is thus ideological in the sense that this social organization preserves conceptions and means of description which represent the world as it is for those who rule it, rather than as it is for those who are ruled.[7]

Adult education is also not unique in its marginalization of women and feminist work. Feminists working in other disciplines and professional schools face the same problems and are also engaged in revitalizing and inclusive projects.[8] Although women's omission comes as no surprise, it is at the same time dismaying given the wealth of material being written, mainly by feminist activists, practitioners and scholars, about the experiences and contributions of women.[9] The marginalization of women's activities is also alarming given that the history and foundation of adult education, at least in Canada, is so closely related to the activities of various social movements for social justice.

---

[5] See, for example: Elisabeth Hayes, "The impact of feminism on adult education publications: an analysis of British and American journals," *International Journal of Lifelong Education 11*, 2 (April-June 1992) pp.125-138; Jane Hugo, "Adult Education History and the Issue of Gender: Toward a Different History of Adult Education in America," *Adult Education Quarterly 41*, 1 (Fall 1990) pp.1-16; Joyce Stalker, "Women and Adult Education: Rethinking Androcentric Research," *Adult Education Quarterly 46*, 2 (Winter 1996) pp.98-113; and Melody Thompson and Fred Schied, "Neither Polemical Nor Visionary: Language, Professionalization, and the Representation of Women in the Journals of Adult Education, 1929-1960," *Adult Education Quarterly 46*, 3 (Spring 1996) pp.123-141.

[6] Barbara Houston "Gender Freedom and the Subtleties of Sexist Education," *Educational Theory*, 35(4) (Fall 1985) pp.359-369.

[7] D. Smith, "The Social Construction of Documentary Reality," *Sociological Inquiry 44*, 4 (1974) p.267.

[8] Exploring the underlying practices that maintain women's invisibility throughout many of histories of various disciplines and fields of practice would take longer than space permits. I share the understanding and belief of others who work in movements of social justice, particularly anti-racist and anti-sexist struggles, that the histories that get written and seen as the truth and authority are usually the result of privilege. Privilege means that one's experiences are of a particular kind and are indeed limited, thus producing a narrow view and understanding of the world. My arguments here reflect a perspective that has been identified as "standpoint" epistemology, a perspective based on the belief that one's location is always significant.

[9] I invite those unfamiliar with this literature to begin to explore this material and to note that there is diversity and at times vigorous debate occurring—a sign, I would argue, of one of the strengths of feminist efforts that it engages in self-critique, which is difficult, painful and necessary. Recent debates in the feminist literature(s)—particularly those produced by women of colour, lesbian women, women living with disabilities and the post-modern and post-structuralist discussion—also highlight the difficulties of any discussion that assumes an unproblematic approach to the notion of being a woman.

Social justice, particularly as it relates to challenging and transforming un-equal power relations perpetuated by sexist structures and practices, is the fundamental goal of feminist efforts.

Beyond Political Correctness—A Clearer Vision

Expanding our knowledge about the foundations of adult education in Canada by including information about various women who have been leaders in the adult education enterprise and including material that highlights the ground-breaking contributions of women's organizations and the women's movement is essential to an understanding of what adult education is all about. Such an effort must not be seen as something that simply appeases those calling for such inclusion. Rather it is part of the *responsibility* of those who have the *privilege* of writing the histories of adult education, of those who assume some authority over what counts as knowledge in the field and of those who play key roles in the learning process of students of adult education.

Another argument for creating a more inclusive story about the foundations of adult education is that women make up significant (and, in particular contexts, are the majority) of participants in a wide variety of adult education activities, including workplace-based educational activities.[10] Women are also the educators, the organizers, and the planners of many adult education activities. Few women, however, are positioned in the academy as scholars and professors of adult education where the narratives about adult education foundations are constructed. This situation in the universities contrasts sharply with a feminization of adult education practice, reflecting some of the changes that are taking place as the economy shifts toward more job growth in the service sector. More historical and current analysis is needed to document and explore the contribution of women as the workers in the field of adult education, in particular women working in the greatly expanded private-training and not-for-profit training sectors.[11]

In the following discussion about women in adult education, I begin by revisiting some of the now-familiar moments in Canadian adult education history in order to shed some light on the women who played a significant role in these activities. Then I outline some of the women's organizations, many of which began in the 1800s that played a significant role in the provision of adult education activities for women. Following this, I examine some

[10] Canadian Association for Adult Education, *"Survey of Trends in Adult Education in Canada (1985-1995)."* Prepared for Canadian Commission for UNESCO, May 1997.

[11] See Shauna Butterwick, *"The Politics of Needs Interpretation: A Study of Three CJS-Funded Job-Entry Programs for Women,"* Unpublished Doctoral Dissertation (Vancouver, University of British Columbia, 1993). This research explored women's re-entry programs and illuminated the significant role women play as coordinators and instructors of these programs.

more recent developments in feminist adult education organizations and then point to the adult education activities of a variety of women's organizations that are commonly understood to be examples of the second wave of the women's movement. The chapter concludes with some thoughts on priorities for future action in relation to women's interests and welfare as learners and adult educators.

Familiar Stories and New Faces

In 1982, the annual Atlantic Institute, held at St. Francis Xavier University focused on women in the Antigonish Movement.[12] At this meeting, Sister Irene Doyle, Kay Desjardins, Zita Cameron, Ida Delaney and Ellen Arsenault met to discuss and share with the participants their work in the St. Francis Xavier Extension Department as secretaries, organizers, writers and indispensable assistants. It was noted at that meeting that much that had been written about the Antigonish Movement was from the perspective of outsiders rather than those working within the various study clubs, co-operatives and credit unions. With some sense of urgency, given that few of the fieldworkers were still living, Ida Delaney set about to write about her experiences. Her book is a refreshing account of the complexity of the activities and support needed to achieve the goals of the movement. Ida Delaney worked as a field worker for the Extension Department, which involved setting up a library, teaching many of the short courses, supporting study clubs and making public speeches.

Kay Thompson Desjardins joined Dr. Moses Coady and A.B. MacDonald as the first staff member. Together with Sister Marie Michael, they gathered together the reading material to be used in the study clubs. These two enterprising women collected material from everywhere, mainly in the form of pamphlets. Kay Thompson also wrote one of the pamphlets ("Maritime Techniques in Consumer Co-operation") that was required reading for all groups. Kay Thompson Desjardins also became editor, succeeding George Boyle, of the *Maritime Co-operator,* which became the central adult education journal of the Antigonish Movement (replacing the Extension Bulletin). Other women who contributed to both the *Bulletin* and the *Maritime Co-operator* included Sister Marie Michael, Zita O'Hearn, and Mary MacIntryre McNeil. The *Maritime Co-operator* was managed entirely by women for a substantial period of time, an unusual situation at the time in the field of co-operative presses. Another important figure was Norah Bateson, a librarian who had set up the library system in Prince Edward Island. She worked with Father Tompkins, another champion of libraries, in setting up libraries in Cape Breton.

---

[12] I. Delaney, *By Their Own Hands—A Fieldworker's Account of the Antigonish Movement* (Hantsport, NS: Lancelot Press, 1985).

The Canadian Reading Camp Association, which became Frontier College, is well known for its literacy and citizenship education programs for men working on the Canadian frontier.[13] Little is known, however, about the women involved as both educators and participants.[14] In the early stages of Frontier College, women's participation was strongly encouraged by the founder, Alfred Fitzpatrick, but those who followed him did not share his progressive views. Fitzpatrick was also active in the homesteads-for-women movement (1909-1913). Nonetheless, a few women served as instructors during the early years including Mrs. Alex Scott, B.M. Laverie, Miriam Chisholm, Isabel Mackey and Margaret Strang (who graduated in medicine). Jessie Lucas worked for forty-three years, initially as Secretary-Treasurer and later as Registrar. Wigmore notes that Lucas's records of the activities of Frontier College are "one of the most remarkable adult education archival resources in Canada" (p.263). These women worked mostly with men, but Miriam Chisholm and Isabel Mackey[15] also worked with female workers in different factory and retail settings. The work and perseverance of these women is notable given that, with the exception of Fitzpatrick, the leaders of Frontier College did not encourage women to take leadership positions until the 1970s. For the last three decades women have played a significant role as coordinators, instructors, community development workers, and tutors—including women who broke the gender barrier as workers/instructors in mining and the railway.

Just as the Antigonish Movement is a familiar story in adult education, the role of the Canadian Association for Adult Education (CAAE), which began in 1935, is commonly regarded as another cornerstone in the foundation of the field. Yet, we hear few stories of the women who have assumed leadership roles in that organization. Isabel Wilson served the CAAE from 1943 until 1970 and was instrumental in the development and success of the CBC's *Citizens' Forum*. It was she who edited the study pamphlets (over 300 of them) for the program series, exhibiting an extraordinary skill in showing both sides of an argument with fairness and integrity and in her ability to take lengthy and complex documents and translate them into simple and concise language. Following her death in 1983, the CAAE established a fund in her

---

[13] I use the term "frontier" advisedly, given the problematic assumptions underlying a notion that renders invisible the long history of native peoples living on lands that eventually became Canada under confederation.

[14] I am indebted to the research conducted by Shirley Wigmore, Ontario Institute for Studies in Education, who wrote about her work "The Hidden History of Women in Frontier College" in the *Proceedings of the 10th Annual Conference of the Canadian Association for the Study of Adult Education*, pp.262-267. See also M. Forrest and J. Morrison, "The women of Frontier College." *Canadian Women's Studies 9*, 3-4 (Fall/Winter 1988) pp.21-23.

[15] M. Zavitz, "Isabel Kelly: Pioneer Literacy Worker." *Canadian Women's Studies 9*, 3-4 (Fall/Winter 1988) pp.24-25.

name.[16] Anne Ironside, who played a leadership role in the University of British Columbia's Continuing Education Division, was the first female president of the CAAE (1983-1988). Ironside was also one of the founding members of Canadian Committee for the Continuing Education of Women (CCCEW) which began in the early 1970s as a subcommittee of the CAAE and which later became the Canadian Congress for Learning Opportunities for Women (CCLOW). Dr. Teresa MacNeil served as the second female president of CAAE from 1987-91. She was the Director of Extension of St. Francis Xavier University and also served from 1985 to 1989 as the Chair of the Cape Breton Development Corporation, a position which followed her work as Chair of a 1985 task force on the economy of Cape Breton.

Much work is needed to uncover other women who played leadership roles within adult education organizations as well as in government departments. We need to know more about women such as Florence Mary O'Neill who received her doctorate in adult education from Columbia University in 1944. Prior to that she had worked as a school teacher and principal and "itinerant" teacher in the Department of Adult Education in Newfoundland. In 1949, she became the Director of Adult Education, the same year as Newfoundland became a province. Dr. O'Neill continued to provide leadership within government circles on issues that related to adult education, working from 1962-1970 as the Director of the Adult Education Section of the federal Department of Indian Affairs and Northern Development.[17]

First-Wave Women's Organizations

During the nineteenth and early part of the twentieth centuries a number of women's voluntary organizations were founded that, to a greater or lesser extent, focused on the education of women. These organizations played a significant role in valuing women's domestic responsibilities and fighting against sexist rules and regulations that prevented women from participating at a public level. They were for the most part initiated by middle- and upper-class women of European ancestry. Their work can be considered as examples of liberal-feminist strategies; that is, strategies that focused on supporting women's access to educational, employment and civic leadership. More research is needed to further appreciate the contributions of these organizations to the history of adult education in Canada. It is important to note as well that further research will help to expand our knowledge of the women's move-

---

[16] The Isabel Wilson Fund was established to support the cost of facilitating and disseminating a speech (focused on citizenship and adult learning) at an important event sponsored by a voluntary organization.

[17] I am indebted to the historical work of Katherine McManus, doctoral candidate in the Department of Educational Studies, University of British Columbia.

ment. The women's movement did not disappear in the 1920s, after suffrage had been achieved, and then reappear with the "second wave" in the 1960s. Instead, many women expanded their work to include the goal of democratic socialism.[18]

Efforts by feminist scholars have illuminated the activities of these individuals and groups, shedding light on a vast array of initiatives that have been largely ignored. However, generally speaking, voluntary organizations have not been the focus of analysis for historians, and women's voluntary organizations even less so, a situation lamented by many feminist historians. As Anne Firor Scott pointed out: "Analyzing nineteenth- or, for that matter, twentieth-century American social development without understanding the part played by women's voluntary associations is a little like trying to understand photosynthesis without knowing about chlorophyll."[19]

Most students and academics in adult education are aware of the Young Women's Christian Association (YWCA) and the Women's Institutes and their work will be briefly elaborated on in this chapter.[20] Before doing so, several other national organizations and their local chapters must be noted as well, including the Women's Christian Temperance Union,[21] the National Council of Women,[22] the Women's International League for Peace and Freedom,[23] the Home and School Associations,[24] the Canadian Federation of University Women,[25] and the Elizabeth Fry Society.[26]

---

[18] For this chapter, I will not expand on the role of women in the CCF and the Canadian Left, but readers should note that they were active and occupied significant leadership roles in the creation and persistence of these democratic socialist movements. See J. Newton, *The Feminist Challenge to the Canadian Left 1900-1918*. (Montreal: McGill-Queens Press, 1995).

[19] Anne Firor Scott, ibid., p.9.

[20] My understanding of these organizations has been much enriched by Susan Witter's master's thesis (1979, UBC, Adult Education) entitled *"An Historical Study of Adult Education in Two Canadian Women's Organizations: The Federated Women's Institutes of Canada and The Young Women's Christian Association of Canada 1870-1978."* There is a wealth of information about women's organizations and women's participation in adult education in the unpublished master's and doctoral theses in our universities. We need to make this material more accessible and part of the public and published story of adult education in Canada.

[21] See, for example: Sharon Anne Cook, *"Through Sunshine and Shadow"—The Woman's Christian Temperance Union, Evangelicalism, and Reform in Ontario, 1874-1930* (Montreal: McGill-Queen's University Press, 1995); Wendy Mitchinson, "The WCTU: 'For God, Home and Native Land': A Study in Nineteenth-Century Feminism," in Linda Kealey (Ed.), *A Not Unreasonable Claim—Women and Reform in Canada, 1880s-1920s* (Toronto: Women's Educational Press, 1979); Harold Tuttle Allen, *Forty Years' Journey—The Temperance Movement in British Columbia to 1900* (publisher unknown); and Jan Noel, *Canada Dry—Temperance Crusades before Confederation* (Toronto: University of Toronto Press, 1995).

[22] Veronica Strong-Boag, *The Parliament of Women: The National Council of Women of Canada 1893-1929* (Ottawa: National Museums of Canada, 1976); Gillian Weiss, "Education is Better Than Agitation: Vancouver Clubwomen 1910-29," in Michael Welton (Ed.), *Educating for a Brighter New Day: Women's Organizations as Learning Sites* (Dalhousie: School of Education, 1992).

[23] Beverly Boutillier, "Making Peace as Interesting as War: The Educational Strategies for the Women's International League for Peace and Freedom in Canada During the 1920s," in Michael Welton (Ed.), *Educating for a Brighter New Day: Women's Organizations as Learning Sites* (Dalhousie: School of Education, 1992) pp.89-112.

Similar to the YWCA in England, the Canadian YWCA focused on assisting immigrant women arriving in the large urban centres. In many respects the local organizations of the YWCA were functioning as the first women's centres where a plethora of activities and services were provided, including evening classes, lending libraries and reading rooms, residences, gymnasiums, and working women's clubs. The YWCA served both young immigrant women newly arrived to the city and local clubwomen. Between 1870 and 1930, thirty-nine branches of the YWCA were established in Canada. The YWCA also played a role as an employment agency, particularly for domestic workers.[27] This organization was instrumental in the establishment of Domestic Science and the first cooking school. The activities of the YWCA, like many other organizations, were informed by the sensibilities of middle- and upper-class women who brought a form of maternalism to their work, fuelled by the view that their task was to "shepherd" young women during what was viewed as dangerous periods of their lives—that is, young women working in offices, factories, shops and domestic services. There was a concern on the part of some leaders that "the experiences of employment, education and living independently might result in a substitutions of material values and 'selfish' personal ambition."[28]

The first Women's Institutes (WI) began in Canada and became the building blocks for the development of an international organization. "The success of the Women's Institutes," Crowley notes, "stemmed from being firmly rooted in local communities where women took action on their own behalf."[29] Adelaide Hoodless, a board member of the Hamilton YWCA, is well known as the founding member of the Women's Institutes. She had already been active through the YWCA in the establishment of a Domestic Science school and had become an outspoken critic of Farmers' Institutes and their lack of attention paid to the importance of women's activities in the home. She came

[24] Kari Dehli, "The Role of Home & School Association in the Education of Women in Toronto," in Michael Welton (Ed.), *Educating for a Brighter New Day: Women's Organizations as Learning Sites* (Dalhousie: School of Education, 1992) pp.79-88.

[25] Barbara Lathan & Cathy Kess (Eds.), *In Her Own Right: Selected Essays on Women's History in B.C.* (Victoria, BC: Camosun College, 1980).

[26] Lee Stewart, *Women Volunteer To Go To Prison—A History of the Elizabeth Fry Society of B.C. 1939-1989* (Victoria, BC: Orca Books, 1993).

[27] Robin John Anderson, "Domestic Service—The YWCA and Women's Employment Agencies in Vancouver, 1898-1915," *Social History 25*, 50 (November 1992) pp.307-333.

[28] Recent feminist scholarship has been critical of the motivations of the early YWCA women for their evangelical, individualistic and heterosexist orientation to reform. See Diana Pederson, "Keeping Our Good Girls Good: The YWCA and the 'Girl Problem,' 1870-1930," *Canadian Woman Studies* 7, 4, p.21.

[29] Terry Crowley, "Educating for Home and Community: The Genesis of the Women's Institutes in Ontario," in Michael Welton (Ed.), *Educating for a Brighter New Day: Women's Organizations as Learning Sites* (Dalhousie: School of Education, 1992) pp.1-16.

to her activism through her experience of losing her fourth child due to contaminated milk. Her inspiring speech to over 100 people at Stoney Creek in the winter of 1896 prompted the local women to establish the first Women's Institute in February of 1897. The focus of WI activities was to bring farm-women together for socializing and for education in home management. Even that does not capture the breadth of the activities and the impact these groups had on women's lives. As Linda Ambrose pointed out in a book written for the centennial anniversary of the Women's Institutes, "many women point to the WI as the group that first empowered them to speak in public, learn parliamentary procedure, or get involved with efforts to lobby the government for change."[30]

Looking back on these activities from the perspective of the current women's movement, these organizations may not appear revolutionary. Nevertheless, their efforts must be compared with the expectation of the time, that "women's place was in the home and she was expected to stay there venturing outside only to do church work or perhaps attend the WCTU [Women's Christian Temperance Union] ... "[31]

Second-Wave Women's Organizations—Rocking the Boat

The 1960s and early 1970s witnessed the emergence of hundreds of women's organizations with different concerns and politics. During this time consciousness-raising groups were forming throughout North America, places where women came together to discuss their experiences—discovering in the process that they were not alone in their struggles and that what appeared to be the private individual situation of women was linked to larger social, cultural economic and political structures and power relations. The well-known feminist slogan "the personal is political" emerged from these gatherings. Consciousness-raising groups have received little attention in the adult education literature. This is a curious absence given the fascination the field has had for Paulo Freire, a Brazilian adult educator whose literacy work was based on a conscientization process which bears remarkable similarity (although there are significant differences) with consciousness-raising groups in North America.[32]

---

[30] Linda Ambrose, *For Home and Country—The Centennial History of the Women's Institutes in Ontario* (Erin, ONT: Boston Mills Press, 1996) p.11.

[31] Ruth Howes, "Adelaide Hunter Hoodless," in Mary Quayle Innis (Ed.), *The Clear Spirit: Twenty Canadian Women and Their Times* (Toronto: Canadian Federation of University Women, 1961) pp.110.

[32] See Shauna Butterwick, *"Learning Liberation: A Comparative Analysis of Feminist Consciousness Raising and Freire's Conscientization Method,"* (1987). Unpublished Master's Thesis, Department of Administrative, Adult and Higher Education, University of British Columbia.

During the second wave of the North American women's movement, several women's organizations emerged that focused particularly on adult education opportunities for women. This history and the activities of some of these groups are outlined below, beginning with the development of the only feminist adult education organization in Canada, the Canadian Congress for Learning Opportunities for Women (CCLOW).

As has been mentioned, CCLOW began its life as CCEW, a committee of the CAAE.[33] At its inception, the focus of concern was with "transitional women"—mature women who were facing the challenges of moving into paid work after working in the unpaid labour market and whose needs were not being addressed at the local, provincial or federal level. In 1976, an application was made to the Women's Program of the Secretary of State to establish an autonomous committee which, at that time, was referred to as the Canadian Committee on Learning Opportunities for Women. Funding was approved, a coordinator was hired (Janet Willis) and, in 1977, work began on the creation of a national network, the collection of information on innovative programs for women, and the preparation for a national workshop (which was held in Winnipeg in October of 1977). At that workshop it was determined that a national organization be formally established. Dorothy Smith, a well-known feminist sociologist, played a key role as advisor and evaluator of the organizational planning. Reports were prepared and submitted to three political parties, an initiative that began the advocacy work that CCLOW has continued with since. The founding Congress was held in Banff, Alberta, in April 1979 at which Greta Hoffman Nemiroff, a well-known Canadian feminist educator, gave the keynote address. Marie St. John Macdonald was elected as the first national president at that time.

Many women who assumed leadership roles in this organization have also contributed to scholarship in the field of adult education. Dorothy MacKeracker, adult education professor at the University of New Brunswick, has written for years on the barriers women face as adult learners and more recently on women's informal learning in the workplace.[34] Dr. MacKeracher wrote some of the early reports and studies for CCLOW, reports that were instrumental in CCLOW's advocacy work with the federal government.[35]

---

[33] I am indebted to the historical research conducted by Edith Smith. See Edith Smith, *"Convergences and Divergences in Feminist Theorizing and Organizing Practices during the Second Wave Women's Movement: A Case Study of the Canadian Congress for Learning Opportunities for Women,"* Unpublished Doctoral Thesis (1996). Department of Sociology, Carleton University.

[34] See Dorothy MacKeracher, "Women as Learners," in B. Barer-Stein and J. Draper (Eds.) *The Craft of Teaching Adults* (Toronto: Culture Concepts, 1993); Dorothy MacKeracher, Joan McFarland, Margaret Wall, & Bonnie Wood, "Women's On-the-Job Procedural Knowing," in *Proceedings of the 9th Annual Conference of the Canadian Association for the Study of Adult Education* (1990).

[35] Dorothy MacKeracher, "Roadblocks to Women's Learning: Issues for Advocacy," (Toronto: Canadian Congress for Learning Opportunities for Women, 1978).

In addition to establishing a strong national voice, CCLOW provincial and territorial networks played active and often ground-breaking roles in advocating for policies and creation of innovative programs for women. CCLOW has continued to play a pivotal role in researching issues related to women's learning, creating networks, and advocating for policies to support women's learning. Literacy has been the focus of a national participatory research project, several conferences, and the development of innovative feminist curriculum materials.[36]

CCLOW is officially a bilingual organization, but in 1981 a separate francophone organization was formed—Réseau National d'Action Éducation Femmes (RNAEF). One of the key tools used by CCLOW was its journal, *Women's Education des femmes* (WEDF), the only national feminist adult education journal in Canada. In 1997, due to funding cutbacks, CCLOW ceased publishing WEDF. CCLOW also is an active member of the National Action Committee (NAC) on the Status of Women and has played a role in developing the Women's Reference Group, a network of women's organizations that supports the women's representative to the Canadian Labour Force Development Board (CLFDB). The significance of the advocacy and organizing efforts of women and different women's organizations in relation to the establishment of new federal and provincial training boards (several are no longer operating) is not commonly acknowledged nor recognized. Without their efforts and those of women working within government bureaucracy, women and the other "equity" groups (people with disabilities, Aboriginal peoples, visible minorities) would not have a place at the table.[37]

During the last two decades, other women's organizations that have focused on adult education opportunities for women, particularly as they relate to entry to the paid labour force, have been active in advocating for changes to policy and in the development of women-centred job training programs. The Association for Community Based Education for Women (ACTEW) grew out of the Committee for Alternative Training and Education for Women, which was an informal network of eighteen groups in Metro Toronto providing pre-employment for women. In 1985, ACTEW was incorporated as a provincial coalition, which continues today—focusing on advocacy work, public education, and research and supporting community-based trainers with meetings, special workshops, a resource centre and a newsletter.[38] In the same year

---

[36] See Betty-Ann Lloyd (with Frances Ennis & Tannis Atkinson), *The Power of Woman-Positive Literacy Work* (Halifax: Fernwood Publishing, 1994); *Making Connections—Literacy and EAL Curriculum from a Feminist Perspective* (Toronto: Canadian Congress for Learning Opportunities for Women, 1996).

[37] See Shauna Butterwick, "The Labour Force Development Strategy: Tripartism and the Inclusion/Exclusion of 'Equity' Groups," *Policy Explorations 6*, 1 (Spring 1992) pp.14-21.

[38] For further information, contact ACTEW, 801 Eglinton Avenue West, #301, Toronto, ON M5N 1E3.

(1985), the Women's Employment and Training Coalition (WETC), a Vancouver-based group, was formed. WETC works in a similar fashion as ACTEW, focusing on meeting with government officials to advocate changes to policies affecting women's access to training. WETC also provides networking activities, such as monthly meetings and a newsletter.[39]

The 1980s also saw the formation of a number of local Women in Trades (WIT) networks that focus on women's access to training and employment in trades, technology and blue-collar work. After a number of national meetings (1980 and 1988), a national network was officially formed in 1992. Included in their activities and services has been the development of national standards for WIT courses and a bibliography of resources and innovative programs.[40]

I have highlighted several "second-wave" women's organizations that have focused on women's access to adult education opportunities and the creation of alternative adult education programs for women. There are many more organizations and groups within the women's movement in which adult education practices have been central to their work (e.g., anti-violence groups, Native women's organizations, environmental and peace groups, Lesbian organizations, and organizations for women with disabilities).[41] The powerful role these groups and other new social movements play as learning sites is beginning to be recognized.[42] From my own experience within many of the women's organizations I have examined in this chapter, I believe that one of the biggest challenges is learning how to create a collective out of a group of individuals. Learning to acknowledge and respect our differences and seek common visions is a crucial issue in this process:

> When there is no vision, the people perish. But when together we can dream a world of collective survival, we all flourish. This is the urgent challenge that is before us as feminist educators, workers, activists, mothers, artists, community organizers, dreamers, doers, survivors and sisters: bridging our differences and finding our power. That is the task we must turn to quickly, with all our collective energies.[43]

---

[39] See Lucy Alderson, *"The Women's Employment and Training Coalition—Advocating for Equity in Adult Education,"* (July 1994). Unpublished Paper, Department of Administrative, Adult and Higher Education, University of British Columbia.

[40] For more information, contact Women in Trades and Technology National Network, 10 Douglas Court, Unit 2, London Ontario, N5W 4A7.

[41] The Women's Research Centre, a national organization formed in 1973 and based in Vancouver, is an interesting example of a feminist organization that has employed and transformed adult education practices through their development of action research strategies, evaluation methods and community workshops. For more information, contact Women's Research Centre, 101-2245 Broadway, Vancouver, BC, V6K 2E4.

[42] See, for example: Matthias Finger, "New Social Movements and Their Implications for Adult Education," *Adult Education Quarterly 40* (1989) pp.15-21; and Michael Welton, "Social Revolutionary Learning: The New Social Movements as Learning Sites," *Adult Education Quarterly 43* (1993) pp.152-164.

[43] Lisa Albrecht & Rose Brewer (Eds.), *Bridges of Power—Women's Multicultural Alliances* (Philadel-

Within the process of coalition building are many significant, if not transformative learning moments. Learning to build coalitions is critical to democratic and planetary survival.

Just the Tip of the Iceberg

A number of themes seem to be threaded through the stories brought forward in this chapter. Women who worked in those movements and organizations that are familiar to us—such as the Antigonish Movement, Frontier College, and Citizens' Forum—were essential to the success of these activities. They were not the visible leaders but they were often the front-line and behind-the-scenes workers, weaving a web of relations and acting as the "social glue" that sustained the organizations. The women who worked in organizations such as the YWCA and the Women's Institutes brought a sense of caring, often articulated through their maternal and domestic roles, to their approach.

The women's organizations that have emerged during the last three decades reflect both of these characteristics (i.e., the behind-the-scenes, everyday work of sustaining organizations and caring) as well as a kind of double vision. By double vision, I am referring to a critical analysis of the power relations and structures that devalue women's labour—an analysis that frames their understanding of women's struggles generally as well as their own struggles against marginalization as feminist organizations.

My hope is that this chapter provides a glimpse at some of the women, and women's organizations, who have contributed to the field of adult education in Canada. More work is needed to uncover other organizations, individuals, and experiences in order to create a more accurate picture of the foundations of adult education in Canada. I began with a quote, which raised several questions including "what must happen to bring some hitherto unseen part of past reality into visibility?" Two tasks face us—first, we must be vigilant and take notice of what has been ignored and raise questions about why this is happening; and, second, we must build new areas of knowledge and work to have this wisdom accepted as part of the knowledge base of the field.

Uncovering/creating the stories and including the voices of women who have been silenced or obscured from discussions of adult education is not enough. Bringing in new voices requires that we also listen, so that there is an *audience* for these accounts. And sometimes, being able to hear and understand requires that we also rethink or reconceptualize the frameworks that are familiar to us. To quote Anne Firor Scott once again: "Like the unexamined life, the unexamined discipline is unlikely to achieve its fullest potential."[44]

---

phia, PA: New Society Publishers, 1990) p.ix.

[44] Anne Firor Scott, ibid., p.21.

5

Participation, Participants and Providers

The Interest in Adult Learning

Every day and each evening in Canada a significant number of adults are involved in learning activities of one kind or another. They pursue their learning in a variety of settings and with the assistance of numerous kinds of organizations. Evidence of this pursuit of learning include cars parked around school buildings in the evenings, displays of course brochures in public settings and impressive industrial training centres.

Two observations are at the root of the interest which adult educators hold in studying adults' participation in learning. The first is that the greatest amount of adult learning is done completely on a voluntary basis. Even when freed from the compulsion to attend grade school, adults in substantial numbers choose to continue learning. In most cases the choice is entirely of the individual's own volition, while in some cases there are compelling reasons to participate, such as keeping up in one's employment. For the most part, however, participation in adult education is based on adults exercising their free will. The second observation is that adults need to continue learning in order to maintain and advance themselves in their society. Whereas in earlier times continuing one's education was seen as a way of getting ahead, particularly in the context of the workplace, nowadays continued learning is necessary just to keep current with the ever-quickening pace of change. Taking both observations, a common question arises which adult educators are interested in having answered: Why do some adults continue with learning while others do not? While much is known about the factors which both promote and discourage participation, our understanding is by no means complete, and this chapter will address the question rather than answer it.

The term which has been favoured to describe adults who are active learners is "participants," and the observable behaviour of adults who are active in their learning quest is described as "participation." This seems reasonable enough, and hence to define the term "participation" as it relates to adult education would appear to be straightforward. After all, by definition to participate is to join; thus participation in adult education is the act of joining some form of adult learning activity. As with much in adult education, however, it is not quite that simple, and one of the purposes of this chapter is to help clarify what is meant by participation. As an example of the difficulty, the initial question might be asked: Is it necessary that an adult, in order to participate in adult education, must join in with others to learn, or can an adult also learn in a solitary manner? As we shall see, there is debate on this question, and has been for some time.

Before starting to examine adult participation, it will be helpful to first identify why the concept of participation in adult education is seen as being important. This can be done by adopting the viewpoint of the several "stakeholders" in adult education, i.e., those with a particular interest in it. To begin, there is the viewpoint of Canadian society. Numerous writers on adult education point to the need of adults to participate actively in the affairs of the society in order to preserve and strengthen the democratic ideal.[1] As citizens we are aware that, given Canada's ethnic mosaic, beginning with the Native peoples, then the dual cultures of the French and the English and its current evolution to a multi-cultural society, there is an ever-increasing reliance on a tolerance of differences in order for the weave of Canadian society to remain strong. We know tolerance is derived from understanding that is based on knowledge, as opposed to intolerance which is based on ignorance and fear. In addition, Canada is faced with perplexing and often conflicting issues such as environmental protection and economic development, individual rights and community welfare, and national priorities and regional recognition. In our democratic society it is ultimately the citizen who must make informed choices, and participation in adult education is seen as an important way to become informed.

The next viewpoint is that of the providers of adult education, whether they be large institutions such as a community college or small associations such as an Alzheimer's Disease support group. These providers all offer what they believe to be interesting and useful programs, some of which are intended to have a general appeal while others are directed at specific groups. In desiring

---

[1] For example, G. Hawkins (Ed.), *A Design for Democracy* (New York: Association Press, 1956); J. Draper (Ed.), *Citizen Participation: Canada* (Toronto: New Press, 1971); G. Selman, "Adult Education and Citizenship," in Cassidy & Faris (Eds.), *Choosing Our Future: Adult Education and Public Policy in Canada* (Toronto: OISE Press, 1987); G. Selman, *Citizenship and the Adult Education Movement in Canada* (Vancouver: University of B.C., 1991).

to fill the available space in the class—that is the number of seats for atten-ders—these providers need to know how to promote attendance. Further, once a person is motivated to attend, it is the instructor (or facilitator) who needs to be aware of participation factors in order to design the appropriate instruc-tional strategy to meet the learning need.

Another viewpoint is that of adult learners. Generally speaking, the more that is known about adult learning needs and desires, and the factors which influence the decision to participate, the more that will be able to be done to meet these same needs and desires. This should in turn increase the availabil-ity of opportunities to participate. Not only will there be more opportunities, but these opportunities will be more accessible to adults as the sponsoring organizations become more adept at overcoming the difficulties which stand in the way of adult participation. For example, in an effort to enable home-bound parents to enroll in a course on child development, the course which is normally offered in the evening at a far-off community college might now also be offered during the daytime at a neighbourhood church hall with child minding provided.

Another viewpoint is that of adult educators who believe fervently that through continued learning an adult enjoys a more productive and satisfying life. By increasing the number of adults who successfully participate in learn-ing activities, the adult educator is fulfilling a role, indeed a mission, that contributes to the well-being of individuals and society alike. This is a moral viewpoint, and differs completely from a self-serving one which simply seeks participation for participation's sake, thereby providing employment for adult educators. At the same time it is important for adult educators to be able to point to high enrollment figures as an indication of adult learning. Such fig-ures help to advance the day when decision makers accept lifelong learning as the basis for all educational policy.

In summary, Canadian society places a very high value on learning by youth and adults alike, and large amounts of public resources are made avail-able to enable learning to take place. Because in adult learning the basis for participation differs in a number of significant ways from that of youth, and adult learning has no prescribed format, the concept of participation in adult education is of particular interest. Participation is viewed as being admira-ble—even virtuous—and non-participation, rather than being viewed disdain-fully, is instead understood in terms of the presence of some impediment to participation which must be overcome. The admirable traits of participation include the following:

- it is a manifestation of the concept of lifelong learning;
- it is an indication of a learning society, with the likelihood of greater understanding and tolerance existing among citizens;

- it reflects a constructive use of leisure time and a productive use of work time;
- it is an available mechanism for people in the conducting of their lives, i.e., staying abreast with change, coping with problems, taking advantage of opportunities, bringing understanding to perplexing situations;
- it represents activity versus passivity, striving versus stagnation, enterprise versus indolence, positiveness versus negativeness;
- it is reminiscent of an earlier time in Canada when small communities depended on participation to sustain a quality of community life.

Three Central Ideas to Participation

There are three ideas which are central to the topic of participation: (1) determining what is meant by participation in adult learning; (2) examining who participates and for what reasons; and (3) identifying the providers of adult learning activity. As a backdrop to examining these ideas the methodology and findings of major surveys conducted on adult education in Canada will be presented.

There have been at least four attempts in recent decades to provide a comprehensive picture of participation in adult education in this country. Three of these have been conducted by public agencies (the Dominion Bureau of Statistics/ Statistics Canada in co-operation with government departments) and one by the private sector (the two national adult education associations). The earliest, conducted by the Dominion Bureau of Statistics, was carried out as part of the monthly Labour Force Survey in 1959-60 and indicated that 3.6 percent of Canadians over fourteen years of age (approximately one in twenty-five) participated in adult education in the ten-month period covered.[2] The second study was carried out for the two national adult education bodies, the Canadian Association for Adult Education (CAAE) and the Institut canadien de l'éducation des adultes (ICEA), by the Gallup organization in 1982 and was based on a very much smaller sample. It surveyed persons eighteen and over and produced a participation rate of approximately 18 percent.[3] There was some scepticism about this study, the sample of those surveyed having been relatively small, but the trend which showed enormous growth of participation in adult education was confirmed by a study carried out early in 1984 by Statistics Canada in co-operation with the Secretary of State's Department. Entitled *One in Every Five*, this report was based on a very large sample and concluded that of those seventeen and over (excluding full-time

---

[2] Dominion Bureau of Statistics, *Participants in Further Education in Canada*, (Ottawa: DBS Education Division, 1963).

[3] CAAE/ICEA, *From the Adult's Point of View* (Toronto/Montreal: CAAE/ICEA, 1982).

students), 19 percent of Canadians had participated in adult education in 1983.[4] Alberta led the nation with a participation rate of 25 percent. The fourth survey was again a broadly based one, carried out by Statistics Canada (as part of its Labour Force Survey) on behalf of Human Resources Canada and examining participation in the year 1991 by Canadians seventeen years of age and older. If those in that group who are still involved in full-time education are excluded, the study indicates that approximately 33 percent of Canadians took part in adult education in 1991.[5]

The Idea of Participation

As noted above, the term "participation" has become accepted as a way of describing the act of engaging in adult learning. There are two reasons which can be advanced for this acceptance, both of which indicate the importance of nuance when describing aspects of adult education. The first is that by using the term the operative notion of voluntarily engaging in adult learning is thereby emphasized. One participates by choosing to join, and one can also choose to discontinue participating. This contrasts with the synonym "enrollment" which, even though the enrollment may be voluntary, still suggests the giving of oneself over to the organization which accepts the enrollment. The second reason is that in adult education the common term used to identify an adult learner is "participant" rather than, for example, student. This use is by no means universal but just as participation is suggestive of voluntary involvement, so participant is suggestive of one who joins to share in the learning experience with the "facilitator" (as opposed to "teacher"). The voluntary nature of joining gives the participant a greater sense of equality with the facilitator in the learning activity. Thus the subject of this examination is the act of participation on the part of the participant.

There are two approaches to understanding participation as it relates to adult education. The first approach can be thought of metaphorically as a turnstile. With this approach it is the act of entering, of being counted as one attends at a certain time and place, that denotes participation. While the turnstile description of this approach seems somewhat crass, the approach is based on the administrative necessity found in any formal system of keeping count. Such systems have a constant need to justify their existence, and the easiest way of doing so is to employ quantitative measures to denote activity. Thus departments of continuing education within institutions are able to report on the number of persons who participated, that is enrolled, in their various programs during a given period of time. The label "enrollment" would well

---

[4] Statistics Canada/Secretary of State, *One in Every Five: A Survey of Adult Education in Canada* (Ottawa: Statistics Canada/Secretary of State, 1984).

[5] Statistics Canada, *Adult Education and Training Survey* (Ottawa: Statistics Canada, 1992).

apply to this approach, but labelling this as the enrollment approach to participation is not intended as a condemnation. The very fact that an organization
continues to have statistics to report indicates its adult education operation is
viable. The point, though, is how with this approach emphasizes the statistical
fact of initial participation, i.e., enrollment, rather than the purpose of the
participation, namely learning.

The second approach looks at the ways in which adults engage themselves
in learning beyond their formal education. This meaning emphasizes the occurrence of adult learning wherever and however it occurs. It acknowledges
that beyond one's formal education an adult may exercise freedom of choice
in deciding to continue to be engaged in learning and is free to engage in
learning in whatever way desired. It may involve enrolling in a course at a
night school or it may involve learning at home with the assistance of a
self-study manual purchased at a book store. With this meaning the importance is placed on the act of learning rather than the fact of enrolling. The
label "engagement" would well apply to this second approach as its emphasis
is on the variety of ways in which adults continue to engage themselves in
learning.

Of the two approaches, enrollment and engagement, the former is the more
readily understood. There is a numeric simplicity to it, a mere matter of
counting individuals who sign up and attend. As noted this is an important
measure of participation in adult education. From the viewpoint of the
providers of adult education courses, this approach is basic to their ability to
continue offering courses, dependent as they are on people enrolling. The
latter approach of engagement, however, is more attuned to the activity of
learning as construed by adult learners. To pursue an understanding of this
approach, it is helpful to first liberate one's traditional understanding of learning.

Learning is a natural activity of the human species. All of us take on
extraordinarily complex learning tasks at the outset of our lives, such as
learning to talk, to walk and to discriminate shapes and sizes. By necessity we
are innate learners. We also discover that our innate ability to learn is enhanced by having another person (and even through a stimulus such as a
television) assist us in our learning efforts. Indeed these efforts can be made
much more effective and efficient by having another person direct them in a
manner which they prescribe for the learner. This all-important role is filled
by a person acknowledged by the designation "teacher."

The role of a teacher is introduced very early in a child's life. In the
example above of learning to talk, walk and discriminate, it is usually a
child's parents who perform as teachers. Before long the child is introduced to
school, and it is here that the roles of teacher and learner become formalized.
An indication of the powerful influence of the role of the teacher is to observe

how, for many children, teachers quickly become role models, and in games of, "Let's play school," it is the role of teacher, not student, which is coveted. This role of teacher is important to consider because all societies have built their educational systems around it. When parents enroll their child in school it is the teaching resource it contains which they desire for the child.

It is precisely because a system must be organized in order to place students with teachers that learning becomes the subject of an administrative orientation. Students are arranged into classes, provided with text books and accounted for each school day morning. The taxpaying public demands such efficacy in the school system. What occurs as a result of this efficacy, however, is that learning becomes highly administrated, and this dominates our view of the human learning process. It is no wonder then that this administrative view carries forward into adulthood once a student's formal education is concluded. Most significant for adult education, however, is the understanding that this view no longer needs to dominate the conception of how individuals engage in learning activities.

The view in adult education is to return the learner to the pre-eminent role. This return is heralded by the fact that the adult enjoys the freedom to choose whether to continue learning or not, and also to choose the circumstances in which any learning will take place. It is precisely this freedom of choice that gives "engagement" participation its meaning. That adults do continue to engage themselves with learning in the ways they do constitutes the true phenomenon of participation. Equally, though, the phenomenon includes reasons for adults who are not continuing to be engaged with their learning. These reasons for non-engagement suggest impediments which, if overcome, might well lead to participation. This latter point will be examined further in this chapter under the heading of "Barriers to Participation." For the present the emphasis will be on those who are considered participants.

From this discussion it is seen that the idea of participation in adult education is associated with learning. This association requires, however, that there also be an understanding of what is meant by learning, and it is here that there exists a divergence of thought as it relates to adult learning. One direction leads along the path of learning theory as developed by educational psychologists and emphasizes the importance of planned learning, i.e., instruction, to learning. In this direction every effort is made to understand the internal mental processes connected with learning so as to determine the instructional strategies most likely to influence learning. It is apparent that this direction is of particular interest to the professional educator, whose task it is to direct the strategies which will likely have the greatest potential for bringing about learning in the individual. Indeed the presence of an educator is seen as being necessary in order for planned learning to take place.

The second direction leads along a path where there is much less emphasis on the role of an educator in bringing about planned learning and instead sees the adult learner as being capable of assuming some or even all of this task. Adherents of this direction regard the adult learner as having reached a state of both self-awareness and self-determination sufficient to make his or her own learning decisions. Thus it is the adult learner who intentionally and voluntarily places himself or herself in a learning situation and measures it to determine the extent to which learning will occur so as to meet personal learning objectives. This direction is not to be seen as being counter to that of the educational psychologists; indeed the definition of learning is common to both, incorporating as it does the elements of a change which is brought about in physical or mental ability and which is sustained over time.[6] Instead an adult is viewed as being in a position to exercise considerable autonomy and discretion over his or her learning, and this includes the option of taking on some or all of the responsibility for planning the instruction, including the evaluation criteria. As Brookfield notes, "At the heart of self-directedness is the adult's assumption of control over setting educational goals and generating personally meaningful evaluative criteria."[7] Indeed the ultimate situation for any teacher must be when the teaching which has been provided enables a person to become an independent learner. Thus participation in adult education, when understood in terms of the presence of learning, can include much more learning activity than occurs when only a teacher or facilitator is instructing.

In light of the suggestion that the presence of learning indicates participation, it would be wrong to suggest that whenever learning takes place there is necessarily participation. The respected adult education theorist Gale Jensen referred to learning which takes place as a result of the everyday experiences of life as being learning in the "natural societal setting." This learning he characterized as being both casual and serendipitous and in terms of this discussion would not be associated with participation. Jensen contrasted the natural societal setting with the "formal instructional setting," which includes the presence of an educational "agent" (teacher) to guide and direct learning.[8]

---

[6] For example the educational psychologist Robert Gagne describes learning as "a change in human disposition or capability, which can be retained, and which is not simply ascribable to the process of growth." R. Gagne, *The Conditions of Learning*, 2nd ed. (New York: Holt, Rinehart & Winston, 1970) p.3. The adult educator, Alan Thomas, similarly describes learning as being "a voluntary act, which occurs each time a member of society comes to know something, to be able to do something, or to be able to feel something he or she could not previously." A. Thomas, "Learning in Society—A Discussion Paper," in *Learning in Society—Toward a New Paradigm* (Ottawa: UNESCO, 1985) p.21.

[7] S. Brookfield, *Understanding and Facilitating Adult Learning* (San Francisco: Jossey-Bass, 1986) p.19.

[8] G. Jensen, "The Nature of Education as a Discipline," in G. Jensen (Ed.), *Readings for Educational Researchers* (Ann Arbor: Ann Arbor Publishers, 1960).

For many adult education theorists it is the formal instructional setting that constitutes adult education's field. (The term formal instructional setting is intended to emphasize the necessity of the educational agent, and not to imply an actual classroom.) By this is meant that purposefulness is necessary to distinguish intended learning from that which occurs serendipitously. The responsibility of the educational agent, then, is to ensure the purposefulness of the learning activity. The educational agent accomplishes this by designing "a sequence of tasks using specific learning procedures to help an adult achieve a mutually agreeable learning objective."[9] Thus another respected adult education theorist, Coolie Verner, defined adult education as being, "a relationship between an educational agent and a learner in which the agent selects, arranges and continuously directs a sequence of progressive tasks that provide systematic experiences to achieve learning."[10]

The delineation of the field of adult education in terms of the formal instructional setting, with its inclusion of organized educational activities and an ongoing relationship between learner and educational agent in order to ensure purposefulness in the learning activity, has more recently been challenged by researchers of adult learning. They have concluded that adults can and do learn in a purposeful manner without necessarily needing to be in an organized educational activity complete with an educational agent. Further, their findings indicate that adults are capable of conducting their own learning activities and that the role of the educational agent (teacher) is one that the learner can assign to another as he or she sees fit. In some cases the learner will assign this role to a class instructor; in other cases the learner might assume a large portion of it, thereby enabling the learner to self-direct much of the learning activity, consulting with a subject expert only if assistance is required. In fact this is a distinguishing aspect of the engagement approach to adult education, namely the belief that the learner can assume some or even all of the responsibilities of the "agent." In this approach the learner is participating, but this act of learning, this engagement, may never be evidenced on any class list.

It is apparent that the view of adult learning which gives credence to the idea of self-directed learning embraces both directions to learning noted above, that is the need for a professional educator to direct learning and the ability of the learner to assume responsibility for planning his or her own learning. In self-directed learning the role of the educational agent can be divided between the learner and the educational agent, as determined by the

[9] C. Verner & A. Booth, *Adult Education* (Washington: The Center for Applied Research in Education, 1964) p.1.

[10] C. Verner, "Basic Concepts and Limitations," in J.R. Kidd (Ed.), *Learning and Society* (Toronto: CAAE, 1963) p.235.

learner. There is even the option of the learner assuming all of this role. In this latter option, however, the educational agent will still be present in an impersonal form, for example, as the author of a book, the organizer of a lecture series, or the script writer of a television documentary. (Note, however, that in such cases the term "educational agent" would be inappropriate as the author, the lecture organizer and the script writer are not acting in the capacity of a professional educator, as is intended by the term.) This self-directed view should not be associated with serendipitous learning in the natural societal setting, as the essential element of purposefulness is still present.

The person most identified with self-directed learning is Allen Tough of the Ontario Institute for Studies in Education. According to Tough, adults commonly undertake "learning projects," which he defines as being "a series of related episodes, adding up to at least seven hours. In each episode more than half a person's total motivation is to gain and retain certain fairly clear knowledge and skill, or to produce some other lasting change in himself."[11] Tough's research work confirmed the idea that adults were competent in directing their own learning and, when necessary, even teaching themselves. The term "adult's learning projects" was introduced by Tough to emphasize the intentionality with which adults commit themselves to their learning.

The findings by Tough and others as to the extent of adult participation in learning projects are most revealing:[12]

- almost everyone undertakes at least one or two major learning projects a year, and the median number of projects conducted annually is eight;
- it is common for an adult to spend 700 hours a year engaged in learning projects;
- almost 70 percent of learning projects are self-planned.

By adopting the understanding of participation as purposeful learning which utilizes both enrollment and engagement approaches, it is possible to appreciate the shortcoming of using enrollment figures alone to measure the extent of participation. Enrollment figures indicate some, but not all, of the adult learning phenomenon. To illustrate this point the Statistics Canada Adult Education Survey determined that approximately 20 percent of Canadian adults took at least one course, class or instructional activity in the calendar year 1983 (up from 4 percent in 1960). Another finding, this time from research conducted earlier by Tough, determined that virtually all adults engage in several "learning projects" each year, and were thereby participating in

---

[11] A. Tough, *The Adult's Learning Projects: A Fresh Approach to Theory and Practice in Adult Learning*, 2nd ed. (Toronto: OISE, 1979) p.6.

[12] A. Tough, *The Adult's Learning Projects*, p.1.

adult education. Tough's research concluded that 90 percent of the adult population is engaged in carrying out their own "learning projects."[13]

The discrepancy between the two findings is easily enough explained by the approach to identifying participation. In the case of Statistics Canada's survey it was enrollment while in the case of the research on learning projects it was engagement in learning. Further, the Adult Education Survey (and many similar surveys) defined adult education in terms of a course, class or instruction, i.e., the formal instructional setting, whereas for Tough's purposes learning was defined in terms of an adult learning project, which is "a major, highly deliberate effort to gain certain knowledge and skill (or to change in some other way)."[14]

From reviewing the findings of both Statistics Canada's and Tough's efforts at quantifying participation in adult education, one is left with two distinctly different impressions. According to the engagement approach to participation (as posited by Tough and embodied in self-directed learning), most adults are satisfying their learning needs and wants, while the enrollment approach to participation used by Statistics Canada suggests cause for great distress, considering the high level of non-participation (80 percent). What is to be concluded from such an apparent discrepancy?

Firstly the reasons for the gap can be readily determined, i.e., the definition of the term participation and the basis for measuring participation (enrollment versus self-directed learning project). Secondly, adult education researchers continue to grapple with the phenomenon of adult learning and with efforts to describe it accurately. This means rethinking many of the conventional ideas about education, even adult education, such as the requirements for learning: a classroom, a collection of students, a curriculum and a teacher. Adult education is still an emerging field of research and practice. Thirdly, when one uses the term participation, the approach to its meaning—enrollment versus engagement—must be made clear.

In summary it is recognized that while participation in adult education is an empirical fact, there are different points of view regarding the idea of participation. Depending on how one believes that the learning process takes place, the rate of participation in adult education in Canada varies from a discouraging low level (20 percent) to an encouragingly high level (90 percent). Whatever one's point of view, however, behind these statistics are the participants, and it is helpful to appreciate their individual circumstances.

---

[13] A. Tough, "Major Learning Efforts: Recent Research and Future Directions" in *Adult Education* (USA) *28*, (1978) pp.250-263.

[14] A. Tough, *The Adult's Learning Projects*, p.1.

The Idea of Participants

Who exactly is a participant in adult education? It is interesting when walking down a busy street or riding on the public transit to speculate on whether individual adults one encounters are participants, and what might be the subject of their learning interest. Initially by way of intuition, and more recently by way of surveys and research, a fair amount of knowledge has been gained about participants and their motivations for learning. Using the enrollment approach, these are the 20 percent recorded in the Statistics Canada Adult Education Survey and from whom information has been gathered as to their reasons for participating. Of equal if not greater interest to the adult educator are the other 80 percent, but our knowledge of this group is scant by comparison. It is easier to ask an adult who is participating why he or she chose to participate than to identify a non-participant and ask why he or she is not participating. Further, in the case of the non-participant it is difficult to determine whether he or she would in fact participate if the declared impediment to participation were to be removed.

One of the first questions which arises when determining who is a participant is what constitutes adult education. Is a thirty-year-old university graduate student a participant? Is an eighteen-year-old school dropout who is now enrolled in a high school completion program a participant? There is no categorical answer to these questions; rather it depends on the context of the question. In the two instances raised here, both persons may be identified as adult learners by virtue of their age. Also both are accumulating a growing amount of life experiences, and these experiences influence their ways of thinking and provide them with an adult self-concept. But because the university student is registered in the formal educational system, which is considered outside of adult education's purview, while the high school dropout is registered in a program sponsored by a school board's adult education department, administratively one will not be counted as an adult participant while the other will. In adult education, then, it is helpful to take a broad view of who is a participant. The motive for identifying a participant is not to draw a line of demarcation so as to arbitrarily separate participants as being either included or excluded. Instead the emphasis is on identifying the individual's circumstances, and using these to suggest that he or she is a participant. Three factors are used in determining an individual's circumstances so as to distinguish them as being a participant in adult education: age, psychological maturity and social role.[15] Each will be examined in turn.

One apparently straightforward approach to identifying who can be considered as an adult participant would be to use the age separating youth from

---

[15] C. Verner, "Definition of Terms," in Jensen et al. (Eds.), *Adult Education: Outlines of an Emerging Field of University Study* (Washington: Adult Education Association of the USA, 1964).

adult and suggest anyone who has achieved chronological adulthood is thereby automatically an adult participant. What, then, might be the age? Not too long ago in Canada and elsewhere the so-called "age of majority" signifying adult status for such purposes as voting in national elections and purchasing liquor was twenty-one years. This arbitrary age has subsequently been lowered to eighteen years. At eighteen, however, an individual may already have taken on considerable responsibilities normally ascribed to adulthood, such as marriage, parenting and soldiering, and because of this it is usual to bestow adult status and privilege on the individual. Another approach, that of using the official school leaving age (usually sixteen years), poses similar difficulties. Can we consider the significant numbers of students who remain in school beyond this age in order to complete their high school matriculation as suddenly being different, i.e., adult, and thus deserving of adjusted teaching methods? Such a suggestion would be totally impractical, just as the basis for it is fallacious. Age alone, therefore, is not a means of distinguishing an adult participant.

Psychological maturity refers to the point in time when the individual is prepared to assume responsibility for him or herself and at the same time assume a productive role in the community. Seen in these terms it is the individual's state of mind as evidenced by social maturity which indicates when the individual is prepared to enter adulthood. While every society has developed certain bench marks leading up to a complete acknowledgment of adulthood, for example, ascribing legal adult status, granting privileges such as driving a car and bestowing the right to vote, the total elapsed period for all this to come to pass may be several years. Thus an individual who considers him or herself to be an adult, and is accepting of adult responsibilities, should be so acknowledged and supported by the society, even though all the "rights of passage" might not yet have been attained.

The third factor is that of social roles. As this factor will be elaborated on shortly, for now the essence of the idea will suffice. Throughout life there are social roles appropriate to certain ages which individuals assume as they grow and develop. For example a child must learn to relate with other children of the same age. Somewhat later in life a young adult must learn to live with a marriage partner. There is a difference, however, in how the learning is acquired. Whereas a child for the most part learns about these social roles from teachers in the school and from parents in the home, for the adult the onus is on the individual to seek out other opportunities for learning about the social roles which they as adults are now assuming. Thus an adult participant is one who is assuming a social role appropriate to adulthood, and sets out to learn about it.

There have been recent efforts in Canada at developing a working definition of an adult so as to enable the collection of participation data. In 1982, the CAAE and its francophone counterpart, the ICEA, commissioned a Gallup survey to examine the state of adult education and training in Canada, and they defined adult to include "all persons beyond the compulsory school attendance age in each Canadian jurisdiction who have interrupted their continuous attendance at an educational institution for a significant period of labour-force participation or other activities."[16] Subsequently the Statistics Canada Adult Education Survey of 1984 defined adult participant as an individual seventeen years and over who did not attend an educational institution full time, unless as a full-time student that person took a course, class or instruction on a part-time basis in addition to his or her full-time course load.[17] In terms of the three factors noted above, both definitions incorporate the age factor while only the CAAE/ICEA definition additionally implies the presence of the psychological maturity factor with its reference to labour-force participation "or other activities." The Statistics Canada definition obscurely hints at the social role factor by its suggestion of a full-time student taking a course in addition to his or her course load. Neither definition is seen to be totally satisfactory as both of necessity employ arbitrary distinctions. For instance in the case of the CAAE/ICEA definition, all full-time students beyond compulsory school attendance age seem not to be adults for the purpose of adult participation statistics, even though they may participate outside of their full-time studies. In the case of the Statistics Canada Survey definition it suggests that a woman who returns to college after raising a family in order to complete a diploma program is not an adult participant. Both examples of exclusion are quite unsatisfactory and point to the limitations—and difficulties—in developing working definitions in adult education.

There is an approach to identifying an adult participant other than by using the factors of age, psychological maturity and social role already noted, and that is to use the content and sponsorship of the education as the distinguishing criteria. Using the approach of formal, non-formal and informal education as presented in Chapter 1, the suggestion is that persons involved in more precisely registered informal education are not considered as participating in adult education, even though they may unquestionably be considered as adult, as in the example of the middle-aged woman returning to college to complete a diploma. The reasoning is that the formal education system has conditions which it imposes on students in order to award credentials, and that the various requirements which are a necessary part of academic conformity are incompatible with the tenets of adult education. For instance, one of these conditions is that the student learn at a certain rate or else suffer consequences such as failing the course, being denied the certification or being forced to

---

[16] CAAE/ICEA, *From the Adult's Point of View*, p.4.

[17] Statistics Canada, *One in Every Five: A Survey of Adult Education in Canada*, p.1.

withdraw. Adult education practice, by comparison, acknowledges that adult learners learn at varying rates and good practice makes provision for this without the consequence of failure, denial, or withdrawal. Adult education's purview, then, is seen as being with non-formal and informal education.

In some respects this distinction seems clear enough but it is certainly one which does not see the matter from the adult participant's point of view. By way of example, is an adult who registers full time in a community college's diploma program a different learner from another adult who registers for a course offered part time by the same community college through its continuing education department? From an administrative and even conceptual point of view the answer is "yes," while from the adult's point of view it is "no."

It is necessary to further understand this administrative arrangement because it is telling of adult education's status within the formal educational system, and thus the status of adult learners. It is the educational planners (be they policy makers, administrators or whoever is part of making the educational opportunity available to adults) who must plan and manage the formal educational system established for that society. Because resources for this purpose are finite and because the system needs to be coherent in order to best serve the society, it must be structured on an organized basis. For this system to function, distinctions must be made so as to determine for whom it does and does not have legislated responsibility for providing education. Beyond this mandate the system can then determine who it does or does not desire to serve. Because for the most part the legislation governing the formal educational systems in the provinces does not provide for non-formal adult education, adult education has existed by and large on sufferance within these systems. Using the example above, the adult who is registered full-time is considered a bona fide student at the college while the adult who is registered in the continuing education course is distinguished as being a "participant."

In keeping with the formal educational system's need to define as a way of distinguishing, it will be helpful to now provide a definition of an adult participant. The definition is simple enough, and it is contained in a broader UNESCO definition of adult education adopted at its 19th Session held in Kenya in 1976.[18] This definition acknowledges that adulthood is a stage of social development, and the age at which this stage is attained by the individual varies from society to society. For this reason the definition remains open, and adult participants are defined as "persons regarded as adult by the societies to which they belong." By way of the content of their learning, these adults participate in the "entire body of organized educational processes, whatever the content, level and method, whether formal or otherwise, whether

---

[18] UNESCO, *Recommendation on the Development of Adult Education* (Ottawa: Canadian Commission for UNESCO, nd).

they prolong or replace initial education in schools, colleges and universities as well as in apprenticeship ... " This definition would suggest that for the purpose of identifying an adult learner in Canada, the federal voting age of eighteen would be accepted as when society regards an individual as being an adult by way of enjoying full citizenship.

Before leaving the discussion on who is a participant, it is fair to suggest that adult participants have caused some difficulty for formal educational systems. Most often educational systems have sought to distinguish adult participants for reasons of exclusion or for separate treatment, for example, the setting of academic admission requirements or the charging of cost recovery fees. The paucity of legislation recognizing adult learning needs is one indication of the difficulty which adult education poses for the formal educational system. As a consequence, adult education's frequently described marginal status as viewed by the formal educational system is often visited upon the adult participant, or would-be participant.

Having answered the question of who is an adult participant from various perspectives the next question to address is, Why do adults participate? (See also Chapter 1 for a discussion on the functions of adult education.) The common conception about education is that it is something one does during the early part of life in order to then get on with the business of living. "First learn, then earn" has been viewed as the logical life sequence upon which educational systems are built. Indeed, while attending school, college or university, the goal of attending is typically described as being to "complete" one's education or to be "finished with school." With these limiting notions in mind, the fact that adults choose to continue their education understandably raises the curiosity of those who observe the phenomenon. Because this phenomenon is neither recent nor incidental, however, and because the curiosity of researchers and theorists have been piqued and their findings publicized, it is possible to interpret the motivations of participating adults. This interpretation is contained in the adult education literature on motivation, and it is by studying motivation that a clearer picture emerges of learning's pervasive influence on the lives of adults.[19]

Motivation to Participate

As human beings, adults are motivated by needs, wants and desires. There is a considerable degree of conformity among adults in the objects of these three motivators, as well as some individuality. For many the strength of the motivation is not sufficient to bring about action on the part of the individual,

---

[19] See for example R. Wlodkowski, *Enhancing Adult Motivation To Learn* (San Francisco: Jossey-Bass, 1985) and P. Cross, *Adults as Learners: Increasing Participation and Facilitating Learning* (San Francisco: Jossey-Bass, 1981).

while for others their motivation leads to, in the case of adult education, participation. By simply being attuned to the normal circumstances of adulthood and the influences of socio-economic conditions, it is possible for an adult educator to determine which compelling needs, wants and desires are likely to solicit a participatory response by at least some adults.

A particular set of assumptions about the learning needs of individuals has been gathered together under the heading of andragogy, meaning the art and science of helping adults learn. In his acclaimed book, *The Modern Practice of Adult Education*, Knowles identifies four assumptions of andragogy, one of which describes adults' readiness to learn.[20]

> Adults are aware of specific learning needs generated by real life tasks or problems. Adult education programs, therefore should be organized around "life application" categories and sequenced according to learners' readiness to learn.

This readiness to learn refers to the learning needs of adults as they develop through their adult life. Adult education as a field of practice has been greatly influenced by developmental psychology, and an understanding of it can provide insights into why adults learn.

One of the earliest proponents of the relationship between developmental psychology and adult learning was Robert Havighurst.[21] Havighurst identified and sequenced what he called the "developmental tasks" of childhood and adulthood, and suggested that these tasks are faced in turn by the individual as he or she grows in age and maturity. Havighurst believed that in order to meet the demands of each developmental task, learning was required, and that this need for learning gave rise to a "teachable moment," i.e., a point in time when a person is most receptive to learning information and skills pertaining to the particular task. Havighurst further indicated the importance of successfully achieving each developmental task in order for the individual to contend with life in a satisfying manner.

There are three periods of adult life identified by Havighurst which contain developmental tasks appropriate to that life period. These are:

Early Adulthood, ages 18-30
- selecting a mate
- learning to live with a marriage partner
- starting a family
- rearing children
- managing a home

---

[20] Malcolm Knowles, *The Modern Practice of Adult Education* (Chicago: Follett Publishing Co., 1980) p.43.

[21] R. Havighurst, *Developmental Tasks and Education*, 3rd ed. (New York: McKay, 1972).

- getting started in an occupation
- taking on civic responsibility
- finding a congenial social group

Middle Age, ages 30-55
- achieving adult civic and social responsibility
- establishing and maintaining an economic standard of living
- assisting teenage children to become responsible and happy adults
- developing adult leisure time activities
- relating to one's spouse as a person
- accepting and adjusting to the physiological changes of middle age
- adjusting to aging parents

Later Maturity, age 55 and over
- adjusting to decreasing physical strength and health
- adjusting to retirement and reduced income
- adjusting to the death of a spouse
- establishing an explicit affiliation with one's age group
- meeting social and civic obligations
- establishing satisfactory physical living arrangements

In addition, Havighurst identified ten social roles which adults might assume during adulthood, namely: worker, mate, parent, home maker, son or daughter of aging parents, citizen, friend, organization member, religious affiliate, and user of leisure time. As an individual moves through the three phases of adult life there is adjustment in the carrying out of these social roles, and this gives rise to additional developmental tasks.

Other writers have built on this notion of developmental tasks in an effort to increase their knowledge of what the learning needs of adults are at stages of their adulthood, and what the implications are of these learning needs for adult education practice. For example Alan Knox's book *Adult Development and Learning* is subtitled "A Handbook on Individual Growth and Competence in the Adult Years for Education and the Helping Professions."[22] Because of this enhanced understanding of adult learning needs, adult educators are in a better position to anticipate what adults are most likely to want and need to learn, and why. A simple example will illustrate this point. A young couple wishing to get married has the opportunity to attend a marriage preparation course covering such topics as finances, inter-personal communication and family planning. The course has been developed to deal with the nuptial issues the couple is now facing. Still later on, after several years of marriage,

---

[22] A. Knox, *Adult Development and Learning* (San Francisco: Jossey-Bass, 1981).

the couple might well attend a parenting course in order to strengthen their relationship with teenage children. Still later yet, one marriage partner might need to join a support group concerned with caring for a loved one who suffers from Alzheimer's disease.

Arguably the most lucid thinking on the question of why adults participate is that of Cyril Houle. In his book *The Inquiring Mind*, Houle identified three major types of adult learners on the basis of their motivational orientation to learning: the goal oriented, the activity oriented and the learning oriented.[23] According to Houle the goal oriented are those who use education in order to accomplish fairly clear cut objectives, for example, a person wishing to advance within his or her work situation. The activity oriented are those who partake because they find in the circumstances of learning a meaning which has no necessary connection, and often no connection at all, with the content or announced purposes of the activity. This recognizes that many persons participate in continuing education courses, for example, because they provide a break from routine and an opportunity to meet new people. The learning oriented are those who seek knowledge for its own sake. Such persons are often described as having a thirst for knowledge because of the satisfaction it brings to them.

Houle constructed his typology on the basis of extensive interviews with twenty-two acknowledged continuing learners. Since reporting his findings in 1961, there has been considerable further investigation by other researchers to corroborate and elaborate on Houle's conclusions.[24] While others have indeed elaborated on the categories none have surpassed the clarity of Houle's typology, with its readily identifiable categories.

Houle's conclusions as to motivational orientation to learning are compatible with the engagement approach to adult learning. Another effort at determining motivational orientation, in this case consistent with the enrollment approach, is the 1984 Statistics Canada Adult Education Survey. Its findings are based on data which have been subjected to statistical analysis. Whereas Houle deduced his typology from the interviews which he conducted, the Adult Education Survey's findings were simply reported, leaving any deduction up to the user of the data. It is interesting to note that while both efforts are subject to criticism for their respective methodological shortcomings, each provides additional insight into the complex and highly personal realm of individual motivation.

---

[23] C. Houle, *The Inquiring Mind* (Madison: University of Wisconsin Press, 1961).

[24] For corroboration see R. Boshier, "Motivational Orientations of Adult Education Participants: A Factor Analytic Exploration of Houle's Typology" in *Adult Education* (USA) *21*, 2 (1971) and for elaboration see Morstain and Smart, "Reasons for Participating in Adult Education Courses: A Multivariate Analysis of Group Differences" in *Adult Education* (USA) *24*, 2 (1974).

The Adult Education Survey questioned participants as to their motive for participating, using five motivational categories: (1) academic, (2) job related, (3) personal development/general interest, (4) hobby/craft/recreation and, (5) other. (It will be recalled that these participants were not attending an educational institution full time, rather, they were part-time learners.) Included in each category were the following topics: "academic" referred to courses taken at a high school, college, or university for credit toward a diploma, certificate or degree; "job related" referred to courses which provide skills applicable to either the job held by the participant or for a prospective job; "personal development/general interest" referred to courses which are taken for the benefit or interest they provide to the participant without that person wanting to accumulate credits leading to some form of certification; "hobby/craft/recreation" referred to courses taken as a leisure pursuit by the participant, for example, photography, woodworking. (It was possible to include job-related topics in this category if the participant's motivation was leisure oriented, not job related); "other" referred to courses which did not reasonably fit into one of the four specified categories, for example, marriage preparation. Table 1 shows the percentages of total number of participants for type of course taken.

Table 1: Adult Education Survey: Percentages of Total Number of Participants for Type of Course

Job related	41%
Personal development/general interest	23%
Hobby/craft/recreation	20%
Academic	12%
Other	2%
Don't know/not stated	1%

This data has been analyzed using variables such as age, gender, educational attainment, mother tongue, place of birth, the respondent's employment status and the institutional provider of the instruction. (The data has also been prepared for each province.) When so analyzed the data becomes more revealing. For example, in the case of gender, 57 percent of the men who participated took job-related courses compared with only 28 percent of the women who participated. This is contrasted with the finding that 27 percent of the women participants took personal development/general interest courses compared with only 18 percent of the men. Interestingly enough, in the case of job-related courses, 56 percent of the men, compared with 44 percent of the women, had their fee paid by the employer.

Another example indicates that while 21 percent of Canadian adults have zero to eight years of education, only 4.7 percent of them participated. This is contrasted with the 10 percent of adults with a university degree, of whom 40.8 percent participated.

The survey's findings provide illuminating statistics which suggest some of the reasons why adults participate; however their use must be prefaced with caution. The specific findings are like a photograph in that they capture only a point in time and space and, like the lens of the camera, the survey questionnaire can only focus on a certain area. Thus the findings describe but one "episode" of participation, using definitions and parameters chosen by the researchers. It is possible to compensate for this by conducting the survey in a like manner on more than one occasion, as in a longitudinal study, so as to develop something like a motion picture. This allows for useful comparisons to be drawn which in turn permits more reasonable inferences to be made. Unfortunately such has not been the case with the Adult Education Survey. Nonetheless there has been sufficient research into motivation to enable the drawing of some conclusions.

In reviewing the literature on motivation to participate in adult education, Rubenson came up with the following summary:[25]

- the strongest motives for participating are "work" and personal satisfaction;
- typically about one-third give personal satisfaction as their main reason for participation;
- one powerful reason for participating is the desire to make practical use of the knowledge acquired;
- preparation for new jobs are mainly emphasized by persons under thirty and by women in the process of changing from child care to gainful employment;
- interest in job-related goals begin to decline at age thirty and drops off sharply after age fifty;
- professionals and college graduates are more likely to be seeking advancement in current jobs than blue collar workers;
- pensioners look for courses where they can acquire knowledge which will help them to adjust to their new role in society;
- women working at home tend more than others to state that they participate to "get out of the rut" and "see new faces";
- personal satisfaction is a stronger motive among the upper classes than among the lower;
- there is a steadily growing number of people taking courses for recreational reasons.

---

[25] K. Rubenson, "Barriers to Participation in Adult Education," Background Paper 4 prepared for the Report of the National Advisory Panel on Skill Development Leave, *Learning for Life* (Ottawa: Supply and Services Canada, 1984) p.9.

Barriers to Participation

Knowing why adults participate enables adult educators to better meet learning needs. Participants, however, are those who have acted on their motivation. Much more difficult to determine are the reasons why adults do not participate. While non-participants may be equally motivated by their circumstances as participants, and in some respects more so, for some reason or reasons they do not act on this motivation. One of the concerns of adult educators has been to identify and if possible remove these so-called barriers to participation.

Just as studies have been conducted to determine what it is that motivates an adult to participate in adult education, similarly studies have been conducted in an attempt to determine why such a large percentage of adults—approximately 80 percent in Canada according to the Adult Education Survey—do not participate. The question is asked: Is there some impediment, some barrier, to their being able to participate—or feeling inclined to participate? Presumably if providers could determine the barrier(s) which stands in the way of participation, removal of the barrier would result in a measurable increase in participation figures. Thus considerable effort has gone into identifying these barriers and assessing their metaphorical height.

Before looking at the barriers to participation in adult education it is wise to introduce a caution. While indeed numerous barriers can be identified, it is important to understand that there is not a simple "cause and effect" relationship between any one barrier and participation. To suggest that by simply removing a particular barrier, for example a substantial tuition fee, an oversubscription of a class will automatically result is to ignore the intensely individual make-up of voluntary action (in this case participation) on the part of the adult learner. Thus our understanding of non-participation must not be based on the assumption that all adults are eager to participate but for the fact that barriers stand in their way. As discussed earlier this notion of participation is based on the enrollment approach. According to the engagement approach, where studies have found participation rates ranging from 70 percent to 100 percent, adults are able to conduct their learning without necessarily needing to enroll. Expressed another way, it might well be that many adults simply prefer not to enroll and instead to be completely self-directed.

Research into non-participation has found that it is possible to divide barriers into three categories: situational, dispositional, and institutional.[26] The situational barriers are the circumstances of the potential learner and include such describable items as disposable income, means of transportation, and availability of child-minding services. The dispositional barriers likewise be-

---

[26] See P. Cross, *Adults as Learners* (San Francisco: Jossey-Bass, 1981).

long to the learner, but in this case are a function of the individual's personality. Psychological factors such as fear of returning to the evaluative attention of a teacher, the feeling of intellectual inadequacy after being away from schooling for a long time, or a general disinterest in learning once a good job has been secured are three examples of dispositional barriers. The last category of barrier, institutional barriers, are those put up by the institutional sponsor of the learning activity. These barriers are not seen as being intentionally erected by the institution to discourage participation; rather they reflect the operating practices of the particular institution which have adverse consequences. Thus the decisions taken by the institution in offering an adult education course, such as scheduling, class location, pre-requisites, instructor selection and so on, will for some potential participants become reasons for their not participating. Of the three barriers to participation, then, it is evident that "ownership" of the situational and dispositional barriers resides with the individual while the institutional barriers resides with the provider. Thus any attempts to lower these barriers to the point where participation is enabled requires understanding and communication between the non-participant and the provider.

The number of specific barriers which can be identified is endless, and hence the need for a grouping. As an indication of the more prominent barriers, the findings of the participation study undertaken by the CAAE and the ICEA are presented. These barriers were derived from a series of consultations with "persons who come from social groups known to experience difficulties when they seek to access learning opportunities from public institutions."[27] Out of these consultations emerged fifteen consistent themes:

1. financial aid policies which have the effect of discouraging learning by imposing penalties on recipients who enroll in courses, or where the financial aid in support of learning is inadequate;

2. lack of co-ordination between referral agencies and educational institutions;

3. lack of support systems such as orientation, counselling, child care and tutoring;

4. lack of information on available courses;

5. geographic barriers which discriminate against those in rural areas due to the concentration of educational opportunities in the urban centres;

6. institutional practices which are incompatible with learner needs;

7. fatigue experienced by part-time learners who have other activities;

---

[27] CAAE/ICEA, *From the Adult's Point of View*, p.11.

8. lack of time to engage in learning due to employment, family and personal reasons;

9. attitudinal barriers either directed by others at the learner or felt from within which cause the learner to be sensitive about learning;

10. fees and other costs;

11. scheduling which is either inappropriate or which changes;

12. employers' recruiting policies whereby unnecessary credential requirements are used as a screening device to employ young graduates in preference to retraining existing employees;

13. residency requirements of universities for degree programs;

14. reluctance of institutions, in the absence of academic credentials, to accredit an individual's life experiences as part of entrance requirements;

15. curriculum and learning are often organized not with anxious learners in mind, but experienced learners.

Ten of the fifteen barriers can be seen as being institutional, while three are situational (#s 5, 7, 8), and two are dispositional (#s 9 and 15).

Much can be made of these barriers and their detrimental influence on participation; however, they should be viewed contextually. At the beginning of this chapter an account of the institutionalizing of learning was presented, and the confining legacy it imposes on the idea of learning in our society and on the lives of individuals. What is lacking is a supportive educational framework which is designed to: (1) remove institutional barriers by eliminating adult education's marginal status; (2) remove situational barriers by providing access; and (3) remove dispositional barriers by uplifting the educational experience. Some of the work necessary for this lies with policy makers and their responsibility for resource allocation, but equally there is the need to develop a shared attitude within the society which views continued learning as central to individual and societal well-being.

The Idea of Providers

It is understandable that most people immediately associate adult education with "night school." After all, the use of grade schools in the evening has historically been the most apparent evidence of adults continuing with their education, and it now serves as a convenient stereotype. Two things, however, indicate that this conception is now misleading: (1) the proliferation of organizational sponsors which provide adult education at all times of the day and evening; and (2) our contemporary understanding of how adults satisfy their needs and interests in learning without necessarily resorting to the traditional classroom setting.

Adult education is now recognized as being sponsored by a large number of agencies and conducted in many settings, be they public lecture halls, workplace training facilities or the privacy of one's home. Thus in considering the providers of adult education it is important to distinguish the provider, i.e., the sponsoring agency, from the particular building in which the activity is conducted. With formal education the sponsor and the building most often go hand in hand, whereas that is not necessarily the case in adult education. Instead the important factor when describing the provider of adult education is the sponsoring agency. As an example, many school boards have converted former grade schools buildings which no longer serve a school age population into adult learning centres. The reason for this is to congregate many of the school board's multiplicity of adult education programs into one facility and offer them during the daytime as well as in the evening. To look at the particular institution, i.e., the building, one would rightly say it was devoted to adult education. The sponsoring agency, however, is a school board which was established with the primary purpose of meeting the learning needs of youth, and its adult education work is secondary to this primary purpose. It is likely that the adult learning centre has been funded with grant monies which, because they are not guaranteed in legislation, can be withdrawn with little notice. This is a different funding arrangement to the grade school system. Another example is the situation of a voluntary association utilizing the facilities of a church hall for its particular weekly program. The provider of the adult education activity is the voluntary organization, not the church.

No one organization is perceived to have jurisdiction over adult education's offerings, nor are its activities required to be conducted in a particular type of institution, for example an educational facility. An agency can be any organization that is involved in sponsoring opportunities for adult education, be it an educational institution, a voluntary association, an industrial concern, a public agency or whatever.

It is also now accepted that many adults are capable of conducting independent learning projects of their own instigation, seeking assistance from an appropriate agency only if needed. Thus adults need not receive their education only through the auspices of some sponsoring organization. Furthermore, because adults have different learning needs at various stages of life, they will turn to different sources for assistance, as suggested by the particular learning need. Thus a vocational institute will provide upgrading in technical areas while an accounting firm will put on a workshop in pre-retirement financial planning. What is needed, then, is a way of identifying agencies which have a place in adult learning, be it through direct sponsorship of courses or through being considered a supporting resource for the self-directed learner.

Various typologies have been developed in an attempt to capture and categorize the number of organizations which sponsor or support adult education.

The one developed by Schroeder[28] is an amalgam of several of these and identifies four types of agencies. These agency types are:

- Type I: Agencies established to serve the educational needs of adults—adult education is a central function. Agencies of this type are not numerous when compared with the number concerned with the educational needs of youth; however the number is growing. Type 1 agencies typically have a specific adult "market" which they are serving. Schroeder identifies proprietary schools (for example, business schools, correspondence schools and technical schools such as are listed in the Yellow Pages of the telephone directory under "schools") and independent residential and non-residential adult education centres (for example, Banff Centre, Frontier College and the Justice Institute of B.C.) as being of this type.

- Type II: Agencies established to serve the educational needs of youth which have assumed the added responsibility of at least partially serving the educational needs of adults—adult education is a secondary function. Agencies of this type are the ones most often identified with adult education, and for the most part are publicly funded (even though their adult education offerings are to a large degree dependent on user fees). Examples include public schools, community colleges and universities, each with their adult and continuing education divisions or departments.

- Type III: Agencies established to serve both educational and non-educational needs of the community—adult education is an allied function employed to fulfil only some of the needs which these agencies recognize as their responsibility. This type constitutes a significant number of agencies (for example, libraries, museums and public health clinics), and many of these recognize the need to educate in a specific area in order to achieve their particular purpose, for example, public health.

- Type IV: Agencies established to serve the special interests (economic, ideological) of special groups—adult education is a subordinate function employed primarily to further the special interests of the agency itself. There is a vast amount of adult education that is conducted by such agencies (for example, churches, advocacy groups, voluntary associations, labour organizations, business and industry). Schroeder suggests that agencies of this type are generally concerned with adult education "to the extent that such education contributes to the effectiveness of the agency in fulfilling its primary purpose ... "[29]

---

[28] W. Schroeder, "Adult Education Defined and Described," in Smith et al. (Eds.), *Handbook of Adult Education* (New York: Macmillan, 1970).

Schroeder's typology serves as a helpful means of differentiating among the numerous sponsoring agencies, and it equally demonstrates the diverse nature of adult education when analyzed according to sponsorship. This diverse nature also indicates the extent to which education is utilized by numerous agencies to promote individual, community and special interests. Adult education does not have a distinct institutional presence in the community, nor is there an institutional hierarchy as in the case of the formal educational system, with its elementary, secondary, college and university institutions. Nonetheless adult education does have a pervasive presence.

Schroeder's typology represents a classical approach to understanding providers of adult education, centring as it does on sponsoring agencies. This typology does not, however, account for self-directed learning, although it is understood that all agency types are available to the self-directed learner (subject of course to institutional policies which may limit accessibility). More recently another schema has been proposed in a new attempt to make coherent the diversity of providers of adult education, and this schema does take into account the self-directed learner.[30] Described by its originator, Jerold Apps, as a framework of providers of adult and continuing education, this classification system places the adult learner rather than agencies at the centre of its consideration. In graphically presenting the framework by way of circles containing the providers types, Apps places the adult learner in a circle at the centre of the diagram and stems the four provider types outwards from there. The four types are: tax-supported agencies, non-profit agencies, for-profit agencies, and non-organized learning opportunities. Apps indicates that the framework "is based on the assumption that adult learners have choices for learning opportunities—a long-standing characteristic of the adult education field."[31] He also acknowledges the existence in some areas of mandatory continuing education, for example, continuing education within some professional groups, but this does not detract from the framework as formulated. As for the self-directed learner, Apps suggests all four provider categories are available to the learner (also subject to institutional policies).

The provider types are described briefly as follows. Tax-supported providers are those agencies and institutions which are fully or partially tax supported and include educational agencies, correctional institutions, libraries, museums and so on. Non-profit providers are self-supporting agencies and institutions typically associated with the voluntary sector and including professional organizations. For-profit providers encompass those companies

---

[29] W. Schroeder, "Adult Education Defined and Described," p.37.

[30] J. Apps, "Providers of Adult and Continuing Education: A Framework," in Merriam & Cunningham (Eds.), *Handbook of Adult and Continuing Education* (San Francisco: Jossey-Bass, 1989).

[31] Ibid., p.279.

whose adult education work is sustained by the profit motive and include the obvious proprietary and correspondence schools as well as conference centres, computer software publishers and workshop facilitators. Non-organized learning opportunities as a provider type is understood to be open ended, and this acknowledges that it is the self-directed learner who selects the provider. By way of illustration of this provider type, Apps includes television viewing and the other mass media, the work setting, and travel and leisure time activities.

Apps' effort to organize providers by way of a systematic framework rather than a classification schema which employs selection criteria (as evident in Schroeder's agency specific typology) is an attempt to reflect, as he suggests, "the situation of adult education in North America in the late 1980s."[32] Thus for Apps the providers of educational opportunities for adults are conceptualized as being all inclusive as opposed to being selective and include agencies, organizations, services, individuals or simply the learning opportunity itself, however provided. Particularly noteworthy for Apps is the amount of adult learning opportunity made available by the for-profit providers, especially as its growth is an indication of successful entrepreneurial efforts to meet adult learning needs and wants. He concludes his conceptualizing by noting that, "we are entering a new era in adult education, and we must change our thinking about the way it is organized."[33]

It is interesting how the categorical aspect of both Schroeder's and Apps's typologies are being eroded by developments in formal education. Even though the categories as designated were intended more to be instructive than to be mutually exclusive, nevertheless a number of trends have appeared which are transforming perceptions and blurring delineations. The most significant trend is towards acceptance by the formal education system of the notion of lifelong learning. The belief that one can be educated for a lifetime within the first twenty years or so of one's life no longer prevails as a defensible idea in formal education. From the point of view of the individual, the rapidity, extent and omnipresence of change have virtually eliminated the grounds for being complacent about learning beyond one's formal education. For example, in the modern era a worker will likely experience more than one career change within the space of a working life, and each change will prompt a need for new learning. As part of this trend, a rather bewildering number of vocations now require educational certification, and this virtually compels an individual to enroll in upgrading programs of one sort or another with each career move. The outgrowth of this trend to lifelong learning by formal educa-

---

[32] Ibid., p.280.

[33] Ibid., p.285.

tion institutions, and especially as driven by job related considerations, has been a re-orientation of emphasis by some agency types.

The Type II agencies of Schroeder's typology (agencies established to serve the educational needs of youth which have assumed the added responsibility of at least partially serving the educational needs of adults) have experienced the greatest developments in adult education. As an example, community colleges, which initially were construed as an alternative to university at the post-secondary level for high school graduates, i.e., youth, have assumed a considerable adult education orientation and thus in certain aspects correspond more to a Type I agency (agencies established to serve the educational needs of adults). Indications of this shift by community colleges include the amending of registration criteria in credit programs to allow for a mature-student category and the advertising in the media of their programs, promoting as they do for adults to return to college to enhance their career opportunities. Certainly the provision of distance education by agencies dedicated to this purpose, such as Athabasca University in Alberta and the Open Learning Agency in British Columbia, particularly accommodates the adult learner.

Another development in formal education concerns public funding. The Type II agencies are understood to be included in Apps's tax-supported category. Apps notes, however, that the public funding of adult education is not secure by way of legislative enactment, as is the case with grade school education. In many cases adult education which is provided by a tax-supported agency, for example, a school board, is increasingly having to pay its own way, thereby diminishing the extent to which adult education is tax supported.

There are two other developments which blur the distinctions among provider types, institutional brokering and institutional collaboration. The brokering idea in education borrows from the free enterprise practice of an individual or company acting as an agent of exchange between two parties. In this case, however, it is not always necessary that there be the usual fee-for-service payed to the broker. In the Saskatchewan community college model, where the college was conceived of as an administrative entity and not as an educational facility, the college's function was to broker with other agencies, both educational and community based, for the delivery of courses, including adult education courses. These courses were intended to meet learning needs as identified from within the community. This represents brokering on a provincial scale. On a smaller scale, brokering often takes place in instances where an educational institution arranges for another institution or organization to deliver instruction on behalf of a group of learners. This often occurs when, for example, an industry or community agency with a corporate learning need will turn to a local continuing education department of a school board or university and ask that it arrange for a particular program of another organization to be presented.

Among educational institutions there is also a trend to collaboration which goes beyond simple co-operation. In this case two or more institutions will formally agree to provide some service or program in combination with each other. An example is in British Columbia where the Open University of the Open Learning Agency is a consortium of three universities: the University of Victoria, Simon Fraser University and the University of British Columbia. By way of this collaboration, an adult learner is able to earn a baccalaureate degree from the Open University, having taking courses from all three universities. Another illustration is where a community agency will collaborate with an educational institution for the delivery of a course of studies at the facilities of the community agency. This often occurs where it is apparent that the learners would not attend the course at the educational institution but are receptive to it being offered at the community agency. There are numerous examples of this in the area of literacy instruction and also with homogeneous groups of learners, for example, Native peoples, who identify with their own surroundings rather than with those of the dominant culture as represented by the educational institution.

These trends which are taking place within many of the providers are symptomatic of the fact there is no assigned institutional form for adult education. As long as adult learning needs continue to be identified and met, whether prescriptively or instinctively, there will always be variations among providers. In Canada the lead role among providers has evolved first from the voluntary sector to, second, the formal education sector and now increasingly to, third, the employer sector. At the same time, however, the importance to adult education is not that there be any dominant provider group but rather that there remain an assortment of providers, each addressing particular learning needs in a fashion helpful to the learners.

A categorizing of agencies which provides a comparison of "market share" among providers is presented in the Adult Education Survey where, rather than utilizing a conceptualization of providers as in Schroeder's typology, there is a simple grouping of agencies most associated with providing adult education. This basis is not very instructive, as a number of agencies are grouped like strange bedfellows or else are grouped in an all-encompassing category. The findings, however, are helpful, particularly in the case of the agencies which enjoy a category unto themselves. The nine categories are: (1) employers, (2) union and professional associations, (3) universities, (4) colleges, (5) school boards, (6) private schools, i.e., proprietary schools, (7) churches, (8) voluntary organizations, and (9) libraries.

In terms of comparisons between provinces and within Canada, the findings for the providers must be viewed in light of the provincial circumstance.[34]

This differs from the participation findings which have national as well as provincial significance when used for comparative purposes. For example, at the time of the Adult Education Survey, Nova Scotia did not have a community college system (although there were some colleges) and it was the school boards which were identified as being the most significant providers of adult education in that province. In Saskatchewan, by contrast, it was the community college system as created in the early 1970s which was identified as providing the greatest amount of adult education. In Alberta, where there is a system of Further Education Councils which works to rationalize the program offerings of agencies within a given area so as to avoid duplication, no one provider dominated. The findings of the Adult Education Survey reflected these provincial differences. The school board provision in Nova Scotia was 25 percent of all courses taken by adults, in Saskatchewan 2 percent and in Alberta 11 percent. College provision was 6 percent in Nova Scotia, 27 percent in Saskatchewan and 17 percent in Alberta. The combined total of school board and community college provision was, however, comparable in all three provinces—Nova Scotia, 31 percent, Saskatchewan, 29 percent and Alberta, 28 percent.[35]

We have already seen how participation in adult education is for the most part a voluntary act, and how for each individual the act of participating is determined by the interaction of several variables—some quite personal (situational, dispositional), others within the control of providing agencies (institutional). The providers of adult education, however, are seen as being very much instrumental to participation, appealing as they do to the learning needs and interests of adults. For this reason in adult education there has always been a widespread interest in providers, whose goals are to serve learning needs in helpful, often creative ways. In Canada, a country with a small population and a short history, there have been and continue to be a remarkable number of agencies providing noteworthy programs, and much of the record of adult education is related by way of accounts of these agencies.[36]

Up to this point the discussion of participation, participants and providers has dealt with these ideas in mainly inanimate terms. Of course nothing could

[34] See Chapter 8.

[35] Statistics Canada, *One in Every Five: A Survey of Adult Education in Canada*.

[36] For descriptions of various providers and their programs in Canada there are three useful overviews: J.R. Kidd (Ed.), *Adult Education in Canada* (Toronto: Canadian Association for Adult Education, 1950); J.R. Kidd (Ed.), *Learning and Society* (Toronto: Canadian Association for Adult Education, 1963); and Kidd & Selman (Eds.), *Coming of Age: Canadian Adult Education in the 1960s* (Toronto: Canadian Association for Adult Education, 1978). In the US, the American Association of Adult and Continuing Education and its predecessor, the Adult Education Association of the USA, have published at intervals of approximately ten years (1934, 1936, 1948, 1960, 1970, 1990) handbooks on the study and practice of adult education, and each has a section devoted to describing agencies. Darkenwald and Merriam have a useful chapter on agencies and programs in *Adult Education: Foundations of Practice* (New York: Harper and Row, 1982).

be further from the fact of the matter: adult education is full of passion. Participants are understood as being human beings with learning needs unique to their individual situations. Providers are not inorganic edifices but rather vital organizations created with purposes sympathetic to adult learners. And participation is understood as being an adult behaviour driven by learning needs and desires which are very much part of the human condition. The dispassionate view develops, however, as it becomes necessary to bring some organization to our understanding of participation for purposes such as conceptualizing the phenomenon for study and advocating to government for financial support. The next chapter, "Elements of Design in Programs," presents several illustrations of programs where it is the passion in adult education which is clearly evident as contrasted with the statistical and categorical presentation of participation.

Having now examined in turn the three central ideas of participation, participants and providers, it becomes clear that in both the study and practice of adult education it is participation which is the underlying phenomenon. It is through participation that adults and agencies are linked for the satisfaction of personal learning needs and the carrying out of agency missions. Adult learners seek out agencies and agencies both receive and seek out adult learners. Whereas in youth education the link between the learner and the providing agency is fixed and is described as attendance, in adult education there are innumerable motivational influences at play in creating a participation link between learner and agency. Further, the nature of the participation link is specific to each situation, whether it be the borrowing of a book from the library or an interactive educational television program via satellite technology.

The goal in adult education is generally understood to be participation by all adults so they may derive meaning in their lives and contribute to the well-being of their communities.[37] Both learner and agency are seen as being active in this effort to bring about participation, as is government through policy initiatives such as employment training. The continued interest by adult educators in the three central ideas of participation recognizes that there is still much to be learned and much to be done in order to reach the goal. Enabling non-participants is the single most important objective in attaining the goal, and for this reason it is necessary that adult educators maintain a perspective on the two approaches to participation outlined earlier. Taking the engagement approach and considering the research findings that the vast majority of adults are engaged in self-directed learning, the argument can be

---

[37] For example see UNESCO, *Recommendation on the Development of Adult Education*; and John Lowe, *The Education of Adults: A World Perspective* (Toronto: OISE Press, 1975) Chapter 1, "Changing Ideas and Functions."

made that the existing provision for adult education must be adequate and that individual adults are apparently quite capable of meeting their own learning needs. This argument is obviously very attractive from a politician's point of view when it comes to allocating budget resources. And yet common sense indicates that with five million adult Canadians functionally illiterate, as determined by a survey in 1987,[38] there must be a very large number of adults who would find it difficult if not impossible to participate in adult education. For these adults alone, not to mention those with other compelling circumstances, government must be involved in making participation possible. When seen in this light, the concept of participation also becomes a matter of public policy.

For adult educators, then, participation is a key concept which must be seen from more than one viewpoint, as it is subject to interpretation. Participation is the dynamic facet of adult education which prompts research by academics and conjecture by practitioners as to what brings it about and what stands in its way. The fact of participation has inspired the creation of many distinctive providers of adult education, and it has resulted in untold numbers of adults being helped in the conduct of their lives. What is clear is that participation for participation's sake is not sufficient in adult education. There must be a purposefulness worthy of the involvement of the various stakeholders identified at the beginning of this chapter. The next chapter examines various elements of design in adult education programs which acknowledge this need for purposefulness.

---

[38] This was the finding of the Southam Literacy Survey and was reported in several Canadian newspapers. These articles have been collected in a booklet published by Southam News entitled *Broken Words* (Toronto: Southam Inc, nd).

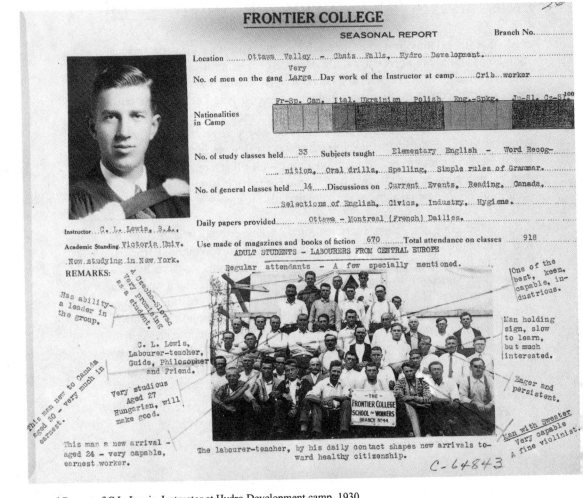

Annual Report of C.L. Lewis, Instructor at Hydro Development camp, 1930.
Courtesy of Frontier College.

6

Elements of Design in Programs

The most conspicuous aspect of adult education is its programs. Programs are regularly promoted in all the media as well as advertised in special catalogues, and they are conducted in any number of locations and at times throughout the day and well into the evening. Those who participate in programs talk about them with family, friends and co-workers. Not infrequently some form of action will result from a program which draws the attention of the wider community, for example, neighbourhood watch programs for deterring crime. Some programs have even become so established as to have their own physical presence in the community—such as religious education centres attached to churches.

Most adults come to adult education by way of participating in some form of organized program. Providers such as school boards, recreation departments, private organizations, voluntary associations, businesses, churches, universities and libraries, to name but a few, offer innumerable programs in a myriad of formats. One can register for a class, attend a public lecture, enroll in a correspondence course, join in a study group, organize a reading program, and so on; the opportunities and options are many and varied.

This chapter is concerned with the idea of program in adult education, and is divided into two sections. The first section presents the main conceptual ideas associated with programs and briefly describes how they are planned. In the second section a number of elements of program design are highlighted by way of examples. The underlying belief expressed by this chapter's organization is that adult educators must draw from two sources when involved in program planning. There is what Knowles calls the "technology of adult education," that is the processes and procedures which have been devised to create programs which meet the needs and interests of adults.[1] There is also,

---

[1] M. Knowles, *The Modern Practice of Adult Education* (Chicago: Follett, 1980) p.130.

however, the wealth of information and inspiration to be found in examining programs which in either the present or the past have proven successful.

The Concept of Program

Program is the basic unit of organized participation in adult education. It describes the bringing together of resources, no matter how modest or elaborate, in order to facilitate learning. The participation is said to be organized by virtue of the fact that someone besides the learner has been involved in planning the participation, and this involvement has resulted in a program being developed. There is a great spectrum of possibilities when considering what might be described as programs, from a reading program developed by a librarian in discussion with a borrower to a province-wide hunter awareness program conducted by a government department. There are no specifications for what constitutes a program other than the existence of a learning need or interest which has caused resources in support of the learning need to be purposefully brought together by an organizer. It is this learning purpose, then, which distinguishes an adult education program from a purely recreational or social program.

Despite the apparent generality surrounding programs in adult education, a few basic elements begin to emerge. Learning is the focus of a program. There is a degree of organization to a program as provided by an organizer. Some resources are necessary for the learning to occur (for example, facilities, instructor). And there needs to be participation in order to make the program viable. These four basic elements of program, then, are present in all adult education programs and they only grow by a matter of degree as programs take on greater complexity.[2] As well, programs with greater complexity in their design will undoubtedly have additional elements associated with them. Thus, just as in Chapter 4 participation was seen as being the underlying phenomenon in adult education, in this chapter program is identified as being the basic learning arrangement.[3] As such, programs hold a particular fascination in adult education, and for a number of good reasons.

One reason is that there are no prescribed formats in adult learning, although there are a number of formats which have proven successful over the years. Thus, the planner or planners of a program typically have several possibilities open for their consideration, and this allows for creative planning. Another reason is that adult education is viewed as being a positive force in

---

[2] Brookfield identifies three features to program: purpose, order and finiteness. S. Brookfield, *Understanding and Facilitating Adult Learning* (San Francisco: Jossey-Bass, 1986) p.204.

[3] For a detailed overview of the concept of program see Alan Thomas, "The Concept of Program" in Jensen, Liveright & Hallenbeck (Eds.), *Adult Education: Outlines of an Emerging Field of University Study* (Washington: Adult Education Association of the USA, 1964).

society, and programs are adult education's main mechanism for contributing to a better society. A third reason is that programs are not the property of any one or a few organizations; rather, a multitude of organizations are involved in conducting programs. A fourth reason appreciates that organizing and conducting successful programs calls for a broad range of abilities and talents on the part of the planner or planners. Lastly there is the recognition that programs tell the observer some things about the organization offering the program, such as its purpose, its philosophy and its resourcefulness. After all, organizations are best understood as the means by which humans are able to collectively address themselves to some mutually agreed purpose. The next aspect of program, then, is bringing some sense of coherence to the array of programs which have developed over the years.

There are two approaches that can be taken in attempting to bring understanding to the array of adult education programs. The first approach is to develop a system for classifying all programs and the second is to identify a number of bases which are helpful in distinguishing among programs while at the same time not attempting to be inclusive. The first approach is useful both from an instructive point of view and as a means of portraying the field of adult education through, for example, comparative surveys of participation in types of programs. The second approach is useful when one is expediently describing a program by distinguishing what it is from what it is not, for example, a credit program from a non-credit program, or simply identifying it for what it is, for example, a university extension program. This second approach acknowledges that most people have a general understanding of the common adult education program types.

As for the first approach, then, the classic conceptualization of the field is based on how participants are organized into programs.[4] This scheme recognizes how the natural pattern of human organization fits with the experience in adult learning, namely that adults can learn individually, they can learn in groups (small and large), and they can learn within the context of the whole community. Thus in adult education programs are developed which organize learners into: (1) individual programs, for example, home study, computer assisted instruction; (2) group programs, for example, classes, workshops, conferences; and (3) community programs, for example, programs which take in the scope of an entire community as in the case of a community development project. These categories, then, of individual, group and community are the three formats for organizing programs.[5] This represents the organizational

---

[4] C. Verner and A. Booth, *Adult Education* (New York: Centre for Applied Research in Education, 1964).

[5] The term originally given by Verner to this classification was "method." Knowles preferred the term "format." For a discussion on this see M. Knowles, *The Modern Practice of Adult Education* (1980) p.131.

system for classifying programs. Another system is to use the content of the program.

The 1984 Statistics Canada Adult Education Survey provides a good example of an effort to classify programs on the basis of their content. For the purpose of this survey five categories were identified: (1) academic; (2) job-related; (3) personal development/general interest; (4) hobby/craft/recreation; and (5) other. The categories were defined as follows:

> Academic courses refer to those taken at a high school, college or university for credit toward a diploma, certificate or degree. Job-related courses are defined as those which provide skills applicable either to the job participants held or a job which they wished to qualify. Included in this category are courses in such areas as word processing, computer programming, auto mechanics, and TV repair. Hobby/craft/recreation courses cover leisure pursuits such as woodworking, pottery, painting, photography, cooking, and sewing. Job-related subjects can also fall into this group if the participant's motivation was leisure-oriented. Personal development/general interest courses refer to classes in history, music appreciation, etc., and academic courses taken on an unstructured basis (as distinct from accumulating credits toward a diploma, certificate or degree). The final type of course—the catch-all "other" category—comprises training that does not fit neatly into one of the foregoing groups. Included here are marriage preparation, prenatal instruction, driver-training, first aid, etc.[6]

It can be seen that this content classification, while initially appearing quite reasonable, has inherent problems when faced with particular situations. For one, the fifth category of "other" is seen as an unsatisfactory way of accounting for a significant number of different programs. For another the categories are not mutually exclusive. It is instead the respondent's perception of the program which determines the category. Take, for example, a university course in art history. For the part-time student working towards a degree the course could be categorized as academic. For an art gallery worker the course could be job related. And for a retired person seeking more knowledge of art the course could be general interest.[7] It should also be noted that there are other program category descriptors besides the ones used in the Statistics Canada Survey that are commonly used to capture program groupings, including liberal adult education, religious education, public affairs, and home and family life education. Attempting to group programs by content is thus seen as a difficult proposition, given the variety of programs in adult education and the perceptions of what they are as seen by the participants.

---

[6] Statistics Canada, *One in Every Five: A Survey of Adult Education in Canada* (Ottawa: Ministry of Supply and Services Canada, 1985) p.19.

[7] This example is taken from P. Dampier & J. Stalker-Costin, "Adult Education in British Columbia: A Discussion of the Statistics Canada Adult Education Survey" in Jindra Kulich (Ed.), *Advocacy for Adult Education in British Columbia* (Vancouver: Pacific Association for Continuing Education, 1988) p.22.

Another approach to this program categorization is to examine the content by way of the adult education function it is believed to serve. Using Bryson's five functions (as discussed in Chapter 1) the content categories in this case would be remedial, vocational/occupational, relational, liberal and political. In this approach, however, it is someone other than the participant who is designating a program as one or the other category. As pointed out, participants very often take the same course for different reasons.

Another possibility is to use the predominant learning domain to which the content is directed, be it the cognitive domain (i.e., learning information, intellectual skills and problem-solving strategies), the affective domain (i.e., interests, attitudes, values, beliefs), or the psychomotor domain (i.e., motor skills). This system is more difficult in that it is often the case that a program will deal equally with cognitive and affective learning—for example, a public affairs program which attempts to help people form a reasoned attitude on an issue by presenting factual information.

From the above examples it can be seen that different approaches can be taken to the classifying of adult education programs. There is no one schema that can be used for all purposes and instead it is necessary to know the purpose for which the classification is intended. As well it is necessary to know from whose perspective the program categories will be selected—that of the adult education theorist/researcher or that of the participant.

The second approach to understanding program types does not attempt to be inclusive by way of a classification scheme but rather distinguishes or identifies a program on a commonly understood basis. The example above used the basis of a credential to distinguish credit programs from non-credit programs. This basis is quite clear cut as programs are either one or the other, i.e., credit or non-credit. Another basis which can be used is the method by which the program is delivered, for example distance education as contrasted with traditional classroom. Other bases have evolved through the generalizing and even stereotyping of programs. An example is the sponsorship of a program where one identifies the provider, for example a night school course (which implies an educational agency as the provider) as distinct from, say, a training course (which implies an employer as the provider) or a Bible study course (which implies a religious organization as provider). Another example of this is to identify the environment in which the learning takes place, such as a home-study program, a residential program, or an educational travel program. Of course this approach to understanding programs is limited because it is neither systematic nor comprehensive; however, it does recognize the general awareness that adults have as to different types of programs.

Having identified the two approaches to understanding programs in adult education—classification systems and distinguishing bases—the question is next raised as to the source of the need for these programs. Three general sources can be identified. The first is the potential learner, the adult who feels within him or herself the need for, or interest in, learning. Often an adult is already conscious of this need or interest, while in some cases this consciousness is brought about through such avenues as a conversation with a friend, a counselling session or, in the work setting, a performance appraisal. In an effort to ascertain the individual learning needs and interests of adults, frequently a provider will conduct a survey and use the results to plan programs.

The second source is that of subject area. Many areas are undergoing change based on new ideas, improved technologies or whatever, and in order for adults to keep up with these developments, programs are offered for this purpose. Examples can be drawn from virtually any subject area, be it history as reinterpreted though revisionist thought, social work identifying new options for dealing with disturbed youth, or computer applications through enhanced programs. Many adults become aware of their learning needs and interests as a result of seeing a program advertised, and the program may have been planned because of developments in that subject area. The third source is that of contemporary society. In order for society to continue to function, and particularly in a democratic society, it is necessary that there be an informed citizenry, able to participate fully in that society. Often it is government which identifies the learning needs of society, or for at least a segment of society, as in the case of job retraining for members of the labour force whose work skills are no longer of productive value. Another example is the need in Canada, as a matter of government policy, for a federal civil service that is able to operate bilingually and hence the need for language training. It is not only government, however, that identifies the needs of contemporary society. Any organization is able to interpret such needs and develop programs to address them. Thus libraries, for example, are able to be part of a municipal effort at reducing the amount of landfill waste by sponsoring a program on residential recycling.

Having examined the three general sources of the need for programs it is possible to suggest that programs satisfy the needs of individuals, of institutions, and of society. In the case of individuals, programs are the main avenue for meeting learning needs through participation. It is important that there be a wide range of programs available as it is only through the opportunity to participate in programs that the multiplicity of individual learning needs can be met. This is reflected in developments in distance education, for example, which seeks to eliminate access barriers such as are imposed by geography and time constraints in order to increase participation. Programs also satisfy the needs of the institutions which provide them. It is through participation that the institution is able to carry out its adult education mandate, whether this be central or peripheral to the institution's mission. For those institutions whose adult education is central to its mission, offering programs which attract participation is necessary for the institution's continued existence. As for society, programs of adult education are a vitally important means for that society to maintain and advance. It is impossible to imagine how the society would function were individuals not enabled, through participation in programs, to continue with their learning beyond the formative years. Thus it is necessary that within the society there be institutions providing programs which allow adults to act on their learning needs.

The foregoing discussion can be summarized by asserting that programs are the most pervasive feature in adult education. The more one delves into the concept of program, the more it is possible to recognize the richness in learning opportunity made possible through programs. This assertion is substantiated by the attention paid in the literature of adult education to the process of developing programs, and this process is introduced in the next section.

Program Planning

In adult education the term used to describe the process of developing programs is program planning (also program development and program design). This term is preferred to the one used in formal education, namely curriculum development, because program planning is seen as being broader in its considerations. There are not nearly the constraints in adult education that there are in formal education, such as prescribed curriculum, levels of academic progression, regulations, and certification. Providers of adult education programs have the ability, generally speaking, to meet learning needs in ways which they believe to be most effective. The person who carries out the planning process is usually referred to as the program planner (also program developer and program designer), and often an important aspect of this person's task is to involve others in the planning, including prospective participants. In many instances the planning process itself becomes a learning experience for those involved, and this is seen as a desirable feature of program planning.

The term program planning has become central in the adult education nomenclature. It describes the process by which programs are researched and developed so as to meet the multitudinous learning needs and desires of adult learners. Its several phases have been variously described and are typically sequenced as follows: (1) diagnose needs, (2) set objectives, (3) plan methods and resources, (4) implement, and (5) evaluate for re-planning.[8] In proceeding through these sequential phases the program planner makes numerous decisions such as matching the identified learning needs with suitable instruc-

---

[8] R. Herman, "Planning for Learning: A Model For Creative Decision-Making," in T. Barer-Stein & J. Draper, *The Craft of Teaching Adults* (Toronto: Culture Concepts, 1988) p.58.

tional resources, securing appropriate facilities and setting fees. The aggregate of these decisions culminates in the final design of the program and it is by this design that the program is commonly recognized and described, be it a women's program, a general interest program, a personal development program, a vocational program, a certificate program or whatever it is that the design suggests. Thus whereas the initial program planning is the process by which a program is developed, the subsequent program design is the overall statement of the program's purpose. Typically the design is perceived by such indicators as the program's title, its duration, the sponsoring organization, the intended participants and so on. While it is obvious that a program's design and the planning process applied to obtain that design are integrally related, for the observer it is only the design which is readily apparent. The decisions taken during the planning process by the planner can only be inferred from the final design.

Program planning is recognized as being a critically important aspect of adult education. As more and more adults act on their needs and desires for learning and turn to the providers for assistance, it is essential that the programs in which they participate satisfy their situations and foster an openness for further learning. This will only be the case if, in the minds of the participants, the programs are successful. For this reason program planning has always held a particular fascination for adult educators in their individual efforts to achieve program success and to avoid failure. Additionally, in many program areas of adult education there is the effort to attract respectability by securing more predictable results, as in the cases of literacy education, skills development and corporate training.[9]

There are two aspects to program planning. The first aspect is the various tasks associated with each of the planning phases outlined above. To take the initial phase of diagnosing needs, there are a host of tasks involved in completing this phase alone. Depending on the situation, a representative group must be identified, a method chosen for soliciting their learning needs (for example, personal interviews, questionnaires, survey of employers), a diagnostic instrument developed, research conducted, results analyzed, and conclusions drawn. These conclusions may then have to be further verified. Thus there are numerous tasks to be carried out if the program is to be successful according to the criteria established for it. The second aspect is very much related to the first, namely the skills and abilities required of a program planner to carry out the various tasks. This, however, involves more than just carrying out the tasks. Using again the planning phase of diagnosing needs, a

---

[9] For a detailed treatment of the junction of adult learning and program planning see D. Brundage & D. MacKeracher, *Adult Learning Principles and Their Application to Program Planning* (Toronto: Ministry of Education, 1980).

program planner might need to be competent in not only the tasks as indicated but also in such areas as committee work, statistical analysis, budget administration and report writing.

It is beyond the scope of this chapter to outline the planning tasks and the planning skills and abilities involved in program planning.[10] Instead a framework will be presented which integrates the concept of program with the dynamics of program planning.

Houle's Fundamental System

In his book *The Design of Education*, Cyril Houle presents what he refers to as the fundamental system of educational design. It is so described because Houle indicates its applicability to any level or type of education, be it youth or adult, formal or informal. Houle directs his thinking, however, to adult educators in particular, and the fundamental system is briefly presented here by way of recommending it as a schema which is useful for both analytical and developmental purposes.

The fundamental system is guided by Houle's conception of adult education, which he describes as being, "the process by which men and women (alone, in groups, or in institutional settings) seek to improve themselves or their society by increasing their skill, knowledge or sensitiveness; or it is any process by which individuals, groups, or institutions try to help men and women improve in these ways."[11] For Houle, the basic way that the process is carried out is through the design of an activity, and he defines activity as, "a specific educational action or succession of actions ... "[12] Thus Houle's activity equates with the concept of program as presented in this chapter.

The fundamental system takes the dual possibilities of people helping themselves to learn and people helping others to learn and develops two distinct but interrelated parts. The first part consists of an enumeration of the educational design situations out of which a learning activity, i.e., a program, occurs. Houle identifies eleven such situations, and categorizes them into four groupings: individual, group, institution, mass. These categories (noted as "C") are as follows:

Individual

C-1 An individual designs an activity for himself

---

[10] There are a number of sources where these skills and abilities are enumerated. A comprehensive treatment is presented in a manual developed for the British Columbia Ministry of Education by B. Lund & S. McGechaen, *CE Programmer's Manual* (Vancouver: UBC Centre for Continuing Education, 1981). See also M. Knowles, *The Modern Practice of Adult Education* (1980) p.256.

[11] C. Houle, *The Design of Education* (San Francisco: Jossey-Bass, 1973) p.32.

[12] Ibid., p.229.

C-2 An individual or a group designs an activity for another individual or group

Group

C-3 A group (with or without a continuing leader) designs an activity for itself

C-4 A teacher or a group of teachers designs an activity for, and often with, a group of students

C-5 A committee designs an activity for a larger group

C-6 Two or more groups design an activity which will enhance their combined programs of service

Institutional

C-7 A new institution is designed

C-8 An institution designs an activity in a new format

C-9 An institution designs a new activity in an established format

C-10 Two or more institutions design an activity which will enhance their combined programs of service

Mass

C-11 An individual, group or institution designs an activity for a mass audience

This enumeration, then, covers the broad range of possibilities for programs in adult education. (The C-1 learning situation is seen as being outside the concept of program, i.e., organized participation, as developed at the beginning of the chapter as this represents self-learning. To the extent that the individual in this situation might also participate in one of the other learning situations, however, then this participation is seen as being organized and hence covered by one of the other categories. For example a person who sets out to learn navigation by reading books has designed a program for him or herself, and is self-learning. At such time as the person might take a night school course on the same subject so as to confirm the knowledge gained through self-learning, then this participation is in a program designed as a result of one of the learning design situations in the institutional grouping, and thus is no longer self-learning.)

The second part of the system consists of the framework through which these activities, i.e., programs, operate. This framework is made up of the several considerations which together capture the planning and conducting of a program. These considerations are Houle's formulation of the phases of program planning, similar to the phases presented above. His phases are:

1. A possible educational activity is identified

2. A decision is made to proceed

3. Objectives are identified and refined

4. A suitable format is designed

5. The format is fitted into larger patterns of life

6. The plan is put into effect

7. Results are measured and appraised.

While there is a natural sequencing suggested by the phases of the framework as presented, Houle advises that these components are to be understood as a complex of interacting elements and not as a logical sequence of steps. Houle notes:

> In theory, the process of education usually goes through the stages of identification of objectives, selection of means of accomplishing them, conduct of the planned activity, and retrospective evaluation of it. If these various elements are to be identified and understood, they must be recorded in some fashion, and the temporal order is as good as any other for the purpose. But practice does not usually follow this logical pattern.[13]

Houle offers a number of possible reasons why there is a disinclination to follow a logical pattern. One is that often an educational activity is launched because some fortuitous resource or circumstance makes it possible for the activity to come to be. In such cases "the objective is chosen to fit the means, not the reverse."[14] Another reason advanced is that "the mind seldom works in a completely logical fashion."[15] Houle notes how the design of an educational activity typically undergoes numerous reformulations prior to its ultimate incarnation. The developmental process often implores spontaneity, and often considerations are dealt with out of their logical order, or are temporarily put aside, so as not to impede creativity.

The Fundamental System can be operated in two "modes." The first mode is to use it when contemplating the offering of a program (be it a course, workshop, public forum and so on) so as to first think through the design options and the planning considerations. The applicable categories can be examined in turn to assess their appropriateness to meeting the learning need. From this review of the options the program can then be planned.

The second mode is to use the Fundamental System to study a particular program which is already planned. Used this way it is possible to place the program in the applicable category and examine its significant design ele-

---

[13] Ibid., p.39.

[14] Ibid.

[15] Ibid.

ments. This mode permits both a comparative and an analytical perspective to studying programs. It is this feature which commends the Fundamental System as a helpful structure for appreciating adult education programs as it offers a complete view of the field of program and a realistic description of the operation of program planning. It is recommended that the reader study Houle's formulation in greater detail as the system outlined here represents only a summary.

Before leaving the discussion on program planning it must be noted that there is a danger in program planning being approached too narrowly, as though the process is able to be carried out on a formulated basis so as to assure that identified learning needs can be met. This susceptibility arises because the steps involved in the process have been variously described in numerous adult education texts and guidebooks, and one might be led to conclude that planning adult education programs is simply a matter of working rationally through the steps. Knowles, for example, refers to andragogy as being "an emerging technology for adult learning."[16] A reasonable extension of this assertion is that those who work in the field are thus adult education technicians. While in some respects this is the case—after all good practice ensues from successful application of insight and knowledge of what has occurred previously—it does not convey the role of creativity, intuition and inspiration as essential ingredients of much that is present in adult education. To balance the view of an adult education technology Knowles also introduces the idea of adult education as an art form, whereby there is also merit to applying art principles to the design of programs.[17] Nonetheless there are a number of strong influences at work on program planners which constantly threaten to restrict the dimensions of their planning considerations.

The first such influence stems from the modern age of high technology. Without doubt, North American society has an infatuation with technology, and we willingly allow our lives to be led by it. With the introduction of succeeding technological innovations, less and less time is required for each to become virtually a household item. Developments in this connection have had a direct influence on education generally as witnessed by the twin terms, "educational technology" and "instructional technology." Examples in adult education include the utilization of computers in adult basic education, the employment of interactive video discs in corporate training departments, and establishing dialogue through telecommunications in distance education. In the area of instructional design there are several "authoring" software programs available that simply prompt the adult educator through a curriculum development process. Technological developments such as these are truly

---

[16] M. Knowles, *The Modern Practice of Adult Education* (New York: Association Press, 1970) p.37.

[17] M. Knowles, *The Modern Practice of Adult Education* (1980) p.127.

dazzling in their capabilities, and their applications hold much promise. Certainly there will be yet further developments of this kind. By way of perspective, however, the place of technology in adult education is seen as being an assist to learning. Verner believed that the rightful purpose of the items of technology was to augment instruction in order to "make learning more certain."[18]

Another restricting influence on program planners results from the quite spectacular expansion in the number of public sector providers of adult learning and due largely to the development of community college systems in the provinces. With the profusion of these institutional providers the scope of the work of program planners has come to be delineated by the bounds which surround these institutions, and which are expressed by such delineators as mandate, geographical service area, subject matter, clientele and so on. These bounds impose practical limitations on program planning which have the effect of introverting the extent of thinking to within the institution. Further, it becomes necessary to harmonize institutional program planning with the instructional time cycle of the institution, such as its semester, term, program period, session or whatever. Program planning in adult education, then, has come to suggest in a significant way the development of programs (courses, workshops and so on) by adult education specialists working for institutional providers and which must fit into the parameters of the institution.

A third restricting influence on program planners is the suggestion of a overly structured approach to planning. Planning by its very nature connotes a set, deliberate and calculated process where everything is predetermined prior to the implementation. Indeed the rationality of planning lies in its promise that there will be no surprises once the program comes to be implemented. This conception of adult education, however, is in many cases much too presumptuous. One of the basic tenets of adult education is that the adult participants bring with them to the learning activity their own ideas and experiences with which to enrich and enlarge the activity. Overplanning has the potential for missing this opportunity as it implies that the planner has the ability beforehand to predict outcomes. Anyone familiar with the community development process, for example, knows that upon entering the process the animator (as the adult educator is referred to in this area) can offer no assurance as to the direction the process will take. Structuredness is not meant to intimate that program planning is counterproductive to good adult education practice; in fact the opposite is the case in that when properly carried out, it is possible for program planning to account for such unknown factors. What is known, however, is that historically many exemplary adult education pro-

[18] C. Verner, *A Conceptual Scheme for the Identification and Classification of Processes for Adult Education* (Washington: Adult Education Association, 1962) p.9.

grams never underwent a systematic program planning process. Rather it was considerable amounts of intuition, creative thinking, and spontaneous decision making that represented the sum of the intellectual control of the specific program.

A fourth influence on program planners is decidedly philosophical in nature and stems from two differing views of the purpose of adult education, namely the liberal view and the social transformation view. In the liberal view the purpose of adult education is to provide opportunities for adults to improve their personal situations. By offering programs which hold promise for individual betterment, adult education is seen to be a means of overcoming societal inequities. Thus it is appropriate for the wide variety of adult education agencies to offer a potpourri of learning opportunities. This offering allows individual adults to choose from among the options in order to improve their social and economic lot in life. Opposed to this liberal view is that of social transformation. This view holds that through adult learning it is possible to bring changes to the social, political and economic structures in society as it is these structures which are responsible for the adverse conditions experienced by certain groups of people. Adopting this view, the purpose of adult education is not simply to serve the particular learning needs and interests of individuals which can bring about individual change but rather to serve the collective needs and interests of groups of people so as to bring about specific social change. The philosophical point to be made is put forward by the social transformationists who argue that there is no neutral education, and that education is either a force for change or a way of reinforcing the status quo.[19]

The implication is that programs developed according to the liberal view only reinforce the status quo because, while individuals might in fact improve their circumstances through participation, the oppressive structures remain. Increasingly, and in fact predominantly, the adult education programs offered in Canada are seen to promote this liberal view, especially as the large institutional providers are publicly funded, and program planning as carried out in these institutions has the effect of reinforcing the status quo. It is this connection of program planning with the liberal view which philosophically introduces a limiting suggestion to the process of program planning.

The above discussion of the restricting influences on program planners points out the need by adult educators to be conscious of the personal orientation which they bring to their planning activity. While there is nothing inherently mistaken about the program planning process, it is important to

---

[19] G. Selman, "Adult Education and Citizenship," in F. Cassidy & R. Faris (Eds.), *Choosing Our Future: Adult Education and Public Policy in Canada* (Toronto: OISE, 1987) p.44. Selman has further developed this idea of adult education being associated with change—change which is not always welcomed. See G. Selman, "The Enemies of Adult Education," *Canadian Journal of University Continuing Education 15*, 1 (1989) pp.68-81.

recognize that adult education, as expressed through programs, communicates the values and beliefs of its planners and sponsors. Wittingly or otherwise these values and beliefs are thus visited upon participants.

Elements of Design in Programs

Having now examined the concept of program in adult education and the program planning process in the abstract, it is fitting to regard some actual programs. As indicated at the beginning of the chapter, adult educators should be as interested in learning from developed programs as from the theoretical conception of program planning. How this can be pursued is a matter of individual appreciation. One way is to use a model such as Houle's Fundamental System in order to single out the different planning considerations which have resulted in a program design and then study the ones which offer the greatest interest. In this section, however, the orientation is away from technical considerations and instead is upon design elements. The intention is to present a more sensitive appreciation, and the term "design element" is used to identify a discernible part of the overall program which in some special way contributes to the program's overall impact on adult learning.

There is not a finite list of design elements in programs; rather the appreciation of the observer can identify any number of individual elements. Likewise a program is not made up of a set number of elements in order to achieve a design. When regarding a program, though, it is often the case that a single design element in a program can be noted which most apparently contributes to the program's impact. What follows is a selection of design elements, chosen on no particular basis, although most would be recognizable in any adult education program. Each design element is elaborated upon by way of a thumbnail sketch taken from a Canadian experience. The intention is that these sketches convey some of the inventiveness, intuitiveness and inspiration which are also very much a part of planning adult education programs. The design elements include:
- the unsettled social circumstances
- the vision and the visionary
- the sponsorship
- the philosophical basis
- the learning tradition
- the collaboration
- the learner/s
- the instructor
- the learning environment
- the learning process employed
- the learning materials
- the educational technology utilized
- the power dynamics

The Unsettled Social Circumstances: Saskatchewan College System

Much of the history of adult education is rooted in the concern for over-coming the arduous social circumstances experienced by adults. Those with little or no education have always been especially susceptible to a life of subjugation at the hands of those with wealth, power and superior education. In addressing this oppressive situation it was recognized by early activists that education was a means of empowering individuals to gain a measure of control over their circumstances, which could lead to a more satisfying existence. Furthermore, education which was undertaken on a community basis and combined with collective action was seen as a way to bring about basic change in a society. It was this conviction and the programs which emerged which provided adult education with its original impetus as a social movement.

Canadian society has not been stratified to nearly the extent as has Great Britain, with its formal system of class distinction. Nevertheless social circumstances in Canada have been adversely influenced by such factors as economic control by foreign interests of many resource-based industries, rapid and unsettling social changes in light of Canada's development as an industrial nation and even extremes in geography and climate. More so in earlier times than at present, for many adults and their families the impact of these factors has meant a life of eking out a minimal existence. Despite this, however, Canadians in the various parts of the nation have always had an idea of the way they believed they should reasonably be able to live, based on the country's rich natural abundance and their willingness to work hard for their living. The example of the unsettled social circumstances comes from Saskatchewan, where aspects of the social fabric were seen as needing to be protected in light of changes to the province's traditional rural way of life.

Saskatchewan in the 1950s was described as being a "province in ferment" where "almost every aspect of the earlier economic and social pattern is shifting."[20] These changes had been brought on by the steady trend to urbanization, resulting in the diminution of values associated with rural living. As an indication of how strongly these values were held, in 1956 a Royal Commission on Agriculture and Rural Life was conducted to examine ways in which the quality of life in rural areas could be stimulated. As well a Centre for Community Studies was established at the University of Saskatchewan to study the changes that were occurring. Nonetheless, throughout the 1960s the shifting continued and the negative consequences to the rural areas was such that the situation called for a positive response. In large measure the response was the development of the Saskatchewan Community College.

---

[20] W.B. Baker, "A Centre for the Study of Community Dynamic," in J.R. Kidd (Ed.), *Learning and Society* (Toronto: CAAE, 1963) p.224.

In 1973, the newly elected NDP government passed the Community Colleges Act, thereby putting in place a provincial community college system unique in all of Canada. The uniqueness stemmed from the expressed desire to sustain Saskatchewan's rural communities and the traditional values associated with them. These values were articulated by the Advisory Committee which had been formed earlier to investigate a suitable college system for the province. "The sense of community in rural Saskatchewan, built on traditions of community participation and co-operation blended with self-help, is among the province's most valuable attributes."[21] The community college system was intended to serve the particular needs of Saskatchewan as opposed to being simply a copy of any one of the systems being developed at the time in other provinces. Specifically, the system was designed to be an instrument of community development whereby each college would provide programs of community education and service as determined by the community. The Advisory Committee Report noted that "a Provincial education system develops within a specific social-historical context. New developments, to be relevant, should be in tune with not only the history, but also the spirit of the people."[22]

The Saskatchewan form of community college was portrayed as "the college is the community, the community is the college." At the outset it was not considered necessary to construct separate college facilities; instead colleges would make use of existing facilities within the community. The staff resource was likewise purposely kept to a minimum. The college was designed to operate with an administrator, an adult counsellor and a small number of community educators whose jobs were to work with the community in identifying educational needs. Instructional staff were, as much as possible, contracted locally for specific programs. As for its academic programs, the college would not grant diplomas but rather would act as a broker of educational services in concert with the province's existing universities and technical institutes. In terms of governance, the provincial government appointed boards for each community college made up of members from within each of sixteen regions in the province. In summary, as one of the principal architects, Ron Faris, described the Saskatchewan community college system, it was made up of "colleges without walls but with foundations."[23]

The colleges were well received throughout the province. One assessment referred to the first ten years of their operation as "an era of remarkable achievement in the area of adult and continuing education" and noted partici-

---

[21] Province of Saskatchewan, *Report of the Minister's Advisory Committee on Community Colleges* (Regina: Department of Continuing Education, 1972) p.6.

[22] Ibid.

[23] Ron Faris, "Colleges without Walls but with Foundations" as quoted in J. Dennison & P. Gallagher, *Canada's Community Colleges* (Vancouver: University of B.C. Press, 1986) p.56.

pation rates as high as 20 percent. Furthermore the original objective of improving the quality of Saskatchewan life, particularly in the rural communities, was judged to be an unqualified success. "As community-based institutions, Saskatchewan's colleges had few equals."[24]

There have been a number of changes to the Saskatchewan college system such that today it has lost much of its original distinctiveness. Some of these changes were inevitable as differences developed between urban and rural colleges in their programming and administration. More significantly, a change in government in 1982 meant a different political philosophy along with a new set of educational priorities, which emphasized economic development as this period coincided with a serious recession. Nonetheless, as in the case of the earlier Antigonish Movement in Nova Scotia, for a time this "great experiment" in community education served to focus attention on unsettled social circumstances which required addressing, and adult education was seen as being the appropriate response.[25]

The Vision and the Champion: Adelaide Hoodless and the Women's Institute

Adult learning needs can arise from any number of circumstances. Whereas the fundamental concern of educators of youth is to provide education which anticipates future circumstances, in adult education the emphasis is much more on responding to the present circumstances of adults in an effort to bring about some change. With adults, however, learning needs often go unnoticed, at least until some progressive individual brings attention to particular needs. Even drawing attention to a learning need is not sufficient: there needs also to be a vision of what will be the new circumstances once the need is addressed. This vision then requires someone or some group to champion it in an effort to bring about the new circumstances.

There are several famous Canadian adult education programs which are examples of this combination of the vision and the champion, including the Antigonish Movement with Fathers Tompkins and Coady, the credit union movement (caisses populaires) with Alphonse Desjardins, and the Women's Institutes with Adelaide Hoodless. These programs were the products of fertile minds, and in each case a perceptive mixture of idealism and pragmatism created a vision of a more desirable circumstance which was possible to achieve using adult education as a means.[26] In every case, rather than simply

---

[24] Ibid., p.113.

[25] Ibid., p.116.

[26] For biographical sketches of these and other early Canadian adult educators see H. Rouillard (Ed.), *Pioneers in Adult Education in Canada* (Toronto: CAAE, 1952).

relating the vision, its champion instead incited others with the vision such that it was acted upon in a large scale. Indeed the factors associated with a vision in the adult education context are that the learning need must be: (1) made recognizable and distinct from the prevailing circumstances; (2) based on a straightforward premise of an achievable change; (3) able to be joined in on and then built upon by other leaders; and (4) able to incite people to action. Further, the champion typically evidences the following attributes: a spiritual concern for the well-being of others, a pioneering determination which deliberates only on success, and an ability to communicate lucidly.

Adelaide Hoodless was an educational reformer devoted to women's causes. Even though her original vision was based on circumstances more prevalent in the nineteenth century, it has maintained its clarity even to the present. The first Women's Institute was founded in 1897 in Stoney Creek, Ontario, and within twenty years similar institutes had been formed in all provinces. In 1919 provincial representatives met in Winnipeg to establish the Federated Women's Institutes of Canada.

The Women's Institute, like several other early women's organizations including the Y.W.C.A., sororities and women's auxiliaries, came about as a counterpart to organizations established for men. In this case Farmers' Institutes had been in existence since the 1880s with the purpose of aiding farmers in adopting more effective farming practices. Hoodless recognized the need for a similar type of organization to assist women in improving their equally important domestic practices. The institutes were particularly suited to the rural setting where opportunities for women coming together were more difficult and hence less frequent than in the urban setting. As well, the mutual dependence which is characteristic of a more rural way of life lent itself well to the sharing aspect of the institutes' activities. Most important, however, was the raised status which the institutes accorded to the role of women and the merit of their views.

The initial concern of the institute was with "domestic science," as home economics was referred to in those days. This base was soon broadened to include other areas such as the arts and citizenship, community improvement projects of various descriptions and advocating on issues of importance to women. (Particularly in the period before women were given the vote, the Women's Institute was one of the few forums in which they could express their views on political matters.) Membership was open to all women and meetings were conducted in such a way that learning and action were shared efforts among the members, without reliance on outside resources. The meetings were usually held in members' homes and the social aspects of gathering together were emphasized. This format had a great appeal, and the institutes both grew in numbers and flourished in their activities under the motto, "For Home and Country."

Hoodless died in 1910 at the early age of fifty-two. In her day the vision she held of the role of women was resisted by many, and she was often referred to with disdain as one of those "new women." Today, eighty years later, the circumstances of women have changed from those seen by Hoodless, yet the vision of women coming together for socializing, edification and action on issues remains unchanged. The Women's Institute continues to serve this vision in mostly rural communities throughout Canada and through its national organization. In other communities where there is no institute, and especially in the cities, there are modern counterparts such as women's resource centres and women's clubs. At the national level there is the Canadian Congress for Learning Opportunities for Women which advocates on behalf of the special needs of women in accessing educational opportunity.

A particular feature of the Women's Institute vision is its international dimension. Not only did the idea of Women's Institutes spread to other countries (due in large measure to the championing efforts of one Margaret "Madge" Watt) but they also provided the basis for an international organization, the Associated Countrywomen of the World. This evolution of the original idea first realized in Stoney Creek in 1897 is a testament to the perceptiveness on the part of Hoodless of a vital human need, one which transcends national boundaries. Her vision and her championing of it serve as an outstanding example of that element of an adult education program which awakens and activates within individuals a deeply felt need for personal discovery and mutual understanding.[27]

The Sponsorship: The Carnegie Corporation of New York

Unlike the education of youth which is predominantly provided for by the state, the education of adults historically owes its presence to sponsorship by independent organizations. From this situation has emerged an array of private sponsors including voluntary associations, religious groups and philanthropic foundations. This private sponsorship has not only been instrumental in shaping the field of adult education but it has also been responsible for enriching its history.

Sponsorship as used here is meant to indicate the financial commitment of an organization which enables a program to go forward. While any organization can sponsor an adult education program without necessarily making a direct or large financial investment, nonetheless the organization is undoubtedly making available other resources (staff time, facilities, supplies) and by

---

[27] For a history of the Women's Institute see E. Rand, *Federated Women's Institutes of Canada: A History 1919-1960* (Ottawa: Federated Women's Institute of Canada, 1961).

virtue of this indirect financial contribution it is still acting as the sponsor. Every program has a sponsor, and frequently there is more than one as in the case of a co-sponsorship. An important distinction is made here between the agency which is offering a program and the agency which is affording it to be offered. While commonly it is the same agency doing both, this need not be the case. Instead it could well be that the providing agency is receiving funding from some other sponsoring agency source for this purpose. The essential question to ask when delineating sponsorship is: Who is affording the program to the point where it is able to be offered? In determining the essential nature of the sponsorship a further question is: What would be the consequence to this program of the sponsor withdrawing financial support?

For the adult participant the question of sponsorship can be either of no concern or of great concern. Some sponsors are seen as being neutral, such as a school board continuing education department, while others· are seen as having a specific purpose, such as a religious organization's educational unit. In other cases the sponsor acts as a "silent partner" in the offering of the program and allows the providing agency complete freedom to offer the program as it sees fit.

Because there is no regulation of sponsorship in adult education, it is enlightening to regard a particular program's sponsor and determine the nature and extent of influence which it has on the program. This is not to imply covertness on the part of the sponsor but rather to suggest that the connection between the sponsor and the program is usually quite informative about both.

The story of the Carnegie Corporation's foundational work on behalf of adult education in the United States is well known and is to be found in other accounts.[28] Less well known, however, is how the Corporation also supported many adult education activities in Canada as part of a provision in its charter, which permitted a small portion of the foundation's income to be used within the British Commonwealth (exclusive of the British Isles, which was separately endowed). In the period between 1925, when the Corporation began specifically to support adult education, and 1959, when the Corporation made the decision to concentrate its "Commonwealth Program" funds on emerging countries, the foundation was involved in financing a considerable number of adult education projects in Canada. This support is seen as being instrumental to the initiation and sustenance of some of Canada's early work of note in the field.

The Carnegie Corporation is one of the philanthropic legacies of Andrew Carnegie, a self-made man who became very successful as an American industrialist in the latter part of the 1800s. Carnegie was born in Scotland in

---

[28] For example see H. Stubblefield, *Towards a History of Adult Education in America* (New York: Croom Helm, 1988).

1835, the son of a weaver. His father experienced difficulties finding work in Scottish factories, and this caused the family to emigrate to America in 1848. Andrew subsequently became involved in the manufacture of steel and, through the Carnegie Steel Corporation, amassed a personal fortune. Believing that the wealthy were "trustees" of their wealth for the good of the public, Carnegie established several endowments for this philanthropic purpose, one being the Carnegie Corporation of New York. This corporation was set up in 1911 to administer the remaining portion of Carnegie's fortune, and Carnegie himself directed the Corporation's activities until his death in 1919. The best-known benefaction of the Corporation are the early public library buildings, most of which were built in North America (2,509 in total, 116 in Canada).[29] This recognizable gift of the foundation is but one aspect of its stated purpose, that being, "to promote the advancement and diffusion of knowledge and understanding."[30] It was this interest on the part of the foundation that caused it to become involved in adult education work in a most vital way.

The Corporation became interested in adult education generally as a result of determining that libraries alone could not carry out the foundation's purpose of diffusing knowledge for general use. Instead it would be necessary to experiment with new methods, and important to this experimentation was the principle that "knowledge should be adapted to make the information appropriate to the recipient and their needs."[31] This interest in adult education by the Corporation was held particularly by its then-president Frederick Keppel, and he initiated a comprehensive program of studies, research, demonstrations and experimentation. Grants from the foundation, rather than creating new, permanent adult education agencies, instead provided temporary support for existing agencies or else created new co-ordinating agencies.

To carry out its adult education program the Corporation provided the necessary impetus, which resulted in the formation of the American Association for Adult Education (AAAE). Subsequently grants for adult education were reviewed by the executive board of the AAAE on behalf of the foundation, and this is the reason for the close links between the American association and many of the Canadian projects so sponsored. (Note: Projects in Newfoundland, until 1949 a British colony, were also supported by the Corporation, on the same basis as Canada.) One of the earlier grants went to assist in the organization of adult education in Canada, and thus the creation of the Canadian Association for Adult Education in 1935.

Specific information regarding the Corporation's Canadian and Newfoundland sponsorship of adult education is too detailed to provide here except in

[29] F. Anderson, *Library Program, 1911-1961* (New York: Carnegie Corporation, 1963).

[30] Carnegie Corporation of New York, *1988 Annual Report* (New York: Carnegie Corporation, 1989).

[31] H. Stubblefield, *Towards a History of Adult Education in America*, p.25.

general terms.[32] Besides the effectual support in establishing the CAAE, the Corporation also supported the co-ordinating efforts of the Newfoundland Adult Education Association and the Quebec Association for Adult Education. In the area of program support, the Corporation made possible expansion of the extension work at the universities of British Columbia, Saskatchewan, Manitoba, McGill, and St. Francis Xavier (the Antigonish Movement). Funds supported programs at Acadia University, Banff School of Fine Arts, the Y.M.C.A.'s Lake Couchiching, Frontier College, and the Workers' Educational Association of Canada and in Ontario. Besides these specific adult education projects, there were numerous other grants made by the foundation which had tangential implications. For example, in 1921, at the request of the colleges and the government of Nova Scotia, the Carnegie Corporation undertook a survey of higher education in the Maritime Provinces.

As indicated, since 1959 the Corporation has directed funds from its Commonwealth Program to educational projects in emerging countries, and since 1979 this program has been referred to as the International Program. In keeping with the Corporation's charter, recipient nations are limited to those countries or territories outside the British Isles which were a member of the British Commonwealth of Nations or were a British colony as of April 1948. Even though Canadian adult education projects are no longer given a priority to receive funds through Carnegie's foundation, the sponsorship which was provided in earlier years remains as a spiritual legacy in the same way as his libraries remain as a physical legacy.

The Philosophical Basis: Education for Co-operative Housing

The coming together by Canadians to form co-operatives for various forms of mutual aid traces its beginnings to the caisse populaire movement, i.e., credit unions, in Quebec starting in 1900. Historically, co-operatives have been rooted in the rural areas of the country where interdependence has always been an essential part of the way of life, given the general condition of economic and social deprivation. Since World War II, co-operatives have also become conspicuous in urban areas, particularly by way of credit unions and, beginning in the 1960s, with the development of housing co-operatives. Like other types of co-operatives, housing co-ops present to Canadians an alternative form of economic and social participation to that provided by the free enterprise system, with its basis in capitalist theory. Thus instead of housing being available by such means as private ownership, rental from a landlord, or

---

[32] For details by way of brief description, dates and amounts see S. Stackpole, *Commonwealth Program, 1911-1961* (New York: Carnegie Corporation, 1963).

social housing, co-operative housing enables people to join together to provide their own housing through joint ownership. A housing co-operative operates as a non-profit business where the members, those people who occupy the housing owned by the co-operative corporation, control the organization.[33] It is this organizational factor which distinguishes co-operative housing from other forms of housing, and it requires that there be an educational resource available to assist members in the successful operation of the co-operative. In short, members have to know how to live co-operatively.

There are two aspects to the educational program for members of housing co-operatives. Not only must the members receive training in the necessary managerial skills to operate a business and the interpersonal skills to live in harmony with one another, but they must also be able to relate these skills to the principles of co-operation. This recognizes the fact that co-op housing as an alternative form of housing has a distinct philosophical foundation upon which all its operations are built. The Co-operative Principles were adopted in 1966 by the International Co-operative Alliance as a set of basic principles that apply to all co-operatives. (These principles are also known as the Rochdale Principles as they are the latest version of the principles adopted by the first co-operative in England.) They are:

1. Open and Voluntary Membership: Membership in the co-op should be voluntary and there should be no artificial restrictions that would prevent anyone from joining who could benefit from its services and is willing to accept the responsibilities of membership.

2. Democratic Control: Co-operatives are democratic organizations. Their affairs should be administered by people who are elected or appointed in a way that members have agreed to and who are accountable to the members. Members should have equal rights of voting and should participate in the decisions affecting them.

3. Limited Interest on Shares: Any share capital that a co-op may have should receive a strictly limited rate of interest, if any.

4. Return of Surplus to Members (Non-Profit Operation): Surplus, or savings, if any, arising out of the operations of a co-op, belong to that co-op and should be distributed so that no member gains at the expense of any other.

5. Co-operative Education: Co-ops should make provision for the education of their members, officers and employees and of the general public in the principles and techniques of co-operation.

---

[33] Co-operative Housing Foundation of Canada, *Communique* (Ottawa: Co-operative Housing Foundation of Canada, May, 1988).

6. Co-operation Among Co-operatives: All co-op organizations, in order to best serve the interests of their members and their communities, should actively co-operate in every practical way with other co-ops.[34]

For many the motive to join an housing co-op has more to do with the shortage of affordable housing than it does with the Co-operative Principles or a sense of participation in what essentially is a reform movement. If, however, co-operative housing is to demonstrate to government and the public that it is indeed a viable housing alternative, then its members must become knowledgable about its philosophy and means of operation, and conduct themselves accordingly. Thus when educational programs are offered by co-op housing federations across Canada on topics such as board orientation, property management, and constructive conflict resolution, the Co-operative Principles provide the philosophical basis for the content, and they must be evident to the participants. The more effective the educational programs are at instilling the philosophical basis, the greater will be the capacity of the co-operative housing movement to offer persons an alternative to the free market housing system.

Indeed this idea of providing alternatives is basic to the philosophy of adult education. A reiteration in 1986 of the CAAE's Declaration on Citizenship and Adult Learning asserts that "the adult education movement is based on the belief that people have, within themselves and their communities, the spiritual and intellectual resources adequate to the solution of their problems."[35] It is understandable, then, that organizations which have been established as an alternative to prevailing social and economic structures would rely on adult education in the effort to educate those who stand to benefit. Additionally, such organizations face the need to constantly work at imparting their philosophical ideals as a means of upholding them.

The Learning Tradition: The Couchiching Institute on Public Affairs

There are some adult education programs which conjure up images of a particular learning tradition. The most widely held learning tradition is associated with "night school." Try as adult educators might to change adult education's image of the night school stereotype with adults utilizing daytime schools in the evening, the term remains as being the most pervasive association of adults with learning. To many the name "Couchiching" similarly connotes an adult learning tradition, in this case the connection being with public affairs programming.

---

[34] Co-operative Housing Foundation of Canada, "Board of Directors' Course" (Ottawa: Co-operative Housing Foundation of Canada, 1986) p.1.

[35] CAAE, *Building the Social Movement* (Vancouver: University of British Columbia Centre for Continuing Education, 1986).

Couchiching takes its name from the lake north of Toronto where the National Council of the Y.M.C.A.s in Canada first conducted a staff and lay training program in 1907. Two years later the property, known as Geneva Park, was purchased by the "Y" and training events continued to be conducted each summer. In the depression year of 1932 the Y extended the philosophy of its training program so that, instead of training strictly young men for their work in the Y, the program emphasized a more worldly outlook. Issues of national and international concern were examined to assess their impact on Canadian society and the work of the Y.M.C.A. This change was inspired by an energetic adult educator who worked with the Y.M.C.A., R.E.G. Davis, and in that year he organized the first conference of the Canadian Institute on Economics and Politics. The program was opened to outsiders as well as Y secretaries (the designation for professional Y staff), and in the second year the outsiders greatly outnumbered the Y trainees. In 1949 the CBC began national radio broadcasts of the conference's sessions, and its involvement made it possible to bring in payed speakers. Subsequently the sessions were even televised.

The learning tradition associated with the Couchiching conference has developed from the special combination of features that have been present from the outset. First there is the reflective setting of Geneva Park itself amidst Ontario's cottage country. Then there is the topic of each year's conference, developed with the awareness of Couchiching's tradition of tackling public affairs issues head on and often in advance of their being generally acknowledged. (For example the 1989 theme was "What On Earth Are We Doing: A Conference on the Environment, Examining the Compatibility of Nature and Civilization.") Thirdly there is the scheduling of the institute each year during the summer, a time when participants are in a relaxed and expansive mood. The fourth feature is the format, consisting of presentations by acknowledged experts followed by informed group discussion. Another feature is the alumni which the conference is able to point to as having been involved with Couchiching, thereby giving it an enhanced reputation by association. Pierre Trudeau, Henry Kissinger, Joe Clark, Lester Pearson and John Diefenbaker are among the notable political figures who have been present.

The conference continues to take place annually at the Y.M.C.A.'s Geneva Park Conference Centre, although the Y.M.C.A. no longer conducts the program and the CBC no longer broadcasts the sessions. Instead the Couchiching Institute on Public Affairs, as it is now called, is a registered charitable organization "dedicated to bringing together interested Canadians to discuss important public policy issues with experts and other members of the general public."[36] While the annual summer program is open to anyone on a first-

---

[36] Couchiching Institute on Public Affairs, membership brochure.

come, first-served basis it has become somewhat of a parochial event in Ontario, although the learning tradition associated with it continues and is described as being "the intellectual Grey Cup of Canada."[37]

There are, of course, other continuing learning traditions in Canada, for example, the Banff Centre (originally the Banff School of Fine Arts), the labourer-teachers of Frontier College and the agricultural extension work of several universities. As well, night school remains as the most universal tradition in Canada, although with the advent of many post-secondary educational institutions it does not connote only the use of a grade school facility. These learning traditions provide reassurance that, in an age of constant change and innovation, there continue to be adult education programs still meeting long-established learning needs in proven formats. This helps to demonstrate the basic nature of many learning needs associated with adulthood. As well, the establishing of any tradition promotes stability, and in the context of adult learning, this promotes acceptance and respect.

The Collaboration: The Open Learning Agency in British Columbia

Many noteworthy programs in adult education are the result of collaboration between two or more agencies involved in the field. Such collaboration occurs on the basis of a synergetic relationship; that is, in order to produce a desired effect a collaborative action is required: a single agency acting on its own could not be successful, or at least not as successful, at conducting the program. An obvious example is the case of the National Farm Radio Forum, conducted through the collaborative efforts of the CAAE, the CBC, and the Canadian Federation of Agriculture. The absence of any one of these three sponsoring agencies would have made it impossible to conduct the program as effectively as was the case.

Because adult education is for the most part free of prescribed curriculum—the exception being where adults are returning to complete academic credentials—it is quite open to opportunities for collaboration. Even in the case of academic credentials, especially at higher levels where program requirements are more flexible than the prescribed curriculum necessary for high school completion or vocational programs, collaboration is increasingly seen as both feasible and desirable. At the root of all collaboration is the intent to bring about the development of programs which are then able to be delivered to the greatest number of adult learners possible. In this way collaboration serves well the interests of both the agencies and the learners; however, as the basis of participation in adult education is its voluntarism, the dominant

---

[37] Gordon Donaldson, "Summer After Summer," *The Review* 3 (1981).

interest to be served by collaboration is that of the learner. To the extent that learners are attracted to programs brought about by collaboration, then the interests of the agencies involved are also able to be well served.

Given the primacy of meeting the needs of learners, what then are the inducements for the agencies to come together in this synergistic relationship? Several can be identified. The first has to do with mandate and purpose. Mandate refers to the authorized mission given to an organization which is established by a superior organization. For example, the federal government established the National Film Board with the broad mission to interpret Canada to Canadians and to other nations through the medium of film. In the 1960s the National Film Board embarked on a bold community development initiative known as "Challenge for Change," which attempted through the use of films to motivate Canadians to address issues of social disparity. However the National Film Board's mandate did not provide for it to assume the role of animator, working directly with community groups to bring about social change. In order to produce the films in the Challenge for Change series, the National Film Board determined to collaborate with various community groups whose purpose it was to animate change. These films then became available for use by other organizations such as university extension departments and the CBC for widespread viewing. In this way the National Film Board's mandate and the community groups' purpose came together in a successful collaborative effort.

Another factor in collaboration is that various agencies and organizations have defined constituencies and rather unique networks. Motivating these constituencies and "working" the networks can most often only be done by the particular agency and thus, when a project is identified that needs to involve the constituencies through accessing the networks, collaboration is called for. An example of this occurred in the late 1970s when the CBC collaborated with the CAAE to conduct the public affairs program "People Talking Back." The CAAE's network of provincial adult education associations was used to provide for local organization of participants in the program.

Collaboration also works where there is a mutuality of philosophy between the agencies, as contrasted with a relationship developed along commercial lines. An example of this is a residential centre owned by a religious organization which collaborates with a church parish in conducting a course, rather than it being held in a hotel conference centre. This example also serves to note how collaboration is a combining of resources, in this case a physical resource with a constituency resource.

Very often collaboration is also driven by financial considerations. An organization may want to develop a program which combines the use of both printed materials and a video tape. While the organization may be well equipped to produce the printed materials, the cost of also producing the video tape portion of the program may be prohibitive. Instead a collaborative arrangement might be worked out with an educational institution equipped to produce video. Examples of this can be found in provinces which have established media production centres as part of their education ministries.

There are also pressures being placed on institutions to collaborate. Institutional mandates are contrived definitions of areas of activity and often the mandates of similar institutions overlap or are in contradiction. With the expansion of provincial educational systems over the last three decades this has been the case on numerous occasions as school boards, colleges, institutes and universities expand to meet educational and training needs and to open new educational "markets." The public as well as policy commentators are demanding that educational institutions increase their collaborative efforts in order to make the educational system more comprehensible and rational as well as cost efficient. The desired result is that the system will be accessible to a greater number of persons. One intriguing example of this prescribed collaboration is the Open Learning Agency of British Columbia.

The creation in 1988 of the Open Learning Agency (OLA) was in response to the need for an even greater access to learning opportunity than was available through the province's already well-developed educational system. Difficulties of geography, the limitations of conventional educational institutions, and a demographic imbalance within the regions of British Columbia were just three of the factors which called for an innovative approach to meeting demands for increased access to higher and continuing education. Making it possible to meet the need were components such as improved distance education technology (for example, the placing in space of the Anik C satellite), a demonstrated success in open learning (the British Open University) and an established educational system of schools, colleges, institutes and universities. What remained was the creation of an agency mandated to integrate the system so as to serve more openly the educational needs and interests of British Columbians.

Open learning as a defined term is still evolving; however, it is used to describe the combining of educational technology with innovative teaching methods into a system of learning which maximizes access to educational opportunity. Because open learning as an approach is designed to be responsive to the diverse needs of adults who wish to continue with their education, it is of considerable interest to adult educators. This is particularly the case as open learning is seen as a significant advance in the providing of an institutional response to the call for lifelong learning. Interestingly, open learning, when organized into a learning system which involves a number of educational agencies as components, is well suited to collaboration. The reason for this is that the component parts are complementary rather than competitive. Educational institutions are typically very protective about their territory, whether it be seen in terms of geographical area, program content, or institute mandate. Anything which threatens to reduce institutional territory is viewed with alarm as any such reduction translates into a reduction of funding to the institution, an undermining of its influence in the territory and a loss of institutional prestige.

Two features of the Open Learning Agency emphasize complementarity and hence enable collaboration. The primary feature is the underlying premise of OLA which places the situation of the prospective learner at the centre of decision making. Programs are designed which recognize the individual's rightful part in choosing when, where and how he or she will learn. (It should be noted that the programs offered by OLA's Open College and Open University are those for which a credential is offered, that is a certificate, a diploma or a degree. It is also possible, however, for persons to take OLA courses out of general interest, and to casually watch programs on OLA's Knowledge Network educational television channel.) As a result of increasing access to programs, due to the lowering of participation barriers, the effect is calculated to enable more participation than previously was the case. The manner in which this feature is made operational (described below) has the desirable consequence of increasing the utilization of local educational resources and facilities.

The second feature is the innovative British Columbia Educational Credit Bank. The purpose of the Credit Bank is to make it possible for open learning students who are working towards an educational credential to be given credits for their previous formal and non-formal learning. Credit Bank advisors assess course credentials awarded by other educational institutions and also skills and knowledge gained through non-formal learning experiences. The effect of this crediting system is to make the educational system considerably more open and responsive to individual learning situations. It does this by recognizing that learning is lifelong, that individuals today are highly mobile and therefore their educational endeavours should also be portable, and that non-formal education is often of very high quality and thus worthy of considered recognition.

The collaboration works between the Open Learning Agency's three program components—the Open College, the Open University and the Knowledge Network—and the other provincial educational institutions. In the case of the Open College this is with school districts, colleges, institutes and private sector organizations where students can combine credits earned through independent learning, i.e., Open College distance education courses, with those earned through traditional methods, i.e., classroom instruction, and through non-formal learning, for example, company sponsored training courses, to earn credentials. Similarly in the case of the Open University, students are able to earn credentials through open learning offered not only by the Open University but also by the province's three other universities. As for the Knowledge Network, this facility acquires, produces and broadcasts educational programs which are both of general interest and which support the province's educational system, including courses of the Open College and the Open University.

As indicated, the Open Learning Agency is an example of prescribed collaboration, bringing a new approach to learning in an era where educational credentials at basic and advanced levels are emphasized. This kind of collaboration is seen to be more difficult to manage than that which occurs willingly. Nonetheless, prescribed or voluntary, the collaboration must work for the benefit of the learner.

The Learners: Elderhostels

Generally speaking, participation in adult education programs is unrestricted by way of enrollment criteria. When attending a class offered by a school board, university extension department or community centre, one is likely to notice among the participants a wide range in age, educational levels, occupational status and other variables. There are programs, however, which are developed for specific groups, and in these cases the criteria for membership become the noteworthy element of the particular program design.

There can be several reasons why a program is developed for a special group of learners. It may be that the learning to be accomplished is specialized, and only needs to be learned by the special group. Technical training is an example of this, where only those who instal and maintain the particular technology need learn about it. Another example is where the specific group has a unique learning circumstance, as in the case of education for those who are incarcerated. A third example is where a "target population" of people are defined in an attempt by the program's organizers to bring a particular homogeneity to the learning group. One such program developed with this in mind is Elderhostel.

Elderhostel is an educational program for older adults which combines travel with intellectual activity. While its start-up is quite recent, its initial inspiration drew on two well-established foreign experiences in adult education. An American social activist and educator, Marty Knowlton, along with David Bianco, Director of Residential Life at the University of New Hampshire, conceived the idea of Elderhostel in 1974. It was their view that older adults were wanting to continue their informal learning, and would be encouraged to do so if novel opportunities could be made available. They looked to the youth hostelling movement in Europe and the folk high schools of Scandinavia for the combination which would become Elderhostel's successful formula. In particular, Knowlton was impressed by the "way in which the availability of a network of modest accommodation encouraged and nurtured an adventuresome hostelling spirit in European youth. He also observed the very positive impact a residential setting had on adult education programs offered by the folk high schools."[38]

A number of factors suggested that a unique form of adult education could be developed with older adults in North America. Generally speaking, older adults enjoy high health standards, have available time, are financially reasonably well off, are mobile and are living in an age of truly fantastic developments. As well, the belief that older persons are incapable as learners, first refuted by Edward Thorndike in 1928, has been further exposed as a falsehood by many subsequent years of adult education programming involving older persons.

The older adult was singled out because of the concern that "one of the major problems of aging lies in the self-image of uselessness and futility that United States society foists on its older members."[39] Retirement is an aging life stage that frequently causes withdrawal from active life by the retiree. It was the belief of the Elderhostel innovators that through a program of physical and intellectual stimulation the withdrawal syndrome could be checked and even reversed. Experience was to bear this out.

The first Elderhostel program was offered in the State of New Hampshire in 1975 using a network of that state's universities and colleges. The experience confirmed the original thinking about the older adult learning audience, and the program expanded the next year to include all six New England states. In 1977 Elderhostel was incorporated as a Massachusetts non-profit corporation and in the following year a national office was opened. Subsequent programs included offerings in Canada (1980), Europe (1981) and Scandinavia (1981). In 1982 a Canadian office was established and in 1986 Elderhostel Canada was incorporated as a non-profit charity with a national office located in Toronto. In 1996 the number of elderhostlers participating in programs was 315,000 and of these 20,000 participated in the Canadian programs.[40]

The Elderhostel program follows, for the most part, a set format. A host organization (such as a university, community college, Y.M./Y.W.C.A. and so on) in a particular locality arranges for three courses to be conducted, the contents of which take advantage of the resources of that locality. The program runs from Sunday afternoon to the next Saturday morning and the classes are held during the Monday to Friday period. Each class runs from one to one-and-one-half hours each day, and it is possible for a participant to take

---

[38] Elderhostel Canada, *Catalog, 12,* 3 (Spring 1990).

[39] M. Knowlton, "Liberal Arts: The Elderhostel Plan for Survival," in *Educational Gerontology, 2* (1977) p.88.

[40] Elderhostel Canada, *Board of Directors Report* (Toronto: Elderhostel Canada, 1996).

all three courses or just one. Participants are responsible for their own travel to the locality of the program. The registration fee covers the cost of the program once there, and includes tuition, accommodation and meals. In 1990 the average cost per week was $275.

There are two important stipulations concerning the Elderhostel curriculum. The first is the requirement that the host organization offer courses which are intellectually challenging and of good educational quality. The second is that courses are not to be designed for the elderly. "Elderhostel is not interested in teaching the elderly how to be old, which is certainly the effect, and often the purpose, of courses designed for the elderly."[41] From these two stipulations has emerged a curriculum based largely in the liberal arts and also in the sciences. At the same time the courses are intended to attract older people regardless of their educational background, and there is no prescribed academic standard. The experience has been, however, that the Elderhostel program "tends to draw persons with higher educational levels, incomes, and community participation rates."[42]

The one proviso of the Elderhostel program is that participants be "retired or about to retire." This way the Elderhostel program can be developed in consideration of this age group's life experiences. Further, and most importantly, the host organization must maintain the special administrative dispensation which the program enjoys on behalf of the participants, namely that tuition, accommodation and meals be provided at cost.

Elderhostel is truly an international movement in adult education, a logical outgrowth of its eclectic genesis. Programs are now offered in 90 countries by approximately 3,400 institutions. Its success clearly indicates how responsive adults can be to an educational program which is planned and organized in such a fashion as to acknowledge adult learning ability. For proponents of adult education, Elderhostel demonstrably confirms the conception of lifelong learning.

The Instructor: Frontier College

Basic to learning in a student-teacher relationship is the nature of that relationship. This can be understood both in terms of personality, i.e., compatibility and mutual respect, and in terms of role definition, i.e., formal expectations of the student and of the teacher. Thus, as individuals grow and mature as persons, similarly they grow and mature as students. This maturing develops in such a manner that the student-teacher relationship is modified and, instead of being understood by way of an hierarchical distinction based

---

[41] M. Knowlton, "Liberal Arts: The Elderhostel Plan for Survival," p.92.

[42] D. Peterson, *Facilitating Education for Older Adults* (San Francisco: Jossey-Bass, 1983) p.251.

on differences in age, life experience and knowledge, in adulthood there is much more of an equality based on a considerable lessening in the significance of the differences. Of course there is still recognition of the teacher's greater skill, knowledge or understanding in a specific content area, and hence the creation of the teaching situation, but this superiority does not formally extend its influence to other aspects of the relationship.

The change in the student role and the need to accordingly alter the teacher role together form the basis of the original distinction made by Knowles between pedagogy—the art and science of teaching children—and andragogy—the art and science of helping adults learn.[43] While Knowles subsequently amended his thinking about pedagogy and andragogy so as to see them not as dichotomous but rather as two sets of assumptions to be made about learners, the andragogical assumptions nonetheless were descriptive of mature learning situations.[44] With this in mind, Knowles summarized the differentiation of pedagogy and andragogy as follows:

> ... andragogy is premised on at least these four crucial assumptions about the characteristics of learners that are different from the assumptions on which traditional pedagogy is premised. These assumptions are that as individuals mature: (1) their self-concept moves from one of being a dependent personality toward being a self-directed human being; (2) they accumulate a growing reservoir of experience that becomes an increasingly rich resource for learning; (3) their readiness to learn becomes oriented increasingly to the developmental tasks of their social roles; and (4) their time perspective changes from one of postponed application of knowledge to immediacy of application, and accordingly, their orientation toward learning shifts from one of subject-centredness to one of performance-centredness.[45]

In order to respond to these changes in the student role brought on by the student's maturation, it is the tenet of adult education that the teacher role must also change. One of the ways this is reflected is by use of the term "instructor." The intent in adult education when using the term instructor is not to deny that teaching is occurring, rather the term more particularly recognizes the varied situations in which adult learning takes place. The use of the term teacher carries with it connotations of a formal learning environment where andragogical assumptions do not prevail. Indeed the role of instructor in adult education has not nearly the formality attached to it as does the role of teacher. This is a reflection of the largely informal nature of adult education, and the absence of an institutionalized tradition which defers to the all-knowledgeable teacher.

---

[43] M. Knowles, *The Modern Practice of Adult Education* (1970) p.37.

[44] M. Knowles, *The Modern Practice of Adult Education* (1980) p.43.

[45] Ibid., p.44.

There is no stereotype which characterizes an instructor of adults. In terms of work it may be a full-time career choice or part-time sideline. An instructor might be an employee of an institution, an independent contractor or a volunteer. The pecuniary rewards can be substantial (in excess of $1,000 per day for trainers in business and industry) to being very minimal when, for example, working for a non-profit agency. In many cases the motivation to be an instructor is intrinsic to the individual and it is often that a person gives of his or her time and talent voluntarily. The credentials required vary according to the course being instructed, and much instruction requires no credential other than an attested interest or ability in an area. Many instructors develop the course which they then teach, while others instruct using a prepared syllabus. There are even some seemingly paradoxical situations with instructors of adults; for example, it is easily possible that the instructor will be younger in age than any of the students. In another example the roles of instructor and student may be exchanged at times during the instructional session if the student has more knowledge, skill or insight in a particular area. These situations are understood by the fact that in adult education the student-teacher relationship is one of adult to adult. There is a basic equality in this fact, and one that exerts a pervading influence on the relationship.

In selecting an instructor for an adult education activity there is usually more to consider than the basic matching of the instructor's content expertise with the learning needs of the students. Very often the instructor's ability to instruct will also be dependent on a sincere motivation which is sympathetic to the students' circumstances, as well as an abundant enthusiasm. An outstanding example of this can be found in the instructors of Frontier College, Canada's premier adult education institution.

Interestingly, the description applied to instructors of Frontier College's original educational work was "labourer-teacher." This description is now very much a part of Frontier College's proud history and tradition, but in light of the above discussion, it does reflect an earlier conception of adult education which was based more on pedagogical assumptions.[46] What the account of the labourer-teacher illustrates so poignantly, however, is the prerequisite of an adult relationship between the learner and the instructor if learning is to be facilitated by the instructor.

The name, Frontier College, conjures a wonderful juxtaposition; the vast and desolate Canadian hinterland being tamed by, of all things, learning, the stuff of civilized centres. And yet that was precisely the conception of Frontier College. Initially (in 1899) it was called the Canadian Reading Camp Movement by its founder, Presbyterian minister Alfred Fitzpatrick. From the modest early objective of bringing a civilizing presence to the rough railroad,

---

[46] See J. Morrison, *Camps and Classrooms* (Toronto: Frontier College Press, 1989).

lumbering and mining camps through the provision of suitable literature in rustic reading rooms, Frontier College soon evolved a more ambitious goal of bringing education to the labourers.

Initially many of the reading rooms had "instructors" assigned to them by the Reading Camp Movement who were supported by church congregations. Because the work day extended virtually from dawn to dusk there was little for the instructor to occupy himself with while awaiting the labourers return to the camp. One early instructor, Angus Gray, determined that he could enhance the rapport between himself and his students by working alongside the labourers by day and being their instructor in the evening. Thus began the celebrated labourer-teacher position with Frontier College.

The labourer-teacher is more than an inspirational happenstance; it is a natural realization of the role of the adult educator in such a circumstance. This role calls for the adult educator to know his or her students in such a way as to then be able to deliver instruction, aware of their learning needs and personal aspirations. Knowles, when examining processes of adult learning, correlates conditions of learning with what he regards as being superior principles of learning. Taking one example and applying it to the labourer-teacher position of Frontier College, it is abundantly evident why the position has enjoyed such success as a model for others to consider. As a condition of learning Knowles indicates, "The learning environment is characterized by physical comfort, mutual trust and respect, mutual helpfulness, freedom of expression, and acceptance of differences." Two of the principles of learning which he correlates to this are, "The teacher accepts the learners as persons of worth and respects their feelings and ideas" and, "The teacher exposes his or her own feelings and contributes resources as a co-learner in the spirit of mutual inquiry."[47]

In both principles it is the teacher who is understood to need to come closer to the students, and not to adopt a posture of aloofness. The labourer-teacher position exemplifies this understanding, and labourer-teacher has become a term which simply means "that teachers of adult learners not only go to where their students are to teach them, but also to work side by side with their students as well."[48]

The labourer-teachers of Frontier College continue to be placed in the various work camps across the country, but new learning frontiers have opened which call for an equally innovative response by committed instructors. While literacy remains the paramount learning need to address, the venue for Frontier College's programs has moved in from the geographical frontier. Now programs exist in urban workplaces, in penitentiaries, in Frontier Col-

---

[47] M. Knowles, *The Modern Practice of Adult Education* (1980) p.57.

[48] J. Morrison, *Camps and Classrooms*, p.3.

lege's own learning centres, and in locations of the students' own choosing. This opening of new frontiers is consistent with the College's fundamental conviction, "to take education to those who do not have it wherever they may be."[49]

A constant with Frontier College is its qualifications for those who wish to be teachers. A contemporary recruiting advertisement for the labourer-teacher program states the requirements to be: "A demonstrated commitment to voluntarism and community development. Experience in teaching and/or tutoring is helpful. Must be fit. Background in heavy labour preferred. Ability to live and work closely with others in an isolated environment." For its other programs Frontier College believes that, with training and support, a literate person can teach another person the literacy skills necessary to function as a proud individual and as a productive citizen. As an example, in the brochure outlining the College's Prison Literacy Initiative, the call for volunteer tutors maintains that, "volunteers, through their willingness to give of themselves and their time, demonstrate that the community cares and that it is prepared to give devalued people a second chance."

In these ways, then, Frontier College continues to attract instructors to carry out its educational mission. Perhaps most effectively, Frontier College is able to act as a connector between the learning needs of educationally disadvantaged adults and the humanitarian commitment of those intent on making enlightenment possible.

The Learning Environment: Residential Centres and the Native Education Centre

There are two illustrations to present regarding the element of the learning environment. The first, residential centres, is by way of general comment as there are numerous such centres across Canada, and all exhibit the same support for learning. The residential learning environment enables adults to leave behind the strictures of routine and instead establish a pattern which has learning as its focus. It is the function of the residential centre to assume for the learners many of the tasks of daily living which otherwise would distract or discourage them from concentrating on the learning at hand. As well, by typically being situated in outlying areas, or at least away from the mainstream of life, the centre offers a contemplative surrounding and a soothing ambience.

Another function of the residential centre is to bring together persons from different localities. This is particularly important in Canada where the country's vast geography mitigates against easy and prolonged contact among

---

[49] Ibid., p.22.

persons with similar learning interests. This coming together for an extended period of time has the intended effect of making possible communication which otherwise might have to be conducted by correspondence or telephone. As well there are many more communication opportunities which are present in a residential setting due to its informality and the occasions it provides for casual contact with resource persons and other learners.

Because attending a residential centre stands out in one's experience as being an uncommon event, the learning episode tends also to stand out and thus learning is reinforced by association. As well there is a heightened intensity to learning which takes place in an unencumbered environment as learners have more energy to devote to learning. This is typically supported by the freedom in a residential centre to manipulate the learning process as it is occurring through various means, including: having the space to easily break into small groups; having groups work on learning tasks with the benefit of generous time allotments; and determining a balance of time between learning sessions, social opportunity, recreation, and individual space.

Most residential centres in Canada are operated by organizations that utilize them for conducting their own programs and also make time available for other organizations. Despite all the attributes connected with learning at these centres, organizing for such learning experiences is often a difficult task. Adults find it difficult to make the time available, there is an accommodation cost above whatever might be the tuition fee, and it often takes longer to become accustomed to the different learning environment than is possible to schedule. Nonetheless residential centres do offer a supportive and interesting environment for adult learning which the program planner should be prepared to consider.

The second illustration of the significance of the learning environment draws on the experience of the Native Education Centre in Vancouver. In this case environment and architecture are dual elements as the learning centre is a magnificent structure, incorporating functional learning space and social area within a northwest coast Native longhouse design.

The Native Education Centre has conducted an adult education program in Vancouver since 1967, and since 1979 this has been operated by an all-Native community non-profit society, the Urban Native Indian Education Society. At its inception the Centre served two broad purposes, namely to assist Native people with their basic education so as to promote the taking of further education or the securing of employment, and to assist Native people in the difficult transition between life on the reserve and life in the urban area by way of life-skills programs. More recently there has been a new sense of urgency to Native people acquiring education and skills training, namely the developments associated with Indian self-government. Until the opening of the present building in 1985, the Centre offered its program using conventional space, and this period was spent proving the need for such a program.

Because Native people place great emphasis on their cultural beliefs and values, it was seen as important to have a learning centre designed not only to support this emphasis but indeed to boldly reflect it. This need is expressed in the Education Society's constitution where one of its goals is stated as being, "To provide central and suitable facilities where educational meetings may be held." This has been successfully accomplished. The Centre is located in a light industrial section of the city of Vancouver and, when sighted, is immediately remarkable. A large totem stands at the street side of the building and serves as a ceremonial entranceway to the longhouse design. The exterior of the building is all wood, allowing the exposed massive beams and posts to make a solid statement about the structure's derivation from traditional Native architecture. Around the building a landscape has been created where students are able to walk among plants and trees that have been selected for their cultural significance. A waft of smoke from the chimney serves to further situate the student in a village setting, not in the midst of Canada's third largest metropolitan area. Upon entering through the main doorway one is greeted by a large social area with a fire pit as its focus. This area is the setting of many of the cultural activities which are part of the life of the Centre. A small kitchen serves up mainly Native foods, with lunch being the time for communal eating. The walls are hung with many reminders of Native peoples and events.

The distinctive aspect of the Native Education Centre's learning environment is how intentional it is, and it is readily apparent that the Centre was created to appeal to Native people. The importance of this appeal to academic achievement is appreciated when one considers how for Native people there is no cultural equivalent to learning which takes place within a building designated for this purpose. For many Native people the association they have of institutionalized learning is in connection with the residential schools, and this experience is seen as having been culturally destructive. Furthermore the learning environments which dominate the educational systems in Canada are large in scale and are built to a design and with building materials which have been selected for practical rather than cultural reasons. Thus the Native Education Centre provides a culturally identifiable space where Native adults are able to learn together in a supportive environment. This illustration should cause adult educators to closely examine the learning environments which they utilize, and the extent to which these environments either support or interfere with learning activity.

The Learning Process Employed: The Lake Cowichan Food Bank

In adult education there is no one way in which learning is deemed to be most efficiently achieved. Partly this is because adult circumstances are complex, as contrasted to the circumstances of youth which are largely given over to the task of learning. Partly also it is because adult learning needs are varying, again as contrasted to those of youth which, because their needs are basic, are much more uniform. The result of this variation in adult education is that there are numerous ways in which learning can be organized so as to meet particular learning needs.

As noted in the first section of this chapter there are three general formats by which adult learning is organized, namely individual programs, group programs and community programs. The individual and group formats of learning are much more contained and predictable than is the case with the community format, which involves learning on a community-wide basis and is most often denoted by the term, "community development." This format is the one which adult educators have the least experience in organizing and yet, when observed and studied, stands out by way of its distinctive learning process.

There is also a touch of intrigue to community development (or CD as it is familiarity known) as the outcome of a particular CD effort is never predictable. By virtue of the involvement of a community of people in its learning process, CD arouses passion and motivates people to action, often embroiling them in contentious issues. With CD, however, the focus is on the learning process in which the participants are engaged: their success from an adult education point of view is not measured so much by whether the desired outcome is achieved but more by what the participants have learned as a result of the CD process in which they are engaged. This learning might be in terms of their personal capabilities, their knowledge of an issue, their ability to organize for collective action, or their understanding of the power structures which control community decision making.

One of the reasons the community format of learning is not prevalent is that not many educational institutions believe they have a mandate to engage in CD, and in fact not many do, at least not officially. Adult educators working in this area typically do so under the auspices of some other organization. Community development is not usually considered as mainstream adult education by institutional providers, even though much profound learning by adults does occur through their involvement in such experiences.

There are several outstanding examples of community development in Canada, including the oft-mentioned Antigonish Movement, the NewStart Corporations of the 1960s and 1970s dealing with adult basic education, and the National Film Board's Challenge for Change film program dealing with poverty and social change.[50] It is not necessary, however, for the community learning method to be organized on a grand scale. An instructive example comes from the logging community of Lake Cowichan on Vancouver Island, British Columbia.

Lake Cowichan is a stable community with a population of approximately 2,500, with another 4,000 or so persons living within the school district catchment area. The school district employs a director of Adult Education, and this fact is instrumental to the community development events which transpired. Dorothy Clode, the school district's first full-time director of Adult Education, was appointed to this position in 1968. She had moved to Lake Cowichan with her family fifteen years earlier and had immediately become an active and respected member of the community, including as a community organizer and as a teacher of adults. Once employed as director, she set about the task of meeting the community's adult learning needs which could be addressed in one way or another through the resources of the school district's adult education program. To enlarge her understanding of the field to which she was now giving leadership, Clode completed a Masters degree in adult education during the initial two years of her directorship.

As with any initiative there are circumstances which precipitate action. In the case of Lake Cowichan, beginning in 1980 there was a serious, virtually unprecedented, downturn in the economy of the small town, long sustained by an abundant natural resource base. The economic downturn which began in 1980 soon made itself felt, and by 1982 the unemployment rate stood at 60 percent. The impact was immediate and devastating to the townspeople who, under normal circumstances, prided themselves on a self-reliant way of life. The only consolation, if it might be considered as such, was that Lake Cowichan was not suffering alone. The whole provincial economy was similarly caught in the grips of the recession. It is fair to say, however, that rural communities felt the blow much sooner and much harder than the metropolitan centres as rural communities were less insulated economically.

The community needed to come together to discuss the deteriorating situation, and Clode worked diligently at organizing a meeting. At this gathering a number of ideas were suggested, the most significant being to conduct a community survey so as to determine the recession's impact on the area and to identify the needs which required addressing. A committee was formed for this purpose and, going by the acronym, LESS—Lake Economic and Social Survey, completed the survey. One of the needs immediately identified was for a food bank, especially as other communities similarly affected by the economic downturn had responded in this manner. While the need to distrib-

---

[50] See descriptions of these and other programs in J. Roby Kidd & G. Selman (Eds.), *Coming of Age* (Toronto: CAAE, 1978).

ute food to the disadvantaged is not a response unique to the 1980s, the extent to which the whole community—individuals, organizations, businesses, agencies—became involved in this activity, and the organization that was brought to the effort, made food banks an expression of community caring in the face of the crisis at hand during that decade. In the case of Lake Cowichan, it also provided the opportunity for community development to take place.

Organizing and running a food bank requires community involvement and the utilization of many skills. Through the fall of 1982 the LESS committee worked to open a food bank in the basement of an Anglican church. Donations of food, equipment and expertise were forthcoming and by November groceries were being made available to those in economic difficulty at wholesale cost plus 1 percent, with the 1 percent mark-up being placed in a special fund to afford groceries for those in greatest need. To run the food bank—which involves maintaining the dignity of the recipients and offering hope as well as distributing food—unemployed volunteers came forward and, where necessary, Clode organized for training in such skill areas as peer counselling, cashiering, book keeping, and general administration. Within a year of opening the food bank had two hundred registered members, most with dependents. (There was a special concern for the needs of wage earners with dependents as it was recognized that in facing the decision about looking for work elsewhere, they could not so easily pick up and move on, plus the community wanted to keep its social fabric together as much as possible.)

Organizing learners by way of a community development effort is viewed by many as an unconventional approach to adult learning,.despite its faithfulness to the tenets of adult education. Clode recalls with some delight an incident in connection with her food bank experience. A very senior official from the Ministry of Education paid an unscheduled visit to the school district and was surprised to find that Clode, rather than being in her office, was instead at the food bank. As a result of this incident Clode was required to officially account for her food bank involvement.

Identifying the need for the food bank and getting it established were immediate responses to the need. Once this need was met, however, attention could be turned to understanding the root causes of economic dislocation and unemployment, and then taking some further action. In the case of the LESS committee, the subsequent action was to develop a three-year plan for social and economic recovery, including projects the citizens could take on themselves to improve the community's prospects. An Economic Development Committee was formed and set about to bolster the community's belief in itself. With the assistance of funding from the federal government, projects were initiated which enabled the residents to make their community more attractive so as to benefit from the tourism industry. Possibilities for new self-help ventures were explored and, for example, a number of people opened bed-and-breakfast type accommodations.

The recovery process continued, although the community did not return to its earlier situation. One of the lumber mills closed down completely and the other was modernized so as to produce greater output with fewer workers. The job market declined and some skilled tradespeople did move away. Nonetheless, new opportunities were opened up including tourism, the export of log buildings, and "twinning" of Lake Cowichan with a city in Japan (also dependent on the forest industry), which resulted in a number of exchanges between school groups. The outcome of these successful ventures is that the Economic Development Committee continues with its efforts and now reports to the Village Council. Most hopefully, with a return to economic health, the need for a food bank has been eliminated.

When asked to reflect on the food bank initiative, Clode stated that the learning to be had through community development is contained in the fact that people are provided with a learning process, "and it's ultimately the process that they remember."[51] This process brings people together who are in some similar need (in this case unemployment) and enables them to organize for action. Learning is seen as being a major part of the action plan as the people involved must take on the responsibility for doing things for themselves, and new skills and knowledge are required for this. The role of the adult educator is to initially animate the community in coming together and then to facilitate the learning process so that the action plan can be carried out. This learning process is understood to empower people at the very time when they are feeling most helpless by building their self-esteem and providing them with their own source of hope. As Moses Coady, leader of the Antigonish Movement, described it in the title of his book, the participants in a community development project are "masters of their own destiny."

The Learning Materials: Citizens' Forum Study Guides

Learning materials are the various items used by an instructor to assist the learner in the learning task. In the case of independent learning these materials serve the additional purpose of providing direction to the learner through the instructions and suggestions incorporated into the materials. Learning materials can be anything which the instructor chooses, be they everyday objects, workbooks, films, audio/cassette tapes and so on. They can be eclectic in nature such as handouts or be a single source as in the case of a text book.

The most pervasive learning materials in adult education are those prepared in printed form. This is not a reflection of the instructional effectiveness of the printed word over, say, a video tape or a computer program. Rather it is an

---

[51] R. Moss, *Dorothy Clode: Community Educator* (University of B.C., Unpublished M.Ed. Thesis, 1988) p.25.

indication of the comparable cost effectiveness of print for preparation, production and distribution and its versatility for use in teaching. Additionally there is both a history and a tradition to the use of print in education and indeed one of the initial learning tasks of an individual seeking to be educated is learning to both read and write. Thus the printed word retains its preeminence as the means of communicating to learners when learning materials are utilized, which is almost always the case. For this reason what follows is exclusively a consideration of print materials, but this is not intended to discount the value of other types of learning materials, nor to suggest the superiority of print.

The printed word has a significance to society beyond its use in learning situations. Indeed, other than through verbal communication it remains as the most important method of common communication. This explains the emphasis placed on an individual having sufficient literacy skills to function as a member of society and as a citizen. Not surprisingly, much of the work in adult education has been directed at literacy instruction, and this is as true for the present as it is the record of the past. (Interestingly 1990 was International Literacy Year while the previous year, 1989, marked the 90th anniversary of the founding of Frontier College, Canada's outstanding institution dedicated to teaching adult literacy.) Historically speaking, an early move to promote adult learning was by the establishment of reading rooms, as was the case in Y.M.C.A. facilities, and the construction of public libraries, for example with funding provided by the Carnegie foundation.

Printed learning materials have several attributes which make them attractive to both instructor and learner. For one, they most often are a way in which the content of the course is "packaged" and, because these materials typically become the possession of the learner, they are retained and thus available for future reference. They also can be used and shared as determined by the learner. Part of the versatility of printed learning materials is their portability, and they can be accessed at the whim of the learner be it while riding public transportation, relaxing on the beach, or wherever.

There is no prescribed format which governs the development of printed learning materials; rather, it is a combination of the nature of the learning and the learning situation which influence the format. Nature of the learning refers to the expected outcome of the learning, be it in terms of the learner acquiring knowledge, understanding, skills, attitudes, values or interests, or some combination of these.[52] Learning for each requires its own approach; for example, skills learning calls for demonstration of the skill, and in learning materials this suggests illustration work. The learning situation refers to whether the course is given on a credit or non-credit basis. Thus, in the case of an adult

---

[52] M. Knowles, *The Modern Practice of Adult Education* (1980) p.240.

education course which leads to some form of certification, the learning materials typically reflect the course curriculum and are even used directly in the
instruction as in the case of a workbook or text book. Included in this are
those printed materials developed with a learning outcome very much in mind
but which are intended for use in self-directed learning such as self-teaching
publications, "how to" guides and manuals of all sorts. In the case of a
non-credit general interest course the learning materials usually are much less
structured from an instructional point of view—if at all—and the content is
often derived from other sources, for example, magazine articles, reports and
excerpts from books.

In adult education there is a relationship between the learning materials
used in a course or program and the intended learning outcome. This relationship is that the greater the specificity in the learning outcome, as indicated by
the stated goals and objectives, the more specific the learning materials will
need to be. This suggests the necessity in many instances of developing
unique learning materials, as adult education is so often called upon to address particular learning needs. As well, because in adult education there are
innumerable sponsoring agencies, each with their own philosophies, the same
content areas are often approached quite differently. Literacy is a good example of this, with differences noted between agencies engaged strictly in teaching literacy skills and those which teach literacy skills in relation to social
justice issues.

The effectiveness of learning materials can be measured by several criteria,
the foremost of which is how they are experienced by the learner. Contributing criteria include: adherence to principles of good typography, including
page layout and use of graphics; clear organization of content; good composi-
tion; correct grammar and punctuation; appropriate use of vocabulary for the
intended reading level; orientation of the content for adult learners; the extent
to which the content is topical. There are numerous other criteria which could
be identified, but the specific learning situation and the nature of the learning
needs also to be considered.

An outstanding example of effective learning materials is found in the
Citizens' Forum program which was jointly conducted by the CAAE and the
CBC between 1943 and its formal discontinuance in 1966. This example is
chosen for several reasons: the significant number of adults from across the
country who were involved as learners; the topical nature of the content; the
development in the participants of knowledge, understanding, skills, attitudes,
values and interests; the long-standing life of the program; and the ability of
the learning materials to be used in conjunction with two different media,
radio and television.

Citizens' Forum was a national discussion group program which utilized
printed study materials and a weekly broadcast to help Canadians form their

opinions and conclusions on matters of general concern. As the name implies, the objective of Citizens' Forum was citizenship education. The format called for discussion groups to be created under the auspices of a number of community organizations such as university extension departments. The groups would then receive study guide materials related to a weekly radio broadcast (and subsequently also television). The program was operated each year between October and April and the discussion groups would meet weekly to consider the topic which had been introduced earlier in the study guide materials and to then listen to the corresponding broadcast. At the end of each broadcast the groups were invited to forward their conclusions on the topic to the program's provincial offices, and summaries were aired as part of subsequent broadcasts.

In order for the program to be successful in attracting and maintaining a large enrollment of discussion groups, the topics presented needed to be challenging, debatable, and of current interest. Examples from the 1953/54 season include: "Is Professionalism Ruining Canadian Sports?"; "Censorship: Safeguard or Menace?"; "Canada: One Nation?". Equally though, the participants in the discussion groups, in order to derive the greatest benefit from each broadcast, needed to be versed in the points of view pertaining to the topic. This was the purpose of the Citizens' Forum Study Guides.

Each study guide was eight pages in length, and was printed in approximately an 8 x 5 inch size pamphlet. The covers contained information on the Citizens' Forum program, broadcast times, sources of additional information, and suggested discussion questions. The contents developed the topic by way of presenting background information and noting differences in points of view. There are several notable aspects about the study guides as learning materials. The first is in regards to their readability. It was necessary for the guides to be comprehensible by persons of varying educational levels while at the same time providing information and opinions on complex issues. This called for good organization of the material and clarity in the writing. Another aspect was the requirement for objectivity while presenting differing points of view on what were often contentious issues. In order to adequately prepare the participants for the broadcasts, where differing points of view would be represented, the materials had to clearly identify the bases of the differences. The materials also had to cover the topic with sufficient thoroughness that informed discussion could take place. While the nature of the program was such that the study guides were not intended as a treatise on each topic, nonetheless a digest was required. Skilled editing was necessary to meet this requirement in the limited amount of space available. In paying tribute to Isabel Wilson, the study guide editor for the life of the Citizens' Forum program, a former executive director of the CAAE, Alan Thomas, noted, "As journalist, Isabel possessed an unmatched skill in reducing numberless pages of public rhetoric,

mazes of statistics, and bureaucratic argument to multiples of eight pages …
Her pages were full of clear, cogent, and thoughtful argument, designed so
that ordinary people might understand these complex issues, and act with
reference to them."[53] Yet another aspect was how the study guides helped to
focus group discussion. This was the intention of the discussion questions
printed in each pamphlet. Isabel Wilson maintained that formulating the discussion questions was one of the most difficult aspects of the program. For
one, the questions as framed might not have the intended result of stimulating
discussion. For another, a question might be ambiguous, causing the group to
be distracted in attempting to clarify the meaning. Yet another difficulty was
creating questions which were sufficiently open-ended while at the same time
allowing for a conclusion to be reached.

What makes these learning materials particularly noteworthy is the sustained period over which they were produced. This effort is all the more
remarkable in that the materials had to be written with a national audience
very much in mind (excluding French-speaking Canadians, who had a similar
program, Les Idées en Marche, on the CBC French network). Interestingly,
the quality and timeliness of the materials was recognized by individuals and
groups such as university classes who were not registered in the Citizens'
Forum program. The use of the study guides in this informal manner was not
at all discouraged. "The pamphlets make a contribution in the general field of
adult education quite apart from their special use in one project."[54] This is fair
testimonial for any learning material but it doesn't stop there. In a reflection
on Citizens' Forum, Selman comments on how with the passage of time the
study guides become "an increasingly interesting reflection of concerns of
Canadians throughout the life of the project."[55]

The Instructional Technology Employed: Image Projection

Today when one walks into virtually any educational facility an immediate
impression is formed of how the stereotype classroom—desks arranged so as
to face an instructor at the front of the room with a blackboard behind—has
been done over. Instead there are numerous indications that what formerly
was considered a classroom now represents a modern instructional setting.
While a blackboard will likely still cover at least one of the walls, the presence of modular furniture will enable the room to be configured according to
the nature of the instructional activity, and undoubtedly there will also be
present audiovisual equipment such as an overhead projector, a television and

---

[53] A. Thomas, "A Memory of Isabel," in *Learning IV,* 1, p.17.

[54] Wilson et al., *Education in Public Affairs by Radio* (Toronto: CAAE, 1954) p.36.

[55] G. Selman, *Adult Education in Canada: Historical Essays* (Toronto: Thompson Educational, 1995)
     p.169.

video tape deck, and perhaps a cart with other pieces of media equipment on it. These are just the overt indications that the modern instructional setting employs a greater variety of instructional techniques than in earlier times.

The changes noted in the modern instructional setting involve all components of the learning process including the classroom environment, the roles of the students and the teacher, the instructional resources available and the educational philosophy which guides the learning. These changes are summarized by the understanding that assisting individuals to learn has in the past thirty years or so become considerably more systematic than simply a teacher facing a classroom of students and delivering instruction. Three of the most obvious influences in creating a modern instructional setting are: (1) new understandings from research about the learning process, (2) technological innovations in communications equipment which are used for instructional purposes, and (3) less tradition-bound approaches to education. Terminology has also changed in keeping with these developments, and whereas in the past the term "teaching methods" described the approach to instruction, today the term "instructional technology" describes all the considerations available to the teacher to facilitate learning. Gagne describes this instructional technology as including "practical techniques of instructional delivery that systematically aim for effective learning."[56] This description embraces the definition of technology as being scientific knowledge applied to practical uses, and this includes the application of research learning as much as the use of audiovisual equipment.

The developments which have had the most dramatic impact on instruction have for the most part originated outside of the field of education but have been readily applied to it, namely technical innovations in communications. Radio, motion pictures, television and computers are striking examples of this. These developments, which will be referred to as media developments, have had such a profound influence on the providing of instruction that they merit closer consideration, particularly as the hardware associated with these media developments, for example, projectors, televisions, computers, screens, are now commonplace in instructional settings. What follows is a brief sketch of this influence, along with an example of how one of these media developments, image projection, was quickly adopted by adult educators in Canada. It must be reiterated, however, that instructional technology refers to more than the use of media equipment alone, and that this use is but one way that technology, i.e., scientific knowledge, has affected the total process of learning and teaching.

---

[56] R. Gagne (Ed.), "Introduction," in *Instructional Technology: Foundations* (New Jersey: Lawrence Erlbaum Associates, 1987) p.7.

The media developments that have occurred in the instructional setting (the successor to the classroom) impact adult education as much as they do the formal educational system. There are several reasons for this. For one, much adult education takes place in the same facilities and so there is an obvious exposure of adult education to these developments along with the opportunity to take advantage of them. For another, much adult education takes place in settings where media innovation is very much the culture, i.e., training for business and industry. Yet another reason is that many of the learning needs which adult education has been called upon to meet have required employing various technological and novel approaches, and adult educators have been forthcoming in this regard. The Farm Radio Forum program, with its national use of radio, is an example of this ingenuity.

There are, however, aspects of adult education that have impeded an awareness and utilization of these media developments within adult education. For example, a significant number of adult education instructors are only part-time: they have occupations other than instructing to which they devote their major attention. Further, many adult education instructors have had no training in instruction, or if they have, it likely represents more of an orientation than training. There are also budget and logistical reasons which often mitigate against the use of new instructional media, as in the case of the programs that take place in settings other than educational facilities and which therefore likely require either renting or transporting equipment, and this can pose difficulties. Nonetheless, because the purpose of instruction is to bring about learning, and developments in media are able to be readily utilized to enhance the learning situation, adult educators should be aware of these developments and be able to take advantage of them wherever possible. In this way they can be more discriminating in their instructional efforts.

There are various terms used to describe the use of media equipment in instructional settings such as instructional media, audiovisual equipment, and media technology. As noted, however, the term instructional technology is used today to note the systematic approach to providing instruction, and is not limited to describing the use of media equipment. At the same time, because developments in media have been so remarkable, it is helpful to trace these developments so as to gain an understanding of their contribution to the current state of instructional technology.

As education for children became organized in the 1800s, one of the first efforts made to improve instruction was to introduce objects which complimented the oral and written instruction. This was intended to assist in the teaching of more abstract ideas by enabling the teacher to use objects to provide meaning to things abstract. The term "object teaching" was used to describe this approach. In the latter part of the nineteenth century, and stimulated by the advent of photography, the first pieces of visual equipment were introduced, the most remembered of which was the "magic lantern." This was a device which, by way of a lamp and a lens, projected an image contained on a glass slide onto a screen so as to enlarge the image. These pieces of equipment began what was called the "visual instruction" movement, which included static visuals such as maps, wall charts and globes. This movement quickly advanced with the introduction of new projection equipment such as the motion film projector. Paralleling these developments were those in the audio field, including sound recordings and phonographs as well as radio. A quantum leap occurred when audio was synchronized with the visual such that the visual movement now became known as the audiovisual movement. Motions pictures, for example, were now referred to as the "talkies."

Use of audiovisual productions was spurred on by the outbreak of World War II as extensive use was made of film for purposes of both military training and propaganda. In peacetime, film became very instrumental as a medium for communicating culture, and in the instructional setting, the increasing availability of films made them a popular aid to instruction. Not only were they capable of stimulating students by their portrayal of reality, as in the earlier case of object teaching, but their range of subject matter was much more extensive and animated. Another major development which impacted on education was the introduction of television in the 1950s. Television technology has continued to be advanced such that much of its earlier unrealized promise for educational purposes is now being achieved, particularly with the use of space satellites and cable networks for transmitting broadcast signals, and dedicated educational channels used by educational agencies. The next innovation of spectacular proportions to be introduced into the instructional setting was the computer, and especially because of its capability to be highly interactive, and even personal, with the learner. Other innovations have followed which are largely hybrids on earlier advances, including video and aspects of telecommunications such as teleconferencing.

By the 1970s the developments in communications were having such an effect on instruction that the various pieces of audiovisual equipment could no longer be considered as ancillary in the instructional situation. This fact, coupled with continued investigation into the learning process and an expanded theoretical understanding that resulted, led to the introduction of the term instructional technology to replace the concentration on audiovisual alone. Instructional technology was intended to describe the "systematic way of designing, carrying out, and evaluating the total process of learning and teaching."[57]

---

[57] R. Reiser, "Instructional Technology: A History," in R. Gagne (Ed.), *Instructional Technology: Foundations*, p.19.

Image projection has an important place in the instructional technology of adult education. Today there are several types of image projection equipment commonly available to the adult educator, such as 35mm slide projectors, 16mm film projectors, and overhead projectors. More recently there has been introduced video technology for displaying not only prepared video materials but also footage created in the instructional setting by the participant and instructor. Another equipment item, liquid crystal display units, are coupled with overhead projectors in order to display information from computer screens. It is interesting to see how these and other media equipment have over time influenced the instructional format in adult education.

An early use of image projection equipment was the stereopticon, more familiarly known as the magic lantern. Particularly in the period when many university extension departments were delivering programs to rural areas, the magic lantern, as its name suggests, was a popular feature of the presentations because of it ability to illustrate the things being discussed. This occurrence has been delightfully recorded from personal experience by Ned Corbett in his book, *We Have With Us Tonight*.[58] The advent of motion pictures, especially when sound was added, resulted in widespread use of this medium in adult education. The establishment of the National Film Board in 1939 gave special impetus to the use of film. In the rural areas, where at that time over half of Canada's population lived, a projectionist with film, projector and screen would travel a "film circuit," showing various educational films. Subsequently, when projection equipment became more prevalent, film councils and film libraries were established throughout the country to distribute films.

Being able to project images enabled adult educators to present more stimulating sessions and to use new formats. The information communicated in this fashion was easier for the learner to retain as it appealed to the two dominant senses of sight and hearing. As well, the information and ideas which film was able to capture and communicate could be complex while still being comprehensible, as the learner was able to see real life situations with cause and effect relationships. Discussion groups could be formed around the content of the film presentation, particularly as the content had been developed with a specific purpose and hence discussion points could be prepared to suit the audience's interests. The adult educator, rather than having to be the subject expert, was able to facilitate the discussion.

In the period prior to television, film projection necessitated that learners (participants) come together for viewing. For this reason film was an excellent medium for promoting group discussion. The advent of the television changed this as it now possible for adults to remain at home and privately view televised programs. This new option, while convenient, was no substitute for

[58] E.A. Corbett, *We Have With Us Tonight* (Toronto: Ryerson Press, 1957).

viewing and discussing in a group. Thus while television increased individual viewing opportunity, it also had the consequence of eliminating the educational process of substantiating individual learning through discussion. Of course film continued to be an important medium. However, the introduction of the video format, including large screen viewing, has become an increasingly convenient substitute to film during the 1980s.

For the adult educator today there is now a greater range of choices involved when selecting the image projection most suited to the learning program, and choosing requires an understanding of the complete process of instructional technology.

Power Dynamics: The Labour Movement

By D'Arcy Martin[59]

In adult education, respect for the learner is a basic guiding principle. This means that the educator is encouraged, and often exhorted, to act democratically, to work from people's lived experience rather than simply lecturing them. And in social movements like unions, participants simply demand respect, and hold the educator immediately accountable in a way unimaginable in a college, university or other formal environment.

Workers often run for union office because they are critical of the incumbents or impatient with passivity among their fellow members. This means that the people who show up in union courses usually have definite views and the spunk to express them. To do adult education in the labour movement, then, is to deal with an empowered and articulate part of the working class, often newly awakened to the potential of a collective, enlightened self-interest as a path of personal development.

For union participants, the goal in a short (two-to-five-day) intensive course is usually very practical and workplace-based. They may want to know how to identify and remove a hazardous substance from the workplace, or how to write out a proper grievance, or how to calm an angry fellow worker. For the educators, their goal is usually tied to convictions about justice, a sense of the values of fairness and dignity for workers on the job and in the society. For the union as an organization, the goals usually include building loyalty to the collective, and even to the incumbent leaders, as well as encouraging people to take on broader responsibilities within the structure. At times,

---

[59] This the second of three sections on adult education in the labour movement written by D'Arcy Martin for this edition of the book. See also Chapters 2 and 12.

these goals are shared by all, but often it is the tension among them which gives energy and colour to the program itself.

An example would be the activity called "Politics of Furniture," which explores non-verbal dynamics. This evolved as a part of the Facing Management course, taught across Canada's labour movement since 1981, which aims to equip union representatives to better understand management thinking and develop strategies to respond to workplace change. During the course, participants engage in role plays of labour-management meetings, and the issue of "body language" is usually brought up. The course leader needs to judge whether a change of pace will improve the energy levels. If so, the course leader might begin by moving in close to a couple of participants, essentially invading their space bubble to the point where they become uncomfortable. By inviting them to say how they feel, the course leader essentially invites them to name and hence resist a use of power. This opens the exploration of how physical layout can affect the power dynamics of meetings, both with management and within the union. Alternatively, the course leader might move to the back of the room, take a seat, and invite people to discuss "what's wrong with this picture." This leads easily into discussion of how managers use desks, chairs and other tools to establish their power in meetings.

This exploration is best done in a way that brings out people's "streetsmart" knowledge of intimidation tactics in a way that validates the people and encourages them to have some fun. By asking participants to describe the course leader's actions, it moves critical scrutiny off them and makes the course leader "uncomfortable." This can be deepened by asking if people have noticed any other ways that room layout and furniture have affected the course leader's authority/power during the week. These can be recorded on a flip chart without comment. Then people can be asked to look at the items already listed in regard to the course and to describe ways that these same tactics have been or could be used in their encounters with management in the workplace. This should generate some funny stories about past experiences, which people can be asked to act out in a short skit.

At this point, the activity moves into a "stop drama," where other participants can interrupt such a skit and propose different ways that the interaction could be played out. For example, they might suggest moving a steward's chair closer to the manager's desk, or having a steward stand throughout the meeting, or having a second person writing quickly to transcribe the manager's comments. These and other tools of non-verbal power playing can be exposed.

The catch in this for the course leader, however, is that once participants have a common language for naming such power plays, they are likely to use it in the course. In other words, the reward for doing this activity well is that the course leader will be challenged. It is apparently perverse, unless one pauses to think that the job of the labour movement is to build resisters to the arbitrary use of power. This exercise, by exposing "under the table" forms of manipulation, has the effect of neutralizing these forms even in the classroom. From this point on in the course, when the course leader sits on the desk or moves among the participants, or uses markers and chalk to emphasize a point, or stands with the window light behind their head, he or she should simply expect a participant to say "Aha, gotcha, you're using non-verbal cues to enhance your authority." Indeed, it is precisely such a challenge that would indicate successful teaching of the concept. From this point on, participants will see desks and chairs and lights differently, and hopefully will use this understanding both to neutralize any intimidation by management and to improve access to union events like monthly meetings by all members. By moving to tips for using space democratically, a course leader can also model inclusive behaviour in a way that doesn't challenge directly any existing power hierarchies within a local union, but gently surrounds those participants who may feel tense and insecure about the discussion.

In a movement based on winning respect in the workplace, any tendency to "talk down" to participants would be met with resistance in a form that is vocal, angry and organized! Consistently, activities like "politics of furniture" have worked to unveil power dynamics in the workplace and in the union, with the result that it encourages the most vocal participants to exercise their power to re-shape agendas and positions, rather than in passive-aggressive undermining of the course leader.

In such a context, much of the "program planning" process used by institutional providers of adult education simply won't work. The pattern of planning, design and facilitation is much closer to a popular education perspective.[60] This means maintaining respect for participants' experience, posing questions in a way that encourages critical dialogue, and committing to share the individual and collective consequences of putting the learning into action.

In the courses themselves lies the richness of group dynamics and spontaneous dialogue. Much of what happens is shaped on the spot by the questions and debates that arise. Like any democratic adult educator, a unionist needs to keep basic objectives in mind rather than sticking rigidly to an outline. Hence, if a discussion of workplace health starts on a particular toxin, and a participant has had experience of identifying and removing that toxin from the workplace, the agenda will wait until the story has been shared.

---

[60] See Rick Arnold, Bev Burke, Carl James, D'Arcy Martin and Barb Thomas, *Educating for a Change*. (Toronto: Doris Marshall Institute and Between the Lines Publishing, 1991), p.34.

Indeed, the course itself may be in response to the discovery of a toxin, or an incident involving harassment in the workplace, or a heated round of collective bargaining. In these cases, the course is not publicized in a course schedule like continuing education programs at a school board, college or university. It is requested in addition to the regular "tool" courses, usually in response to a heavy-handed initiative from management. Hence the account-ability of the educator is immediate: if the course goes badly, the educator cannot "fail" the participants, as in formal schooling. Instead, the participants would have complained to the national leadership of the union about the educator's failure to meet their needs in a time of need.

Labour education, then, is highly practical in orientation. It is often de-signed in reaction to particular problems. Its outcomes rarely advance an individual participant's career, but rather equip that person better to contribute voluntarily to collective progress. And its power dynamics are such that the educator must respect participants, not merely as an ethical guideline but as a practical imperative.

Speculation on Future of Elements

One way of understanding the past is to view time periods as eras. Most often eras are distinguished on the basis of phenomena such as major events, charismatic leaders, and prevailing ideas. The examples of elements of pro-gram design provided above can each be seen to be products of their own eras, however the particular era may be distinguished. For example, the founding of Frontier College by the Reverend Alfred Fitzpatrick was part of the era of the social gospel while the creation of the Saskatchewan community college system was part of the era of expansion in provincial post-secondary education systems. What one can infer from this is that adult educators, when faced with novel situations within particular eras, have managed to create program designs which address these situations. In some cases the situations have been adverse, such as the Lake Cowichan Food Bank. In others the situation has been opportunistic, as in the case of collaboration among agen-cies. Whichever, adult educators have been able to be alive to the moment: they have made a contribution within the context of particular eras. The ques-tion arises as to the continued ability on the part of adult educators to respond to contemporary eras with imaginative program designs.

Certainly there continue to be easily identifiable eras which call for under-standing through adult education. The decade of the 1980s, for instance, was an era of national crisis as evidenced in the constitutional struggles. The 1990s are likely to be viewed as an era where issues of quality of life are seen as fundamental to society's continued functioning, for example, the environ-ment, the redefined family, and cross-cultural understanding. If adult education is to be involved with these issues in a significant way then new program designs need to be found. Is this possible?

There is no question that it is possible to create new program designs to address the modern era. Nothing stands in the way. There are, however, shifts occurring in how adult education is currently patterned in Canada, and these shifts will exert influences on the generation of new program designs. Six shifts are noted here, and there are undoubtedly others.

(1) The Decline of Nationwide Adult Education Programming

Canada as a nation has grown more complex, and one of the notable outcomes has been an increasingly regional and provincial focus on national matters. Even national institutions such as the CBC reflect this fact in their organizational structure and their program delivery. For adult educators it is difficult to believe that in the coming decade nationwide programming such as the CAAE's forum programs could be so readily conducted. The national preoccupation, even at the constitutional level, has been to emphasize regional differences at the expense of national commonality. Within the regions there is increasing suspicion, even disdain, for national initiatives.

(2) The Spectacular Expansion of Provincial Post-Secondary Educational Systems

Beginning in the 1960s and continuing even to the present, provincial governments have developed their post-secondary educational systems as a strategy for ensuring the skills and knowledge necessary for economic and social well-being. This has reduced the influence of the voluntary sector by overshadowing—and even overtaking—many of that sector's adult education efforts. It has also significantly widened the adult education network such that organizing for co-operative programming is made more complex. Whereas, for example, the extension departments of universities were once the adult education contact points in each province (albeit informal), presently many provinces have more than one university and several colleges and institutes as well as a government department or ministry of continuing education.

(3) The Reorientation of Adult Education Values

Adult education has followed suit with society generally in being more comfortable in expressing its value orientation in secular rather than spiritual terms. This reorientation is reflected in the observation that adult education is no longer a movement born of the social gospel but instead is now an enterprise. While this observation is not by any means absolute, few would deny the influence of entrepreneurialism on adult education today. Unquestionably this influence has been forced onto many adult education operations, but adult educators have by and large adapted to the new business practices and concerned themselves more than ever before with the "bottom line."

(4) Episodic Approach to Participation

How adults perceive and use time, and how educational agencies organize activity for adults, has brought about an episodic approach to participation, i.e., participation in courses or sessions which are distinct and of short duration. For so many adults a telling consequence of living in an era which is affluent, highly mobile, and full of competing opportunities—to identify but three indicators—is the necessity of organizing their lives on the basis of a timetable. Such organization means there is only so much time which adults are prepared to make available for continuing education while also attending to other facets of their lives. Educational agencies are cognizant of needing to organize activities which can be fitted into the general patterns of adult living so as to facilitate participation. What has resulted, over time, is a way of arranging adult education into conventional time frames, for example, courses and sessional terms, where the conclusion of the course brings about the completion of a predetermined amount of instruction. This approach is very much reflected in those adult education programs where fees are charged.

The episodic approach to participation is also a function of how adult education is packaged for marketing purposes. With numerous educational agencies involved in providing adult education, and indeed being in competition with one another, this packaging and marketing have developed this episodic approach to a high level, as evidenced by the seasonal catalogues of continuing education courses provided by school boards, colleges, universities, community centres and other agencies.

Decision making by adults on the use of their time is a matter of personal priorities and circumstances. In this regard it is interesting to note how the new learning options of open learning, distance education and independent study are further recognition of how difficult it is for adults to appropriate their time, even with the aid of timetables, and how adult education must come up with innovative scheduling accommodations. As a society, however, we may have reached the point where the episodic approach is proving to be inefficient, and where schemes such as paid educational leave and recurrent education are required to allow for sufficient time for substantive learning to take place.

(5) More Individualized Learning

Two developments have had a profound impact on determining the location where adults engage in learning. The first in a chronological perspective was the automobile. This ready means of transportation allowed adults to travel from their homes to attend a night school, a community centre or wherever a course was conducted. The underlying notion was that people with a certain learning need or interest would join with others who had a similar need or interest and become a group for the purpose of learning. The second development, advances in electronic media, quite reversed this notion of personal mobility. Now it was possible for the learner to stay at home and have his or her learning need met through distance education, even though there was no greater distance involved than before. Thus the traditional arrangement of learning with reference to a group of learners has been undermined. Nowadays an individual's circumstances and inclination can determine when learning will be undertaken, not schedules and requirements. This option of learning on an individual basis is not likely to eliminate learning in a group. However, the trend is there and is further spurred on by the new administrative arrangements as part of the concept of open learning.

(6) Specialization in Adult Education as a Field of Practice

The breadth and depth of adult education has always meant there were particular areas of focus in practice, as noted in Bryson's five functional areas of adult education: remedial, occupational, relational, liberal, political. With these areas being increasingly taken up and even dominated by public educational institutions, and with even larger enrollments, there has been a definite segmenting of the practice of adult education. This trend is quite evident in the array of associations which have been created along these same lines, for example, the Canadian Association for Distance Education, the Canadian Association for Community Education, and the Movement for Canadian Literacy, to name but three.[61] As the field continues to grow, and as adult learning needs are made more divisible and described in more finite terms, such segmentizing will correspondingly increase. There are several likely outcomes of this. Adult education, in order to be comprehensible to ministries of education and to administrators, will need to become more structured along both administrative and content lines. This in turn will have implications for staffing where adult educators' working arrangements will become the subject of negotiation by a staff association or a trade union. Of course, not all adult educators will be employed by large organizations which might be structured along these lines, but even this distinction will further segment the field.

Whatever might be the result of these and other shifts in adult education practice, there is no question but that programs will continue to be offered and that adults will continue to participate. And because adults will always have learning needs to meet and have discriminating interests to satisfy, programs will need to be developed which are perceptive of these needs and interests, and which reflect them in their elements of program design.

---

[61] G. Selman, "Specialization or Balkanization: Organizations of Adult Educators," in *Adult Education in Canada: Historical Essays*.

7

Public Policy Formation

The last several decades have been extremely active in terms of the development of public policy relating to adult education. This has been true of both the federal and provincial levels of government. It is clear that policy makers who have been aware of social and technological changes in society have seen that there have been urgent reasons why a corresponding response was required in order to provide opportunities for adults to learn the things they need to know. At the federal level, there have been several major pieces of legislation concerned with technical and vocational education, generally aimed at the upgrading of the capabilities of the Canadian work force. Federal action has also been taken in areas such as literacy, English and French as a second language, broadcasting policy and health education, to name but several examples. Provincial governments have to some extent been led by federal actions, but as well they have at times acted with vigour in such areas as the creation of new post-secondary institutions (most notably the college systems); the creation of educational broadcasting systems in some provinces; the expansion of various other forms of distance education; and the utilization of public policy to support and encourage adult learning in other ways (for instance, the Further Education Councils and Community School policies in Alberta). It must also be observed that public policy in the last two decades has had a limiting or harmful effect on certain aspects of the field as well, as funds have been available for vocational and technical training and for some academic education, but have been severely curtailed in other areas.

All of these developments have taken place at a time when the need for continued learning in an age of ever-accelerating change was an undisputed fact.[1] What sense, then, can be made of the place of adult education in Canadian society from a public policy perspective?

---

[1] *Employment and Immigration Canada, Learning A Living in Canada*, vols. 1 & 2 (Toronto: Minis-

The diverse nature of adult education once again mitigates against the possibility of a clear depiction, in this case in terms of public policy. Adult education is not organized into a manageable system, nor is it directed by any central authority. Furthermore the matter of just what constitutes public policy itself requires elaboration and qualification as public policy is but one means by which government can take action in any given area. Added to both these qualifiers is the significant factor in Canada's federal structure of the sensitive interplay between the realities of constitutional jurisdiction and government initiative, and matters of adult education policy just happen to fall right in the middle of these two realities. The net result is that in Canada the attempt to understand adult education as indicated by public policy is not straightforward, but it is a matter of piecing together in each of Canada's legislative jurisdictions the situation as it relates to specific areas of adult education.

Because of this uneven nature to public policy development in Canada regarding adult education the subject will be presented across two chapters. This chapter will first present a theoretical understanding to public policy and its formation. Accordingly it begins with an examination of what is meant by the term public policy and then provides a framework for analyzing the process of public policy development. As a means of integrating this theoretical understanding within the Canadian political context, the example of public policy favouring adult literacy is then used as a case study. To conclude the chapter there is a review of international calls regarding public policy and adult education. Chapter 7 reviews the public policy actions which have been taken in Canada at both the federal and provincial levels. To help bring an international perspective to the Canadian situation brief descriptions are also provided of the policy situation in three countries: Sweden, Tanzania and China. To begin, then, we will look at what is meant by public policy.

The Meaning of Public Policy

Generally speaking, the term "public policy" suggests a specific undertaking by government on behalf of the public. In its most forthright expression such an undertaking is made to the people through legislation, thereby ensuring that the undertaking can only be amended or withdrawn by way of a change to the legislation. In reality, however, this is only one form in which public policy can be made. Other forms are often much less explicit, and neither their development nor their pronouncement are necessarily done in a particularly public manner. Examples of this include the specific regulations developed so as to make operational the intent of the more general legislation and the in-camera deliberations and decisions of a cabinet, the executive

ter of Supplies and Services, 1983).

council of government. It is quite often the case that government policy must be inferred from the perceived actions of government as opposed to looking only to its formal expression as communicated by legislation. Several reasons have been advanced for this:

1. the public utterances of politicians do not always reflect the intent of the government

2. statutes are normally cast in rather general language and typically include aspects of permissiveness or provide discretionary powers to various operating levels

3. the general language of a statute is made operational by rules and regulations or orders-in-council which do not require the assent of the legislature

4. the interpretation of statutes and regulations by civil servants may or may not be in accord with a government's intent.[2]

Another difficulty with the term public policy is its implicit suggestion that not only are policies developed publicly but that they are also developed necessarily in the public interest. This suggestion is challenged by Cassidy, who suggests that "many of the policies which are made for the public are made by private rather than public interests. In fact, it is frequently the case that public policy is neither developed in public nor by the public. Public policy is often public only in the sense that it is something which happens to the public."[3] According to Cassidy, when regarding public policy it is necessary to consider whose interests are being served by that policy, and why that might be the case.

A further difficulty with public policy is that we must in many instances look to the absence of an explicit public policy, in whatever form, in order to conclude what the government's policy is regarding a certain issue. This situation is common in the case of adult education where in many jurisdictions there is no specific public policy governing adult education. This does not indicate that publicly provided adult education is taking place outside of a legal framework but rather that the laws which govern and enable it are general rather than specific.[4] The government, while not wanting to forbid adult education, at the same time is not wanting to give it a statutory status equal to that of compulsory youth education which would thereby commit government to a significant level of public expenditure. Using the situation in British Columbia as an example, the legislation governing the grade school

---

[2] J. Ellis, "Government Policies," in I. Mugridge and D. Kaufman, *Distance Education in Canada* (London: Croom Helm, 1986) p.27.

[3] F. Cassidy, "Public Policy Development: A Learning Approach," *Journal of the Alberta Association for Continuing Education*, 13 (1985) p.13.

[4] Ellis makes this point in the case of distance education. J. Ellis, "Government Policies," p.28.

system, School Act (1989), allows for school boards to provide adult education by virtue of Section 94 subsection 8 which says, "A board may permit a person who is older than school age to attend an educational program in accordance with any terms and conditions specified by the board." Such permissive, but not obligatory, wording reinforces the oft-made suggestion of adult education's marginal status.

To this point the consideration of public policy has focussed on policy and regulations enacted by a legislative body, i.e., a provincial legislature, a territorial assembly or the national government. There is also the policy developed by a lesser authority, for example, a school board, and by individual providers, for example, a university extension department, to provide guidelines for administrators as they confront situations, either in the present or in anticipation of the future. Policies made at these levels are also important to take into account when considering the policy provision for adult education. The above example of British Columbia demonstrates this, as the general provincial policy delegates the specific policy to the local school board level. Thus the term public policy is surrounded by a degree of ambiguity, and this situation is summed up in a review of educational policies in the Province of Saskatchewan:

> Broadly defined, policy includes all written documents, statements of philosophy, customary practices (of the Department of Education), and all statutes and regulations regarding administrative procedures (followed by Department officials). Those policies reflected in statutes and regulations have legal implications. Others are largely intended to guide education officials in carrying out duties derived from statutes and regulations ... Formal policy found in legislation and statutes is difficult to read. Less formal policy is not consolidated and is not widely understood or easily communicated.[5]

In this chapter the consideration of public policy will for the most part be kept to its expression in statutory form.

Education and the State

Having reviewed the difficulties in specifying what exactly is public policy it is necessary to step back further yet and take a philosophical point of view about public policy and adult education. In doing so it is necessary to consider all of education as provided by the state, not just adult education. The question is one of determining what the nature of the relationship is between education and society, and appreciating the crucial interdependence that exists between the two. It then becomes possible to see the need for government, through its allocation of resources, to provide direction to the education sys-

---

[5] Minister's Advisory Committee, *Saskatchewan Education: Its Programs and Policies* (Regina: Saskatchewan Education, 1984) p.7.

tem. Once the need for this direction giving is apparent, it becomes further possible to distil the place of adult education within the total provision of state supported education.

Basic to any society is the need to ensure its survival. In most societies this basic need is advanced to a higher order of existence than merely surviving, and in the case of societies governed by democratic ideology, they additionally strive to uphold the principles of democracy. These principles promote the rights of the citizen within society, and this is seen as being the most just means by which people should be governed. In such societies the educational system, with its ability to inculcate beliefs, values and attitudes as well as knowledge, is a primary instrument of government for ensuring the society's continued vital and democratic existence. Much of this is evidenced in the curriculum prescribed for use in the grade school system where socializing students in the dominant values held by the society is as much an emphasis as is the developing of individual intellect. (It also explains why curriculum development is controlled centrally and why grade school attendance is compulsory.) By way of its resource allocation to the educational system, government assumes a controlling interest in the results produced by the system.

At the same time the educational system in a democratic society, while not an independent entity, exercises a degree of autonomy from government and is able in turn to exert influence on the state. This comes about by virtue of the fact that the educational system, and particularly at the higher levels, is the predominant creator and disseminator of the knowledge and skills essential to the continued survival of the society. It is the educational system which has the ultimate ability to respond to circumstances which threaten the continued well-being of the state. (The exception to this is a military threat which calls for a military response.) Because the state exists in an ever-changing world, especially in post-industrial societies there is the need at a minimum to maintain the standard of living which its citizens have come to expect while at the same time making the significant adjustments brought about by changes in the technical, economic and social environments. It is the educational system that plays the crucial part, on behalf of the state, in mediating between the necessary changes and the ability of citizens to respond, thereby making the adjustments possible. An example of this is the Free Trade Agreement between Canada and the United States which has as one of its consequences the exposure of a number of Canadian industries to stiff competition now that protective tariff barriers have been removed. The education system has become involved in at least two ways, the first being the educating of industry managers to new manufacturing and marketing strategies and the second being the retraining of workers who find themselves displaced.

In identifying the mediating role of the educational system it is important to note that the system serves the learning needs not only of the state but also of individual citizens. Free-thinking citizens in a democratic society pursue their learning motivated by personal needs and interests, and these may well be distinct from the specific needs of the state. This is not a discordant situation in a democratic society, although resource allocation by government may be perceived as skewing the balance between individual and state interests if individual interests are thought of as being compromised or even ignored. Thus, for example, government might make large sums available for vocational education, and even provide tuition subsidies, while not supporting at all programs for older workers on retirement preparation.

In Canada and indeed most post-industrialized countries, the educational system has had to make adjustments consistent with changes brought about in the society in order that it better serve the needs of the state. The most pivotal of these adjustments by the educational system is responding to the fact that individuals need to continue their education beyond what was once considered sufficient, i.e., beyond youth and now into adulthood. Thomas identifies two principal sources for this adjustment, one intellectual and the second practical.[6]

The intellectual source is identified as being the report of the International Commission on the Development of Education (Faure Commission) entitled *Learning to Be* and published in 1972.[7] The Commission had been established by UNESCO to review the results of the huge expenditures in education undertaken by most governments in the world since the 1950s. Thomas notes the Report arrived at the conclusion that it had not been a mistake for countries to have invested heavily in education as a means of development but that it had been an error to concentrate the expenditures on the education of the young. According to Thomas, the Report "laid to rest one of the most cherished illusions of the West, that you can bring about positive and controlled change in a society by concentrating on the education of the young."[8]

The practical source identified by Thomas stems from the discovery not only by governments but also by large organizations that "even for the maintenance of their societies and organizations, they are increasingly dependent upon learning, that is, upon learning undertaken by increasing numbers and types of individuals in their populations, over longer periods of their lifetimes—learning which cannot be accomplished by means of exposure to educational resources in the first twenty years of life."[9]

---

[6] A. Thomas, "Learning in Society—A Discussion Paper," in *Learning in Society: Toward a New Paradigm*, UNESCO Occasional Paper No. 51 (Ottawa: Canadian Commission for UNESCO, 1985) p.17.

[7] International Commission for the Development of Education, *Learning to Be* (London: Harrap, 1972).

[8] A. Thomas, "Learning in Society—A Discussion Paper," p.17.

[9] Ibid., p.18.

Distinction between Learning and Education

From the above it is possible to recognize how the relationship between education and society is both essential and dynamic, and that the instrument of education is seen, by some at any rate, to extend to the education of adults as well as youth. There is one further implication to be drawn relating to education and society and that is the distinction between learning and education. Learning is understood as being an intellectual process within the capacity of the individual, an activity described by Thomas as being "voluntary and uncoercible."[10] Education, by contrast, is an organized way of providing for learning to take place, as in the case of a school system or an industrial training centre. This distinction is important when considering public policy in that the state can legislate and regulate education but it cannot do so with learning. This is evidenced in Canada by the fact that significant numbers of students drop out of high school upon, or shortly after, reaching the age where education is no longer compulsory. In terms of the formal curriculum, these persons have chosen to discontinue their education. There may be certain skills or knowledge, however, which these same individuals will subsequently need to learn (or relearn) in order to function effectively, and it is likely only through the opportunity to subsequently continue with their education that this learning will be made possible. Thus while the distinction between learning and education is easily made, managing the interaction between the two is considerably more difficult both for the state and for the individual citizen. The difficulty exists for the state in being able to provide educational opportunity for those times when a citizen has a learning need. For the individual citizen the difficulty lies in being able to access educational opportunity when a particular learning need arises. The appropriate balance is exceedingly difficult to maintain, and it is not easy to determine just what constitutes "appropriate." Of interest to adult educators is the fact that much of this managing needs to occur with persons who are beyond their years of formal education, as this is the purview of adult education.

In Canada the state's involvement in the management of education beyond the formal educational system, i.e., with continuing education, is not a new phenomenon, although particularly during and since World War II its involvement has intensified in response to military and economic threats. The response has been by way of identifiable public policy, and in order to understand why and how these responses were developed it is helpful to have available an analytic framework.

---

[10] A. Thomas, "Government and Adult Learning," in F. Cassidy and R. Faris (Eds.), *Choosing Our Future: Adult Education and Public Policy in Canada* (Toronto: OISE Press, 1987) p.109.

Analytical Framework for Public Policy Formation

It has already been noted that the rendering of public policy is often difficult to discern. This situation is made even more difficult by the fact that public policy formation is sometimes done for reasons that have as much to do with political expediency as with providing good government. Because of this situation, a framework for analyzing the formation of public policy must necessarily be general so as to accommodate the innumerable factors and interests which influence the developmental process. The following framework is put forward as a means of analyzing individual public policies and also of comparing one with another.

Four stages can be identified when analyzing the formation of public policy. These stages are:

1. the precursor circumstances which give rise to a call for a public policy response, and which lead to …

2. the development process of a public policy, which leads to …

3. the implementation of a public policy, which is followed by …

4. the review of a public policy in light of subsequent circumstances.

As noted earlier, public policy, however it is made public, is an indication of a deliberate action on the part of government. Similarly, the absence of a public policy can be construed as a deliberate action on the part of government, in this case one of deliberate inaction which in effect maintains the status quo or which allows developments to occur unimpeded by public policy. To account for this possibility the above framework must be amended in stages 2, 3 and 4 so as to indicate that public policy can be seen in terms of either deliberate action or deliberate inaction. Thus:

1. the precursor circumstances which give rise to a call for a public policy response, and which lead to …

2. the development process of a public policy, which leads to … *or the denial of a process.*

3. the implementation of a public policy which is followed by … *or the refusal or failure to implement a public policy, which is perhaps followed by …*

4. the review of a public policy in light of subsequent circumstances … *or a review of the continued ignoring of the precursor circumstances, or the circumstances as they have since developed.*

Stage 1

By way of elaboration, at stage one there are always innumerable circumstances in a society which need addressing or which call for redressing. To the extent that these circumstances are able to garner sufficient attention and support, an issue may develop which is not only recognized by an advocacy group but is also acknowledged by the government. At stage one, however, the focus is on the garnering of sufficient attention and support for the circumstances. The cause of the modern women's movement, beginning in the 1960s, is an example of circumstances coalescing into an issue. It is important to also note that it is often the case where government itself is the body which identifies the precursor circumstances and initiates the call for a public policy response. The move by the Conservative government to implement free trade between Canada and the United States in light of global economic trends illustrates this point.

Stage 2

At stage two the response to a call for public policy lies squarely with the government. It is here that the government chooses either to acknowledge or ignore the circumstances. This is evidenced by the government either engaging in a public policy development process or denying such a process. The focus is on process in that government, in choosing to acknowledge the circumstances and engage in a public policy development process, may elect to make the process as public or private as it wishes. The appointment of Royal Commissions is an example of a public process which is intended to encourage broad public participation. Most often, however, public input into policy development is controlled or even non-existent. Democratically elected governments are in a position to decide whether public input is required or whether the input as supplied by the elected representatives of the people is sufficient. Political considerations frequently influence a government's decisions in this regard. Regardless of the extent of participation by the public in the policy development process, the next stage awaits.

Stage 3

Ideally, of course, at this third stage public policy flows out of the development process. The government selects what it believes to be the most prudent course of action as identified by the developmental process and begins on that course. However by virtue of engaging in a policy development process the government does not necessarily obligate itself to take action, whether by way of legislative enactment, order-in-council or other methods at its disposal. Indeed one of the strategies employed by government to defuse an issue is to appoint a study into it as part of the policy development process, and to then ignore or only selectively implement the findings of the study. Adult education has fallen victim to this strategy on more than one occasion.

Stage 4

The fourth stage indicates that a particular public policy need not last forever, and is reviewed and evaluated in terms of its effectiveness in addressing or redressing the original precursor circumstances. Similarly, in the event the government initially chooses to ignore the precursor circumstances or subsequent circumstances, it may want to review that decision if the issue still exists or has gathered strength. The situation of industry despoiling the environment illustrates an issue the government was able to ignore for a considerable period of time, but because of growing public concern it has now accepted environmental quality as being an issue which requires control through public policy.

For each stage there are a myriad of considerations which influence the progression or non-progression through the stages. For example, in the first stage—the precursor circumstances which give rise to a call for a public policy response—the existence of precursor circumstances may be a debatable point. A particular advocacy group may be determined that they do exist, while government may disagree or choose not to agree. An illustration of this is where an environmental lobby believes a certain adverse condition exists, such as the polluting of a watershed by an industry, but government studies come up with different findings. Even if the precursor circumstances do exist, their implications may be insufficient to arouse much interest among other advocacy groups, the general public or with government. In adult education there is the example of the move to certify adult educators along lines similar to teacher certification in the grade school system. Nothing has come of this move despite there being proponents of it. Further yet, if sufficient interest is indeed generated the response by government can be something other than to develop public policy. Instead an insignificant enforcement action or the appointment of an inquiry commission might be other responses that have far less policy consequences for government.

Public Policy Consequences

Consequences are a major consideration for any government. In the case of Canada the form of government is the parliamentary system, in which political parties vie for the right to form the government, and this right is for a limited period (maximum five years) when it must again be conferred. This strongly suggests that the policy-making process is prompted by political considerations in addition to the altruistic considerations attached to a particular issue. In reality both altruistic and political considerations must be present for public policy to be developed and the framework as outlined can be made operational by identifying for each stage the altruistic and political considerations which are present. Where the two considerations are compatible, the probability of public policy being developed is greatly increased. Where the two are incompatible, there is little likelihood, unless exigencies exist such as the example of the federal budgetary deficit and the government's introduction of the Goods and Services Tax.

Another consequence for government arises in the process of allocating resources or, more specifically, money. While economists will point out that government's ability to spend money is not restricted, as government has the ability to raise additional amounts through taxation, the situation today of a large public debt is causing government to be particularly conscious of its fiscal responsibility. The outcome of this is that funds available to government must be carefully distributed among different priority areas, and just because a public policy issue has harmonious political and altruistic considerations, it will not necessarily result in public policy if the required budget amounts are not available. An example of this is the long-touted national day-care scheme, a proposal which has remained unimplemented for lack of funding.

There is a further financial consideration for government which bears directly on education and this is the issue of universality. In Canada the notion of universality applies to certain government programs whereby citizen access to the benefits of those programs is not influenced by socio-economic considerations. Health care and child allowances are two such programs of the federal government. Within the provincial jurisdiction, education through the elementary and secondary grades is a universal program for school-age children. Operating this educational system involves hefty expenditures of public money, and this is without adding the equally substantial cost of operating the post-secondary system. Thus for government any extension of universal access to education beyond its current level, replete as it would be with financial implications, is not seen as being an attractive option to pursue when attempting to address the educational needs of adults. An interesting development, however, is that in some provinces access to free education to the high school completion level has now been extended to adults regardless of age.

Four Modes of Government Response to Demands for Learning

To complete this discussion of adult education and public policy there is a categorization of the responses which governments can make to demands for learning, including adult learning, which serves as another assist to analyzing government action. Developed by Thomas, the categorization is made up of four possible modes: Mode 1—to permit, Mode 2—to encourage, Mode 3—to direct, Mode 4—to forbid.[11] Depending on the learning objectives involved in the particular demand for learning, government can choose to respond in

---

[11] A. Thomas, "Government and Adult Learning."

the mode which will most likely bring about the outcome most desired by government.

The first mode, to permit, suggests that unless otherwise prevented by law the citizen is free to pursue learning as a basic freedom. Because learning is so much a part of the classic freedoms of speech, association and movement, it is absolutely necessary to ensure these freedoms remain untethered. These freedoms are part of the "social contract" between the state and its citizens. Providing there is no legal impediment to the learning objectives (Mode 4—to forbid), the response by government from Mode 1 is either to encourage (Mode 2) or to direct (Mode 3) the attainment of the learning objectives.

The second mode, to encourage, indicates that government believes learning per se should be encouraged, and it is thus appropriate that public provision be made for this to occur, even though the objectives of the learning might not be associated with a particular requirement of the government (which is the third mode, to direct). In this second mode the individual is free to choose from among a spectrum of agencies involved in providing learning, from museums, libraries and art galleries through to employers, labour organizations and voluntary agencies. While the form of encouragement made by government is most often financial, for example, capital expenditure or tax credits for tuition costs, there are other means at its disposal to similarly encourage learning. Thomas cites the example of a municipal government's regulatory ability to influence the architecture of buildings so as to make them, in this case, congenial adult learning spaces.

The third mode, to direct, indicates that society, through government, has identified particular learning objectives which warrant a systematic provision at society's expense. Public institutions have been created for this purpose and are readily identified as schools, colleges, institutes and universities. Thomas notes the constant factor with regards to these providing agencies is that they all have the authority, through government, to certify the achievements of their students.

The fourth mode, to forbid, is the antithesis of the first, to permit, and refers to those aspects of teaching which government has identified as being seditious, racist, treasonous, hateful and so on and which are expressly forbidden by law. An example would be the laws against the promulgation of hatred. The maintaining of community standards through censorship is another example.

Thomas indicates there is a dynamic to this categorization, a movement amongst the modes, which directly relates to the management of learning by government. Government is able to determine in which mode it will respond to a demand for learning, and by using this categorization it is possible to ascertain whether a particular response is likely to bring about what government considers to be the desired outcome. This is the topic of the next chapter, in which the responses by governments in Canada to the requirements and demands for adult learning are reviewed.

The foregoing outline of public policy has been general so as to embrace the wide spectrum of possibility regarding adult education and public policy. It will be useful to now "ground" this outline by way of a contemporary example. Because adult literacy has been the subject of explicit public policy in Canada, and calls for policy have come both from within government and from the community, it is an instructive illustration of public policy related to adult education.

Adult Literacy: A Case Study in Public Policy

Beginning with Thomas's four modes, government has always responded to demands for adult literacy education from the standpoint of Mode 1—to permit. What is clearly discernible, though, is that whereas government for many years based its policies on Mode 2—to encourage, more recently, as the problem of adult illiteracy has become a political issue, government has had to shift more noticeably toward Mode 3—to direct. The policy analysis framework introduced earlier is useful in identifying the specific developments which have led to public policy formation in the area of adult illiteracy.

1. The Precursor Circumstances Which Give Rise to a Call for a Public Policy Response

The fact of adult illiteracy in Canada has long been recognized. One of the country's most venerated adult education institutions, Frontier College (established in 1899), early on saw the need to provide adult basic education in an effort to address this very problem. More recently, in 1967 the Canada New-Start Program was launched under the auspices of what was then the federal Department of Manpower and Immigration with the purpose of promoting experimentation in methods which would motivate and train adults who were "educationally disadvantaged." Most recently the federal government has created the National Literacy Secretariat (in 1987) to foster action and promote co-ordination in literacy related programming.

Historically speaking, illiteracy has been considered as a condition afflicting immigrants and the less well educated, i.e., those who never attended school or who dropped out along the way. The earliest attempts at attacking illiteracy included provision by the state for the compulsory education of youth and also the provision by voluntary organizations of language training for immigrants and basic literacy skills for others.

In the span of time from the turn of the century to the present the attitude towards those who are adult illiterates has evolved from them being considered as either foreigners or ill-fated persons by virtue of an incomplete education, to being considered persons who are required to assume their full role in modern Canadian society. The essential factor in this evolution has been the acceptance by government of the responsibility for overcoming adult illiteracy, and with this acceptance provision of public funds has been made for the necessary remedial education.

This acceptance of the responsibility occurred largely as a result of uncovering the extent of illiteracy and the effect it was having on the country's social and economic development. Prior to this, illiteracy remained out of public view; indeed one of the hallmarks of a developed country such as Canada is its educational system with the capacity to effectively deliver mass education. Acknowledging the existence of illiteracy can be seen as a condemnation of the educational system. In Canada the revelation began as a result of the federal government's initiatives in the 1960s with work-force planning, starting with the Technical and Vocational Training Act (1960). As Thomas notes, "Very early in the decade, it was realized that an alarming proportion of those in need of vocational training did not have enough of the academic skills to enable them to participate in the vocational training programs."[12] As a consequence the federal government became actively involved in funding remedial education as part of its vocational training initiatives, beginning with the Adult Occupational Training Act (1967). Adult basic education programs such as Basic Training for Skill Development (BTSD) and innovative approaches such as the NewStart Corporations came into being to compensate for inadequate or incomplete formal education.

The extent of illiteracy has, however, never been a secret. Census figures have regularly reported educational attainment in the adult population and these figures, in the absence of more specific precise literacy statistics, have been used as a reasonable indicator of the number of Canadian adults who, by definition, are functionally illiterate.[13] UNESCO established the standard of less than nine years formal education to indicate functional illiteracy.[14] For the most part, however, the statistics remained cause for individual rather than societal distress, and it was not until much later in the 1980s when the statistics were placed in the compelling context of the cost to Canada's labour market that illiteracy drew concerted attention at both the national and the provincial levels.

Despite the federal provision for adult basic education, illiteracy persisted and even worsened. Aspects of the problem became politically charged when,

---

[12] Audrey Thomas, *Adult Illiteracy in Canada: A Challenge*, UNESCO Occasional Paper No. 42 (Ottawa: Canadian Commission for UNESCO, 1983) p.63.

[13] For example, see E. Adamson, "The Need for Adult Basic Education," in Selman and Kidd (Eds.), *Coming of Age: Canadian Adult Education in the 1960s* (Toronto: Canadian Association for Adult Education, 1978) p.124.

[14] For a full discussion on definitions and standards see J. Cairns, *Adult Illiteracy in Canada* (Toronto: Council of Ministers of Education, Canada, 1988) p.4.

for example, the findings of a Senate committee were published which stated that federal funds were financing the costs of upgrading the adult drop-outs from the provincial school systems.[15] Another Senate committee, investigating poverty in Canada, underscored the connection between educational attainment and economic status and the inevitable link between poverty and illiteracy.[16]

For an economically advanced and democratic country such as Canada, the fact of persistently high illiteracy rates was a source of national embarrassment, not to mention social dislocation. At a time of massive investment in post-secondary education, the adult illiteracy issue remained a perplexing problem, one which called for a direct public policy response.

There are many additional precursor circumstances which could be identified as being influential to the call for public policy. Certainly a number of advocacy groups had been active in the effort to influence governments' increased role in addressing the issue, including Frontier College, the labour movement, World Literacy of Canada, The Movement for Canadian Literacy, the Canadian Association for Adult Education, and Laubach Literacy of Canada. By the mid-1980s the issue was well documented and acknowledged by all concerned.[17] In some provinces special literacy programs had been developed, and in British Columbia during 1982 a policy statement on adult basic education was issued which stated, "It is the policy of the ministry to provide, to adult citizens and landed immigrants residing in the province, reasonable access to high quality adult basic education programs."[18] The major call for action, however, was directed at the federal government, and there was considerable pressure applied. Thus the precursor circumstances had by 1986 led to ...

2. The Development Process of a Public Policy (or the Denial of a Process)

In the Speech from the Throne delivered October 1, 1986, the federal government pledged to "work with the provinces, the private sector and voluntary groups to develop resources to ensure that Canadians have access to the literacy skills that are the prerequisite for participation in our advanced economy."[19] This policy reference signalled the political acceptance of the literacy issue on the part of the Conservative government. By virtue of being

---

[15] Audrey Thomas, "Adult Illiteracy in Canada: A Challenge," p.64.

[16] Government of Canada, *Poverty in Canada: Highlights of the Report of the Special Senate Committee* (Ottawa: Information Canada, 1971).

[17] J. Cairns, *Adult Illiteracy in Canada*, p.13.

[18] As quoted in J. Cairns, *Adult Illiteracy in Canada*, p.42.

[19] Hon. David Crombie, "Message," in *Learning, V*, 1 (1988), p.13.

included in the Throne Speech the reference also signalled the gravity of the issue, and by its wording indicated the concern was framed in terms of the human capital view of adult education. (This view holds that the predominant purpose of adult education is to develop the skills of members of the work force, the "human capital" of the economy.) The government's acceptance of the illiteracy issue, however, was still non-committal in terms of specific actions. Throne speeches typically provide the government in power with the opportunity to acknowledge the existence of a particular issue without having to go further. They are simply an indication of likely future action, and do not outline specific commitments.

The Throne Speech announcement represented, of course, a significant breakthrough for adult literacy advocates. Even though the reference was fleeting, its significance lay in the willing acceptance of the moral responsibility for the issue on the part of the federal government. By taking on the commitment the federal government would not only make available public resources to address the issue but would also be publicly accountable for its actions or inactions. What remained was the development of the specific policy.

As noted earlier, the development process of a public policy has no specified format or procedure. In the case of adult literacy the process was limited to the federal government acting of its own accord, although not without input from other sources. In part this is explained by the delicate jurisdictional issue: education is a provincial, not federal, responsibility, and the federal government had only so much room in which to take initiative. The Department of the Secretary of State was assigned the task of developing a national strategy for substantially reducing illiteracy, and the Department undertook consultations with provincial governments, with groups from the voluntary, educational, labour, and private sectors and with other federal government departments.

The reference in the Throne Speech had the effect of galvanizing the voluntary sector into action. A coalition was formed of national organizations concerned with promoting adult literacy. Under the leadership of the Movement for Canadian Literacy, the coalition embarked on a campaign of public awareness by way of placing an open letter to the prime minister, the provincial premiers and the territorial government leaders in two mass circulation publications, *Macleans* magazine and the *Globe and Mail* newspaper.[20] This letter summarized a statement on public policy, known as the Cedar Glen Declaration, which the coalition had produced shortly after coming together in December 1986.

---

[20] *Macleans*, February 22, 1988, p.27.

The Council of Ministers of Education was also part of the consultation process. This body of provincial ministers of education is, among other things, a focal point for consultation on education-related matters between the provinces and the federal government. Always mindful of the provincial prerogative in the field of education, and not wishing to be usurped on the literacy issue, the Council embarked on its own survey of the issue and followed this publication with the provincial response outlining provincial measures already being taken to eradicate adult illiteracy.[21]

The single most influential contribution to the policy development process came unsolicited to the federal government. During September 1987, newspapers of the Southam News chain published articles on adult illiteracy based on the findings of a literacy survey commissioned by Southam News. The survey determined that five million Canadians were functionally illiterate, according to criteria developed specifically for the survey.[22] The national impact of the findings was enormous, all the more so due to such shocking revelations as illiteracy existing even among university graduates.

The results of the Southam Literacy Survey gave rise to another study being conducted, this time by the Canadian Business Task Force on Literacy, in February 1988.[23] The purpose of the Business Task Force study was to estimate the cost of illiteracy to business in particular and society in general so as to instigate a serious dialogue on the problem of illiteracy. The intended outcome of the dialogue was to have government and business "allocate resources adequate to the dimensions of the problem." The study, undertaken by an accounting firm, estimated that the direct cost to business of illiteracy was $4 billion and to society as a whole it was $10 billion. The report's authors noted that, "These estimates are published not with absolute conviction of their accuracy, but from a need to contribute to the debate on the position that literacy should occupy on the national agenda." The findings, although not as widely reported as the findings of the Southam Literacy Survey, were nonetheless astounding.

The purpose of the Business Task Force study was well served. The Southam Literacy Survey had brought the issue into full public view and "established beyond a reasonable doubt the existence of a literacy problem in Canada."[24] It was the quantification of that problem, however, which confirmed the insidious economic effects of illiteracy, and this was a clearly understood consequence, free of the entrapping of "softer" social concerns.

---

[21] J. Cairns, *Adult Illiteracy in Canada*.

[22] P. Calamai, *Broken Words* (Toronto: Southam Newspaper Group, 1987).

[23] Canadian Business Task Force on Literacy, *Measuring the Costs of Illiteracy* (Toronto: Business Task Force, 1988).

[24] Ibid., p.3.

Writing in response to the Southam Literacy Survey but before the publication of the Business Task Force study, Darville had noted in regard to maintaining literacy on the national policy agenda that "the development, or lack of development, of a conception of costs may make or break the literacy issue as a focus for long-term government attention."[25]

Two years after the reference to literacy in the Throne Speech, the policy development process within government, both planned and in response to unfolding developments, had received all the necessary input. (Darville refers to these inputs as being a discourse, "that kind of conversation in texts through which 'issues' in our society are defined, and terms are devised to describe 'problems' and what should be done about them. Many texts (speeches, policy statements, committee and commission reports, scholarly articles, media accounts) make up this conversation.")[26] More than ever the issue was ready for direct policy action.

3. The Implementation of a Public Policy (Or the Refusal to Implement a Public Policy)

There were two initial policy initiatives announced by the federal government prior to the revelation of the major policy initiative. The first, in March 1987, was the Solicitor-General's announcement of a significant program to address the high illiteracy rate among the prison population, it being estimated that nearly one-half of the inmates were functionally illiterate. The second, in September 1987, came when the Secretary of State announced a $1 million allocation for the establishment of a National Literacy Secretariat and the granting of funds in support of literacy initiatives. The major policy initiative occurred on International Literacy Day, September 8, 1988, when the Prime Minister announced the federal government's National Literacy Strategy consisting of a $110 million fund to be made available over five years. This amount was earmarked to support literacy partnership initiatives with voluntary associations and joint program initiatives with provincial governments. "Funds are available for pilot or demonstration projects, but not for ongoing delivery. Other projects funded include research and needs assessment studies, conferences and public awareness initiatives, development of materials, resource networks and provincial coalitions."[27]

The question arises as to whether the National Literacy Strategy can properly be defined as a public policy. In an operational sense it is. Public commit-

---

[25] Richard Darville, "Framing Il/literacy in the Media" in *Learning*, *V*, 1 (1988) pp.9-11.

[26] Ibid., p.10.

[27] Provincial Literacy Advisory Committee, *Opening the Doors to Lifelong Learning: Empowering Undereducated Adults* (Vancouver: Ministry of Advanced Education, Technology and Job Technology, 1989) p.9.

ments have been made by the Prime Minister (who announced the National Literacy Strategy), resources have been allocated ($110 million), and a bureaucracy established (the National Literacy Secretariat). In a strict policy sense, however, it is not. There is no legislation which outlines the government's policy towards literacy. There is no official definition of literacy against which to measure the outcomes of the National Literacy Strategy. The partnership arrangement of the strategy distributes decision making among numerous partners and thereby reduces the policy's cohesiveness. It also makes the avenues for accountability unclear. Lastly, the funding commitment is for five years only. In this regard the public policy is seen as not having gone far enough to ensure the policy's objectives can be met, i.e., the substantial reduction of adult illiteracy. This is compared to, for example, the National Training Act (1982) in which the federal government's job retraining policy was spelled out by way of legislative enactment and unilateral action. Despite this definitional question, the federal government has clearly acknowledged its lead role in bringing resources to bear on the literacy issue. Attention turns, then, to stage 4 of the policy development process.

4. The Review of a Public Policy in Light of Subsequent Circumstances (A Review of the Continued Ignoring of the Precursor Circumstances, or the Circumstances as They Have Since Developed)

With federal and most provincial policies concerning illiteracy/literacy being relatively new, the major emphasis up to this point has been in the area of development and implementation rather than in review and evaluation. The Literacy Secretariat has developed its research activities, however, and among other things has attempted to apply to Canada the criteria developed by UNESCO and other international bodies for assessing the state of literacy. In 1989, Statistics Canada conducted a Survey of Literacy Skills Used in Daily Activities, and this had the effect of raising some policy issues related to the field.[28] The most recent and substantial study of the literacy skills of Canadians was carried out by Statistics Canada in 1994, as part of the International Adult Literacy Survey of that year. Statistics Canada and the National Literacy Secretariat released the Canadian findings in the fall of 1996 in a report entitled *Reading the Future: A Portrait of Literacy in Canada.*[29] The results of that study indicated that literacy levels in Canada had not changed substantially in the five years between the two surveys. For present purposes, and

---

[28] Statistics Canada, *Survey of Literacy Skills Used in Daily Activities* (Ottawa: Statistics Canada, 1989).

[29] Statistics Canada and National Literacy Secretariat, *Reading the Future: A Portrait of Literacy in Canada* (Ottawa: Statistics Canada, 1996).

combining the findings on three "types" of literacy (prose literacy, document literacy and quantitative literacy), the results showed that on a five level scale, 22 percent of Canadian adults fall into "Level 1" (may be able to read but have serious difficulty dealing with printed material) and approximately a further 25 percent fall into "Level 2" (can deal with simple material that is clearly laid out). Compared with some of the other industrialized countries, Canadians test at lower levels in both document and quantitative literacy. Canadian skilled craft workers and machine operators have lower literacy levels than their counterparts in Germany and the Netherlands. There are more than 1.6 million seniors in Canada at Level 1, the lowest level. These are just a few sample findings from the surveys, the results of which are useful guides to the use of resources, both at the time they are taken and over time, as an evaluation of efforts and a guide to future action.

In addition to such survey work, the National Literacy Secretariat co-operates with provincial ministries of education in providing leadership and financial support to regional literacy organizations across the country and support to curriculum development, and experimental and demonstration projects. Most provinces and territories have literacy "coalition" organizations, all of which are members of the Movement for Canadian Literacy, which was formed in the late 1970s. When opportunities arise for useful advocacy activity at the federal level, several national organizations interested in literacy work, such as the Movement for Canadian Literacy, Frontier College, Laubach Literacy of Canada and la Federation canadienne pour l'alphabetisation en française, make representations on behalf of the work. There has been concern in recent years about the level of federal government support of the National Literacy Secretariat, but at the time of writing, support for that agency seems to be secure.

The manner in which Canada is responding to the literacy issue is also of international significance. Canada sees itself as a responsible member of the international community, a view that is reinforced by its "middle power" status. This status positions Canada between the superpower nations and the developing Third World countries, thereby enabling it to be influential in mediating differences and in exercising leadership in the promotion of peace and human well-being. As evidence of this Canada participates thoughtfully at international gatherings, and often guides the deliberations so as to produce constructive outcomes. This certainly describes Canada's actions in the area of international adult education, and this country has participated at all four of the United Nations Educational, Scientific and Cultural Organization (UNESCO) sponsored international conferences on adult education (Elsinore—1948, Montreal—1960, Tokyo—1972, and Paris—1985).[30] As a recent

---

[30] For reports on these conferences see UNESCO, *Summary Report of the International Conference on*

example of Canada's role in these deliberations, at the 1985 Paris conference Canada introduced the Declaration on the Right to Learn which was subsequently passed by the assembly.[31] It is useful, then, to briefly examine the international calls for public policy regarding adult education.

International Calls for Public Policy

The work of the United Nations agency, UNESCO, has been particularly instrumental in bringing adult education into the mainstream of educational policy planning. One manner in which this has occurred has been the convening of the above noted international conferences on adult education. Three other items also stand out: the establishing of an International Commission on the Development of Education in 1971, the adoption of a Recommendation on the Development of Adult Education in 1976, and the appointment of the International Commission on Education for the Twenty-First Century, which reported in 1996.

The International Commission on the Development of Education was established by UNESCO to look at the development of education worldwide, to study its problems and to put forward new strategies for planning educational systems. Its conclusions were published in a landmark report entitled *Learning to Be*, and which is commonly referred to as the Faure Report after the Commission's chairman, Edgar Faure. In a broadly considered approach to the provision of education worldwide, the Commission reviewed the adequacy of existing educational systems and their abilities to be responsive to both the requirements of their societies and the needs of individuals. The whole concept of education was examined in terms of its pedagogy and its occurrence throughout life. The report's conclusions were necessarily general, given the scope of the inquiry and the international community to which they were addressed. Twenty-one conclusions were advanced with the intention that they become "elements for contemporary strategies" within individual countries in the desire to engender "learning societies." As an example, the first conclusion asserted the principle that "every individual must be in a position to keep learning throughout his life. The idea of lifelong education is the keystone to the learning society." From this principle came the recommendation that lifelong education be considered as "the master concept for educational policies in the years to come for both developed and developing countries."[32]

Adult Education (Paris: UNESCO, 1949); UNESCO, *World Conference on Adult Education: Final Report* (Paris: UNESCO, 1960); UNESCO, *Third International Conference: Final Report* (Paris: UNESCO, 1972); UNESCO, *Fourth International Conference on Adult Education* (Paris: UNESCO, 1985). An excellent synthesis of the Third Conference is contained in J. Lowe, *The Education of Adults: A World Perspective* (Toronto: OISE Press, 1975).

[31] Desmond Berghofer, "The Right To Learn," in *Learning, IV*, 2 (1985) p.11.

[32] International Commission on the Development of Education, *Learning To Be: The World of Educa-

A subsequent UNESCO General Conference, held in Nairobi, Kenya, in 1976, adopted a Recommendation on the Development of Adult Education.[33] The principles contained in the Recommendation were commended to the signatory nations for attention and implementation by "authorities, departments or bodies responsible for adult education and also of the various organizations carrying out educational work for the benefit of adults, and of trade union organizations, associations, enterprises, and other interested parties." This Recommendation is significant on many counts, one being its effort at integrating into a policy document the products of previous international gatherings which dealt with aspects of adult education. The Recommendation is also comprehensive in its consideration of the areas of adult education which call for policy development, as seen in its organization under the following headings: (1) Definition, (2) Objectives and Strategy, (3) Content of Adult Education, (4) Methods, Means, Research and Evaluation, (5) The Structures of Adult Education, (6) Training and Status of Persons Engaged in Adult Education Work, (7) Relations Between Adult Education and Youth Education, (8) Relations Between Adult Education and Work, (9) Management, Administration, Co-ordination and Financing of Adult Education, and (10) International Co-operation. The Recommendation has no binding authority on those governments which supported it, including Canada. Instead the Recommendation points the direction for member states as they develop their provision of adult education "to give effect to the principles set forth in this Recommendation."

A quarter century following the Faure Commission, described above, UNESCO established another international committee to study the future of education. This one was officially named the International Commission on Education for the Twenty-First Century and was chaired by another Frenchman, Jacques Delors. Their report was published in 1996[34] and in many respects it was an elaboration and update of the Faure Commission's ideas. Lifelong learning (frequently referred to in this more recent report as "learning throughout life") was still seen to be the central idea. Like its predecessor, too, it grounded the necessity for lifelong learning in the problems facing contemporary society. Much was said about "the prevailing mood of disenchantment" abroad in the world and the importance of education and learning in relation to dealing with violence within and among societies, fostering international understanding, facilitating economic development, fostering "a

---

tion Today and Tomorrow (Paris: UNESCO, 1972) p.181.

[33] UNESCO, *Recommendation on the Development of Adult Education* Occasional Paper 34 (Ottawa: Canadian Commission for UNESCO, nd).

[34] UNESCO, *Learning: The Treasure Within*, Report of the International Commission on Education for the Twenty-First Century (Paris: UNESCO, 1996).

deeper and more harmonious form of human development," and perhaps most basic of all, the "renewal of practical democracy." There was comment on all levels of education, with some emphasis particularly on adult basic education. Canadian adult educators are presumably particularly interested in the fact that there are echoes of Moses Coady's ideas in the report, with some emphasis on the fact that people have come to feel helpless amidst forces over which they have no control and need to be helped, through education, "to retain mastery of their own destinies." Like its predecessor, the report, which is entitled *Learning: The Treasure Within*, is a very humanistic document. Delors, in his substantial introductory essay to the report, sums up much of the flavour of the document in stating that "the concept of an education pursued throughout life ... should command wide support. Lifelong education must constitute a continuous process of forming whole human beings—their knowledge and aptitudes, as well as the critical faculty and the ability to act."[35]

Other UN agencies which have also been active in calling for adult education measures include the International Labour Organization and the Food and Agriculture Organization, although these calls have been limited to the context of the specific mandate set out for each. In other global initiatives, adult education has been identified as a means to achieving particular objectives set by the UN General Assembly in its attempt to create a more just world economic and social order. Examples of this include the sustained effort to reduce the gap between rich and poor nations during the First and Second Development Decades of the 1960s and 1970s, and the declaration of international years to focus attention on specific areas of concern such as International Literacy Year in 1990.

Another international organization, the Organization for Economic Co-operation and Development (OECD), through its Manpower, Social Affairs, and Educational Directorate and its Centre for Educational Research and Innovation, has also been active in advocating to national governments various adult educational policies for implementation. In particular the OECD, beginning in the early 1970s, embraced the concept of recurrent education.[36] As proposed by the OECD, a recurrent education policy would consist of three main elements:[37]

1. that individuals, at the end of compulsory schooling, should have the right to defer the continuation of their education up to higher levels, to times of their own choosing, together with the right to re-enter the educational cycle;

---

[35] Ibid., p.21.

[36] OECD, *Recurrent Education: A Strategy for Lifelong Learning* (Paris: OECD, 1973).

[37] As noted in Employment and Immigration Canada, *Learning a Living in Canada, 1*, p.47.

2. that individuals should have the right to such occupational training as may be required to enable them to upgrade their job, to change it or to find a new one should they become redundant;

3. that positive measures should be taken to ensure that the expansion of adult learning opportunities should not accentuate inequalities.

In 1976 the OECD conducted a review of Canada's educational provision and in its subsequent report urged Canada to adopt the idea of recurrent education as the master strategy for its educational system.[38]

The Council of Europe is an organization of European countries which has also researched the need for adult education among its member nations.[39] The Council champions the concept of permanent education, which it describes as being a coherent and integrated educational system for all stages and sectors of life. In studying the existing provision of education, the Council found a significant lack in the ability of educational systems to respond to new social and economic realities. By member nations adopting a system of permanent education, the arbitrariness of educational provision which is made only for youth would be supplanted with a system which acknowledges the need for providing ongoing educational opportunity. This need arises because both developed and developing countries must continue to expand their economic and social systems in a world that is ever changing. While the concept of permanent education is particularly applicable to economic development with respect to education and training for work, its proponents also include all social and cultural activities with an educational content so as to additionally promote social development.

There are also many international non-governmental organizations concerned with adult education which have been active within their own spheres of influence at calling upon governments to support the provision of adult education. The International Council for Adult Education (ICAE), founded soon after the Third UNESCO Conference in Tokyo in 1972, is but one example. In 1976 the ICAE adopted a position on adult education and national development known as the Declaration of Dar es Salaam.[40]

There are also a number of individuals whose ideas have had a marked impact on international thinking about education, including adult education. The two who are arguably the best known due to the radical nature of their views on the educational process are Paulo Freire (*Pedagogy of the Oppressed*) and Ivan Illich (*Deschooling Society*). There are others, however,

---

[38] OECD, *Reviews of National Policies for Education—Canada* (Paris: Organization for Economic Co-operation and Development, 1976).

[39] Council for Cultural Co-operation, *A Contribution to the Development of a New Education Policy* (Strasbourg: Council of Europe, 1981).

[40] *Convergence, IX*, 4 (1976) p.9.

who through publications and attendance at international gatherings have lent their thoughts to the call for public policy. Two Canadians who are notable in this regard are Alan Thomas of the Ontario Institute for Studies in Education and the late Roby Kidd.

The effect of all these calls for public policy has been to influence and guide discussion within the educational jurisdictions of individual nations. The most important effect has been to promote adult education and its several conceptions (such as lifelong learning, recurrent education, learning society) to the point where these conceptions are accepted by educational planners and even, in some cases, by policy-making bodies. The rate of acceptance is ever increasing, particularly as those precursor circumstances, which are the products of a rapidly expanding and ever changing world, force policy makers to take action on specific issues. The purpose of the next chapter, then, is to examine the policy situation within Canada with respect to adult education.

Since World War II, and particularly since the 1960s, there has been an expansion of the vocational/technical institutes and community colleges. Adult education is seen to be an included function of these institutions and distinct departments carry out "continuing education" work. Photo above was taken at Humber College of Applied Arts and Technology, Toronto. Courtesy of Gary Gellert.

8

Public Policy in Canada: A Synthesis and an Appraisal

In 1966 the Canadian Association for Adult Education (CAAE) issued a paper outlining its ideas on the development of a Canadian policy for adult education (referred to in the paper as continuing education).[1] In its call for an articulated system of continuing education the CAAE insisted that its development could not be left to chance. Rather it needed to develop on the basis of an overall conception of learning where learning and the learner were placed in a central position in society. "Underlying all is the premise that all citizens should have reasonable access to any part or level of the system at any time in his [her] life and with reasonable convenience to his [her] circumstances." Numerous provincial and national studies on aspects of adult education have been prepared both before and since but the element of chance concerning its development persists to this day. There is more that is implicit than explicit about policy respecting adult education.

Many reasons are advanced for the lack of an explicit Canadian policy on adult education, and always the first to be cited is the constitutional provision in the Constitution Act 1867 (known as the British North America Act prior to 1981) which stipulates that education is a matter of provincial, not federal, jurisdiction (Section 93). Many in the adult education field consider the advancing of this reason as a subterfuge in that Section 93 deals only with provincial jurisdiction regarding youth education, and particularly to the guaranteeing of the right to sectarian education.[2] The suggestion of a subterfuge is supported by the fact that at the provincial level there are only a few govern-

---

[1] CAAE, *A White Paper on the Education of Adults in Canada* (Toronto: CAAE, 1966).

[2] For example, A. Thomas, "Other Voices, Other Rooms: The Emergence of New Educational Constituencies in the 1980s," in Ivany & Manley-Casimir, *Federal-Provincial Relations: Education Canada* (Toronto: OISE, 1981) p.84.

ments which have embraced a broad conception of adult education and have developed policies to support its development. In the 1990s, many provinces (New Brunswick and Ontario are two good examples) have committed considerable resources to labour-adjustment programs in addition to their traditional adult education programs. Thus, they might take exception to this analysis. Nonetheless, it is our view that provincial adult education policies, where they exist, are corollaries of general educational or job training policies. No province, with perhaps the exception of Alberta, has a comprehensive set of policies guiding the development and delivery of adult education.

Federal Government Policy Initiatives

Despite the apparent exclusion of the federal government in matters of education by virtue of Section 93 of the Constitution Act, the national government has had, and continues to have, a quite considerable involvement. Prior to the 1950s this involvement was predominately in the area of technical and vocational education encompassing both youth and adults. Beginning in the 1950s, and using the 1951 Report of the Royal Commission on National Development in the Arts, Letters, and Sciences (Massey Commission) as a marker, the federal government also committed itself to the support and development of provincial post-secondary educational systems, i.e., universities, colleges and institutes.[3] More recently, with the passage of the Official Languages Act and with the influx of large numbers of non-English or French-speaking immigrants, the federal government has funded language training in both official languages at the elementary and secondary school level. In each of these cases the involvement has been justified by the general commitment of the federal government to national interests such as economic and social development.[4]

Specific federal policy developments in support of technical and vocational education and occupational training programs begin with the appointment in 1910 of the Royal Commission on Industrial Training and Technical Education and with the first legislative enactments, the Agricultural Instruction Act of 1913 and the Technical Education Act of 1919. Ever since, the federal government has maintained its presence in these areas through the funding of different initiatives in conjunction with the provinces.

Whereas the earlier fiscal interventions of the federal government were directed at supporting programs at the secondary school level, beginning in

---

[3] For an account of this involvement see Secretary of State, *Federal and Provincial Support to Post-Secondary Education in Canada: A Report to Parliament, 1987-1988* (Ottawa, Secretary of State, 1988).

[4] For an elaboration on this involvement see E.D. Hodgson, *Federal Intervention in Public Education* (Toronto: Canadian Education Association, 1976).

1937 with the Unemployment and Agricultural Assistance Act, it also became involved with supporting the training of unemployed youth and, during the war, the training of skilled workers.[5] This increased involvement was prompted by the immense dislocation in the work force brought about by the Great Depression. The outbreak of World War II provided added impetus to the need to prepare persons for new occupations, in this case to sustain the war effort through the training of both armed forces personnel and civilian production workers. Thus, the federal government was now proactive in not only supporting programs conducted in educational institutions but also training initiatives addressed to the needs of those requiring training beyond their formal schooling, and particularly the unemployed. The significance of this federal involvement was the precedent it set for future interventions. "This pairing of federal support to educational institutions with federal training initiatives to combat unemployment, all via the intermediary of the provinces, was to be the hallmark of [federal] postwar policy."[6]

The federal involvement in occupational training increased by a quantum amount with the passage of the Technical and Vocational Training Assistance Act (TVTA) of 1960. This legislation was part of the government's response to the sluggish economic condition of the country at the time when, for example, in the summer of 1960 the unemployment rate was at a postwar high of 8 percent. Particularly noteworthy for the interests of adult education was that some of the measures in the TVTA were directed at the retraining of workers threatened with job obsolescence. The significance of this is its foreshadowing of a greatly expanded federal government role in human resource planning and policy from the mid-1960s to the early 1990s, when national economic interests would be allowed to supersede jurisdictional reservations surrounding the provision of education. This expanded federal role was proclaimed in the heady year of 1967, which marked Canada's centennial of confederation and witnessed the exhilaration of Expo 67 in Montreal.

The Adult Occupational Training Act of 1967 represents a watershed event in federal involvement in matters of education. At the 1966 Federal Provincial Conference Prime Minister Lester Pearson stated, "We propose to change the emphasis of our policy for training in a way that accords with the national economic priorities which are the inescapable concern of the federal government. That is to say, we propose to clarify our purposes and expand our activities in adult training."[7] The explanation put forward justifying this assertive action was that the federal government had "a constitutional and neces-

---

[5] Dupre et al., *Federalism and Policy Development: The Case of Adult Occupational Training in Ontario* (Toronto: University of Toronto Press, 1982) p.14.

[6] Ibid., p.15.

[7] As quoted in Dupre et al., *Federalism and Policy Development*, p.26.

sary role in the training and development of our adult labour force for economic growth and full employment."[8] By way of circumventing the jurisdictional issue of provincial autonomy in matters of education the federal government accentuated an existing artifice so as to serve its constitutional needs, namely making formal a distinction between training and education. In order to directly influence the availability of particular skills and knowledge necessary for economic development the federal government couched its manpower initiatives by designating them as the training of adults, a specific area not dealt with in the Constitution Act under Section 93. At the same time, and so as not to raise the ire of the provinces by appearing to infringe on their educational jurisdiction, the federal government concurrently provided generous funding to the provinces by way of cost sharing arrangements so that each could continue to develop and operate their particular post-secondary educational system free of federal interference.[9] The impact of these measures on adult education was twofold. For one there was now considerable federal funding available to support job training programs, including adult basic education. For another the expansion of provincial post-secondary educational institutions had the unspecified effect of making considerably more adult education opportunities available, as departments of continuing education or similar structures were created in the new colleges, institutes and universities.

The Adult Occupational Training Act (1967) marks the first time in Canada that adult learning needs have been explicitly identified and singled out in public policy. (Note: For the purposes of the Act an adult was defined as a person who had been out of the school system for at least three years and who was attached to the labour force.) The provisions of the Act were such that the federal government would pay both the training costs and living allowances of persons assisted under the Act, and that citizens could deal directly with federal agencies in accessing the various training programs and benefits available. In turn, however, the federal government was still obliged to look to provincial institutions to provide the requisite training.[10]

It is important to note that the learning needs addressed in the Adult Occupational Training Act were those as perceived by the federal government. In terms of public policy the federal adult training initiative represents one of the two major views on the purpose of adult education, namely the "human capital" view as contrasted with the "humanistic" view. These views are not to be seen as in opposition to each other; rather, they represent a placing of empha-

---

[8] Ibid.

[9] This was by way of the Federal-Provincial Fiscal Arrangements Act (1967) and subsequently in 1977 by the Federal-Provincial Fiscal Arrangements and Federal Post-Secondary Education and Health Contributions Act.

[10] A. Thomas, "Legislation and Adult Education in Canada: A Comparative Study," *International Journal of Lifelong Education, 8*, 2 (1989) pp.103-125.

sis. According to the human capital view the economy requires a skilled and knowledgeable work force capable of creating wealth. This work force forms the human capital which, along with investment capital, ensures a vital economy. Just as investment capital moves around to seek out opportunities with greatest profit potential, so must the human capital be available to take advantage of these opportunities. Thus, skilled and knowledgeable workers form part of the economic equation for a healthy economy, which is measured by such indices as the Gross National Product (GNP), employment levels, and international competitiveness.

The humanistic view of adult education takes a different point of view by looking at the whole person and appreciating the individual as capable of achieving his or her full potential as a human being. Rather than the individual being seen in terms of an economic unit, as in the case of the human capital view, the humanistic view instead values the individual in terms of his or her total life contribution including at work, in the community, with family and through self-actualization. The purpose of adult education, then, is to enable individuals in achieving their full potential.

As noted, the two views are not in opposition to one another. However there can be, and often is, disagreement as to the emphasis placed on one over the other. This is particularly the case when emphasis gets translated into policy, which has definite implications for resource allocation. This resource allocation can then be interpreted as an expression of philosophic orientation on the part of government in its relationship with its citizens. There is, of course, more sophistication to the two views than sketched here; for example, it is easily argued that only through economic independence, made possible by the human capital emphasis, are workers better able to pursue their humanistic interests. Another example, arising from the Adult Occupational Training Act (1967), is how the Act enabled a considerable amount of adult basic education to be provided, and this opened the doors of possibility and opportunity for trainees. In analyzing policy, however, one looks for the underlying assumptions and the evenness of the policy's application to the general situation. Thus, in the case of the human capital view, it is only those who are part of the work force, or potentially part of it, who are singled out for attention. There are many adults who are not part of this group and thus not in a position to benefit, such as adults with handicaps, those retired from the work force, and those who are devoting full time to domestic life, including child rearing.

The consideration of adult education in the last quarter of the twentieth century must be situated in the context of economic globalization where so-called "human capital" has become among the most valuable resources. Human capital connotes a work force who has access to information and who has a high degree of knowledge and professional skills. Politicians and business have been quick to designate vocational training as the miracle solution.

Hence, the federal government emphasis on labour-force planning and adult training has grown steadily in this period. This led to an updated National Training Act in 1982. The thrust of this Act was to assert that the federal government had the right to determine the providers of federally funded training, outside of being bound to provincial educational institutions as had been the case with the Adult Occupational Training Act. The federal government declared that henceforth it was free to develop contractual relationships also with employers, private training establishments, and other training entrepreneurs.[11] This policy shift was amplified in 1985 with the introduction of the federal government's new job creation program called Canadian Jobs Strategy.[12] In 1989, a further initiative was taken by the federal government with its introduction of a new strategy for equipping the labour force to adapt to changes and meet new requirements. Referred to as The Labour Force Development Strategy, this initiative was launched in response to "an evolving work environment brought on by technological and demographic change."[13] The strategy proposed to focus on the plight of displaced older workers and their need for training rather than entrants to the labour force.

The Labour Force Development Strategy led to the creation of the Canadian Labour Force Development Board (CLFDB) and parallel boards in most provinces. In the early 1990s, an enormous amount of energy was devoted to establishing these boards and to agreeing on their mandate, their scope of activity and their structure. Of all the provinces, Ontario responded most aggressively by creating the Ontario Adjustment and Training Board (OTAB) with an annual budget in excess of $400 million and wide-ranging authority for apprenticeships, labour-adjustment programs, pre-employment training, literacy and numeracy programs, and upgrading of employed workers. The Quebec version, Société québécoise pour le développement de la main d'oeuvre (see Chapter 4) had a similarly large mandate. A few other provinces, like New Brunswick, created small offices and boards with very limited power. Many never got beyond the organizational stage before the winds of political change swept them to the sidelines.

The second edition of this volume is being written at the end of the 20th century. It is an appropriate time to review the results of the federal policy initiatives with regards to adult education which are described in the preceding paragraphs of this chapter. Unfortunately, there is little evidence that

---

[11] Collins and Long, "Federal and Provincial Adult Education Agencies in the United States and Canada," in Merriam and Cunningham (Eds.), *Handbook of Adult and Continuing Education* (San Francisco: Jossey-Bass, 1989) p.390.

[12] F. MacDonald, *The Canadian Jobs Strategy* (Ottawa: Employment and Immigration Canada, 1985).

[13] Canadian Labour Market and Productivity Centre, *Report of the CLMPC Task Forces on the Labour Force Development Strategy* (Ottawa: Canadian Labour Market and Productivity Centre, 1989) p.1.

policy making in Canada is guided by a vision of adult education as a central element in building the "good society." At its best, a coherent adult education policy at the federal level and a strong integration with provincial initiatives could make a major contribution to building citizenship, national cohesion, community development and economic prosperity for Canada. As it is, both federal and provincial initiatives have generally been piecemeal and inconsistent.

It is the eve of a new millennium. In Canada, the period can be characterized by very rapid change, considerable confusion about national identity, uncertainty about the future of the country, economic instability, continuing high rates of illiteracy and major external pressures as a result of globalization. In order not to be swept away by these pressures and uncertainties, our country needs citizens who have vision, self-confidence, a commitment to participatory democracy, a profound sense of community and a broad set of appropriate work skills. A coherent national adult education policy is key to equipping Canadians with these qualities.

Adult Education Policy in the Provinces and Territories

The development of provincial educational systems has historically been focussed on providing publicly supported education for youth. Initially this was directed at the grade school system and then expanded from there to the post-secondary system, first with its universities and latterly with its colleges, institutes and an increased number of universities. Only since the 1960s, however, has there been comprehensive development of the post-secondary system in most provinces to parallel that of the grade school system.

By way of generalization, the pattern respecting the development of publicly provided adult education has followed that of the formal educational system, with the significant exception being the absence of enabling legislation. Initially, adult education was associated with the night school offerings of the public grade schools, then additionally with university extension departments and vocational training centres and, more recently, with the continuing education units of community colleges and institutes. As noted, these are institutions which are part of the formal educational system. In addition to these institutions it is readily possible to identify other publicly funded institutions which provide adult education such as libraries, community centres and various government departments (for example, departments of health and of recreation). This review will confine itself, however, to the formal educational system, as it is possible to trace this system's gradual acceptance of the responsibility for the education of adults as well as youth. As pointed out in Chapter 7, this acceptance by way of statutory provision carries with it considerable financial implications, and explains why Thomas describes it as being for the most part "benign and enabling."[14] The acknowledgment of the need for adult education, however, is now as undisputed as was the need for youth education a century ago. This acknowledgment is evidenced by the widespread use in official documents of such terms as adult learning, continuing education and lifelong learning.

The point has already been made that learning is pervasive regardless of the age of the individual. With youth, however, the organizing of learning into a formal educational system makes it possible to easily observe and analyze its component parts, such as its enabling legislation, its level of funding, its structuring and its physical presence. With non-formal education, by contrast, there is no containment into a particular system, but rather a multiplicity of independent systems, for example, school boards, voluntary associations, trade unions, employers, and so on, which are involved in addressing the gamut of adult learning needs. Because of this multiplicity, and because of the absence of any coherence among the various systems, it is impossible to observe and analyze non-formal education as an entity in the same terms as formal education.

A particular anomaly of adult education is how it sits astride both systems of formal education and non-formal education. Seen in terms of structure, a significant portion of its activity comes about by virtue of its direct association with the formal educational system, for example, an adult education department within a school board or an extension department within an university. Equally, it is possible to see training departments within corporations and adult education sections within voluntary organizations. Seen in terms of program content, many programs can be offered as readily by a community group or another government department as by an institution attached to the formal educational system, for example, a course on coping with stress. Because of this dual existence in both formal and non-formal education it has proven difficult to circumscribe adult education for the purpose of public policy development. It is this fact which makes it difficult to pinpoint specific instances of public policy supporting adult education. The diverse nature of adult education has mitigated against the development of a cohesive public policy. Instead, the pattern is much more of a patch work.[15] For this reason it is necessary to first determine what it is we are looking for when we search out public policy in support of adult education.

---

[14] A. Thomas, "Legislation and Adult Education in Canada: A Comparative Study," p.123.

[15] In taking this point further, Alan Thomas of OISE, who has been researching the legal foundations for adult education in Canada for a number of years, observes the diverse nature of its statutory provision. He notes that the diversity "reveals something about the nature of adult education which is both necessary and desirable" and that the aspiration to have all concerns for adult learning contained in legislation exclusively designed for adults "seems to be vain and not very constructive." See A. Thomas, "Policy Development for Adult Education: The Law," in Rivera (Ed.), *Planning Adult Learning: Issues, Practices and Directions* (London: Croom Helm, 1987) p.60.

It is ironic that so much publicly supported adult education is in fact conducted when there is such a paucity of explicit policy. In attempting to explain this situation the first item to search out is the source of the statutory authority which enables the particular adult education activity to be conducted. Even when found the source may only make an oblique reference to adult education; for example, the enabling legislation establishing community colleges in several provinces appends adult education as one of the functions of a college. There is no further mention made, and it is up to the individual college to then sort out the extent of its offering in this area. Thus, legislation is often an insufficient indicator of adult education policy and it is necessary to look for other sources.

Because the wording of enabling legislation does not usually spell out the administrative details necessary to carry out the statutory provision, regulations are developed for this purpose. These regulations are approved by the executive council of government, i.e., the cabinet, or by executive committees of individual ministries. With regard to regulations, Thomas makes the point that they are less public in their pronouncement and much more difficult to track. He makes the further point regarding the harmony between legislation and regulations that "regulations are not supposed to contradict the letter of the law, and they rarely do, but they often impede or destroy what many supporters of the legislation believed to be the spirit."[16]

Legislation and regulations result in some level of provision being made, and it is this provision which indicates the extent of the actual commitment to adult learning. Indicators of this commitment include:

- the published goals and objectives which promote the commitment;
- the level of funding provided to support the commitment;
- the type of leadership provided to direct the commitment, i.e., how adult education is placed within the bureaucracy and what the capabilities are of the persons employed;
- the comprehensiveness of the provision which makes up the commitment, i.e., what range of programs is provided to whom;
- the results of the commitment, i.e., how many people participate and what is the extent of the learning;
- the extent to which adult education is incorporated into other areas of policy, i.e., adult education is recognized as an instrument of change;
- the degree to which adult education has become established as a necessary and integrated part of the public educational system.

These are but some of the indicators that might be used to determine the presence and certitude of adult education.

---

[16] A. Thomas, "Policy Development for Adult Education: The Law," p.63.

Before looking at specific provincial policies it is possible to make some generalizations about the Canadian situation regarding public policy and adult education, even though individual provinces have exercised their autonomy in educational matters in several distinct ways.

1. Initially adult education was conducted as part of the work of provincial departments of agriculture, public health and education. In the case of departments of education, it developed as an adjunct to the public school system, and this arrangement has remained strong.

2. In the post-World War I era universities conducted extension work, initially in agriculture and then in areas of social development and liberal education. University extension departments remain as important providers of adult education, with a proud tradition in this field.

3. The dislocation of the depression years and World War II gave impetus to the federal government to fund vocational training programs for adults. Since then there has been considerable direct federal funding made available in support of occupational training.

4. Since World War II and particularly since the 1960s there has been considerable expansion of the post-secondary educational system in terms of vocational/technical institutes, community colleges and universities. Adult education is seen to be an included function of these new institutions, and distinct departments carry out "continuing education" work.

6. The amount of adult education, broadly defined, being conducted has grown significantly, and publicly supported educational institutions have become the largest providers.

7. The expansion of provincial education systems in the period since 1960 has resulted in some provinces splitting their ministries of education into dual ministries, approximately along the lines of grade school education and post-secondary (advanced) education. The post-secondary system is often described as providing "continuing education" to distinguish it from "youth education" as provided by the grade school system.

8. With the splitting of a single education ministry into dual ministries, adult education is left straddling both, and a not insignificant amount of bureaucratic time is spent attempting to bring co-ordination to the now divided work.

9. The prevailing emphasis on occupational training in the post-secondary education system has in some cases resulted in "training" or some such synonym being included in the names of post-secondary education ministries.

10. While many provinces have acknowledged the role of adult education, and have appointed commissions which have studied this role, adult education has not been officially recognized as a distinct system, likened with the grade school system and the post-secondary educational system. Instead adult education continues to have a secondary status within most provincial education systems.

11. While correspondence study has always been one means for adults to complete their grade school education, the introduction of distance education technology has allowed some provinces to venture into technologically based distance education, and much programming has been designed to meet the needs of adults.

12. Government-sponsored adult education is not limited to education ministries. Instead several ministries are involved in sponsoring a variety of programs.

13. The economic recession of the early 1980s and the consequent fiscal restraint by government adversely affected support for adult education, and particularly general interest and community education. Provincial governments cut back on funding and forced the emphasis on a "user-pay" approach.

14. In the 1990s, private training institutions and private trainers have emerged as a major player in the adult education field. The federal government has withdrawn from the block purchase of seats in colleges and put this money more directly in the hands of "buyers." This shift combined with the growing emphasis on the "user-pay" approach means that there are excellent opportunities for providing adult education on a for-profit basis. For-profit agencies may have greater flexibility than their publicly funded counterparts because they are not subject to the same government control or labour agreements. Some provinces are beginning to study the policy implications of this development.[17]

15. Most of the inquiries into provincial education systems have acknowledged the essential place of adult education and have made recommendations for adult education to be a legitimate function of the post-secondary system.

All the provincial and territorial jurisdictions make provision for adult education in one form or another, and some are more deliberate in this regard than others. While there is a discernable pattern of development, there is no uniformity in either philosophy or structure. Each jurisdiction has determined

---

[17] In response to a series of post-secondary review panels, the Saskatchewan government introduced amendments to the Private Vocational Schools Regulation Act in 1995 which address consumer protection, tuition refunds, program quality and co-ordination with the educational system.

its provision in keeping with its particular social-historical context.[18] What follows is an overview of key initiatives within each province (with the exception of Quebec) which have influenced in some way the development of public policy related to adult education.[19] The situation in Quebec is described in detail in Chapter 3.

Alberta

Statement of the General Situation

Adult education is offered by all provincial educational institutions although not all have discrete adult education departments. These institutions have latitude in their governing legislation which enables them to be active in this area. A particular feature of the Alberta system is the policy involvement by the government through a network of Community Adult Learning Councils (originally Further Education Councils). The government's formal recognition of, and involvement in, further education (a synonym for adult education) dates from the early 1970s, and specifically with the publication in 1975 of the policy statement *Further Education Policy, Guidelines, Procedures*.[20] By establishing the councils the government acknowledged the large number and variety of public educational institutions and voluntary organizations engaged in offering adult education courses, and the councils provided a mechanism for co-ordinating government services in this area at the local level.

An analysis of the Alberta data from the 1992 Statistics Canada Adult Education and Training Survey shows that participation in adult education and training is almost 20 percent greater than the Canadian average. In addition, although huge gaps in participation rates exist between the most advantaged and the most disadvantaged persons in the province, these gaps are smaller than those in other Canadian jurisdictions.[21]

The Banff Centre for the Arts is another unique feature of the Alberta situation. It was under the governance of the University of Alberta from 1935

---

[18] There is, however, increasing collaboration among the provinces in educational matters as evidenced by the formation in 1967 of the Council of Ministers of Education. The Council is a national forum which serves to enable the provinces to speak collectively to the federal government on educational matters and which also promotes inter-provincial consultation and co-operation. The Council has no constitutional authority, nor are its decisions binding. It does select delegates to international conferences sponsored by the United Nations Educational, Scientific and Cultural Organization (UNESCO) such as the International Conference on Adult Education and by the Organization for Economic Co-operation and Development (OECD).

[19] For an early assessment of this work see P. Sandiford, *Adult Education in Canada: A Survey* (Toronto: University of Toronto, 1935).

[20] Province of Alberta, *Further Education Policy, Guidelines and Procedures* (Edmonton: Ministry of Advanced Education and Manpower, 1975).

[21] Canadian Association for Adult Education, *Adult Education and Training in Alberta* (Toronto: CAAE, 1994).

to 1966. From 1966 to 1978 it operated under the aegis of the University of Calgary. It became autonomous in 1978.

There are two departments responsible for education, the Department of Education and the Department of Advanced Education and Career Development. The latter has full responsibility for all adult education programs.

Historical Developments

The origins of adult education in Alberta stem from the first legislative session of the new province in 1906 when a bill was passed creating the University of Alberta.[22] Soon after opening in 1908, the university became very active in extension work, particularly in providing service to Alberta's rural population. The provincial Department of Agriculture also carried out a noteworthy program of adult education. A second development of note occurred in 1958 when Lethbridge Junior College opened, thereby becoming one of the first public two-year community colleges in Canada.[23] Included in its functions was the provision of community education. The further development of colleges was stimulated that same year when the Public Junior Colleges Act was passed and when, in the next year, a Royal Commission on Education delivered its findings which helped clarify the role of the new colleges. Additional definition was provided in 1969 with the passing of the Colleges Act, and Alberta's colleges were confirmed in providing, among other things, access to "wider educational opportunity to a broader segment of society."[24]

Another key element in the foundation of adult education in Alberta was the creation of the Alberta Vocational Colleges. They were created between 1965 and 1972 with a mandate to provide education and training opportunities to undereducated adults up to the high school level. In 1997, responsibility for these four colleges will pass from the government to independent boards of governors.

The pivotal thinking with respect to public policy and adult education in Alberta stems from the appointment in 1969 of the Educational Planning Commission, chaired by Dr. Walter Worth. The Commission was given a broad mandate in order that it might make recommendations to guide the Alberta government in developing its system of public education for the next decade.[25] While a change in government occurred in the interval of the Com-

---

[22] For an historical account see D. Berghofer and A. Vladicka, *Access to Opportunity, 1905-80: The Development of Post-Secondary Education in Alberta* (Edmonton: Alberta Advanced Education and Manpower, 1980).

[23] J. Dennison and P. Gallagher, *Canada's Community Colleges: A Critical Analysis* (Vancouver: University of B.C. Press, 1986) p.19.

[24] Ibid., p.22.

mission's appointment and the tabling of its report, *A Choice of Futures*, and this mitigated against many of its recommendations being adopted, nonetheless the document contains important statements about the place of state-supported adult education in Alberta. Much of the thinking in this regard was done by the Lifelong Education Task Force appointed by the Commission.[26]

The first explicit policy on adult education in Alberta was introduced in 1975 when the Department of Advanced Education published the document *Further Education Policy, Guidelines and Procedures*.[27] The distinguishing feature of this policy was the Local Further Education Council (LFEC) designed to co-ordinate all the available resources for adult education in a given community. In 1994, the government released a revised policy and guideline document in which the LFEC's were renamed Community Adult Learning Councils. The revised guidelines emphasize the councils' role in meeting learning needs of the respective community, in facilitating study circles, and in promoting literacy programs. Councils are encouraged to use their resources to increase access for those learners who cannot afford to pay for the programs they need. The revised policy states that Community Adult Learning Councils will

> meet the learning needs of adults through systematic inter-agency communication, co-operation and co-ordination especially for those whose participation in threatened by financial or other barriers.[28]

In spite of a 21 percent reduction in funding between 1993 and 1996, there are some eighty-four councils operating across the province. As a result of the revised policy, councils offer more programs for marginalized groups (single parents, people living below the poverty line, isolated seniors). These programs tend to focus on personal development issues such as life skills, conflict resolution and independent living. Councils continue to offer a wide range of general interest programs on a cost-recovery basis and some of the more entrepreneurial ones generate surplus revenues from this activity. Alberta's councils represent a particularly outstanding example of an adult education policy which has had a direct impact on accessibility for the learner.

The original 1975 policy has recently been restated and now asserts that "Alberta Advanced Education will facilitate involvement in further education by adult Albertans, and encourage systematic inter-agency communication,

[25] H. Roberts, *Culture and Adult Education: A Study of Alberta and Quebec* (Edmonton: University of Alberta Press, 1982) p.69.

[26] Commission on Educational Planning, *A Choice of Futures* (Edmonton: Queen's Printer, 1972).

[27] Province of Alberta, *Further Education Policy, Guidelines and Procedures*.

[28] Alberta Advanced Education and Career Development, *Community Adult Learning Program* (Edmonton: Alberta Advanced Education and Career Development, 1994), p.3.

co-operation and co-ordination in the provision of learning opportunities for adults."

Alberta has long been an innovator in adult education. There have been many examples in Alberta of public policy favouring adult education. These include provision by the Department of Education for adults who are completing their high school education, the creation of the Community Educational Consortia to facilitate credit programming at the community level, the Extension Grant Program (terminated in 1997), the establishment in 1972 of Athabasca University to provide distance education, the Skills Development Program (annual budget of $90 million) and the formation in 1973 of the Alberta Education Communications Corporation—popularly referred to as ACCESS Alberta—for the production and broadcasting of educational programming. (A sign of the times, it was sold to a private broadcaster, Moses Znaimer, in the mid-1990s.) Additionally, the Banff Centre for the Arts has enjoyed an international reputation as a unique adult learning centre.

In 1997, Alberta boasted sixty-five Volunteer Tutor Literacy Programs supported through the Community Adult learning Program in partnership with the local Adult Learning Councils. These programs have been part of Alberta's further education efforts since 1979. As part of the program, the department publishes 34,000 copies of *English Express*, a tabloid for adults who are learning to read.

In the 1990s, the government made *de facto* policy changes by introducing major cuts to base funding for adult education. In 1994, Advanced Education and Career Development released a strategic plan for adult learning in the decade ahead. [29] The document identified four key priorities—access, responsiveness (i.e., creation of new paths for competing degrees), affordability and accountability. Incentive grants in support of these priorities restored some of the base funding that had been cut. In 1995, a formative discussion paper entitled *Vision for Change: A Concept Paper of the Development of a Virtual Learning System*[30] gave impetus to innovations in delivery and new distance education initiatives. In response, the government introduced the Learning Enhancement Envelope, a $30 million incentive program to encourage the development of "a system-wide virtual learning environment."[31] It is hoped that this fund will lead to an adult learner support network which can be accessed in any community across the province.

---

[29] Alberta Advanced Education and Career Development, *New Directions for Adult Learning* (Edmonton: Alberta Advanced Education and Career Development, 1994).

[30] Alberta Advanced Education and Career Development, *Vision for Change* (Edmonton: Alberta Advanced Education and Career Development, 1995).

[31] Alberta Advanced Education and Career Development, *Enhancing Alberta's Adult Learning System Through Technology* (Edmonton: Alberta Advanced Education and Career Development, 1996) p.4.

In 1996, Alberta became the first province to sign a deal with Ottawa to take control of job counselling, training, work placement and other labour-adjustment programs. The agreement gave Alberta full control over $317 million of federal funds. The federal plan is designed to allow each province to tailor job-related adult education programs to the emerging economic needs in its territory. The plan will also strengthen the trend of focussing adult education efforts increasingly on work-related training.

Alberta's progressive policies in adult education appear to have borne fruit. A 1985 report from Statistics Canada showed that adults in Alberta are the most active in Canada in pursuing their continuing education.[32] Subsequent surveys have invariably indicated higher participation rates in Alberta than in any other jurisdiction in Canada. A 1996 report indicated that 40 percent of adult Albertans enroll in adult learning programs each year.

Nonetheless, during this same period, Alberta has made substantial cuts to funding for adult education and has given increasing priority to work-related training. A 1996 concept paper entitled *Employability and Beyond* indicates that the purpose of adult development system is "to provide a continuum of learning opportunities for individuals ... to enable them to obtain and retain work and to pursue further training or education."[33] Later in 1996, a discussion paper entitled *People and Prosperity* gave further priority to human resource development and especially to the task of increasing workers' skills and employability. While the paper espouses a vision of Albertans being able to participate in the work force *and* contributing to their communities, the goals and actions proposed focus exclusively on work-related initiatives.[34]

The Alberta experience is an encouraging one. Participation rates continue to grow. In spite of significant budget cuts, the government of Alberta has maintained its commitment to a broad range of adult education programs and has pursued new policy initiatives in many areas. Adult education advocates will want to encourage policy makers to continue to expand this broad-based approach rather than one that focuses narrowly on job-related training as the panacea for progress in the province.

---

[32] Statistics Canada, *One in Every Five: A Survey of Adult Education in Canada* (Ottawa: Ministry of Supply and Services Canada, 1985).

[33] Alberta Advanced Education and Career Development, *Employability and Beyond* (Edmonton: Alberta Advanced Education and Career Development, 1996) p.3.

[34] Alberta Advanced Education and Career Development, *People and Prosperity* (Edmonton: Alberta Advanced Education and Career Development, 1996).

British Columbia

Statement of the General Situation

Most of the province's public educational institutions offer adult education programs, although there is no comprehensive policy providing for this. Instead, legislation gives sufficient latitude to the public educational system to be active in adult education. In the early 1970s many school districts gave over their adult education programming to the newly created community colleges. In 1988, the Ministry of Education extended free education at the public schools to adults over nineteen years of age, to the Grade 12 level.

In 1986, the British Columbia government created the Ministry of Advanced Education and Job Training. In 1996, it was re-integrated with other educational programming into the Ministry of Education, Skills and Training.

Historical Developments

In 1854, a group of settlers at Craigflower, outside Victoria, formed a study group and took turns presenting papers to each other on such subjects as theology, natural history and geography. This is the first recorded example of the strong commitment to continuing education in British Columbia.[35] In 1994, a multivariate analysis of work-related and employer-supported courses prepared by the University of British Columbia's Centre for Policy Studies in Education showed that the likelihood of work-related or employer sponsored training is 50 percent greater in British Columbia than in Ontario. [36]

One of the earliest policy development in support of this interest in adult education occurred in 1910 when the province's Public Schools Act was amended to permit school boards to conduct night school courses. In 1915 the University of British Columbia was established, and extension work began shortly thereafter. In 1963 the Public Schools Act was again revised in a way favourable to adult education, this time to allow for the formation of community colleges. Over the next fifteen years, fifteen colleges and five institutes were created. Also in 1963, the Universities Act (B.C.) created Simon Fraser University and the University of Victoria. Both developments were as a result of a report by the then-president of the University of British Columbia entitled *Higher Education in British Columbia and a Plan for the Future*.[37] Continu-

---

[35] G. Selman, "The Invisible Giant" in *Adult Education in Canada: Historical Essays* (Toronto: Thompson Educational, 1995).

[36] Rubenson, K. & Xu, Gongli, *Adult Education and Training in British Columbia: An Analysis of the 1994 Adult Education and Training Survey* (Vancouver: Centre for Policy Studies in Education, University of British Columbia, 1997).

[37] J. Macdonald, *Higher Education in British Columbia and a Plan for the Future* (Vancouver: University of British Columbia, 1962).

ing education was included in the mandate of all these new post-secondary institutions. Additionally the province took advantage of federal funding under the federal government's Technical and Vocational Training Assistance Act (1960) to expand its occupational training programs and facilities.

In 1976 the government appointed committees to investigate three aspects of the province's educational system: the Commission on University Programs in Non-Metropolitan Areas (Winegard Commission); the Commission on Technical, Vocational, and Trades Training (Goard Commission); and the Committee on Continuing and Community Education (Faris Committee).[38] The outcome of this activity was the passage of the Colleges and Institutes Act (1977) which, among other things, created the Open Learning Institute with responsibility for developing a provincial distance education program. Educational broadcasting was begun in 1980 with the formation of the Knowledge Network of the West Communications Authority (KNOW-BC). In 1988, the province's initiatives in distance education, educational broadcasting and open learning were brought together under the aegis of the Open Learning Agency.

Despite these institutional developments, there have been significant inconsistencies in the government's commitment to adult education broadly defined. A Division of Continuing Education, established within the Ministry of Education in 1977 and later transferred to the new Ministry of Advanced Education and Job Training, was systematically dismantled by 1987. In 1988, Selman wrote that "the improvements which appeared to have been made during the 1970s in government's acceptance of responsibility for leadership and support for adult education have proven to be illusory, or at best, short term."[39] Perhaps the observation was too harsh since the unit was resurrected in 1994 as the Innovation and Continuing Education Branch.

From 1990 to 1996, there were a number of major initiatives to increase access to adult education. The Skills Now program injected $200 million into post-secondary education in 1994 and 1995. Nearly 70 percent of all approved projects involved application of new learning technologies. For example, some twenty community skill centres were created with a goal of increasing access to new learning technologies and providing infrastructure for a new

---

[38] There had been an earlier Task Force appointed to review the role of the community colleges in the province, in 1973 under the NDP administration. Its report made a number of recommendations supporting continuing education in the colleges, even to the extent that the colleges should become the public agency responsible for the funding, provision, and (or) co-ordination of adult and continuing education in each college region. The report was not acted on when the NDP was voted out of office in 1975. Task Force on the Community College in British Columbia, *Towards the Learning Community* (Victoria: Department of Education, 1974). See also the *Report of the Committee on Continuing and Community Education in British Columbia* (Victoria: Ministry of Education, 1976).

[39] G. Selman, "The Invisible Giant" in *Adult Education in Canada: Historical Essays*, p.305.

Learning Network which connect all schools in the province with colleges, universities, libraries and museums.

The provincial government protected education from the full impact of nearly $2 billion cuts in federal transfer payments from 1995 to 1997. In particular, post-secondary tuition fees were frozen and grants to most public educational institutions were maintained. At the same time, recent British Columbia governments have emphasized vocational and technical education as priorities. Other kinds of adult education are supported only on a user-pay or for-profit basis.

The British Columbia Labour Force Development Board was created and abolished within a three-year period in the mid-1990s. Like many of its sister boards, it fell victim to cost-cutting measures of the provincial and federal governments before it really got off the ground.

As part of the policy development process initiated through the Division of Continuing Education, a policy statement on adult basic education (ABE) programs was adopted in 1982. This policy recognized the responsibility of the Ministry of Education to "foster learning opportunities for adults in British Columbia who have not had the opportunity to develop some or all of those skills required to function successfully in Canadian society."[40] The policy of the Ministry is to provide "to adult citizens and landed immigrants residing in the province, reasonable access to high quality adult basic education programs." A more recent expansion on this policy is the provision for adults over nineteen years of age to receive free education to the Grade 12 level in the province's public schools.[41] This policy has helped to insure continued support for adult basic education in the public school system in spite of the fiscal restraints of the 1990s. The college system has all but abandoned ABE because they receive no funding for these programs.

As the end of the century approaches, adult education policy in British Columbia is still piecemeal and fragmented. In the latter half of the 1990s, the emphasis is on prior learning assessment and recognition, distance education and learning outcomes—in each case, with particular reference to work-related training. Private, for-profit training is increasing while publicly funded adult education in support of citizenship, culture and community building languishes in a policy vacuum.

---

[40] Province of British Columbia, *A Ministerial Policy on the Provision of Adult Basic Education Programs including English Language Training in the Public Education System of British Columbia (1982)* (Victoria: Department of Education, 1982).

[41] Ministry of Education, *Ministry of Education Information Circulars # 275 and # 353 (1988)* (Victoria: Ministry of Education, 1988).

Manitoba

Statement of the General Situation

There is a well-developed system of government support for adult education in Manitoba. Manitoba was the first province to conduct a Royal Commission solely on adult education (1945) and at that time the importance of co-operation and co-ordination in the provision of adult education was emphasized. Today the Ministry of Education and Training, through the Adult and Continuing Education Branch of the Division of Post-Secondary, Adult and Continuing Education, gives tangible support to the adult education which is conducted through the school districts, community colleges and community-based organizations. Priority for this funding assistance is given to those groups which are seen as educationally disadvantaged. Many policy documents make specific reference to the needs of Manitoba's Aboriginal population. The province's four universities offer a variety of continuing education programs that also support the adult education needs of Manitobans.

There is one department responsible for education, the Department of Education and Training.

Historical Developments

The promotion of rural life has historically been important to Manitoba's social and economic fabric, and in the earlier years the absence of publicly funded institutions active in adult education work saw the co-operative movement play a lead role in this area. As an example, from 1939 onwards the Manitoba Federation of Agriculture and Co-operation encouraged and supported study groups through supplying speakers for meetings, organizing film circuits, and maintaining a central lending library.[42] Exigencies of World War II caused the Manitoba government to become active in the area of vocational training, and this was stimulated by the federal government's Vocational Training Co-ordination Act of 1942 which provided for generous joint funding arrangements. This work continued at war's end as part of the resettlement process for returning veterans under the terms of the Veterans Rehabilitation Act (1945), which assisted veterans wishing to pursue vocational or post-secondary education.

Soon after the war the Manitoba government was lobbied to appoint a Royal Commission on Adult Education with the hope that increased co-ordination and co-operation, including government involvement, would result from such a study. The Commission was chaired by Dr. A.W. Trueman, President of the University of Manitoba, and reported in 1947.[43] Its two principal

---

[42] B. Fairbairn, *Building A Dream* (Saskatoon: Western Producer Prairie Books, 1989) p.84.

recommendations were: (1) that a Manitoba Adult Education Council be established, and (2) that an Inter-departmental Committee on Adult Education be established to make most effective use of federal assistance, to establish more efficient co-ordination of provincial government adult education programs, to avoid duplication and waste and to co-operate with voluntary agencies. There were, however, no policy developments on the part of government, as had been anticipated. However the influence of federal assistance to Manitoba's vocational training remained strong and accounted in large measure for developments in the late 1960s.

The next major development was the adaptation of Manitoba's vocational institutions into three community colleges in 1969. By this date vocational training had become a significant portion of the adult education provided in the province, due mainly to the funding made available under various federal programs. This change had a general effect of increasing the number of adults participating in a variety of both formal and non-formal programs. In 1993, the community colleges were incorporated and began operating under the governance of their own boards.

Within a few years the government determined that a study of the province's post-secondary system was required, and in 1972 a Task Force on Post-Secondary Education was appointed.[44] The subsequent report did not specifically address the area of continuing education (which it defined as "education that does not lead to a high school or college diploma or to a university degree") but it noted how lifelong learning had become an "articulate public demand." Particular concern was expressed for the ability of disadvantaged groups to access and participate in continuing education. The report put forward the consideration that "continuing education—a co-ordinated system of life-long learning—may provide some solutions to the problems of accessibility and participation."[45] Despite this inclination the report further noted the difficulty of finding a systematic way to fund and support such a system. Regardless, one of the hallmarks of adult education in Manitoba continues to be the attention paid to the disadvantaged referred to in the report. An example is the ACCESS programs which were designed to increase access for groups (northern residents, Aboriginal people, single parents, immigrant students, women learners) that face systemic barriers to adult education. The ACCESS programs allow them to participate in a variety of post-secondary programs that lead to professional designations.

---

[43] Royal Commission on Adult Education, *Report* (Winnipeg: King's Printer, 1947).

[44] Province of Manitoba, *Report of the Task Force on Post-Secondary Education in Manitoba* (Winnipeg: Queen's Printer, 1973).

[45] Ibid., p.179.

Through a reorganization of the Department of Education in 1982 a Post-Secondary, Adult and Continuing Education division (PACE) was created with the following as part of its mission:

- To increase accessibility to post-secondary education for Manitobans who have participated only marginally in post-secondary education;
- to increase the system's ability to respond to the diversity of learners' needs in the province;
- To contribute to human resource development in the province.[46]

In 1993, the PACE division disappeared when the Advanced Education and Skills division was created. In particular, its mandate focussed on labour-force analysis, on labour mobility and on improving the linkage between training and labour-market needs. The new division brought together a range of adult education initiatives including youth programs, employment development programs and training for social welfare recipients. In 1994, it was replaced with a new division called Training and Advanced Education. The new division, under its own deputy minister, indicated the higher profile and key role for this area of education in Manitoba's strategic plans.

In 1989 the responsibility for the education of adults, including employment services and job training initiatives, was consolidated in a new Department of Education and Training. Within the PACE division there is an Adult and Continuing Education Branch which in turn is composed of a Continuing Education Unit and an Adult Language Training Unit. One of the programs of the Continuing Education Unit is to provide grants to school districts for part-time adult programs and grants to rural school divisions for evening use of facilities for adult education programs.[47]

The Manitoba Task Force on Literacy released a major report in 1989 which advocated pluralistic literacy development that was learner-centred, community based and accessible across the province.[48] It called for the creation of a Manitoba Adult Literacy Council as well as a Literacy Office within the Department of Education and Training and adequate funding to support the proposed policy objectives. Finally it called for special attention to the literacy needs of the Aboriginal community in both English and mother tongues. The report defines literacy as a set of skills that enable individuals or groups to fulfill their own self-determined objectives as individuals, family and community members, workers and members of various groups. In other words, it recognized the essential connection between literacy and full citizen-

---

[46] Manitoba Education, *Annual Report 1987-88* (Winnipeg: Manitoba Education, 1988) p.33.

[47] Ibid., p.41.

[48] Manitoba Education and Training, *Pathways for the Learner* (Winnipeg: Government of Manitoba, 1989).

ship. As a result of this report, funding for literacy in the province increased dramatically, reaching a level of $850,000 annually by 1996. Many of the other recommendations were implemented in the succeeding years, though literacy programs in Aboriginal tongues were never put in place.

Manitoba made a strong pitch to move skills training to the top of the adult education agenda in 1989 when it released the report of the Skills Training Advisory Committee. In his introduction, then-Minister of Education and Training Len Derkach stated that "a skilled, adaptable and productive labour force is essential to Manitoba's ability to compete during this period of rapid market and technological change."[49] He announced his intention to introduce a skills-training strategy as a blueprint for developing a strong training culture throughout the province. The language and the recommendations in the report mirror similar reports from other provinces written during this period. They emphasize the need for improved basic education and literacy skills, the shift from a resource-based to an information-based economy, the mismatch between labour and demand, the need to share responsibility for labour-force development among government, private sector, labour and educational institutions and the need for market-driven training. The recommendations proposed the creation of Community Training Committees, a Manitoba Skills Institute to advise on public policy and to promote a training culture, a strengthened community college system, increased focus on human resources planning and special attention to the education needs of Native communities. While the Community Training Committees and the Manitoba Skills Institute did not materialize, most of the recommendations were implemented. The report led to the creation of sectoral committees in seven high priority areas and served as the foundation for the 1990 provincial training strategy Work Force 2000.

In 1993, a new policy statement stressed further the need to use education to increase the province's human resources capacity. "Our educational investment must be channelled into meaningful skills training that will match the talents of Manitobans with emerging opportunities in business and industry."[50] The statement applauded the creation of the Skills Training Advisory Committee in 1989, and the Work Force 2000 strategy. It announced a $250 million agreement with the federal government for joint labour-force adjustment programs, the creation of labour-force development boards and a task force on distance education. Above all, the document affirmed, "government, business, labour, educators and communities must work together to develop a

---

[49] Manitoba Education and Training, *Partners in Skills Development* (Winnipeg: Government of Manitoba, 1989) Introduction.

[50] Economic Development Board, *Framework for Economic Growth* (Winnipeg: Economic Development Board, 1993) p.39.

province-wide commitment to knowledge and skills training, and lifelong learning."[51] The distance education task force gave birth to MERLIN (Manitoba Educational Resources Learning Information Network) which supports all educational institutions in the province in increasing the use of educational technologies. On the other hand, the recommendations regarding labour-force development boards were never implemented because the province anticipated the shift in the federal approach to this work.

In 1993, former premier Duff Roblin chaired a provincial commission to review university education. The report[52] called for an expansion of the community college system, an increase in the use of technology for education, the creation of a First Nations Post-Secondary Education Authority and greater flexibility for part-time students. While the First Nations Post-Secondary Education Authority was never created, Aboriginal leaders were appointed to the boards of all the community colleges and their Aboriginal programs were expanded. In 1996, the Post-Secondary Education Council was established, creating one administrative body to guide the development of post-secondary education. Among other things, it is hoped the Council will promote more prior learning assessment and recognition, increased laddering among institutions and improved articulation agreements.

Leading up to the 1995 provincial elections, incumbent premier Gary Filmon released a policy platform entitled *The Filmon Vision*.[53] The document integrated a number of themes and priorities from the work of the department of Education and Training including substantial statements on skills training, lifelong learning, building healthy communities and "pioneering tomorrow's education frontier." It promised a tax credit for post-secondary learning, an increase in community college funding and additional funding for literacy. It also declared again that skills training would be the cornerstone for a prosperous Manitoba. *The Filmon Vision* appeared to equate lifelong learning with skills training, improved literacy and greater computer literacy. It argued that productive citizenship and economic security is the result of building a learning culture in the province. According to the vision statement, a learning culture means increased access to education, more involvement by business in education, job readiness programs for youth, making colleges more responsive to industry training needs, changes in funding policies and further emphasis on literacy. The statement made no reference to issues related to adult

---

[51] Ibid., p.41.

[52] University Education Review Commission, *Post-Secondary Education in Manitoba: Doing Things Differently* (Winnipeg: Government of Manitoba, 1993).

[53] Manitoba Progressive Conservative Party, *The Filmon Vision* (Winnipeg: Manitoba Progressive Conservative Party, 1995).

education and its role in areas like nurturing citizen participation, linking culture and community building, or revitalizing rural life.

As it heads toward the year 2000, Manitoba, like many other provinces, has a policy agenda for adult education which is heavily weighted in favour of skills training and economic prosperity.

New Brunswick

Statement of the General Situation

Adult education is provided by all levels of New Brunswick's educational system: school districts, the community college and the four universities. As well, several government departments conduct occupational training. It is the New Brunswick Community College, however, which has a particular mandate to meet all the post-secondary, non-university education and training needs in the province. In the area of academic upgrading for adults (adult basic education, English as a second language, and so on) the community college reimburses school districts who plan and conduct this work. The community college instead focuses on providing continuing education in its various program areas. In 1992, the province merged its employment and labour department with its advanced education and training portfolios to create the Department of Advanced Education and Labour. This merger put increased emphasis on the close relationship between adult education programming and the needs of the provincial labour force.

Development of general interest and citizenship programming is left to the voluntary and non-governmental sector. However, the government encourages the use of public schools by community groups in the carrying out of their educational, cultural, recreational or other activities.[54]

Historical Developments

An early public provision was made for adult education in New Brunswick in the case of the adult vocational night program conducted by the Department of Education, which followed on the 1918 Vocational Act and the opening of Carleton County Vocational School a year later. By 1930 there were nine centres operating with an enrollment of 2,556.[55] The Department of Agriculture also conducted courses to promote improved farming techniques.

Similar to Nova Scotia, New Brunswick has a rich history of university-level higher education, and this includes extension services. As late as 1969

---

[54] New Brunswick Department of Education, *Policy Statement: Community Use of Schools—Schools Act, Section 67* (Fredericton, 1990).

[55] P. Sandiford, *Adult Education in Canada: A Survey*, Chapter 2, p.1.

studies on post-secondary education in New Brunswick were still committed to maintaining the province's system of higher education.[56] By the early 1970s it was evident, however, that the universities were not able to readily respond to training needs as they existed in various parts of the province. To address this situation the government in 1973 passed the New Brunswick Community College Act, thereby establishing a single community college with campuses in each of the province's five regions. The purpose of the new college was to meet the needs of all post-secondary, non-university education on a regional basis.[57] The college was described as being "neither a school nor a training programme but it is a comprehensive educational institution designed to provide a wide range of educational opportunities throughout the province."[58] This philosophy was reaffirmed in a 1978 planning document on the future of the New Brunswick Community College, *Quinquennial Plan, 1978-1983.*

Originally the New Brunswick Community College Act was administered by a new Ministry of Continuing Education which was renamed in 1983 as the Ministry of Community Colleges and is now the Ministry of Advanced Education and Training. When first established, the college absorbed the Vocational Branch of the Department of Education, which included two institutes of technology and five trade schools.

The college is intended to provide a wide range of educational opportunities, including adult education programs offered through the community service sections of each college campus. The primary focus of adult education delivered through the college remains, however, with vocational training programs and programs of continuing education for occupational groups.

Since 1987, New Brunswick has been aggressive in developing and piloting new work-related training programs. The provincial government has seen such programs as a way of increasing the capability and productivity of its labour force. It also believes it can lower its social assistance costs by increasing the employability of assistance recipients. Generally, these programs were designed to parallel changes in the federal social security and unemployment insurance systems.[59] Many of them were developed in close collaboration with the federal government.

These initiatives have included new training programs for aquaculturists and fish plant workers, FOCUS (Future Opportunities to Combat Unemployment Successfully), Opportunity Corps, NB Works—a $178 million demon-

---

[56] J. Dennison and P. Gallagher, *Canada's Community Colleges*, p.58.

[57] Government of New Brunswick, *A Statement of Policy and Intent* (Fredericton: Government of New Brunswick, 1974).

[58] W.B. Thompson, "The New Brunswick Community College," *Canadian Vocational Journal, 10,* 4 (1975) p.32.

[59] Government of New Brunswick, *From Options to Action: A New Social Assistance Blueprint* (Fredericton: Department of Human Resources Development-NB, 1994).

stration project aimed at long-term social assistance recipients combining work and education activities, the Self-Sufficiency Project, NB Job Corps—a workfare project where participants received $12,000 for 26 weeks of work on a community development project.

From 1990 forward, New Brunswick also gave literacy a high profile through the Premier's Advisory Council on Literacy. This initiative led to the formation of Literacy New Brunswick Inc., to the creation of some 650 Community Academic Services Programs (CASP's) and to the appointment of the only provincial Minister of State for Literacy. CASP's involve communities, the private sector, voluntary agencies and government in literacy training. Government sources claim that, as a result of the CASP initiative, the literacy rate in the province has increased from 76 percent to 80 percent. This data clashes with the results of the International Adult Literacy Survey which found little change in the literacy rate in New Brunswick over roughly the same period.

In 1993, the Commission on Excellence in Education released its report *To Live and Learn: The Challenge of Education and Training*. In responding, the provincial government gave priority to expanded distance education and the formation of TeleEducation NB. The report also highlighted the implementation of a prior learning assessment system throughout New Brunswick Community College by 1994. Additional steps during this period focussed on greater transferability of credits between universities and colleges.

The New Brunswick Labour Force Development Board (NBLFDB) was one of six established across the country.[60] By late 1996, only the boards in New Brunswick, Saskatchewan and Nova Scotia still remained. The NBLFDB differed from the others inasmuch as it was jointly funded by the federal and provincial governments. As labour market responsibilities shifted primarily to the provinces in the late 1990s, provincial support for the NBLFDB remained apparently solid. However, it should be noted that the board has no formal role in the development of adult education policy and operates at arm's length from government's key policy-making bodies in education and human resources development.

It is important to note how New Brunswick, Canada's only officially bilingual province, has stressed accessibility issues for each linguistic group. The province recognized this challenge when it stated: "Our education and training system must be made fully accessible to all New Brunswickers, so that all of our citizens may participate fully in the province's economic life."[61]

---

[60] The others were in Newfoundland, Ontario, British Columbia, Nova Scotia and Saskatchewan. Quebec's Société pour le développment de la main d'oeuvre was of a different structure with related objectives.

[61] Province of New Brunswick, *Toward 2000—An Economic Development Strategy for New Brunswick* (Fredericton: Province of New Brunswick, 1989) p.14.

New Brunswick presents an interesting case for the student of adult education policy since there has been significant activity in terms of policy formulation, program development and funding, especially in the ten-year period
from 1987 to 1997. As in other provinces, the bulk of that activity focuses on
job-related training and is largely divorced from considerations about adult
education as a tool for building citizenship and community. Critics in New
Brunswick argue that many of the initiatives are political window dressing
that have had little impact on the real needs of adult learners. Government
reports on these initiatives tend to evaluate them in terms of inputs (dollars
spent, number of participants) rather than using outcomes-based indicators
that give a more meaningful measure of impact.

Newfoundland

Statement of the General Situation

In many cases, some of the most innovative and influential developments
in adult education take place at the periphery of public policy. The story of
adult education in Newfoundland— Canada's most easterly, most remote and
most economically depressed province—offers some outstanding examples of
this fact. One such example is described later in this section.

All of Newfoundland's public post-secondary institutions offer adult education programming. In 1987, the province's post-secondary system expanded
to include community colleges. In the early 1990s, the proliferation of funding through the Atlantic Groundfish Strategy (TAGS) resulted in the creation
of a large number of private colleges as well. These latter played a major role
in literacy and upgrading programs while the community colleges have
focussed increasingly on technical and vocational training. It was decided, in
1996, to bring the province's five colleges together under one administration
in Stephenville. It is unclear what impact these changes and the termination of
the TAGS funding will have on adult education in the late 1990s.

Historical Developments

The provision of education in Newfoundland and Labrador has always
been made difficult by such overwhelming factors as rugged geography, scattered settlement and limited budget. Despite this, governments over the years
have recognized the importance of adult education as a means of helping the
working population especially to cope with the vagaries of the economy and
the resulting impact on their livelihoods. Newfoundland has a proud adult
education tradition, established well before the province entered Confederation in 1949.

The founding of Memorial University College in 1925 and the initiating of
its evening and extension classes shortly thereafter marks the first consistent

offering of adult education classes in the then-colony of Great Britain. An-other development occurred in the early 1930s as a result of funding from the Carnegie Foundation. In a concerted effort to reach the isolated communities and provide academic upgrading classes, "Opportunity Schools" were estab-lished whereby instructors would travel from one community to another, pre-senting eight-week courses in each location. By 1936 a total of 140 of these schools had been conducted with some 5,000 adults participating.[62] Recogniz-ing the importance of adult education work, the government in 1936 formed an Adult Education Branch within the Department of Education. Under the direction of this branch a varied program was offered in St. John's (where a permanent centre for adult education was established) and in nine other cen-tres.

The entry of Newfoundland into Confederation precipitated further devel-opments. Memorial University was accorded university status, and this pro-vided additional stimulus to its adult education program of evening classes and extension services. To give greater guidance to this work a Director of Extension Services was appointed by the university in 1959. The next signifi-cant development saw Newfoundland in the post-World War II era taking advantage of the federal programs supporting technical and vocational educa-tion. Initially federal funding went to programs at the secondary school level only but, beginning with the TVTA Act of 1960, funding went to the construc-tion of eleven separate vocational schools. As well, two colleges were estab-lished, the College of Trades and Technology and the College of Fisheries, in addition to two training centres at Stephenville in connection with the con-struction of the Churchill Falls Hydro Project.

The 1960s was a time of change in Newfoundland's educational system, as reflected in the appointment of a Royal Commission on Education and Youth in 1964 (P.J. Warren, Chairman). The Commission reviewed the entire provin-cial educational system and in its recommendations proposed that six regional colleges be established. These colleges would improve access to post-secon-dary education throughout the province and would also support continuing education for adults. The recommendations regarding the college regions were not acted upon and instead resources went into constructing additional vocational schools.[63] As for the Department of Education's Adult Education Division, its name was changed in 1959 to the Division of Adult Continuation Classes. The division retained responsibility for "the organization and super-vision of adult education centres (night schools), the institutional pro-

---

[62] F. Rowe, *The Development of Education in Newfoundland* (Toronto: Ryerson, 1964) p.167. There is an updated version of this work by the same author entitled *Education and Culture in Newfoundland* (Scarborough: McGraw-Hill Ryerson, 1976).

[63] For additional commentary see J. Dennison and P. Gallagher, *Canada's Community Colleges*, p.66.

grammes, and adult education projects generally."[64] This name change reflected the orientation of the division's work to academic upgrading. In 1965
the responsibility for adult education was transferred to the division of Technical and Vocational Education and then, ten years later, reinstated as a separate division of Adult and Continuing Education. The emphasis of the division
was on adult basic education as well as continuing and community education.

The idea of community colleges was again recommended in the 1980
report of a task force investigating Newfoundland and Labrador's post-secondary system. The community colleges would be assigned responsibility "for
all post-secondary non-university education and for adult and continuing education, with the exception of those functions specifically assigned to other
institutions."[65] Again this recommendation was not acted upon, although other
developments at the time resulted in a campus of Memorial University being
established outside of St. John's and with the institutions at Stephenville being
amalgamated into what effectively was a community college. The impetus for
change in the provision of post-secondary education continued, however, and
in 1984 a new Department of Career Development and Advanced Studies was
established which included responsibility for both adult and vocational education as well as manpower planning. The divisions of Adult and Continuing
Education and of Technical and Vocational Education moved into the new
department. One of the initial policy initiatives of the department was the
release in June 1985 of a planning document, *White Paper: Reorganization of
Vocational School System.*[66] In this paper the government outlined its intention
to reorganize the provincial vocational school system into a provincial college
system. This change took place officially in June 1987 with the passage of An
Act to Establish a Community College System in the Province. Changes
brought about as a result of the Act included a new Fisher Institute of Applied
Arts and Technology being created and the two existing institutes being renamed as the Cabot Institute of Applied Arts and Technology and the Newfoundland Institute of Fisheries and Marine Technology. As well, the one
community college at Stephenville and the fifteen district vocational institutes
were regrouped into five multi-campus community colleges serving all the
regions of the province.[67] At this time the government moved out of the
delivery of adult education services and turned this responsibility over to the
community colleges. The services of the Division of Technical and Vocational

---

[64] F.W. Rowe, *Education and Culture in Newfoundland*, p.176.

[65] Task Force on Education, *Improving School Retention and Post-Secondary Participation: Educational Challenge of the 80s* (St. John's: Province of Newfoundland and Labrador, 1980).

[66] Department of Career Development and Advanced Studies, *White Paper: Reorganization of Vocational School System* (St. John's: Department of Career Development and Advanced Studies, 1985).

[67] P. Gallagher, *Community Colleges in Canada: A Profile* (Vancouver: Vancouver Community College Press, 1990) p.14.

Education, which also accounted for a considerable amount of adult training, were similarly absorbed by the colleges.

From 1959 to 1991, many ground-breaking experiments in adult education took place under the aegis of Memorial University's Extension Service.[68] The Extension Service was unique in that it engaged with rural people where they lived and worked, it avoided the language and conventions of schooling and its curriculum was the experience and problems of rural communities. It maintained a network of field offices which had a specific mandate to promote community development through adult education. It nurtured close links with the visual and performing arts community in the province. The Extension Service also had a media unit through which it pioneered the use of film as a tool for adult education. The unit worked in close collaboration with the National Film Board's Challenge for Change program. The strategies it developed were subsequently adapted for use in community development work in the United States, Asia and the Arctic.

This innovative work went on for over twenty-five years with virtually no public policy support. It was often criticized for a lack of results i.e., measurable data (inputs) like registrations, course calendars and tuition fees collected. To prove the worth of the Extension Service's work, its supporters pointed to communities which found the political will and self-sufficient mechanisms for maintaining their economic viability. Ultimately, the Extension Service was closed in 1991 when then-President Dr. A. May stated that its activities were not essential to the university's primary responsibility of teaching and research. In the public debate that followed, the premier of Newfoundland indicated in the House of Assembly that the university was an autonomous body and not subject to the dictates of government.

Like other provinces, Newfoundland tried a variety of new approaches during the 1990s. The Newfoundland Labour Force Development Board was short-lived because of tensions between labour and management. In any case, the TAGS funding dominated labour-adjustment schemes in the mid-1990s, leaving little room for other initiatives. In 1994, the Department of Education spun off literacy to an arm's length body called the Literacy Development Office. The move was intended to generate more local involvement and raise private sector funds for literacy work. Human Resources Development Canada set up drop-in centres across the province to deliver adult basic education

---

[68] There are a number of papers which describe the Extension Service's work including E. Harris's *Fogo Process in Communication* (St. John's: Memorial University, 1972), "The Buchans Community Learning Process: Not Essential to Teaching and Research" (Unpublished article) and *Dreaming Reality: Small Media in Community Development as Critical Educational Practice* (Unpublished Doctoral Dissertation, University of Toronto, Toronto, 1992); B. Gilbert's *Speaking of Fish* (Unpublished Master's Thesis, St. Francis Xavier University, Antigonish, 1993).

in the hopes of increasing access. The impact of these changes remain to be seen.

At the end of the century, Newfoundland continues to grapple with the connections between adult education and economic survival. It is a province, perhaps more than any other in Canada, where this is an essential question. Federal and provincial governments are looking anxiously for policies and programs in the areas of adult basic education, literacy, prior learning assessment and college-university articulation agreements that will strengthen the human resource capacity and economic potential of the province.

Nova Scotia

Statement of the General Situation

Until quite recently the school boards throughout the province were the main providers of adult education. This work was co-ordinated by the Continuing Education Division in the Department of Education. Specialized vocational and technical institutions and the several universities in Nova Scotia also offered extension services. In 1988, the Nova Scotia Community College system was created with six regional campuses and a provincial francophone campus. It is the mandate of the community college to provide and co-ordinate adult education and training in the respective regions, especially related to occupational training. The school boards continue to be active in offering their long-standing adult education programs.

There are two departments responsible for education, the Department of Education and Culture and the Department of Advanced Education and Job Training.

Historical Developments

Nova Scotia can claim a long history of both public and private support for adult education. As early as 1889 the provincial government was operating Coal Miners' Schools and in the next year it was conducting Government Night Schools for Adults.[69] St. Francis Xavier University established an Extension Department in 1928, with Father Moses Coady as its first director. From this event developed an internationally acclaimed adult education program known as the Antigonish Movement. Nearly seventy-five years later, St. Francis Xavier University carries on the tradition through its Coady Institute and a range of innovative adult education programs. The Nova Scotia Depart-

---

[69] Province of Nova Scotia, *Report of the Royal Commission on Post-Secondary Education* (Halifax: Province of Nova Scotia, 1985) p.227.

ment of Agriculture also played a leadership role by incorporating adult education into its field work program.

The province's formal commitment to adult education began in 1945 when the Adult Education Division was established within the Ministry of Education and, two years later, a Vocational Education Division. From the outset the purpose of the Adult Education Division was to provide "a variety of educational services designed to aid adults in enhancing the quality of life in their communities."[70] This work of continuing education was promoted by field representatives who assisted in the organizing and instructing of many courses, workshops and demonstration projects at the local level. One example of the community development philosophy guiding the Adult Education Division's work is the residential Folkschools that were conducted to foster active participation in community affairs.

By 1979 the adult education work had expanded to the point that, in addition to the field representatives, there were part-time and even a few full-time local administrators appointed by the school boards. Another feature of the division's leadership was the encouraging of school boards to operate community schools so as to provide recreational and general interest courses for all members of the community.

As for the Vocational Education Division, it also carried out an active program throughout the province, in this case primarily of evening classes. This form of vocational instruction had been initiated by the Department of Education beginning in 1907, and was an important aspect of its mandate. In the area of technical education, the division took on the responsibility for such programs as the School for Marine Engineers, the Land Survey School and the Navigation Schools at Yarmouth and Halifax. Other technical training institutions were subsequently established, the Nova Scotia Institute of Technology and the Nova Scotia Eastern Institute of Technology, as a result of federal assistance made available through the Technical and Vocational Training Assistance Act of 1960. Also as a result of federal training initiatives, a number of Adult Vocational Training Centres (AVTCs) were established to deliver occupational courses to unemployed adults.

The extent of adult education being conducted by the Department of Education by the end of the 1960s was such that the responsibilities of the two divisions were reorganized and brought under a single administration in 1969. The new unit was referred to as the Adult Education Program and consisted of three activity areas: Continuing Education Activity (to serve the general adult education needs of the population), the Applied Arts and Technology Activity and the Adult Vocational Training Activity. The work of this unit continued to

---

[70] F.K. Stewart, *Learning Opportunities for Adults: A Study of Adult and Continuing Education in Nova Scotia* (Halifax: Department of Education, 1981) p.29.

expand in all areas through the 1970s such that one knowledgable observer commented that "adult education—continuous learning has obviously become a significant, essential, and integral part of the total educational system."[71] The shortcoming that was noted, however, was the absence of any formal statement by the Department of Education outlining its responsibility and support for adult education. This absence was echoed in the report of the Royal Commission on Post-Secondary Education in 1985. The commissioners noted particularly that the area of continuing education had not been "as fully recognized or accepted as part of the lifelong process of education as it should be."[72] This observation very much reflected what was happening in the continuing education area.

The Adult Education Program unit was reorganized within the Department of Education such that continuing education was now a division of the subdepartment of Vocational and Technical Training. Fiscal restraint brought on by the recession of the early 1980s caused the government to amend the financing of continuing education as provided through the school boards. The provincial co-ordination and support for continuing education all but vanished when the Department of Education's field staff was reduced from six to a single person, and then to the point where no one was given responsibility for this work. Meanwhile other developments in Nova Scotia's post-secondary system were beginning to unfold which were about to have a considerable influence on the structuring of adult education.

In the 1970s, at a time when other provinces were developing their post-secondary education systems with the creation of community colleges, Nova Scotia maintained its existing system of universities and specialized vocational and technical institutions. In its 1974 report, the Royal Commission on Education, Public Services, and Provincial-Municipal Relations (Graham Commission) examined the idea of a community college system but did not recommend it over what already existed in Nova Scotia. The Report of the Royal Commission on Post-Secondary Education in 1985 did not consider such a system, given the advanced nature of the existing post-secondary institutions. The government began a process in 1986, however, of discussion, debate and public hearings on the idea of a community college system. Subsequently, in February of 1988, a blueprint of the system was revealed in *A White Paper on a Community College System for Nova Scotians*.[73]

In promoting the idea of a community college system, the Nova Scotia government was responding to the dual influences of technological advance-

---

[71] Ibid., p.48.

[72] Province of Nova Scotia, *Report of the Royal Commission on Post-Secondary Education*, p. xi.

[73] Province of Nova Scotia, *Foundation for the Future: A White Paper on a Community College System for Nova Scotians* (Halifax: Province of Nova Scotia, 1988).

ment and structural change in the economy. It maintained that Nova Scotians needed to continuously "upgrade and update their education achievements and work skills in order to remain competitive in a changing world economy."[74] Six regional colleges were proposed along with a provincial college for francophones. Their mandate was to provide training and education on both a full-time and part-time basis to students with or without Grade 12 graduation who entered directly from school or at other times in their lives.

The community college proposal was implemented in 1989 and the new colleges began as a consolidation of the facilities and programs of existing institutions. The ministerial responsibility for the colleges lies with the Department of Advanced Education and Job Training. This department has its genesis in 1985 when a Department of Human Resources and Training was created and then renamed the following year as the Department of Vocational and Technical Training. In 1987 it became the Department of Advanced Education and Job Training.

From the outset, the community colleges were mandated to offer a varied program including academic upgrading, trades training, applied arts, technical and technological training, community-based education, and courses targeted to groups with special needs. While the emphasis throughout is on training and occupational education, the colleges were also mandated to co-operate with local school boards and universities to provide continuing education classes. "Regional college administrators or Community Education and Training Officers will work with directors of continuing education programs offered by school boards and universities to determine the courses most appropriately delivered by each type of educational institution."[75]

In fact, college programming in the early 1990s was driven to a considerable extent by the availability of federal grants for customized skill development programs to meet the needs of employers. The Nova Scotia Teachers College was converted to a community college to deliver federally funded training programs related to community economic development and other innovative areas. However, this activity declined sharply and five college campuses were closed in 1995-96 when the federal government announced its intention to discontinue direct purchase of training. At the same time, Regional Industrial Training Committees were set up to support the Canadian Jobs Strategy program. These committees helped strengthen the emphasis on job-related training.

Nova Scotia established its Labour Force Development Board in 1992. It was slow to get started but received strong federal support and eventually mounted a modest program. There was little provincial support for the initia-

---

[74] Ibid., as quoted in the foreword.
[75] Ibid., p.97.

tive and the Board will likely not exist beyond 1997 with the end of federal funding.

Like other provinces, Nova Scotia invested substantially in distance education in the 1990s. All major Acadian communities have access to an interactive program through the Collège de l'Acadie. In 1995, the Atlantic premiers agreed to a plan for a common first and second year general undergraduate program to be made available by distance throughout the Atlantic region. Other policy initiatives during this period centered on improved articulation among Atlantic region colleges and universities, prior learning assessment and workplace literacy.

It is hard to see in Nova Scotia's current policy and programs much of the innovative character that marked its early contribution to adult education in Canada. Its current focus on job-related training is fairly typical of most provinces across the country.

Ontario

Statement of the General Situation

All components of Ontario's public education system provide adult education—the public schools, colleges and universities. In the case of the public schools and the colleges, this activity is carried out with the clear support of the provincial government, although there is an absence of policy specific to adult education. The college system, however, has been developed with adult education intentionally as a major aspect of its mandate. School boards have the authority to admit adults to day school programs, evening classes, summer school and vocational courses.[76]

As in other provinces, the number of departments responsible for education has grown and shrunk in response to political and fiscal exigencies. In the late 1980s, Ontario had three departments handling various aspects of adult education, the Ministry of Education, the Ministry of Colleges and Universities and the Ministry of Skills Development. By 1993, there was only the Ministry of Education and Training. This repeated restructuring adds to the difficulty of developing a thoughtful and comprehensive adult education policy for the province.

Historical Developments[77]

Similar to two other provinces (Nova Scotia and Saskatchewan), Ontario established an official adult education body at the end of World War II. In the

---

[76] Ministry of Education, *Continuing Education: A Resource Document* (Toronto: Ministry of Education, 1987).

case of Ontario, the Department of Education initially formed a Universities Adult Education Board, consisting of representatives from the universities, voluntary organizations and other interests. The board was given the following duties:

1. to promote adult education throughout the province;

2. to encourage the formation of local councils for adult education;

3. to make provision for the training of leaders in adult education;

4. to co-operate with all voluntary agencies in the promotion of adult education;

5. generally to co-operate with educational authorities and government departments, municipal, provincial or dominion, in promoting the purposes of the Board.[78]

Two years later the Department of Education established a Division of Adult Education and, until the mid-1960s, adult learning opportunities were provided by public schools through night classes and by the universities through extension courses.

As early as 1950 the idea of developing a system of junior colleges was proposed for Ontario.[79] While no action was taken at that time, in 1963 a committee of university presidents issued a report which advanced ideas to remedy a number of perceived deficiencies in Ontario's educational system.[80] The first deficiency was "a striking lack of opportunity for adult education in the province."[81] In the context of the report, adult education referred to learning opportunity for those who were high school graduates and who desired to continue their education, although not at a university level. This report and other developments at the time, including the federal government's post-secondary funding initiatives through the 1960 Technical and Vocational Training and Assistance Act, were influential in Ontario establishing a college system. In May 1965, amendments were introduced to the Department of Education Act that resulted in the creation of a provincial system of Colleges of Applied Arts and Technology.

The new colleges were given an explicit mandate to provide adult education. When the Minister of Education (and future Premier), William Davis,

---

[77] In 1996, the government of Ontario created an Advisory Panel on Future Directions for Post-Secondary Education in Ontario. The final report, entitled *Excellence, Accessibility, Responsibility*, includes an excellent background paper by David Cameron and Diana Royce entitled "Prologue to Change: An Abbreviated History of Public Policy and Post-Secondary Education in Ontario."

[78] As quoted in *Royal Commission on Adult Education, Report*, p.153.

[79] Royal Commission on Education in Ontario, *Report* (Toronto: King's Printer, 1950).

[80] Committee of Presidents of Provincially Assisted Universities and Colleges of Ontario, *The Structure of Post-Secondary Education in Ontario*, Supplementary Report No. 1 (Toronto, 1963).

[81] J. Dennison and P. Gallagher, *Canada's Community Colleges*, p.33.

introduced the college legislation, he outlined the colleges' adult education and vocational and technical emphasis as being to offer the following types of courses, among others:

- general adult education programs, including cultural and leisure time activities
- programs of recreation including physical education
- general or liberal education courses, including remedial courses in basic subjects
- re-training, upgrading and updating courses
- other courses to meet local needs.

The colleges were to be comprehensive institutions, "providing a wide variety of programs of varying lengths including work experience programs, by day and in the evening, for adults as well as for youths, and for probably more part-time than full-time students."[82]

An early affirmation of adult education's role in Ontario occurred in 1972 when the Commission on Post-Secondary Education in Ontario (referred to as the Wright Commission after its chairman) issued its report entitled *The Learning Society*.[83] In this report "continuing education" was given great credence within a process of "lifetime learning," and this laid the groundwork for further study by government.[84]

In 1981 the joint Ministries of Education and of Colleges and Universities issued a discussion paper entitled *Continuing Education: The Third System*.[85] In this document a conceptual distinction was made between the educational process which takes place on a full-time basis, and that which occurs after a learner ceases to be a full-time student. Two systems serve the full-time student, the first one being the elementary/secondary system (elementary and secondary schools, separate schools, private schools) and the second one being the post-secondary system (colleges, universities, and private vocational schools and colleges). The paper posited that continuing education represents a third system in the educational process, made up of "educational resources and agencies through which adults obtain learning opportunities throughout their lifetime after their initial schooling is terminated."[86] Included in this

---

[82] As contained in *Continuing Education: The Third System. A Discussion Paper* (Toronto: Ministry of Education and Ministry of Colleges and Universities, 1981) p.103.

[83] Commission on Post-Secondary Education in Ontario, *The Learning Society* (Toronto: Ontario Ministry of Public Services, 1972).

[84] For an assessment of the impact of this report and others of the time see G. Selman, "1972—Year of Affirmation for Adult Education," *Canadian Journal for the Study of Adult Education*, 3, 1 (1989) pp.33-44.

[85] Ministry of Education/Ministry of Colleges and Universities, *Continuing Education: The Third System*.

[86] Ibid., p.3.

system are both the continuing education available through the two established systems of education and the full spectrum of learning activities available outside of the traditional institutions. The paper identified twenty-one issues specific to the third system which pertained to the two ministries, and noted that a fundamental question was the extent to which they should commit themselves to a philosophy of lifelong education. As for policy, the paper suggested that at least a clear policy statement needed to be issued so as to clarify that which was implied in existing regulations and other documents.

In response to this call for clarification the government in 1983 issued a statement, *Continuing Education in the Schools, Colleges and Universities in Ontario*. This statement, while consolidating the government's views on various aspects of adult education, did not provide any clarification by way of specific policy. Instead, the next year a Continuing Education Review Project was initiated by the two ministries to provide recommendations on policy, organization and funding for continuing education as supported by the two ministries. (When the project submitted its findings in 1986, a new Ministry of Skills Development was included in the report.)[87] Again, there was a call for formal recognition of lifelong education and for policy which provides for adult education, for example, "that adult continuing education which addresses the civic, social and economic needs of adults through their various phases of development be formally recognized as being as important as that of the education of children and youth."[88]

In the 1990s, adult education policy and practice in Ontario has been subject to the same pressures as in other provinces. The primary concern of the Ontario government has been to reduce the cost of education and to increase investment by labour and the private sector in work-related training. Significant cuts in provincial and federal funding have caused a decline in adult education programs in school boards, colleges and universities. Among the casualties are upgrading programs for adults in the school boards, community development and outreach programs in the colleges, and any non-credit programs in colleges and university that don't generate a profit.

From 1992 to 1996, Ontario's community colleges made a substantial investment to set up prior learning assessment and recognition (PLAR) systems in response to growing interest and policy support from the provincial and federal governments. However, the procedures are sometimes confusing or onerous for the learner. College faculty do not always support PLAR because they fear it may lead to job losses. PLAR is integrated into many secondary systems and the Council of Ontario Universities has initiated some demon-

---

[87] Continuing Education Review Project, *Project Report: For Adults Only* (Toronto: Ministry of Colleges and Universities, 1986).

[88] Ibid., p.15.

stration projects. However, the full impact of PLAR for adult learners still remains to be seen.

Ontario's NDP government responded strongly and quickly to the creation of the Canadian Labour Force Development Board and the call for provincial boards. Almost immediately, it set up the Ontario Training and Adjustment Board (OTAB) and gave it a budget of over $400 million annually. The Board was given responsibility for a wide range of labour-related training programs including apprenticeships, upgrading of employed workers, labour-adjustment programs, and literacy/numeracy skills. It also undertook valuable research projects. For example, OTAB commissioned the CAAE to do a study of the Ontario data in 1992 federal Adult Education and Training Survey.[89] However the experiment was short lived. In 1996, OTAB was one of the first casualties of Ontario's new Conservative government. The agency was closed and its functions re-integrated into the Ministry of Education and Training.

In 1992, the Ontario Institute for Studies in Education (OISE) released its ninth Survey of Educational Issues.[90] This survey offers a rare example of a regularly administered and publicly disseminated survey. Surveys like these provide essential data and current profiles of public support for educational programs and proposed policy changes. The section on adult and continuing education reported participation rates in Ontario have grown by 5 percent to 36 percent. Much of the increase was related to a greater emphasis on the development of new occupational skills.

It is noteworthy that in the 1990s OISE was merged into the University of Toronto and its Adult Education Department was incorporated with Community Development and Counselling Psychology. These are two examples of how restructuring has lowered the profile of the adult education enterprise at a time when all sectors of society are putting increased emphasis, in their rhetoric at least, on the importance of continuing education and lifelong learning.

In 1996, the Ontario government established a panel to review post-secondary education in the province. The goals and the recommendations of the review demonstrate the policy objectives of the government, namely increased sharing of the costs by students and the private sector, increased collaboration among educational institutions and increased access for a growing number of students. The recommendations were largely instrumental in nature and focussed primarily on more sharing of costs, more flexibility in delivery and the need to equip learners for a changing workplace. The report contained little statistical information about participation, a reflection of the fact that

---

[89] This is one example of unpublished research work which could inform the public policy process. However, because the field of adult education is so fragmented in Canada (cf. Chapter 10), there is little opportunity to share or learn from these resources.

[90] Ontario Institute for Studies in Education, *Public Attitudes Toward Education in Ontario 1992* (Toronto: OISE, 1993).

there are no longer published reports of participation statistics in Ontario. For example, the report failed to note any increase in the average age of college learners. In fact, in many urban colleges, the average age of students is twenty-five years or older, so that colleges have increasingly become adult education institutions. Sadly, the report made no reference to adult education, continuing education, lifelong learning or to the role of post-secondary institutions in these endeavours.

Given Ontario's economic position, it is reasonable to anticipate continued growth of job-related adult education, especially in the area of high technology and financial services. However, a broader vision of adult education and lifelong learning is not so likely until the fiscal and political environment changes.

Prince Edward Island

Statement of the General Situation

Adult education services in Prince Edward Island are, for the most part, provided by Holland College, the province's only community college. Vocational education and academic upgrading are the two major programs offered to adults at the College's three campuses—Charlottetown, West Royalty and Summerside—and in other centres throughout the island. The University of Prince Edward Island also conducts non-credit extension courses for adults, both on and off campus. Additionally, there is the Prince Edward Island Association of Community Schools which is organized on a co-operative basis and which offers general interest programs during the winter months. Modest financial assistance is provided by the provincial government to assist with the co-ordination of community schools.[91]

The Department of Education is responsible for all levels of education including adult education. In 1994, an Office of Higher Education, Training and Adult Learning was established within the department in recognition of the growing importance of this area within the educational life of the province.

Historical Developments

A range of adult education programs, particularly vocational training, have been part of Prince Edward Island's educational activities for many decades. However, it was only with the creation of Holland College in 1969 that adult education has been given a distinct role in the province. Prior to this time, there were only intermittent efforts to meet adult learning needs. For a few

---

[91] E. MacDonald, *A Community of Schools* (Charlottetown: Institute of Island Studies, 1985).

years following World War I vocational courses were conducted in the evening for veterans. Beginning in 1934 and continuing through the depression and war years, the Extension Department of St. Dunstan's University initiated an adult education program for the province's rural population which addressed the difficult social and economic problems associated with these troubled times.[92] After World War II, vocational courses were once again provided to returning soldiers, this time through the Department of Education's Division of Vocational and Continuing Education. With the funding assistance for vocational and technical education made available by the federal government in the early 1960s, Prince Edward Island in 1962 built the Prince County Vocational High School in Summerside and two years later the Provincial Vocational Institute in Charlottetown. Both provided trades training for adults as part of their curricula.

The report of a Royal Commission on Higher Education (J.S. Bonnell, Chairman) in 1965 precipitated significant changes in the province's post-secondary system. Following this report the government made clear its intentions for post-secondary education in a policy statement delivered by the premier to the legislative assembly.[93] By way of restructuring the system, the two existing, tradition-bound institutions, St. Dunstan's University and Prince of Wales College, were transformed into the University of Prince Edward Island, and a community college, Holland College, was created. Both events occurred in 1969.

The college initially conducted a program of applied arts and technology and then, beginning in 1976 when the responsibility for the two vocational centres was added to the college by the Department of Education, vocational education was also offered. To reflect this addition, the mandate for the college was expanded: "The object of the college is to provide a broad range of educational opportunity particularly in the fields of applied arts and technology, vocational training and adult education."[94] This change took place in 1977 when the Holland College Act was amended.

The Prince Edward Island Department of Industry is responsible for channelling both federal and provincial funding to the adult basic education and pre-vocation training programs offered by Holland College. An example of this is the Adult Night Class Program of academic upgrading which is pre-

[92] M. McKenna, S.C., "Higher Education in Transition, 1945-1980," in Smitheram et al. (Eds.), *The Garden Transformed: Prince Edward Island, 1945-1980* (Charlottetown: Ragweed Press, 1982) p.206. For an account of the program see J. Croteau, *Cradled in the Waves: The Story of a People's Co-operative Achievement in Economic Betterment in Prince Edward Island* (Toronto: Ryerson Press, 1951).

[93] Hon. Alex Campbell, "Policy Statement on Post-Secondary Education" (Legislative Assembly, Prince Edward Island, April 2, 1968).

[94] As noted in J. Dennison and P. Gallagher, *Canada's Community Colleges*, p.106.

sented in a night school format.[95] It is offered free of charge to those eighteen years of age or greater who have been out of school for at least one year.

The changing nature of Prince Edward Island's economy away from dependence on the fishery and into new areas of economic activity has considerably influenced the provision of adult education, which has a decided vocational orientation. At the same time, the strong Maritime tradition of co-operation ensures a continued role of the community schools as a method for developing individuals and their communities.

The transfer of labour-market training from the federal to the provincial government will likely have an impact on adult education policy and programming in the late 1990s. The emergence of private trainers and private schools may increase in response to this shift.

Quebec

A detailed treatment of public policy issues in Quebec can be found in Chapter 3 of this book and therefore is not covered in this chapter.

Saskatchewan

Statement of the General Situation

The early provision of adult education in Saskatchewan was associated with non-government organizations, including the Women's Institutes, agricultural societies and the Saskatchewan Wheat Pool, and with university agricultural extension work. In 1973 comprehensive provision of adult education was made available by way of a unique community college system. In the latter part of the 1980s, this system was restructured, however, such that adult education programming is now dispersed among public institutions and community agencies on the basis of its content.

In the new structure, regional colleges were given a mandate to provide the rural and northern areas of the province with adult basic education including literacy, English as a second language, and high school completion, in addition to university and technical institute programs. The Saskatchewan Institute of Applied Science and Technology (SIAST) was created to serve urban areas. SIAST was created through an administrative amalgamation of several technical and vocational institutes and the urban community colleges. As part of its program offering, SIAST, like the regional colleges, offers adult basic education courses.

---

[95] Prince Edward Island, *Evaluation of the Adult Night Class Program* (Charlottetown: Department of Industry, 1988).

Community interest, hobby and leisure courses do not fall within the mandate of the regional colleges. These are offered by local interest groups. Until 1995, Saskatchewan's two universities, the University of Regina and the University of Saskatchewan, offered an active adult education program through their extension departments. However, the University of Regina discontinued non-credit courses at that time. Distance education has become a significant mode of delivering adult education programs in the province, particularly through the Saskatchewan Communication Network.

As in other provinces, the education portfolio is reorganized regularly. In 1995, the single Department of Education was divided into a Department of Education with responsibility for K-12 and a Department of Post-Secondary Education and Skills Training. At the time of publication, the Minister of Labour also served as Minister of Post-Secondary Education and Skills Training. This restructuring would seem to mirror the trend in other provinces of giving increased attention and profile to job-related adult education.

Historical Developments

Within four years of Saskatchewan becoming a province in 1905, the University of Saskatchewan was formed.[96] Early on the extension work of the university was connected with the College of Agriculture, as the provincial government mandated the college to teach agricultural education in the farming communities. (It was not until 1965 that the Extension Department received a mandate to work on a university-wide basis.) The voluntary sector also played a significant role in providing adult learning in the province, consistent with the community based self-help values associated with rural living. By way of public provision some limited amount of community education occurred with government assistance by way of the "lighted schoolhouse" idea, i.e., evening classes for adults.

Beginning in 1944 an Adult Education Division was established within the department to bring a level of co-ordination to this work. The impetus for this development was the election of the first socialist government in Canada, the CCF under Tommy Douglas.[97] The department's aims were announced as being:

1. to liquidate social, scientific and language illiteracy;

2. to help clarify the thinking of citizens regarding fundamental issues confronting modern society;

---

[96] For more historical information see R.F. Harvey, *Middle Range Education in Canada* (Toronto: Gage, 1973).

[97] For an insightful account of this event see M. Welton, "Mobilizing the People for Socialism: The Politics of Adult Education in Saskatchewan, 1944-45," in M. Welton (Ed.), *Knowledge for the People: The Struggle for Adult Learning in English Speaking Canada* (Toronto: OISE Press, 1987).

3. to promote responsible and co-operative citizen action;

4. to encourage integrated and creative community life.[98]

The bold initiatives that were begun to carry out these aims were short lived, however, for reasons of a political nature.

An overriding concern to preserve the quality of rural life in the province moved the Saskatchewan government in 1956 to appoint a Royal Commission on Agriculture and Rural Life. This commission singled out the role of adult education in its broadest terms as being integral to supporting community life and the particular social values associated with it, especially in the face of the changing economic and social environment. The next year a Centre for Community Studies was established as a project of the province and the University of Saskatchewan, and for the next seven years it produced research and resource materials for use by those working in the field.

In 1962 a Minister's Committee on Continuing Education was formed and given the task of delineating a policy of continuing education for the province. This included determining roles and responsibilities of various agencies and voluntary organizations which were active in the field. The following year the Adult Education Branch became the Community Education Branch and began to provide leadership for adult education in rural communities through the efforts of regional field staff. Three years later, however, following a change in government in 1964, the branch was phased out as the emphasis in adult education in the province "shifted away from community programming to the pressing need for expansion of technical training capabilities in the Institutes of Applied Arts and Sciences."[99] The confusion caused by this action, along with other expansionary developments in the education field during the 1960s, suggested the need for a re-assessment of post-school education in the province. In 1967 a committee on higher education had issued a report (Spinks Report) calling for a system of "middle range" education in the province. This was followed four years later by the McLeod Report which, as part of its review of the role of the University of Saskatchewan within the community, considered the part that community colleges could play in the province's total educational system. Prior to the government taking action on establishing junior colleges, however, the provincial election of 1971 resulted in the return of the New Democratic Party, and implementation plans were put on hold.

An early action of the new government was to establish a separate Ministry of Continuing Education in an effort to oversee the system of post-secondary learning in Saskatchewan. In turn the minister appointed a Minister's Advi-

---

[98] Province of Saskatchewan, Department of Continuing Education, *Report of the Minister's Advisory Committee on Community Colleges* (Regina: Department of Continuing Education, 1972) p.5.

[99] Ibid.

sory Committee on Community Colleges, chaired by Dr. Ron Faris. Subsequently, in 1973, the Community Colleges Act was passed, which introduced a unique community college model with an emphasis on community development and community service.

Faris described the Saskatchewan version of the community college as being "colleges without walls but with foundations."[100] They were without walls in that, rather than constructing college institutions in each region of the province, the community colleges were instead to serve the various communities within their regions by utilizing existing facilities. This reinforced the decentralized approach to providing adult education services. As well, rather than employing faculty, the community colleges instead acted as a broker with other educational institutions for delivery of instruction, or else hired instructors on a temporary, fee-for-service basis. The foundations were firm, however, in that they rested on the sense of community in rural Saskatchewan ("traditions of community participation and co-operation blended with self-help") and on the ready access to learning opportunities throughout life.[101]

In their review of Saskatchewan's community colleges, Dennison and Gallagher claim that "in terms of the original goal of improving quality of life, particularly in rural communities, the colleges had proved to be a remarkable success."[102] However, the province's paramount requirements by the mid-1980s were deemed to be in the area of occupational training. A change of government in 1982 and the general economic recession at that time were two precursors of a general assessment of the community college system. In a preliminary move the new government consolidated all post-secondary education, including the Department of Continuing Education, into a single Ministry of Advanced Education and Manpower.

In 1987 the government implemented a major restructuring of the province's educational system. To begin, the total education system in the province was brought together into a single Ministry of Education. In the post-secondary sector a planning document, *Preparing for the Year 2000: Adult Education in Saskatchewan*, was presented in 1987 which reoriented the community college system to emphasize skills training.[103] A new institution was established, the Saskatchewan Institute of Applied Science and Technology (SIAST), which served the urban settings by bringing under one administrative

---

[100] R. Faris, "Colleges without Walls but with Foundations" (Unpublished Speech, Lambton College, Ontario, 1974), as referenced in J. Dennison and P. Gallagher, *Canada's Community Colleges*, p.56.

[101] Province of Saskatchewan, *Report of the Minister's Advisory Committee on Community Colleges*, p.7.

[102] J. Dennison and P. Gallagher, *Canada's Community Colleges*, p.113.

[103] Province of Saskatchewan, *Preparing for the Year 2000: Adult Education in Saskatchewan* (Regina: Saskatchewan Education, 1987).

umbrella several vocational and technical institutes and community colleges. To better serve the rural and northern portions of the province, regional colleges were formed out of the rural community colleges and given the mandate to make post-secondary education accessible within the regions. In addition, distance education became a major method of delivering adult learning.

Adult education programming was considerably altered in the new system. While the regional colleges and SIAST continued to provide literacy training, English as a second language, adult basic education, and high school completion, they were no longer mandated to provide community interest, hobby and leisure courses. Instead these courses were to be conducted by "local interest groups."

The change in emphasis in Saskatchewan's college system away from community education to occupational training effectively ended what Dennison and Gallagher referred to as the "great experiment" in community education.[104] The exigencies of the economy dictated that adult education now carry out its several functions in a much more prescribed manner, with some functions, such as those focussed on the interests of the individual and the community, no longer included as part of the colleges' sphere. This change reflected a different set of circumstances in the province from those which had existed some fifteen years earlier.

In the 1990s, Saskatchewan undertook a number of policy-related initiatives to align its adult education activities with the demands of the times. In 1992, the provincial government established panels to review four sectors of the post-secondary educational system; namely, the universities, SIAST, regional colleges and private vocational schools. The four panels generated 172 recommendations dealing with the structure and governance of the universities, collaboration among post-secondary institutions, post-secondary education for Aboriginal people, international education, funding and labour-force adjustment. In general, the recommendations focussed on strategies for maximizing the post-secondary educational resources in a period of fiscal restraint. They made very little reference to Saskatchewan's remarkable history in adult education, to innovation in continuing education and lifelong learning or to new public policy in the area of adult education.

In 1996, the government commissioned the MacKay Report on university revitalization. Following MacKay's report, the minister released a formal response which repeated many of themes of the 1993 reviews (in particular the Johnson Commission on Universities).[105] The response gave prominence to the universities' responsibility to meet the learning needs of society in general

[104] J. Dennison and P. Gallagher, *Canada's Community Colleges*, p.116.

[105] Saskatchewan Post-Secondary Education and Skills Training, *Public Interest and Revitalization of Saskatchewan's Universities* (Regina: Post-Secondary Education and Training, 1996).

and of the "new economy" in particular. It also focussed on the needs of Aboriginal people and of rural communities. Finally, it reminded the universities of their role in community service and in social/cultural development. The report contained no policy prescriptions but did set some broad parametres for future policy development.

In 1995, the Department of Post-Secondary Education and Skills Training was established as a separate entity in order to handle the growing training agenda which the province will inherit from the federal government in the latter half of the 1990s. It is noteworthy that the Minister of Labour was given responsibility for the new department. In 1996, the new department issued a working paper entitled *Choices for a Saskatchewan Training Strategy* [106] in which it outlined the now-familiar arguments for a co-ordinated provincial training strategy, increased labour-market information and planning, more skills training for a rapidly changing labour market, integration of programs and services. Only the specific attention to the needs of Aboriginal learners distinguished it from other such documents from across the country.

Saskatchewan was one of six provinces to establish a provincial labourforce development board in the early 1990s. The Saskatchewan Board was initially funded by the federal government. In 1996, it was funded jointly by the federal and provincial governments. Funding beyond 1997 is uncertain once federal funding ends. The board focussed on developing sectoral initiatives, on conferences to examine a range of issues including the economy, barriers to employment and skills training. It also initiated a program to recognize excellence in labour-market development programs at the provincial level.

In spite of a difficult fiscal environment, literacy work grew in the province in the 1990s. The Saskatchewan Literacy Network acts as a co-ordinating group for literacy providers and, through effective lobbying, has gained a commitment from the provincial government that it will help compensate for lost federal funding for literacy and adult basic education.

Typically for Saskatchewan, volunteer involvement in adult education has remained strong in the 1990s in spite of the cutbacks in funding and the lack of policy innovations. The active groups include the Saskatchewan Association for Lifelong Learning, the provincial membership of the Canadian Congress for Learning Opportunities for Women and the Saskatchewan Educators for Non-English Speakers. Such groups will have a vital role to play in advocating for progressive policies that support lifelong learning for all Saskatchewan citizens.

---

[106] Saskatchewan Post-Secondary Education and Skills Training, *Choices for a Saskatchewan Training Strategy* (Regina: Post-Secondary Education and Training, 1996).

The Yukon and the Northwest Territories

Statement of the General Situation

The Yukon and the Northwest Territories represent a very special case in adult education given the disparate and conflicting needs of a small, heterogeneous population across a vast geographic region. Any discussion of policy in this region must be considered in the light of these unique circumstances.

Adult education, including academic upgrading for adults, is for the most part provided through the post-secondary systems of both territories. These systems include Yukon College in the Yukon, Aurora College which serves the western part of the Northwest Territories with three campuses and some fourteen community learning centres and Nunavut Arctic College which serves the eastern region with three campuses and twenty-one community learning centres. This latter division of the former Arctic College corresponds to the new territorial division of the region.

In the Yukon, adult education is co-ordinated through the Advanced Education Branch of the Department of Education. Yukon College is responsible for developing and delivering adult education programs that respond to local needs. The college provides a broad range of full-time and part-time programs throughout the Yukon using a network of Community Campuses.[107]

In the Northwest Territories, the responsibility for adult education rests with the Culture and Careers Branch of the Department of Education, Culture and Employment. Aurora College and Nunavut Arctic College have a mandate to deliver adult education programs, certificate and diploma programs, career studies and various part-time programs. Each of the community learning centres has an adult educator who organizes continuing education programs in response to local needs.

Historical Developments

There has been a strong tradition of adult education in the Northwest Territories and the Yukon since the 1960s when population levels began to rise and municipal developments occurred. Unlike the provinces who were able to rely on institutions of higher education to initiate extension services, it was voluntary organizations such as the Y.W.C.A. and Frontier College who took the lead in providing adult basic education in the north. As regional education offices were established by the respective governments, these took on a growing role in adult education in conjunction with the development of the school system. However, the primary concern of the respective departments of educa-

---

[107] Secretary of State of Canada, *Federal and Provincial Support to Post-Secondary Education in Canada: A Report to Parliament 1988-89* (Ottawa: Ministry of Supplies and Services, 1990) p.32.

tion focussed on providing grade-school education to the children of the region. The development of adult education got a substantial boost with the creation of the post-secondary systems in each jurisdiction.[108]

The Yukon portion of this overview draws heavily on Aron Senkpiel's article on post-secondary education in that region.[109] In it, he points out that the development of adult education policy in the Yukon must be understood in the context of its population (4,914 in 1941 and 31,000 in 1992). The formal history of adult education in the territory began in 1963 when the Whitehorse Vocational Training School opened. Similarly, the formal story begins in the Northwest Territories with the establishment of the Northwest Territories Adult Vocational Training Centre (AVTC) in 1968. The creation of these institutions mark the beginning of formal adult education in these regions. The programming has expanded steadily to the present time, especially through an increasing number of community learning centres. With the development of a decentralized college system in the 1980s, delivery of adult education programs was consolidated within the college system. The colleges, through their regional campuses and community learning centres, have been able to be increasingly responsive to local adult education needs.

Further Developments—Yukon

Senkpiel describes the 1960s and 1970s as a time of aspiration and the 1980s and 1990s a time of realization. The Whitehorse Vocational Training Centre was established in 1963 with a particular focus on increasing the employability of Yukon residents. By the mid-1970s, there was an anticipation of a new prosperity in the northern territories because of the Alaska Highway Natural Gas Pipeline, the work of the Berger and Lysyk inquiries, the feeling that the settlement of land claims was in sight and a growing spirit of self-determination in the region. All of this fuelled the demands for increased educational opportunity for adults in the Yukon and a variety of initiatives to address these needs. One group secured letters patent to establish the University of Canada North, though the institutions was never created. The Science Council of Canada called for the creation of a northern university in 1977, but this idea responded mostly to the desires of southern scientists. Around 1978, the Yukon Native Brotherhood was exploring potential linkages with the Saskatchewan Indian Federated College.

---

[108] In the case of the Yukon the territorial Department of Education was established under authority of the Yukon Territory Act (1898) while in the Northwest Territories it was only in 1968 that the Department of Education was formed to take over the school system, run up to that time by the Department of Indian Affairs and Northern Development.

[109] A. Senkpiel, "Post-Secondary Education in the Yukon—The Last Thirty Years" in *The Northern Review, 12*, 13 (Winter 1994).

The confluence of these aspirations motivated the government to invite the University of Alberta's Centre for the Study of Post-Secondary Education and Department of Education Administration to carry out a study on how to best meet the growing needs for adult education in the region.[110] Among its observations, the report drew particular attention to the cultural polarization between Natives and non-Natives, the unique needs of small communities and the lack of interest in the creation of a university. It recommended the establishment of a comprehensive community college for the Yukon. Interestingly, the authors recommended that the new college play a role as an investigator and social critic, a role that is normally attributed to universities or other institutions.[111]

The new college was created in 1983 under the authority of the Deputy Minister of Advanced Education. In 1986, the government invited Lionel Orlikow, a veteran leader in adult education from Manitoba, to study the adult education needs of the region. His report *The Option to Stay* [112] argued that a community-based and autonomous adult education system was needed in order to support people who wanted to live and learn in the region. By 1988, Yukon College had its own new facility called *Ayamdigut* (the house that moved) and a new College Act put the direction of the college in the hands of an independent board of governors. The majority of seats on the new board belonged to Native and rural representatives.

In 1988, the government adopted the college's proposal to create a diploma in Northern studies focussing on Native studies, northern science and northern outdoor and environmental issues. It also contributed $1 million to establish a Northern Studies Research Fund. By 1990, the college was serving very broad education and cultural needs from basic literacy training to first- and second-year university level programs. It has adapted popular education strategies, community development values, adult education principles and traditional academic approaches to meet the diverse needs of its constituency and context.

Yukon College uses its community campus network effectively to support and facilitate community development initiatives. This is especially important in addressing the needs of the territory's First Nations. The college has a Vice-President First Nations who plays a vital role in identifying, interpreting and advocating for First Nations' interests in adult education. For example, the VP First Nations has enabled the development of curriculum dealing with

---

[110] E. Ingram et al., *Toward a Yukon College. Continuing Education Opportunities in the Yukon* (Edmonton: University of Alberta: Department of Educational Administration, 1979).

[111] Ibid., p.ix.

[112] L. Orlikow, *The Option to Stay: An Education Strategy for the Yukon* (Whitehorse: Government of the Yukon, 1986).

the changing context created by the settlement of land claims in the north. The college's structure and approach demonstrates how an adult education institution can play a vital role in nurturing citizenship, autonomy and community development.

Assured access to adult education is fundamental to the future of the region. As the adult education work in the region evolves, it will be important to further entrench the commitment to the needs of adult learners. The most recent Education Act does not refer to adult education or continuing education.[113] More policy work will be required to determine the most appropriate way of meeting the needs of Aboriginal adult learners.

Further Developments—Northwest Territories

The provision of home-management training in the 1960s marked the formal beginning of adult education in the Northwest Territories.[114] In the 1970s there was a considerable infusion of federal funds through different government departments to support various training initiatives. It was the formation of the Northwest Territories' own Department of Education in 1968, however, which provided the opportunity for an indigenous approach to educational planning for the territories.

The educational needs to be met were quite considerable, as culture, geography, history and language were all factors in attempting to provide for a small and dispersed population. As well, educational attainment levels were generally lower than in the rest of Canada.[115] Some adult education services were delivered by authorities responsible for schools in various areas of the territory and by other government departments. In the area of vocational training it was the opening of the Adult Vocational Training Centre in 1968 which initiated concerted efforts on behalf of adult learners.

A major study into all aspects of education in the Northwest Territories was established by the Legislative Assembly in 1980. Its subsequent report, released in 1982, stated the conviction that learning is a lifelong activity and made eleven recommendations specific to adult education.[116] One of the most significant outcomes of this report for adult education was that responsibility for all post-secondary education was consolidated into Arctic College in 1985.

---

[113] D. Burgess, "The Yukon Education Act: Commentary and Discussion on Recent Legislation," in *McGill Journal of Education*, 25, 2 (1990).

[114] Northwest Territories Special Committee on Education, *Learning: Tradition and Change in the Northwest Territories* (Yellowknife: Northwest Territories Legislative Assembly, 1982).

[115] Secretary of State for Canada, *Federal and Provincial Support to Post-Secondary Education in Canada: A Report to Parliament 1988-89*, p.34.

[116] Northwest Territories Special Committee on Education, *Learning: Tradition and Change in the Northwest Territories*.

In turn, Arctic College was divided into two colleges in 1995—Aurora College serving the western region and Nunavut Arctic College serving the eastern region.

To emphasize the importance of adult learning, the Department of Education in 1984 had established an Advanced Education Program (formerly the Vocational and Higher Education Division) to be responsible for delivering post-school programs including adult education in communities. Initially thirty-four community adult educators were employed by this section to conduct this work in conjunction with divisional boards of education. With the passing of the Arctic College Act (1987) they became part of the college system which has the mandate to deliver post-secondary education throughout the territory.

In 1996, the Culture and Career Branch of the Department of Education began to develop a Labour Force Development Plan. It is expected that this plan will support the economic strategy developed by the Resources, Wildlife and Economic Development Department and the anticipated transfer of federal training programs to the territory. Also in 1996, the federal government established a $39.8 million fund to support incremental training related to the creation of the Nunavut Territory. The goal of the training is to achieve a level of 50 percent Inuit employees in the Nunavut Public Service by 1999 when the territory is officially established. By 2010, it is hoped that 85 percent of the public service will be Inuit.

In 1990 the territorial college system, in co-operation with Department of Education, Culture and Employment, established an adult basic education program across the territory. This program included consistent delivery standards for all centres. In 1994, this program won the Program Excellence Award of the Association of Canadian Community Colleges. In 1997, the government plans to release a report on adult basic education which will likely lead to new policy initiatives in this area. As well, the government has had a Literacy Strategy in place since 1990. The strategy has emphasized the delivery of community-based literacy programs. In 1996, a Workplace Education Strategy was launched to increase the involvement of employers in literacy education.

****

The special character of these northern regions of Canada provides a unique context for the adult education enterprise. Policy makers need to develop approaches which respond creatively to the needs of this diverse and exceptionally vast territory. The history and practice of adult education in this region merits further reflection and study.

Federal and Provincial Policy Making: A Proposed Agenda

As the foregoing chapter illustrates, for much of the 1990s federal and provincial policy initiatives and new spending programs were largely concentrated on job-related training to the detriment of citizenship education and other non-vocational dimensions of adult education. This trend is likely to continue as national and provincial economies try to adapt to major shifts in the labour market caused by technology, globalization and restructuring of the social service and health-care systems. In its 1994 Labour Force Development Review, the CLFDB described the situation as follows:

> The Canadian labour market is characterized by a high degree of job insecurity. Workers are worried and experiencing stress. Business is struggling with pressures from increased global competition, technological change, deteriorating economic outcomes, the regulatory environment and changes in the labour force ... [117]

The changes in health-care delivery, for example, have caused major displacements of workers and created high demands for retraining. At the same time, governments want to reduce the role of the state in education and subordinate their policies to the requirements of economic growth. As long as these pressures exist, the policy-making process will undoubtedly be skewed in the direction of work-related training. The Canadian Association for Adult Education and the Institut canadien de l'éducation des adultes, among others, have repeatedly raised concerns about the narrow focus of adult education policies in the last two decades and the longer term erosion of citizenship education as a result.

This tension between job-related training and citizenship education is one of several pivotal policy issues that have emerged, largely since 1990. The future of adult education in Canada depends to a great extent on how these issues are addressed, both at the federal and the provincial level. Other key issues include:

(a) *Transfer of Federal Responsibility and Funding for Training.* In 1996, the federal government announced a $2 billion plan to help unemployed Canadians get back to work. The plan anticipates the federal withdrawal from labour-market training. It is intended to allow for training programs that are tailored to regional needs and eliminate duplication federal and provincial programs. While this plan may ease federal-provincial tensions in some jurisdictions, it does nothing to enhance the framework for adult education work in Canada. It may only serve, on the one hand, to erode the already weak potential for a coherent national strategy in adult education and, on the other, to add

---

[117] Canadian Labour Force Development Board, *The 1994 Labour Force Development Review* (Ottawa, CLFDB, 1994) p.3.

further weight to the bias for job-related training to the exclusion of other areas of concern.

(b) *Prior Learning Assessment and Recognition (PLAR)*. It is increasing important to develop reliable and workable mechanisms for recognizing learning that has been acquired outside the formal learning environment. The emerging paradigm for lifelong learning is one which gives formal recognition to learning acquired in either formal or non-formal teaching/learning environments. The challenge consists in developing national standards and consistent practices across all sectors (business, labour, education, government). Effective policies for PLAR will increase access for adult learners, reduce redundancies in a student's academic career and encourage lifelong learning by giving people formal credit for what they know. The Canadian Association for Prior Learning Assessment, formed in the early 1990s, could play a leadership role in this task.

(c) *Mobility, Portability, National Standards*. The Council of Ministers of Education want and need to bring some coherence to the transfer of credentials between jurisdictions. Together with PLAR, national standards and a seamless system for recognizing credits will lower costs and increase employability for adult learners. It is also a vital next step in creating greater mobility at an international level.

(d) *Literacy*. In 1994, Canada participated with eight other industrialized countries to carry out the International Adult Literacy Survey. The report *Literacy, Economy and Society*[118] shows that significant numbers of adult Canadians continue to manifest low-level literacy skills that constrain their participation in society and in the economy. For example, 22 percent of adult Canadians fall in the lowest level of literacy while a further 24 percent fall into the second lowest level. There has been no appreciable improvement in literacy levels since 1989. Further, the report demonstrates the high correlation between literacy and social well-being.

The report underlines Canada's failure, to date, to deal effectively with this central challenge in adult education. The creation of the National Literacy Secretariat in 1988, the appointment, in 1993, of Senator Joyce Fairbairn as Minister with special responsibility for literacy and a range of provincial initiatives constitute positive steps which have not, as yet, had a measurable impact on literacy skills.

(e) *The Information Highway*. The explosion and popularization of information technologies in the 1990s constitutes another pivotal issue in adult education. On the one hand, these technologies may enable a quantum leap in access to adult education. They permit tremendous flexibility in terms of

---

[118] OECD/Statistics Canada, *Literacy, Economy and Society* (Paris: OECD, 1995).

location, delivery modes, timing, points of entry, access to resources and other components of effective adult education. On the other hand, they give rise to important policy and pedagogical questions that are discussed in Chapter 12 of this volume. As well, policy makers need to consider how to insure that we don't create a new category of disenfranchised adults who are left on the sidelines of the information highway. Ideally, Canada will develop a policy framework and funding programs to maximize the potential of these technologies and to integrate them into an overall national strategy for adult education. The creation of the Office of Learning Technologies by the federal government in 1996 suggests that they recognize the import of this issue and are prepared to invest in the developmental effort.

(f) *Collaboration.* The enterprise of adult education is increasingly diverse and complex. The competition for adult education dollars, especially publicly funded activity, will continue to grow. The public will demand improved accountability and better co-ordination of adult education activity. Governments will need to develop policies that foster effective and meaningful collaboration among public and private institutions.

The Sectoral Partnerships Initiatives (SPI) offers a good example of new collaboration. SPI bring employer groups, unions and other interested parties together from a given sector (for example, tourism, textiles, auto repair) to address common training needs within that sector. From 1986 to 1996, the federal government, through Human Resources Development Canada, provided $176 million to support sectoral partnerships and the private sector contributed a further $264 million. Proponents of SPI argue that it leads to a better match between occupational needs and educators and improves the focus of spending on adult education. Others note that SPI compounds the concentration of adult education spending on activities that are exclusively related to job-training.

One of the most urgent needs for collaboration rests at the level of improved articulation between colleges and universities. In many jurisdictions, college credentials are not recognized for credit by universities. As a result, learners are forced to repeat courses and the cost of post-secondary education is artificially inflated. British Columbia has shown leadership by developing its university college system.

(g) *Cultural Institutions.* Canada's cultural institutions, especially the CBC and the NFB, have been vital instruments in Canada's adult education efforts. The pressures of deficit reduction which have driven political decisions since 1990, combined with the absence of an adult education strategy which recognizes their unique role, have made these institutions extremely vulnerable. In 1995 and 1996, both the CBC and the NFB suffered devastating cuts which have significantly diminished the scope of their activity. Regional and local services have been drastically reduced in the CBC. Similarly, the closure of many NFB distribution outlets has negatively affected access to their films. Production capacity in both organizations is only a fraction of what it once was. Unless these cultural institutions are recognized as essential components of Canada's adult education strategy, this erosion is likely to continue in the coming years.

(h) *Commitment to Research.* Support for research and gathering of data related to adult education in Canada has been weak and inconsistent. Over the years organizations like the Canadian Association for Adult Education, l'Institut canadien de l'éducation des adultes, the Canadian Association for the Study of Adult Education, the Centre for Policy Studies in Education at the University of British Columbia and the Canadian Commission for UNESCO have undertaken important research projects over the years, but these organizations are chronically underfunded. A report on research trends in adult education in Canada, prepared under the aegis of the Canadian Commission for UNESCO, was presented in 1994 and will be ready for publication in 1997. The report offers a helpful overview of current research work in adult education and contains an excellent bibliography of recent Canadian research projects.[119] Statistics Canada has carried out several Adult Education and Training Surveys, but these only capture a small portion of the data required for comprehensive longitudinal and multivariate analysis. The policy making will only be informed if it is rooted in reliable and current research.

****

The foregoing lists constitutes an ambitious agenda for federal and provincial policy makers and adult education advocates. Given the challenges facing Canada today, it behooves us to approach this agenda with determination, coherence and vision.

Conclusion

This volume goes to press at a time when educational policies in many jurisdictions and in many areas of adult education are being narrowed to meet only the immediate needs of the economy or are simply being pushed to the bottom of the agenda in favour of deficit reduction. The policy documents and options of the last ten years rarely address the broader and more essential questions of how we shall live together in the global village, how we will create a sustainable world order, how we will nurture healthy local communi-

---

[119] This report will be available in 1997 from the Canadian Commission for UNESCO in Ottawa.

ties, how we participate in public life. These questions are fundamental to democracy and to educational policy making.

Under the banner of "human resources development," most provinces in Canada have limited their policy interventions to a very narrow band of adult education activity (work-related training, application of new technologies, articulation in post-secondary institutions, adult basic education and literacy work). Canada is not alone in this approach. A 1994 study of training reforms in five OECD countries (Australia, England and Wales, New Zealand, Scotland and the United States) identified nine key reform initiatives related to adult education that were common to all five countries. In general, they focussed on more "multi-skilling" training, articulation, applied technologies, increased flexibility and accountability, and broader participation in funding (i.e., greater share of costs to be borne by users and by the private sector).[120] Human resources development is the order of the day in Canada and internationally.

Support for research and statistical reporting are virtually non-existent. Policy related to adult education and community development, citizenship and the civil society, national unity, and cross-cultural communication have been pushed to the back burner or have simply disappeared from the government's agenda. Yet we know that economic growth and technological development can never be the sole guarantors of progress for humanity. In fact, they are often the source of new problems that challenge the well-being of the planet and the social fabric of nations. Adult education policy must support programs that help ordinary citizens reflect on the impact of these changes and develop appropriate individual and community responses. Adult education that simply assists citizens to submit and adapt to change without regard for its impact is not adult education.

The report of the International Commission on Education for the 21st Century (the "Delors Commission") provides an excellent framework for the policy development work that is required today and tomorrow.[121] The report proposes four pillars:

- *learning to live together*—policies which help us understand others, their history, traditions and spiritual values;
- *learning to know*—policies which insure that we combine broad general education and in-depth knowledge of specialized subjects as a basis for lifelong learning;

[120] R. Faris, *Major Reforms in Training Systems in Five Countries* (Victoria: Ministry of Skill, Training and Labour, 1994).

[121] International Commission on Education for the 21st Century, *Learning: The Treasure Within* (Paris: UNESCO Publishing, 1996).

- *learning to do*—policies that insure we know how to work, how to be a team player, how to deal with new situations and how to alternate between study and work;
- *learning to be*—policies that insure that every citizen can combine independent judging and acting with a clear sense of personal responsibility for the common good.

If Canadian policy makers adopt such a framework for setting the adult education policy agenda for the year 2000 and beyond, there can be much hope for the future role of the adult education enterprise.

Instructor R. Lindsey (at blackboard) and class, Newfoundland, 1951.
Courtesy of Frontier College.

9

Adult Education as Discipline and Vocation

The Emergence of a Sense of Vocation

The term adult education is generally credited to Thomas Pole, whose history of the Adult School movement was first published in 1814.[1] But although activities which we would term adult education, or the teaching of adults, went on for centuries before that, and although Pole may well have coined the phrase early in the nineteenth century, the development of the modern adult education movement did not take place until the present century.

C.H. Grattan, in his *In Quest of Knowledge,* and Thomas Kelly in his history of adult education in Great Britain have made it clear that the teaching or education of adults has a long history in Western society.[2] Grattan takes us back to "preliterate man" and stresses the educational meaning of the concepts of enculturation and acculturation, the processes by which people achieve competence in their own culture, or in moving from one culture to another. He reminds us of Socrates, who taught only adults and who "must rank as the greatest adult educator of all time."[3] Kelly begins with the Anglo-Saxons and identifies the Christian missionaries of the period who came "to convert the heathen" as "the first recorded adult educators" of that nation.[4] In somewhat the same spirit, J.R. Kidd has traced the beginnings of adult educa-

---

[1] C. Verner (Ed.), *Pole's History of Adult Schools* (Washington: Adult Education Association of the USA, 1967); T. Kelly, *A History of Adult Education in Great Britain* (Liverpool: University of Liverpool, 1970).

[2] C.H. Grattan, *In Quest of Knowledge* (New York: Association Press, 1955); T. Kelly, *A History of Adult Education in Great Britain.*

[3] C.H. Grattan, *In Quest of Knowledge*, p.35.

[4] T. Kelly, *A History of Adult Education in Great Britain*, p.1.

tion in Canada to 1605, the earliest days of settlement, when Champlain and Lescarbot founded "l'Ordre de bon temps," an organization which by utilizing "good talk, good books, good music, good food and good plays" helped our earliest settlers get through "the winter's perils."[5] Choosing a more traditional view, E.A. Corbett, in his brief histories of adult education which he wrote in the late 1940s, began the Canadian story with the mechanics' institute movement of the 1850s[6] and the university extension work of the 1890s.[7]

Before the arrival on the scene of a self-conscious adult education movement in the present century, there were clearly large numbers of persons who performed the functions of adult educators, even if they did not use such a term in describing themselves. At least as far back as the thirteenth century, the guild system functioned to protect its members and promote high standards of performance, the craft master teaching the mastery or "misterie" of his craft to the apprentices.[8] The co-operative movement, the Chartist movement, the adult schools and mechanics' institutes, the agriculture and university extension movements, Chautauqua, the Y.M. and Y.W.C.A. organizations—in these and other settings, the teaching or education of adults was being conducted on a very large scale long before those who were engaged in such work thought of themselves as "adult educators." (Indeed there are still many persons today who are in fact educators of adults—some industrial and vocational trainers, agricultural and other "field men"—who do not feel a sense of common interest with "adult education" as they understand the term.)

The terms "adult education" and "adult educator" in their generic sense are generally seen to have been a product of the period between the two World Wars. The landmark "1919 Report" of the Adult Education Committee of the Ministry of Reconstruction in Great Britain helped to put adult education on the map. A combination of the high profile of those involved, the penetration of the arguments stated and the power of the language in which the report was phrased have contributed to its becoming perhaps the most frequently quoted document on the subject of adult education in the English language.[9]

It is generally agreed that a sense of vocation in the field of adult education, at least one which spanned many of the different settings in which adult education functioned, emerged in the inter-war period, and most strongly in

---

[5] J.R. Kidd (Ed.) *Learning and Society* (Toronto: Canadian Association for Adult Education, 1963) p.1.

[6] E.A. Corbett, *A Short History of Adult Education* (Toronto: Canadian Association for Adult Education, 1947).

[7] E.A. Corbett, in J.R. Kidd (Ed.), *Adult Education in Canada* (Toronto: Canadian Association for Adult Education, 1950).

[8] See for instance R.A. Leeson, *Travelling Brothers* (London: Geo. Allen & Unwin, 1979); T. Girtin, *The Triple Crowns* (London: Hutchinson, 1964).

[9] *The 1919 Report*, Report of the Adult Education Committee of the United Kingdom Ministry of Reconstruction (Nottingham: University of Nottingham, 1980 [1919]).

the United States. Before this there was presumably an awareness within particular settings—the Y.M.C.A., the folk schools, university and agricultural extension—of a specialized interest in and practice of the education of adults, but little sense of common interest or common cause with those involved in adult education elsewhere. A World Association of Adult Education was formed in 1919, based in Great Britain, and this organization held a somewhat limited "world conference" at Cambridge in 1928 and for a time published a journal. Its influence, however, was not felt widely within participating countries and the organization disappeared during World War II.[10]

The emergence of a more cohesive adult education movement, which spanned the various settings in which the work was carried out and which was accompanied by the development of professional training for the field, came first in the United States. The key elements and mileposts of this evolution are seen to be the decision on the part of the Carnegie Corporation of New York to fund development in this area; the formation in 1926 of the American Association for Adult Education (with financial support from Carnegie); the creation by Columbia University of the first academic department of adult education (in 1930); and the publication in 1936 of what is generally regarded as the first textbook in the field, Lyman Bryson's *Adult Education*.[11] Webster Cotton has interpreted these and related events as signs that adult education was moving from what he termed an "idealistic" phase, in which the education of adults was seen to be for the purpose of transforming society, to a more practical approach. In this newer phase, according to Cotton, adult education became "essentially an *educational* enterprise concerned with the life of the mind, with ideas and the use of intelligence," not as an instrument of social change.[12] It was willing to leave to the individual learner the decision as to the use to which the newly acquired knowledge would be put rather than to harness adult education to a particular view of the direction of social change. The aim was the democratization of learning and culture—what Stubblefield and others have termed the "diffusion of knowledge," rather than a social transformation of a particular kind.[13]

The idealistic view of adult education which Cotton described in its American setting (and which did not, of course, disappear completely) was well

---

[10] J. Lowe, *The Education of Adults: A World Perspective* (Toronto: OISE, 1982).

[11] See L. Bryson, *Adult Education* (New York: American Book Co., 1936); W.E. Cotton, *On Behalf of Adult Education* (Boston: Center for the Study of Liberal Education for Adults, 1968); C.O. Houle in G. Jensen, A.A. Liveright & W. Hallenbeck (Eds.), *Adult Education: Outlines of an Emerging Field of University Study* (Washington: Adult Education Association of the USA, 1964); M.S. Knowles, *A History of the Adult Education Movement in the United States* (Huntington: New York, Robert Krieger, 1977); H.W. Stubblefield, *Towards a History of Adult Education in America* (London: Croom Helm, 1988).

[12] W.E Cotton, *On Behalf of Adult Education*, p.5.

[13] H.W. Stubblefield, *Towards a History of Adult Education in America*.

represented in Canada, although the volume of literature was much smaller north of the border. The Canadian expressions of such views, rather than take the form of substantial series of published volumes of the type identified by Cotton and Stubblefield in the case of the United States,[14] must be sought out in such places as *Adult Learning*, the journal published by the Canadian Association for Adult Education (CAAE) from 1936 to 1939, and in the pages of its successor, *Food for Thought*. What Cotton terms idealistic views of the field may also be found in the works of some of the great pioneer figures in Canadian adult education, Alfred Fitzpatrick's account of the early years of Frontier College, *University in Overalls*, Coady's account of the Antigonish Movement, *Masters of Their Own Destiny*, and Corbett's episodic autobiography, *We Have With Us Tonight*.[15] In the case of the Canadian literature, which tended to appear later than its American counterparts, the idealistic views tend to be linked with the account of particular educational programs rather than be stated as general philosophical positions.

Whereas Cotton and other prominent writers in the United States date the beginnings of a more professional approach to adult education from the events in the 1920s and 1930s which were mentioned above,[16] it has been argued that a strong trend towards a more professional approach did not emerge in Canada until the 1950s.[17] This is not to say that the earliest indications of a more professional approach did not appear until that decade. That goes back at least to the 1930s, when the Canadian Association for Adult Education was formed. The CAAE, in connection with its founding conference, conducted a survey of the field throughout Canada. The report of the survey was edited by Peter Sandiford, a psychologist from the University of Toronto, and judging by the terms of the report, there was an obvious assumption that the leadership of adult education in Canada would be an increasingly professionalized group, and that the field would become more tightly co-ordinated at the provincial level.[18] At the first Western regional conference on adult education, held in Saskatoon in 1938, the need for trained leaders in the field was stressed.[19] When, for instance, the Public Library Commission of British Columbia conducted a comprehensive survey of the field of adult education in that province

---

[14] W.E. Cotton, *On Behalf of Adult Education*; H.W. Stubblefield, *Towards a History of Adult Education in America*.

[15] A. Fitzpatrick, *The University in Overalls* (Toronto: Hunter-Rose, 1920); M.M. Coady, *Masters of Their Own Destiny* (New York: Harper & Bros., 1939); E.A. Corbett, *We Have With Us Tonight* (Toronto: Ryerson, 1957).

[16] See note #11.

[17] G. Selman, "The Fifties: Pivotal Decade in Canadian Adult Education," *Adult Education in Canada: Historical Essays*.

[18] P. Sandiford, *Adult Education in Canada: A Survey* (Toronto: University of Toronto, 1935).

[19] J.G. Rayner, "Four Western Provinces Discuss Adult Education," *Adult Learning, 2*, 6 (1938) pp.18-21.

in 1941, the recommendations in its report called for a co-ordinated system of adult education, led by "specialists in adult education, not child education-ists."[20] During the 1940s, at least three Canadians earned doctoral degrees in adult education in the United States—Roby Kidd, Florence O'Neill and John Friesen.[21] During the latter years of the 1940s, articles of interest to professional practitioners began to appear with increasing frequency in the CAAE journal, *Food for Thought*. These included items about the history of the field, comments on related public policy and at least one about the training of adult educators. Soon after he joined the staff of the CAAE in 1947, Roby Kidd formed a committee which looked into the matter of professional training in Canada for adult educators.

The 1950s: Pivotal Decade

Kidd was to be the key person in promoting the professionalization of the field during the 1950s, the period in which he served as director of the CAAE. During the decade, he travelled back and forth across Canada in connection with his work, was one of a handful of Canadians who had doctoral qualifications in the field, and in the context of his CAAE duties had access to leaders of educational institutions, ministries of government and heads of other organizations, as well as to adult educators themselves. He lost no opportunity to promote the cause of training and other professional development activities for adult educators.

The work of Kidd and others in promoting a more professional approach to adult education in Canada during the 1950s, which has been described as the "pivotal decade" in this respect,[22] may be summed up under four headings: the emergence of a sense of vocation and professionalism in the field; the development of training opportunities; institutional development; and the growth of a body of literature for the field.

A Sense of Vocation and Professionalism

Those working on a full-time basis in the field of adult education in Canada prior to this period saw themselves mainly within the institutional systems within which they carried out their duties, be it agricultural extension, voluntary bodies such as the Y.M. or Y.W.C.A., library work or university extension. The formation of the CAAE in 1935 and its various meetings and publications provided means by which a relatively few of those working in the field began

[20] British Columbia Public Library Commission, *A Preliminary Study of Adult Education in British Columbia: 1941* (Victoria: B.C.P.L.C., 1942).

[21] C.O. Houle & J.H. Buskey, "The Doctorate in Adult Education 1935-1965," *Adult Education, 16*, 3 (1966) pp.131-168.

[22] G. Selman, "The Fifties: Pivotal Decade."

to see themselves as part of a larger social enterprise, and a few short-lived organizations of adult educators functioned briefly in some parts of the country in the 1930s and 1940s.[23] Some Canadian adult educators were aware of developments in other countries, especially in the United States, which were making the field more visible and increasing its sense of importance. But on the whole, Canadian adult educators still had a relatively narrow view of their field, often one which did not extend much beyond the organizational setting in which they happened to be working. The 1950s brought significant change in this respect in the thinking of many adult educators, and Roby Kidd was clearly an important influence in this regard for many people. He has rightly been described as "both architect and symbol" of the development of adult education in this period.[24]

Kidd seemed to lose no opportunity to emphasize the importance of adult education and of the adult educator's calling. In his personal contacts and in his extensive writings about the field during the period, he repeatedly stressed the significance of adult learning for the lives of individuals and for society as a whole. In his contacts with senior people in both government and educational institutions, he emphasized as well the need to recruit able persons to take charge of adult education activities and to provide them with satisfactory status and career opportunities. In his contacts with adult educators themselves, he encouraged them to address and make use of the increasing knowledge that was becoming available about how adults could be assisted in their learning. A study of the major addresses, reports and publications produced by Kidd and his organization during the 1950s reveals what a consistent theme this was.[25] For example, in his Director's Report to the CAAE in 1956, which was devoted in large part to professionalism in the field, Kidd spoke strongly about the need for able personnel and for training.

> I have only one serious apprehension about the future. More and more the conception of continuous learning is being accepted. But will we have the staff who are numerous and talented enough? Every year several important positions are open which require men and women of considerable capacity and long experience. So we quickly look around for a suitable person as if we did not fully understand that such people aren't just found, they must be "grown," and the growing period starts many years before.[26]

[23] G. Selman, "Early Adult Education Associations in Canada," in *Adult Education in Canada: Historical Essays.*

[24] A.M. Thomas in J.G. Schmidt (Ed.) *J.R. Kidd: A Bibliography of His Writings* (Toronto: Ontario Institute for Studies in Education, 1988) p.vii.

[25] G. Selman, "Roby Kidd and the Canadian Association for Adult Education 1951-1961," in *Adult Education in Canada: Historical Essays.*

[26] Quoted in G. Selman, "The Fifties: Pivotal Decade," in *Adult Education in Canada: Historical Essays*, p.42.

Later in the decade, when he was commissioned by the Toronto Board of Education to prepare a major report and set of recommendations on the future development of their work in adult education, he used that opportunity to publish strong recommendations about according appropriate status for adult education personnel.[27]

In addition to appeals to employers of adult educators, Kidd repeatedly addressed adult educators themselves about these issues. He saw to it that a great deal more attention was paid in the association's journal to matters of professional concern.[28] He spoke to many groups of adult educators across the country and also restructured the activities of the CAAE itself so as to encourage the development of the field in the regions. In 1950, at Kidd's suggestion, the CAAE decided to hold national conferences only every second year, and to sponsor regional conferences in the Western and Atlantic regions in the intervening years. The chief reason for this suggestion was that the regional meetings would be more accessible to practitioners than were national ones and could serve as a vehicle for strengthening both the development of the field and opportunities for in-service professional education. The Atlantic region was the first to pick up on the idea; the "First Atlantic Region Conference" was held at Amherst, Nova Scotia in June of 1951.[29] Further meetings followed every second year throughout the decade, the programs focussing mainly on the social and economic development of the region. In the West, the meetings did not begin until 1953, the first being held in Banff, but were held regularly thereafter. Although the conferences in the West, like those in the Maritimes, devoted some attention to social development, there was much more focus in the West on the formation of provincial organizations of adult educators, their functions and their relationship with the national organization. It is clear from the reports of these meetings, East and West, that the decision to facilitate the holding of regional meetings under CAAE sponsorship was an important factor in stimulating in-service development activities in both regions.[30]

There had been a few local and regional associations of adult educators in Canada prior to the 1950s—in Newfoundland (not then yet part of Canada) as early as 1930,[31] in Winnipeg in the mid-1930s, in Ontario and the Eastern

---

[27] J.R. Kidd, *18 to 80: Continuing Education in Metropolitan Toronto* (Toronto: Board of Education, 1961).

[28] W. Stewart, *A Comparison of A Historical Model of the American Literature in Support of Adult Education with Literature in the Journals of the Canadian Association for Adult Education* (Vancouver: Unpublished Graduating Essay, University of British Columbia, 1983).

[29] "Maritime Conference," *Food for Thought, 12,* 1 (1951) pp.32-33.

[30] G. Selman, "Roby Kidd and the CAAE."

[31] "Newfoundland and Adult Education," *Bulletin* (World Association for Adult Education) *XLIII* (1930) pp.19-21.

Townships of Quebec in the early 1940s, and in Alberta beginning in 1943.[32] But by the late 1940s, no such organizations were functioning. Arising out of suggestions discussed at Banff in 1953, steps were taken in British Columbia to create a provincially based organization. An organizational dinner in September of 1954 led to the first of what were to be a continuing series of semi-annual conferences on adult education which continued on a regular basis until 1961. The British Columbia organization was a council of agencies rather than a personal membership body, but the British Columbia Adult Education Council sponsored a significant series of in-service professional development activities within the framework of the semi-annual conferences. In 1956, all four Western provinces held provincial conferences of adult educators, and in all but British Columbia (where an organization already existed), plans were discussed for the possible creation of provincial bodies.[33] As it turned out, things developed more quickly in Saskatchewan than in the other two provinces, and under the terms of a revision in the CAAE constitution passed in 1958, the British Columbia and Saskatchewan organizations became "affiliated" with the CAAE and had representation on that organization's national council. In the Atlantic region, that development did not take place until the following decade.

Apart from the CAAE, there were other organizational developments in the field at the national level. The French language national body, l'Institute canadien de l'éducation des adultes, which had developed out of a standing committee of the CAAE, was reorganized in 1952 and became a more vigorous and effective instrument for that language group. Those who worked in the field of university extension, after a period of consultation with an already existing organization of colleagues responsible for summer session activities, joined with them in 1954 in forming the Canadian Association of Directors of Extension and Summer Sessions.[34] Educators interested mainly in the rural and agricultural aspects of adult education had formed an Extension Group under the Canadian Society of Technical Agriculturalists in 1940, but this organization met only sporadically during the following decade and disappeared by 1953. In 1959, a decision was made to revive such a body, and the Canadian Society of Rural Extensionanadian Society of Rural Extension came into existence the following year.[35]

---

[32] G. Selman, "Roby Kidd and the CAAE."

[33] G. Selman, "Western Variations on the Theme," *Food for Thought, 18*, 1 (1957) pp.5-9.

[34] J.R. Kidd, *Adult Education in the Canadian University* (Toronto: Canadian Association for Adult Education, 1956).

[35] G. Selman, "Specialization or Balkanization: Organizations of Adult Educators," in *Adult Education in Canada: Historical Essays.*

Training Opportunities

Opportunities in Canada for acquiring training in adult education expanded very greatly during the 1950s. There had been some work of this general kind going on for many years in certain quarters. The literature of the 1940s contains many accounts of "leadership training" activities in fields such as group work, recreation and, especially late in the decade, human relations training. The Y.M. and Y.W.C.A. and other voluntary organizations, the folk school, co-operative and labour movements were active in this work. Roby Kidd recalled that he had been a student in a credit course in adult education at Sir George Williams College in 1934-35, which may have been the first such course in Canada.[36]

When Kidd returned from his doctoral studies in 1947 and joined the staff of the CAAE, the promotion of training opportunities for adult educators was one of his priorities. He suggested the formation of a CAAE Committee on Personnel in Adult Education, whose initial report was discussed at the annual conference in 1948. It indicated that of the eighty-six full-time adult educators who responded, only two had any training in the field, even a single course. The committee recommended that the CAAE take a lead in the promotion of both formal and non-formal training programs.[37] The endorsement of this report provided Kidd with a mandate for his continuing efforts to these ends during the 1950s.

Non-credit in-service development activities for adult educators were an important new feature of the period and Kidd played a leading role. A few examples will indicate the types of programs which were organized. The first training course for adult educators in the Western region, a two-week program on "Extension Methods and Techniques," was held at Banff in 1949, co-sponsored by the CAAE and the University of Alberta. Kidd frequently taught courses for adult educators in the labour movement. In 1951, he secured a foundation grant to support a two-year series of training programs designed for workers in the outports of Newfoundland. The first regional training course for the Atlantic region was organized by the CAAE in 1958.

Reference has already been made to the role of CAAE regional conferences—East and West—to the in-service development of adult education leaders.

A further aspect of working towards adequate training opportunities for adult educators involved efforts directed at employers in the field, most notably educational institutions, school boards and provincial departments of education. At the CAAE conference in 1950, a working group gave attention to

---

[36] G. Selman, "Roby Kidd and the CAAE."

[37] J.R. Kidd, *Adult Education in Canada.*

"Provincial Divisions of Adult Education" (meaning units within departments of education). In 1957, 1959 and 1961, conferences on the role of governments and school boards in the field were organized in co-operation with the Canadian Education Association. Beginning in the late 1950s, the CAAE had standing committees on governments in adult education and on school boards in the field. In 1950, Kidd published a pamphlet dealing with the role of school boards in the field, and reference has already been made to the study of adult education which he carried out for the Toronto Board in 1961. The committee organizing the Second Canadian Conference on Education, to be held in 1962, commissioned Kidd to write a background study on adult education, one of several on specialized topics published in advance of the meeting. By means of this substantial pamphlet, he made the most of the opportunity to address the educational establishment of Canada with respect to the system's responsibilities in adult education.[38]

Kidd was also active in raising funds from foundations for the purpose of financing training opportunities. The funds he obtained for the training of workers in Newfoundland have already been mentioned. In 1953, a party of leading adult educators from English and French Canada was enabled, with funds secured from Carnegie, to visit outstanding projects in Europe. In 1955, school board adult educators from Nova Scotia and New Brunswick were assisted with a study tour to American and Canadian centres. For several years in the late 1950s, some $15,000 a year, which he secured from the Fund for Adult Education in the United States, was used to make study tours or degree study possible for individual Canadian adult educators.

This was also the period during which academic degree programs in adult education were inaugurated in Canada. With his doctoral degree, Kidd was clearly qualified to be appointed to teach university courses. In the late 1940s and during the 1950s he taught credit courses in adult education at several Canadian universities (frequently the first such course the institution had offered). In 1951, he taught the first graduate course to be offered in the field in Canada, at the Ontario College of Education. A course he taught at the University of British Columbia in the summer of 1956 was utilized by that institution as the first step in developing a masters degree program in the field, which when introduced in 1957 became the first degree program in adult education in Canada. (By this time there were at least twelve universities in the United States which were offering advanced degree programs in the field.)[39] The University of Guelph became the second institution to offer such

---

[38] J.R. Kidd, *Adult Education and the School* (Toronto: Canadian Association for Adult Education, 1950); J.R. Kidd, *18 to 80*; J.R. Kidd, *Continuing Education* (Ottawa: Canadian Conference on Education, 1961).

[39] C.O. Houle, in M.S. Knowles (Ed.), *Handbook of Adult Education in the United States* (Chicago: Adult Education Association of the USA, 1960).

a program when it admitted its first masters candidates in this field in 1960 to a Master of Science degree, with a specialization in agriculture and extension work.[40]

It is apparent from the foregoing that during the 1950s considerable advances were made in both providing various kinds of training opportunities and also attempting to convince both adult educators and their employers that such training was desirable.

Institutional Development

The matter of institutional development has already been touched upon in several ways. The efforts made during the decade to convince the public educational authorities were in large measure directed to this end. Kidd made use of the available opportunities, at meetings and in the course of his constant travel back and forth across Canada, to promote the field and the need for adequate institutional provision for this work. Leading adult educators in the various provinces were also working to this end. CAAE standing committees on school board and government adult education work have already been mentioned, as have several conferences held during the decade with representatives of those sectors of the field. The consultation carried out by Kidd for the Board of Education in Toronto and the opportunity to write one of the study pamphlets for the Second Canadian Conference on Education in 1962 were high profile opportunities to address the educational establishment in Canada. Another opportunity presented itself in 1953, when the National Conference of Canadian Universities commissioned Kidd to write a study concerning adult education in the university. The outcome was a volume entitled *Adult Education in the Canadian University*, which was published in 1956.[41]

There were grounds for encouragement, particularly with respect to provision for adult education within the structure of the provincial departments of education. Saskatchewan had created an adult education unit in 1944. When the government of Nova Scotia created a Division of Adult Education in the late 1940s, Kidd gave great prominence to that development, carrying frequent news items in the journal and printing a full account of the work as one of several pamphlets he arranged to have published in the early 1950s.[42] By 1961, all ten provincial departments had such a unit.[43]

---

[40] G. Moss, "A Brief History of the Development of Graduate Studies in Adult Education in Canada," in *Papers Presented to a Conference on Research in Adult Education* (Vancouver: Canadian Association for the Study of Adult Education, 1980).

[41] J.R. Kidd, *Adult Education in the Canadian University*.

[42] G. Henson, *Adult Education in Nova Scotia* (Toronto: Canadian Association for Adult Education, 1954).

[43] J.R. Kidd, *Continuing Education*.

Literature of the Field

The literature on adult education in Canada was another area in which there was significant advance during the 1950s. It is generally understood that a field of practice, in order to advance towards professional status, must have a body of knowledge on which to base its growth and development. While adult education in Canada could not be said to have reached the stage of theory building or other advanced forms of research and scholarship at this time, what was attempted was to document the nature and history of the field in Canada and to assist adult educators who were ready to do so to take an increasingly serious interest in the methods and problems of practice.

There was very little literature about the field in Canada published before the 1950s. There were the accumulated files of the two CAAE journals, *Adult Learning* (1936-39) and *Food for Thought* (1940-61), Fitzpatrick's plea for and account of the early years of Frontier College (1920), the survey of adult education activities edited by Sandiford (1935) as part of the process of founding the CAAE, and Rev. Moses Coady's account of the philosophy and methods of the Antigonish Movement (1939).[44] Aside from a few other articles, institutional and government reports, and a very few pamphlets, these seem to be the only published works on adult education in Canada prior to 1950.[45] Due to the efforts of Roby Kidd as both author and publisher, and those of a growing but still small circle of practitioners in Canada, this picture changed substantially during the 1950s.

Walter Stewart, in his study of the content of the CAAE journals over the years, perceived a distinct shift of emphasis in *Food for Thought* in 1950 compared to five years earlier.

> The clearly intended audience of the 1950 issues is those who are engaged in educating adults and not those who were being educated, as had been true in the 1940s.[46]

He commented further that at this time the journal became "a magazine about adult education rather than an instrument of adult education."[47]

Kidd's own writing about the field during the period was prolific, extremely varied, and may be seen to fall into four categories.[48] The first, that of descriptive studies of the field in Canada, is represented by two of his major works, *Adult Education in Canada* and *Learning and Society*,[49] both collec-

---

[44] A. Fitzpatrick, *The University in Overalls*; P. Sandiford, *Adult Education in Canada: A Survey*; M.M. Coady, *Masters of Their Own Destiny*.

[45] J.R. Kidd, *Adult Education in Canada*.

[46] W. Stewart, *A Comparison of A Historical Model*, p.36.

[47] Ibid., p.45.

[48] For greater detail, see G. Selman, "Roby Kidd and the CAAE."

[49] J.R. Kidd, *Adult Education in Canada*; J.R. Kidd, *Learning and Society*.

tions of articles which reflect the development of the field in Canada up to approximately 1960, and which in the absence of any general histories of the field continue to be especially valuable resources. A second category consisted of publications which resulted from consultations he carried out, the two most substantial of which were *Adult Education and the Canadian University* and *18 to 80*, the study commissioned by the Toronto Board of Education.[50] Kidd was becoming progressively more active at the international level during the 1950s. Most of his publication in that connection during the decade was in the form of articles, but one major study resulted from a consultation in the West Indies in 1957-58.[51] The fourth category of his writings had to do with the methodology of the field. Several pamphlets he wrote during the period, about such matters as film utilization, field work and discussion group techniques, fall into this category, as does his most notable publication of the period, a textbook entitled *How Adults Learn*, the first edition of which appeared in 1959.[52] This text was the first to be published in Canada and was a significant departure from those written by others in at least one major respect, the relative prominence given to learning theory. The book was well received in the field, in North America and beyond, and it has since been translated into at least five other languages and has been used as a text in at least forty countries.[53]

Over and above Kidd's own writing, the field benefitted from his efforts in encouraging and publishing a great deal of material through the CAAE. Soon after his publication of *Adult Education in Canada* in 1950, he secured a grant from the Fund for Adult Education, an American foundation, to make it possible to continue the program of documenting Canadian achievements in the field. The result was a series of eleven substantial pamphlets (up to 120 pages in length) in a series entitled "Learning for Living," which appeared between 1952 and 1954. A few other representative examples of CAAE publications during the decade were: a survey of labour education in Canada, a bibliography of Canadian writings in adult education, and a study of residential education.[54] There were as well several other notable volumes about the field which were published commercially at this time. They included Donald Cameron's history of the Banff School of Fine Arts, E.A. Corbett's reminis-

---

[50] J.R. Kidd, *Adult Education and the Canadian University*; J.R. Kidd, *18 to 80*.

[51] J.R. Kidd, *Adult Education in the Caribbean* (Mona, Jamaica: University of the West Indies, 1958).

[52] J.R. Kidd, *How Adults Learn* (New York: Association Press, 1959).

[53] N. Cochrane et al., *J.R. Kidd: An International Legacy of Learning* (Vancouver: University of British Columbia/Centre for Continuing Education, 1986).

[54] D. Smith, *A Survey Report on Labour Education in Canada* (1951); M. Thomson & D. Ironside (Eds.), *A Bibliography of Canadian Writings in Adult Education* (1956); E. Loosley, *Residential Adult Education: A Canadian View* (1960): all Toronto, Canadian Association for Adult Education.

cences, *We Have With Us Tonight*, and at the end of the decade, A.F. Laidlaw's history of the Antigonish Movement.[55]

Other organizations at the national level were publishing material at this time: the Canadian Labour Congress, the Canadian Library Association, the Canadian Film Institute and the Canadian Citizenship Council. As well, an increasing amount of material about adult education was being published at the local and provincial level. The bibliography published by the CAAE in 1956, already referred to, contained a number of items related to adult education from *Saskatchewan Community* and *Community Courier* (Ontario) and listed a number of other newsletters and bulletins published at the provincial level.

At the beginning of the 1950s there was very little Canadian literature about adult education, whereas by the end of that decade, practitioners and students had a considerable and growing body of writings from Canadian sources on which to call, covering not only aspects of practice, but also Canadian perspectives, policies and achievements.

Since the 1950s: Towards Professionalism

In a widely cited article which appeared in 1960 in the *Handbook of Adult Education in the United States*, C.O. Houle described the work force of adult education as a "pyramid of leadership."[56] The large base of the pyramid was made up of volunteers, who served as teachers, planners and organizers of adult education. The intermediate sector was made up of the smaller number of persons—usually teachers of adult classes—who worked mainly at other activities but were employed on a part-time basis to teach adults. The top of the pyramid, and the smallest group of the three, was made up of full-time, career adult educators, with "basic career expectations in the field."[57]

This has generally been accepted as a satisfactory representation of the leadership of the field at that time—in Canada as well as in the United States. It was recognized that a great deal of non-formal education took place outside of educational institutions, organized and conducted in the main by volunteers. Within educational institutions and in many other settings, teachers were employed on a part-time basis because of their expertise developed elsewhere. The career adult educators were relatively few in number, were frequently the organizers and administrators of educational programs, were

---

[55] D. Cameron, *Campus in the Clouds* (Toronto: McClelland & Stewart, 1956); E. A. Corbett, *We Have With Us Tonight*; A.F. Laidlaw, *The Campus and the Community* (Montreal: Harvest House, 1961).

[56] C.O. Houle, in M.S. Knowles, *Handbook of Adult Education*.

[57] Ibid., p.120.

often full time in those roles, and usually made up the best paid sector in adult education.

Increasing Numbers of Adult Educators

It is useful to speculate as to the degree to which Houle's pyramid is relevant today, some forty years later. We know that the extent of adult education has increased many times over in the intervening period. But have the relative proportions of the three sectors of the adult education work force, as described by Houle, stayed roughly the same? The author has discussed this matter with a number of experienced adult educators in recent years and several points have been made. The first is that likely the number of paid persons—part and full-time—in the field has increased, compared to the volunteers. It is recognized that a great deal of adult education in our society goes on in the voluntary sector—voluntary associations, health associations, hobby and interest clubs, churches—which is largely invisible to the general public view. But systematic attempts in recent years to survey participation in adult education, although they likely do not do full justice to the private, volunteer sector, nevertheless show it to be only a modest portion of organized adult education overall.

The second main observation is that with the increasing acceptance by government in recent decades of the need for adult education, vocational and technical training and so on, vastly increased funding has been provided for various forms of adult education. As is described elsewhere in this book, the percentage of adult Canadians who take part annually in organized adult education has increased at least seven-fold in the last forty years. This trend has no doubt brought a disproportionate increase in the numbers of full-time, career adult educators, and also in the number of part-time paid teachers of adults. At this point one is once again brought up against the definitional question. Is the full-time faculty member of a community college, who teaches adult students, daytime or evening, as part of a regular teaching load to be considered an adult educator? Certainly such persons are teachers of adults, but we do not normally see them as "adult educators." Even if we steer clear of such moot points in the field, it seems abundantly clear that the number of paid teachers, organizers, counsellors, curriculum developers in adult education has grown enormously since Houle devised his pyramid. What sort of geometric representation one might appropriately make today in describing the "work force" of adult education would perhaps vary, depending on one's answer to the definitional question raised above, but it is the general view that the number of paid workers in the field has increased greatly in comparison with the volunteers.

In addition to the remarkable expansion of the number of adult educators in recent decades, there have been many signs of a growing awareness on the part of those involved in the field that they share interests and concerns with those involved in other sectors of adult education. At the international level, Lowe, Hely and others have described the evolution of adult education towards becoming an increasingly professionalized field.[58] The CAAE, under the leadership of Alan Thomas, continued throughout the 1960s to promote aspects of professionalism. A review of the contents of the Association's journal, renamed *Continuous Learning* in 1962, reveals a conscious policy of supporting such a trend. There were articles about professionalism and about professional aspects of adult education. There were annual listings of professional training opportunities in the field. In 1966, the CAAE held a national conference on the theme, "Adult Education: An Emerging Profession," which was attended by some 225 persons. Thomas strengthened the library of the CAAE as a research centre for the field, published aids to research activity, and launched several newsletters for specialized areas of practice. He saw the promotion of such professional activities as crucial to the welfare of both the field as a whole and his own organization, telling his board of directors in 1966 that "it is our ability here that will either assure us a commanding place in adult education or condemn us to watch the steady erosion of any imaginative unity in adult education."[59]

The emergence of a large number of organizations of adult educators, both nationally and provincially, and of organizations devoted to research in the field, both of which are described in some detail later, are further evidence of the growing number of persons who were ready to identify themselves with the field.

The Roles of Adult Educators

Accompanying the overall growth and institutionalization of adult education activity has come an increased specialization for those who work in the field. Several areas of specialization will be described.

Guidance to the learning process. The role which comes to mind first is that of teacher. The master craftsmen and their apprentices, the literacy teachers of the early Adult Schools, the lecturers at the mechanic's institutes—from the earliest days of the adult education movement up to the present time, the teacher or expert who imparted knowledge to others has been a prominent feature of the work. The teacher has passed on knowledge, has demonstrated how things are done and has directed the educational process. Students have

---

[58] A.S.M. Hely, *New Trends in Adult Education* (Paris: UNESCO, 1962); J. Lowe, *The Education of Adults*.

[59] Minutes of the Board of Directors, Jan. 21-23, 1966, quoted in G. Selman, "Alan Thomas and the Canadian Association for Adult Education 1961-1970," in *Adult Education in Canada: Historical Essays*, p.215.

in many instances decided to take part in the educational activity in the expectation that there would be such an expert present "from whom they could learn." In Houle's "pyramid," referred to in the previous section, the large middle portion of leadership in the field was seen to be made up of persons who were teachers and whose expertise was acquired from their work and study in some other setting or occupation—as accountant, artist, technician, academic, professional, and so on.

From the earliest days of the adult education movement, there was also a second tradition in the guidance of learners, which was based not, or not only on knowledge of the subject which was being mastered, but on the nature of the educational activity or the study materials. The Methodist Bible classes, the local meetings of those taking part in the "corresponding societies" of the 1790s, the groups interested in forming co-operative organizations, the local chapters of the Chartist movement—these are a few among many examples where the leadership or guidance of learners came from persons who may not have been much, if any, better informed in the content of what was to be learned than the rest of the group, but whose role was one of guiding a process, showing the way, assisting in ways other than imparting content to the learners.

The vast majority of adult education activity, it would seem clear, is of the first type and is led by a person (or by a correspondence course or a computer program) where the "instructional agent" both imparts knowledge and directs the educational process. This is almost universally the case in the formal educational sector, but is the dominant mode in the non-formal sector as well.

The subject matter or content expert who serves as teacher in adult education usually is a person who does not associate himself or herself in career terms with the field of adult education. In formal educational settings, the teacher is often an employee of the sponsoring institution and has career expectations which relate to that institutional system. For instance, the teacher of mathematics in an adult basic education program of a community college, though teaching full or part-time adult students, may have little or no sense of involvement in adult education, but rather see himself or herself as a college faculty member or as a mathematics specialist. In many non-formal settings, too, the career expectation of the teacher in most cases lies elsewhere, with the person's full-time employer or with the field of specialty. The second kind of leader referred to above—the process specialist—is perhaps more likely to feel part of the field of adult education.

The teacher of adults may have little or no training in the field of adult education. Persons are usually hired as teachers because of the expertise they have in their subject matter, sometimes reinforced by the fact that they already are employed by an educational institution. Neither the organization which hires the instructor nor the student who enrolls in the class care in the first instance about the teacher's instructional skills, but attach priority to the "credentials" of the potential instructor in the subject to be taught. Many such instructors have by various means become very fine teachers. Many organizations provide in-service training opportunities in instructional methodology. An increasing number of persons who find that their career has taken them into teaching adults subsequently seek formal training in instructional procedures. But the overall picture is that the overwhelming majority of teachers of adults, though involved in adult education, do not have a sense of their career being linked to adult education as a field of study and do not seek training in that field.

Program Planners. With the institutionalization of the field in recent decades has come the development of two groups of specialists in the organization and management of the work, here termed program planners and administrators. The two roles tend to merge into one another, and exceedingly few persons perform exclusively one role or the other. The program planner, or "programmer" is concerned with the planning of the educational event or course, perhaps apart from the process of instruction, which is usually left to the teacher or content expert. The programmer frequently decides what courses will be offered, what resources will be required to carry them out, and what the general objectives of the program will be. The programmer is frequently involved in managing or administering the program while it is in operation and may make decisions about any evaluation procedures which are carried out, formative or summative.

The role of the programmer varies greatly from one institutional setting to another. In certain situations the educator is responsible for hundreds of courses a year and the main tasks may be to decide what courses will be given, recruit suitable teachers and arrange space in which the meetings will be held. This is particularly typical of formal settings and the non-formal offerings of institutions in large centres of population. In other situations the programmer may have fewer courses to manage and may play a significant role in the planning and carrying out of the program. This type of participation is more common in the case of short courses—programs which go on for one or several days on a full-time basis—than in connection with the one-evening-a-week sort of course. The programmer usually has considerable administrative responsibility as well, managing budgets, supervising the work of others, seeking financial resources, and organizing a multiplicity of office activities.

The programmer is the category of practitioner who is most likely already to have, or to seek, training in the field of adult education. It has been a fairly typical pattern in adult education that people have by one means or another "found their way" into adult education, have then realized its potential and have been drawn to it as a career. They frequently then become aware of the training which is available in the field and decide to take advantage of it. There is a sense, therefore, that what in other professions is pre-service training has frequently been in-service training in adult education. Presumably as adult education becomes better known as a career choice, more young people will take training in the field prior to entering it (as indeed is the case in many countries in the world), but up to now, at least, students in degree programs in adult education (which are mainly graduate programs) are already engaged in the field, and are usually in their thirties or forties.

Administrator. As has been mentioned, the other specialist in the management and operation of adult education programs may spend most or all of his or her time in the management function, rather than in the planning of programs. This person is frequently the dean, director or head of an adult education organization or unit. In large organizations there may be more than one such position. The administrator has particular responsibility for managing the processes within the unit, acquiring and apportioning resources, developing and administering policy, selecting, developing and supervising personnel, and managing relations of many kinds with forces outside the unit itself—in the institutional hierarchy, with other adult education bodies and in the community. Public relations and publicity, particularly in their institutional dimensions (as distinct from publicity for particular courses) may also be a special concern of the administrator.

The administrator is frequently a person who has had considerable experience in adult education and has acquired advanced training in the field. It is characteristic of the field, however, and perhaps a manifestation of its relative youth and lack of recognition, that this is often not the case. At the time of writing it is not clear that there is even a trend toward a greater reliance in the case of such roles on those who have received advanced training in adult education. Such a state of affairs is a result of several factors. The adult or continuing education unit is frequently a marginal enterprise within the parent organization and factors other than adult education qualifications sometimes take precedence when appointments are made. There is some disagreement in the field too as to whether the "generic" professional training of adult educators is the most satisfactory type of training or whether training in the broader field of education or in the longer-established disciplines is preferable. Many senior appointments have gone to those with advanced training and experience in adult education, but many have not.

Researchers. An increasing number of persons in recent decades have become engaged in research activity in relation to adult education. University faculty members in departments of adult education, of whom there are over one hundred in Canada at the present time, have a professional interest in such activity, as do an increasing number of practitioners, especially specialists in large organizations. Government and other public agencies are increasingly seeking research results as part of the policy formation process, and a growing number of consultants in the field are making a living from research activity. There are currently some four hundred members of the Canadian Association for the Study of Adult Education, a significant proportion of these being graduate students in the field.

There have been persistent efforts over recent decades to interest specialists in other fields to take an interest in research problems of interest and importance to the field of adult education. By and large such attempts have fallen on deaf ears. It has increasingly been realized that adult education has to "grow its own" body of competent researchers if satisfactory attention is to be paid to the research needs of the field. That process is going on apace at the present time, as a subsequent section will document.

Other Specialists. In the last three decades particularly, several other important specialties in adult education have emerged. They will presumably continue to grow in numbers and significance in the future. The first of these is the counsellor of adult learners. The counselling or advising function has of course been performed as long as there have been adult learners, but the number of practitioners specializing in this field has been extremely small until recently. Matters of definition arise in this connection. Is a counsellor employed by a university or college, working largely with full-time (adult) students, an adult education counsellor? At any rate, there are increasing numbers of persons who do specialize in advising adult students, and presumably this trend will continue. This is one of a number of areas in which the women's movement has shown the way for the rest of the field.

Another specialized area of practice which has been emerging is that of curriculum development. Adult education has traditionally thought more in terms of "program planning" than "curriculum development," but in an increasing number of settings in recent years, particularly in post-secondary educational institutions, curricula designed especially for adult education have been required. A great deal of this work has been contracted out to specialists or consultants. This brings us to the third type of specialist emerging in the field, the consultant. Many organizations—educational institutions, government bodies, business and industry and so on—have made it a practice in recent years to contract out certain research and curriculum development tasks to outside consultants. There are now many small firms and individuals in all large population centres in Canada which undertake this kind of work. The final type of specialty developing in the fields is the media specialist. By this is meant not only the "mass media," in the traditional sense of the term (film, video, print and broadcast), but also those who are expert in the use and application of the computer to the instructional process. With the rapid expansion of distance education offerings in recent years, especially computer-based "on-line" courses, the role of the media specialists has become very much more prominent. The foregoing are several among many emerging specialties in the field of adult education which may be expected to grow in size and importance in future years.

Associations of Adult Educators

One clear indication of the growth of adult education in recent decades has been the emergence of a considerable number of organizations which have been formed by those working in the field.[60] This process has been going on since the 1930s, when the Canadian Association for Adult Education was formed, but has accelerated since the end of the 1950s. This development may be seen as a reflection of several factors: the increase in the numbers of people who work in adult education and who have come to associate themselves and their careers with the field; increased specialization within adult education activities; and the political facts of life in Canada—the constitutional role of the provinces in the field of education and the trend within confederation towards decentralization of authority to the provinces.

The development of national and regional adult education associations in Canada does not lend itself to tidy summary, but some general observations can be made. Aside from a few short-lived exceptions at the regional level, the first three decades of development, from 1935 to the early 1960s, saw the formation of mainly national organizations. The 1960s were a period during which provincially based organizations of a general or "umbrella" coverage of the field came into being. The most recent two decades have brought the development of a variety of more specialized organizations at the provincial level, and more recently, at the national level as well.

The Canadian Association for Adult Education was the first national organization of adult educators formed in Canada. A planning meeting was held in 1934, certain preparatory work carried out in the ensuing year and the CAAE was officially formed in 1935. It followed its American counterpart by some nine years, a point that is worth noting mainly because some of the same dynamics were at work in the two countries, including some stimulation and financial assistance from the Carnegie Corporation of New York.[61] There had been some short-lived local associations in the 1930s and 1940s (see above) but the CAAE was alone in the field again by 1950, at least as far as English-speaking Canada was concerned. (In French-speaking Canada, the field was at first represented by a standing committee of the CAAE, but in

---

[60] For details on these developments, see G. Selman, "Specialization or Balkanization: Organizations of Adult Educators," in *Adult Education in Canada: Historical Essays*.

[61] D.P. Armstrong, *Corbett's House: The Origins of the Canadian Association for Adult Education and its Development during the Directorship of E.A. Corbett 1936-1951* (Unpublished M.A. Thesis, University of Toronto, 1968); R. Faris, *The Passionate Educators* (Toronto: Peter Martin, 1975).

1946, a separate organization was formed.) The CAAE and the French language body, the ICEA, remain today as the two "umbrella" organizations in the field, representing the two main language groups, and for some thirty years both have received financial support on a regular basis from the federal government.

More specialized organizations came along in the subsequent decades. The Canadian Association of Directors of Extension and Summer Schools (CADESS, which became the Canadian Association for University Continuing Education) and the Canadian Society of Rural Extension (which later dropped the word Rural from its name) have already been mentioned. In the 1960s, French language university extension departments split away from CADESS and formed a separate body, L'ACDEULF. Following the passage of federal work-force training legislation in 1960, which had the effect of expanding the number of persons engaged in vocational training programs, the federal government supported the formation of a national organization, the Canadian Vocational Association.

The 1960s were an active period in the formation of associations at the provincial level. The main reason for this was active promotion by the CAAE. There had been provincial associations in Saskatchewan and British Columbia in the 1950s. The British Columbia group, which had been in existence since 1954, put forward a proposal in 1961 that the CAAE revise its constitution to allow for the formation of provincial associations, not as separate organizations, but as integral parts or "divisions" of the national body. This change having been brought about, six provinces formed such divisions during the decade: British Columbia (1962), Nova Scotia (1963), Ontario (1966), Manitoba (1966), Saskatchewan (1967) and Newfoundland (1967). By the late 1960s, it became apparent that a change in the CAAE's structure was imminent once again. For this reason and others, adult educators in Alberta, when they formed an association in 1967, decided not to become a part of the national body. After the CAAE changed its structure in 1971, the provincial divisions were all reconstituted as autonomous organizations, affiliated with the CAAE and with representation on its board of directors. A further development provincially was the formation in 1965 of the broadly based Rural Learning Association of Ontario, representing an amalgamation of the Ontario Farm Radio Forum, the Folk School Council and the Rural Leadership Forum.

Because of the growth and increased specialization within the field, the latter years of the 1960s were also the starting point in the development of more specialized associations at the provincial level. The timing differed from province to province, but generally the subsequent two decades saw the formation of organizations which brought together those in such fields as the administration of adult or continuing education in the public educational institutions (especially the school boards and colleges and institutes); teaching

English (or French) as a second language; adult basic education and literacy; training in business and industry; community education and community development; education for handicapped persons; education for women; and educators in health fields.

In some cases, one or more of the provincial bodies took the lead in forming national associations in such fields of specialty. In other cases, it worked the other way around. More recent years have seen the formation of several new national organizations. Although it was not established as an autonomous body until 1979, the Canadian Congress for Learning Opportunities for Women traces its beginnings back to committee status with the CAAE in 1973. In 1967, a number of persons interested in literacy work formed the Movement for Canadian Literacy, successor organization to World Literacy of Canada, which was formed in the early 1950s. Formation of a national organization in the field of teaching English as a second language, TESL Canada, took place in 1979. The Canadian Association for the Study of Adult Education held an organizational conference in 1980 and a formal founding conference the next year. Laubach Canada Inc., which is concerned with the teaching of literacy, was formally established in 1981, though literacy work utilizing its methods and materials in Canada dated back to 1970. Community educators from several provinces established the Canadian Association for Community Education in 1984. And perhaps most recent among these national organizations, at least at the time of writing, is the Canadian Association for Distance Education, which functioned for a year under the auspices of the university extension body, CAUCE, and became an autonomous organization in 1985.

The organizations referred to above are of several main types. The first group are general or "umbrella" organizations. They aspire to represent the field as a whole, rather than any segment of it. At the national level this would include the two language-based national bodies, the CAAE and the ICEA, and also perhaps the Canadian Association for the Study of Adult Education, whose interests span research about all aspects of the field. At the provincial level, there is in almost all provinces an umbrella association.

A second category of groups is organized along institutional lines. The university extension body, now called CAUCE, was the first of these at the national level. Membership is made up of those responsible for continuing education services offered by Canadian universities. At the provincial level, those administering school board and college-based programs have a separate organization in some places, as do those based in privately owned vocational training enterprises. In this category, the common focus of interest is that the members all, or mostly all, function in similar kinds of settings.

The third category—and it is the most numerous—is made up of organizations based on either the content of the programs being offered or the clientele for whom the services are provided. This includes, for instance, associations for teaching English as an additional language, vocational education, literacy education, learning opportunities for women, and the Canadian Society of Extension, which is concerned with agricultural and rural interests. The number of such specialized organizations has increased markedly in recent years, as the field has expanded as particular needs have become more clearly identified.

Finally, there are organizations of adult educators which are based on the methodology of delivery. The most obvious example in this group is the body concerned with distance education. Although it fits a little less comfortably into this category, the field of community education, with its reliance on community-based methods, falls in this group as well.

One may confidently predict that in the next decade or two additional specialized organizations will be established, both provincially and nationally.

Although there are many differences among these organizations, there are similarities as well. They are generally, for instance, aimed at advancing the interests of adult education, or in some cases of a particular sector of the field. They are concerned with fostering communication among their membership. They are in most cases concerned with the promotion of effective practice. A number are concerned also with a critical examination of their work, seeking by means of research, inter-institutional co-operation and demonstration projects to enhance their contributions to the welfare of adult learners.

There are important differences as well, of course, some arising from the very nature of the categories set out above. There are also differences in what might be termed philosophical orientations among the organizations. Indeed it is clear that some of them were established in the first instance because of such differences of view. This would be true of the Association for Community Education, for instance, the founders of which left the previously existing groups largely because they saw them as devoted to institutional or "content" interests rather than the interests of the learners and their communities. Some of the organizations are made up only of adult educators and, especially those which are connected with the large educational institutions, tend to be comfortable with the emerging professionalism in the field. Others, including many in community education, literacy and basic education, are leery of such professionalism, fearing it will tend to increase the "distance" between educator and learner, and fall heir to some of the rigidities and exclusivity which are frequently associated with the older professions. In keeping with this view, a number of associations include in their membership not only the paid adult education workers but also adult learners and representatives of community organizations. Perhaps most basic of all, some organizations—or the vast majority of their members—believe in the "liberal" philosophical approach to adult education and see it as their role to provide services to individuals. In other organizations a "social transformation" view of adult education is held by many members and their aim, beyond that of providing learning opportunities for individuals, is to contribute to social change—through adult education.

Concern has been expressed about the splintering or "balkanization" of the field of adult education which may result from such a proliferation of organizations.[62] While specialization within the field clearly has potential benefits and will presumably continue to be the trend, are there dangers which need to be guarded against? For instance, with respect to advocacy on behalf of the interests of adult learners, if all the organizations in the field are specialized, who will be in a position to take the larger, more comprehensive view? And will governments or institutions respond if they are receiving unco-ordinated, sometimes conflicting recommendations from the field? There is no expectation that the trend towards specialization among adult educators and their associations will not continue. But voices are being raised expressing concern about the possible disadvantages flowing from this development and urging that the associations learn to act together, or at least co-ordinate their actions when that would clearly work to the benefit of the adult learners they are attempting to serve.

Training of Adult Educators

It has been pointed out earlier in this chapter that the first degree programs for the training of adult educators in Canada emerged in the late 1950s at the University of British Columbia and the University of Guelph. The United States had taken the lead in such activity, Houle having traced the beginnings of formal instruction in the field back to 1917, at Columbia University.[63] That university was the first to create an academic department of adult education (1930), and its first doctorates were awarded in 1935. By that time formal courses were also being offered at Ohio State, Cornell, the University of Michigan and the University of California at Los Angeles. Before the decade was over, the University of Wisconsin and Syracuse University were offering degree programs as well. By 1962, soon after Canadian programs began to function, American universities had awarded 323 doctorates in the field.[64] In the case of Great Britain, aside from a short-lived graduate diploma course which was offered by the University of Nottingham beginning in 1921, the University of Manchester was the earliest into the field. A Department of Adult Education was created in 1946, part-time courses were launched in that

---

[62] G. Selman, "Specialization or Balkanization," in *Adult Education in Canada: Historical Essays.*

[63] C.O. Houle in G. Jensen, A.A. Liveright & W. Halenbeck, *Adult Education: Outlines of an Emerging Field of University Study.*

[64] Ibid.

year and full-time graduate certificate and diploma courses inaugurated in 1955 and 1961, respectively.[65] Apart from these ventures, however, formal training was slow to develop in Britain.[66] The Eastern European socialist countries, especially Czechoslovakia, Yugoslavia and Hungary, began to provide training in the field systematically in the late 1940s and 1950s, but major teaching programs did not emerge until the 1960s.[67]

Three authorities in the field have summed up the situation by indicating that although there were notable pioneers earlier (especially in the United States), the 1960s brought the major expansion of academic degree training for adult educators. In his international review of the field, which was commissioned by UNESCO following the Third World Conference on Adult Education in Tokyo in 1972, John Lowe stated that "since about 1966" there had been in some countries "a spectacular increase in the number and variety of training courses designed for full-time specialists."[68] In his study of training and training needs in the field, Duncan Campbell concluded that it had been largely after 1960 that opportunities for training had been developed.[69] A special issue in 1985 of the international journal *Convergence* was devoted to the "Training of Trainers and Adult Educators." In his introduction, Roger Boshier noted "a worldwide increase in the number of adult education planners after 1960,"[70] and the articles in this and the subsequent issue of the journal confirm that the 1960s were clearly a decade of rapid expansion of training activities.[71]

Boshier's comment, just quoted, raises an important point—the distinction between the training needs of teachers of adults, on the one hand, and the organizers of adult education programs on the other. It is fair to say that it is the latter group for whom university-based degree programs have been designed, and Houle's study of the persons who had earned a doctorate in adult education in the United States by 1966 made it abundantly clear that these indeed were the people who sought such qualifications.[72] There is a relatively long history of short, non-formal courses designed for those who teach adults, or administer programs on a part-time basis. Homer Kempfer stated in his

---

[65] T. Kelly, *A History of Adult Education in Great Britain.*

[66] K.T. Elsdon, *Training for Adult Education* (Nottingham: University of Nottingham/Department of Adult Education, 1975).

[67] J. Kulich in R. Boshier (Ed.), "Training of Trainers and Adult Educators," Special Issue of *Convergence, 18,* 3-4 (1985).

[68] J. Lowe, *The Education of Adults,* p.144.

[69] D.D. Campbell, *Adult Education as a Field of Study and Practice* (Vancouver: University of British Columbia/Centre for Continuing Education, 1977).

[70] R. Boshier, Special Issue of *Convergence* (1985) p.17.

[71] See R. Boshier (Ed.), *Convergence, 18,* 3-4 (1985).

[72] C.O. Houle, "The Doctorate in Adult Education," *Convergence, 1,* 1 (1968) pp.13-26.

1955 text that "a generation ago," pre-service education was required for adult education staff functioning under certain federal legislation and he reported that a significant number of states, including New York, were by the early 1950s requiring that staff in publicly funded adult education programs receive at least ten hours of training in the field.[73] The Eastern European countries in some cases required such training by the early 1950s as well. In many cases, where brief training courses of this kind were not actually required, many institutions which maintained large adult education programs, including some school boards and university extension departments in Canada, provided such training opportunities for instructors on an optional basis. In an international review of the field written in 1962, Arnold Hely summed up the present trends (as revealed at the Second World Conference on Adult Education held at Montreal in 1960) as a "process of professionalization" and "the passing of the 'gifted amateur.'"[74]

This may have been a realistic view of the field as seen from an international viewpoint by a person who was dealing with top leaders in the field from various countries, but it hardly summed up the picture in a country such as Canada. As we have seen, there were only two universities offering degree programs in adult education by the beginning of the 1960s, and only a very few Canadians who had advanced training in the field. The 1960s were a period of rapid development in such work in Canada, as elsewhere. Gwenna Moss has indicated in her review of the Canadian situation in the decade that among the significant developments on the academic front were the following: the University of British Columbia introduced a doctoral degree to its program in 1961 (and a diploma program as well in 1966); the Ontario Institute for Studies in Education launched masters and doctoral programs in 1965; the University of Saskatchewan introduced a masters and post-graduate diploma in 1966; the University of Alberta began a masters in community development in 1968; and the following year the University of Montreal introduced masters and doctoral programs.[75] In their summary of the situation in 1970, Draper and Yadao stated that by that time, seven universities were offering a graduate program in adult education, the same number a certificate or diploma in the field, and seven were offering individual courses but no degree program.[76] The most recent survey of opportunities for the study of adult education in Canada, which was conducted in 1987, lists ten universities as offering graduate programs in the field, the six already mentioned, plus the

---

[73] H. Kempfer, *Adult Education* (New York: McGraw-Hill, 1955).

[74] A.S.M. Hely, *New Trends in Adult Education*, p.14.

[75] G. Moss, "A Brief History of the Development of Graduate Studies."

[76] J. Draper & F. Yadao, "Adult Education as a Field of Study in Canada," *Continuous Learning*, 9, 2 (1970) pp.65-82.

Universities of Calgary, Dalhousie, New Brunswick and St. Francis Xavier, of which three—British Columbia, Montreal and OISE—offered doctoral as well as masters degrees. Eight institutions were listed as offering certificates or diplomas, the Universities of Alberta, British Columbia, Calgary, Manitoba, Montreal, OISE, St. Francis Xavier and Saskatchewan. In addition to those already mentioned, several others were listed as offering "degree courses"; that is, individual courses which could be used for credit towards general degrees in the field of education—the Universities of Toronto, Queen's, Victoria and Western Ontario. There were therefore some fifteen universities in Canada which by 1987 were offering degree credit instruction in adult education, three at the doctoral level.[77] The same survey lists a total of 112 faculty who are involved in teaching these programs, 51 of whom are identified as full time in this work. The figure of fifteen Canadian institutions offering degrees in this field may be compared with approximately eighty in the United States.[78]

Several developments in recent years should be mentioned. In keeping with the notable expansion of this sector of the field, several institutions have introduced new courses or specializations within existing programs that focus on distance education as a methodology. Athabasca University, appropriately enough, has been offering a masters degree in distance education for several years. (In addition, several institutions are now offering credit courses in the field by distance education methods.) There has also been increased attention paid at some institutions to the area of human resource development. Majors in this field are available within some degree programs, and at the University of Calgary, there is a Masters of Continuing Education degree which specializes in "Learning in the Workplace." Another significant trend has involved the introduction of undergraduate degree programs in the field. The University of Alberta has developed a B.Ed. degree in adult education designed for those who already have formal qualifications in a teaching subject (usually in a vocational area). This program is offered mainly by face-to-face instruction, both at the university and in remote locations. A further innovation, likely the first of many such programs, has been the introduction of a B.A. degree in Adult Education by the University College of the Fraser Valley in British Columbia. The program was developed in co-operation with the Open Learning Agency of British Columbia, but after Fraser Valley College became one of British Columbia's new "University Colleges," it took over the sponsorship of the program. In the case of both of these bachelor level degree programs,

---

[77] R.E.Y. Wickett et al., *Adult Education Studies in Canada* (Saskatoon: University of Saskatchewan, 1987).

[78] A.B. Knox (Ed.), *Enhancing Proficiencies of Continuing Educators* (San Francisco: Jossey-Bass, 1979); S. Merriam in R. Boshier, Special Issue of *Convergence* (1985).

particular attention has been paid to granting appropriate credit to entering students for non-degree training in the field which they have successfully completed. As already mentioned, there are a number of diploma and certificate programs in the field as well. The most notable development in the last decade, perhaps, has been the creation by five Western Canadian universities (Victoria, Alberta, Calgary, Saskatchewan and Manitoba) of the Certificate in Adult and Continuing Education (CACE), which is offered by both face-to-face instruction or distance education delivery by all five co-operating institutions.

There is a great deal of closely related degree credit work offered in Canada as well. For instance, many of those training in the field of English as a second language are engaged in teaching adult students. Those interested in community school or community development activities frequently seek training in the fields of social work or recreation. And many professional positions in the field of adult education are filled by persons whose backgrounds are in other fields. Boshier has estimated that only one-fifth of the teachers and one-quarter of the planners of adult education see it as their primary professional concern, and quickly adds that these figures are likely too high.[79]

Apart from the degree-credit type of study, on which this account has focussed to this point, a great deal of important training in adult education takes place under other auspices, much of it of a non-formal kind. Large voluntary organizations such as the Y.M. and Y.W.C.A., the Red Cross, the Scout and Guide movements and the churches conduct substantial and sustained training programs in adult education and related matters. Other educational institutions, especially community colleges, carry out adult education training for groups such as vocational instructors and those being trained to work with volunteers. And a number of large business enterprises conduct "training of trainer" activities for those working in their own training programs. It is impossible to provide anything approaching a complete or comprehensive picture of such work. The foregoing are only a few examples of what is clearly a large and growing aspect of training of adult educators in Canada.

Research and Publication

Earlier in this chapter it was pointed out that the 1950s were an important turning point with respect to research and publication for the field. Very little had been published before 1950, but that changed substantially during the decade.

---

[79] R. Boshier, Special Issue of *Convergence* (1985) p.17.

An extremely important factor in the development of research in the field was the formation of academic departments at the universities. There are currently well over one hundred faculty members and perhaps two to three thousand graduate students working in the field in Canada. Most of, if not all, the students in connection with their courses and for graduating essays, theses or dissertations must carry out research activities. Almost all are taking courses in research methodology. The faculty members mainly hold doctoral degrees in the field, have produced research in earning their degrees and must continue to carry out and publish research in order to progress in their academic careers. The establishment of degree programs in the field has undoubtedly been the most important single factor in the very rapid growth of research and publication in the last thirty years or so. All the studies or inventories of research which have been published since 1960, including those concentrating on non-degree research, have demonstrated that the universities were by far the largest source of research activity.

Several attempts have been made over the years to list or describe research in the field. Several persons have played a prominent role in this activity, but James Draper of the Ontario Institute for Studies in Education has been the leading figure. He took up this area of scholarship in the latter part of the 1960s and pursued it, frequently in co-operation with others, until the early 1980s.

Reference was made earlier to *A Bibliography of Canadian Writings in Adult Education*, which was published by the CAAE in 1956.[80] Early work on this project had been carried out by Murray Thomson and was subsequently completed by Diana Ironside of the CAAE staff. More than five hundred items were contained in this bibliography, gathered under a dozen or so topic headings, and each entry was accompanied by a brief annotation. The items were drawn primarily from pamphlet and periodical literature and the selection was based on a fairly expansive view of the field of adult education, with some items dealing with the social and cultural background of the field. The journals of the CAAE itself, *Adult Learning* (1936-1939) and *Food for Thought* (1940-61), understandably featured prominently in the sources, but a fair range of others were used as well. Much of the material was descriptive, historical or philosophical, but there were sections on community organization and group work methods. As part of Roby Kidd's general strategy of making Canadian adult educators aware of the richness and content of their field, it no doubt played a useful part at the time—and indeed is a valuable source today for information about the 1935-1956 period.

The next substantial effort to prepare a directory of research was conducted by Coolie Verner and Margaret Stott of the University of British Columbia.[81]

---

[80] M. Thomson & D. Ironside, *A Bibliography of Canadian Writings in Adult Education.*

Commenting on their publication, Verner identified two problems, ones which have consistently plagued such efforts: that of deciding what limits or boundaries should be used to define the field; and the problem of finding the appropriate items. He also referred to the fact that because adult education had been "rarely recognized as a legitimate category of research," the traditional reference works were of limited assistance.[82] Subsequent researchers tried to cope with the problem of locating the studies by working through personnel in the field and asking them where their reports had been published. The Stott-Verner bibliography contained some 290 items. Compared to the Thomson-Ironside listing of seven years earlier, this one was organized along more professional or technical lines. This may be in part a result of the different orientations of the compilers, but was also no doubt a reflection of the evolution of the field in Canada and of the type of research being carried out. It is uncharacteristic of the compilers of such directories to comment on the quality of the research reported on. Verner, however, had this to say:

> Existing research is severely limited with respect to its use of creative and imaginative processes of social discovery. Most of the research presented in this Trial Bibliography is descriptive and depends largely upon survey techniques. There is little, if any, experimental or analytic research that helps explain our profession. Such research as is here represented is traditionally oriented as well as dull and pedantic.[83]

Four years later, James Draper began his long association with this area of study. In 1967 he wrote an article which appeared in the CAAE journal, *Continuous Learning*,[84] in which he pointed out the advantages for the field of publishing inventories of research on a regular basis. He made reference to the efforts of the American journal *Adult Education* to report annually on research and pointed out that a number of Canadian items were included there. He then set forth a plan for the compilation of Canadian inventories. Draper subsequently pursued this goal and played an important role in such work for at least fifteen years. He was the author, or one of the authors, of three inventories of non-degree research in Canada (1967-68, 1969, 1970), two studies of degree-related research (1968-69, 1970) and one (1970) which included both.[85] In addition, he published in 1974 a study of thesis research related to

[81] M.M. Stott & C. Verner, *A Trial Bibliography of Research Pertaining to Adult Education* (Vancouver: University of British Columbia/Extension Department, 1963).

[82] C. Verner, "Adult Education Research," *Continuous Learning*, 2, 4 (1963) pp.155-56.

[83] Ibid., p.157.

[84] J. Draper, "A Proposal for Systematically Collecting and Reporting Research Relating to Adult Education in Canada," *Continuous Learning*, 6, 5 (1967) pp.211-14.

[85] J. Draper, J. Niemi & C. Touchette, *Degree Research in Adult Education in Canada 1968-69* (Toronto: OISE/Department of Adult Education, 1969); J. Draper & F. Yadao, *Degree Research in Adult Education in Canada 1969* (Toronto: OISE, 1970); Y. Demers, J. Draper & A. Gray, *An Inventory of Degree and Non-Degree Research in Adult Education: Canada 1970* (Toronto/Mont-

adult education which had been written at the University of Toronto from 1900-1970, and in 1981, an inventory of all Canadian theses about adult education prior to that time.[86] Other substantial efforts to describe research in the field include papers delivered at a conference on research in adult education held in Vancouver in 1980[87] and three subsequent surveys conducted by John Dobson of St. Francis Xavier University, which appeared in 1982, 1984 and 1986.[88] In addition to these publications, there are two bibliographies about Canadian experience with community development and "citizen action" which were prepared by Arthur Stinson and appeared in 1975 and 1979.[89]

With James Draper providing much of the leadership, the five major inventories which appeared between 1968 and 1971 were published by three organizations—the two national adult education associations (CAAE and ICEA) and Draper's home Department of Adult Education at OISE. (In the last of the series, the study of research in 1970, the Faculty of Education of the University of Montreal was a sponsor as well.) The publications on non-degree research were bilingual; the first on degree research included reports on activity at the French-language universities but the second did not. The last in the series, the volume for 1970, returned to the bilingual format. Over the four year span covered by these reports (1967-70), there was no evidence of growth in the number of studies. As far as non-degree research was concerned, the second year, 1968, provided the largest number of projects reported—118. Only in the case of non-degree studies was there an attempt to categorize by subject matter. In the first year (1967), "clientele" and "evaluation" were the categories containing the largest numbers of entries. The authors commented in the 1969 study that in French Canada there was a heavy concentration of studies on the "motivation, interests, characteristics and needs" of adult students.[90] There continued to be a preponderance of

real: OISE/CAAE/ICEA/ University of Montreal, 1971); S. Landry, J. Draper & L. Bratty, *Non-Degree Research in Adult Education in Canada—1967-68* (Toronto/Montreal: OISE/CAAE/ICEA, 1968); A. Setchell, J. Draper & P. Belanger, *Non-Degree Research in Adult Education in Canada 1968* (Toronto/Montreal: OISE/CAAE/ICEA, 1969); L. Gagner, J. Draper & A. Setchell, *Non-Degree Research in Adult Education in Canada 1969* (Toronto/Montreal: OISE/CAAE/ICEA).

[86] J. Draper, *University of Toronto Thesis Research Relating to Adult Education: An Interdisciplinary Analysis 1900-1970* (Toronto: OISE/Department of Adult Education, 1974); J. Draper, *Adult Education Theses: Canada* (Toronto: OISE/Department of Adult Education, 1981).

[87] Canadian Association for the Study of Adult Education, *Papers Presented to a Conference on Research in Adult Education—1980* (Vancouver: CASAE/ACEEA, 1980).

[88] J.R.A. Dobson, *A Database Management System for Canadian Adult Education Studies* (Vancouver: CASAE/ACEEA,1982); *A Study of People, Programs, Places and Processes: Canadian Adult Education Literature 1977-1984* (Antigonish: Nova Scotia, St. Francis Xavier University); J.R.A. Dobson, "Canadian Adult Education Literature," *Caravan, 1,* 2 (1987).

[89] A. Stinson, *Citizen Action: An Annotated Bibliography of Canadian Case Studies* (Ottawa: Community Planning Association of Canada, 1975; A. Stinson, *Canadians Participate* (Ottawa: Carleton University, 1979).

[90] L. Gagner, J. Draper & A. Setchell, *Non-Degree Research 1969,* p.4.

university-based research projects in non-degree as well as degree studies. In the report on 1970, it was noted that the provincial government of Quebec was the source of considerable research.

Draper's other two publications, studies of theses from the University of Toronto and the national survey published in 1981, were both pioneering efforts. In the first of these, special efforts were made to identify theses which had been written in other parts of the university—the humanities and social science disciplines and the School of Social Work of the University of Toronto, and the other departments of OISE. A total of sixty-two theses were reported, covering an extremely wide range of subjects, such as learning theory, sociological backgrounds and a range of institutional settings.[91] The national survey of theses on adult education contained a listing and analysis of these prior to 1978, and a "supplement" containing ones reported for 1978 and the following two years. Seven universities supplied information for the study, but in this case all the theses were written within departments of adult education. A total of 326 masters theses and 56 doctorals were reported for the pre-1978 period. A further 106 masters theses and 45 doctorals were reported for the years 1978 to 1980, which provides an indication of the rapid growth of the academic programs and research activity. In the most recent three-year period, St. Francis Xavier was the leader in the number of masters awarded and the University of Toronto/OISE the overwhelming leader in the number of doctorates completed.[92]

The most recent attempts to catalogue what he termed the "literature" of adult education were carried out by John Dobson in the 1980s (1982, 1984, 1986).[93] By this time, the Canadian Association for the Study of Adult Education had been established and it was the publisher of the first two of his reports. Dobson summarized his work in an article which appeared in *Caravan*, a publication of the Conference of Canadian Bishops.[94] He reported that by means of his three biennial surveys he had identified 1,483 publications over the six-year period, written by 551 different Canadians (or landed immigrants). He found that 80.6 percent of the publications were written by men and that 70.5 percent of the published items were written by persons "sponsored by" universities. Eighty percent of the publications were written by persons who listed only one adult education publication and 5 percent by those listing twenty-one or more items. Of this latter group, all were associated with one of thirteen different universities, OISE (7), British Columbia (5), Saskatchewan (4), Montreal (3) and Guelph (3) accounting for most of

---

[91] J. Draper, *University of Toronto Thesis Research.*

[92] J. Draper, *Adult Education Theses: Canada.*

[93] See J. Draper, *University of Toronto Thesis Research.*

[94] J.R.A. Dobson, "Canadian Adult Education Literature."

these more prolific authors. Dobson categorized into six groups the content or "research interest" of the 112 authors who had published more than one item in the period. The category of "instructional methods" was by far the leader, accounting for 30.4 percent of the publications, "community education" (18.6 percent) and "foundations" (16.8 percent) followed in second and third place.

Although no further comprehensive catalogue of Canadian research in the field has been published since Dobson's efforts in the 1980s, significant work of this kind was carried out in the early 1990s in connection with an international review of research trends which was organized by the UNESCO Institute of Education. As part of the preparations for the fifth world conference on adult education, to be held in 1997, the Institute organized a series of regional surveys of research trends, which in turn required individual countries to undertake the task as well. Madeleine Blais of l'Université de Montréal co-ordinated the Canadian response and two significant conferences, one for French-language institutions and a subsequent comprehensive Canadian one, brought together the results of investigations which had been carried out in most provinces and were in turn reported to an international meeting held in Montreal in 1994 on World Trends in Adult Education Research. A number of the papers that were delivered at the Canadian meeting were then published in a special issue of the *The Canadian Journal for the Study of Adult Education,* published in May of 1995, along with two articles (one in each language) containing comments and reflections on the several regional Canadian reports. Alan Thomas's commentary pointed out that four features of Canadian research in the field were noteworthy: that the research reported was largely carried out in pursuit of individual interests of the researchers and were relatively small (and frequently parochial) in scope; that strong ideological differences were apparent; that most research reported was qualitative in nature, with an element of "participatory" research emerging as well; and that reflected also was "the emergence of a new research paradigm in which 'learning' rather than 'education' is the basis."[95]

A major factor in the development and publication of research in adult education in Canada has been the activities of the Canadian Association for the Study of Adult Education (CASAE), which was founded in 1981. For approximately two decades, two American organizations, the Commission of Professors of Adult Education and the annual Adult Education Research Conference, had attracted and served the interests of some Canadian professors and other researchers. There were some in Canada who wished a forum in which Canadian-based research and related concerns could be discussed. Roby Kidd and James Draper raised the issue in the early 1970s and some

---

[95] A.M. Thomas, "Adult Education Research in Canada: A Personal Perspective," *The Canadian Journal for the Study of Adult Education*, *9*, 1, (1995) pp.103-112.

informal discussions took place, but it was not until 1976 that more formal meetings occurred. In that year the Adult Education Research Conference, which usually met in the United States, held its annual conference in Toronto. On the day prior to that conference, a group of Canadians held discussions about matters of mutual interest. This in turn led to a similar meeting the following year in Windsor, Ontario, attached to the conference of the CAAE. By this time, the group was referring to itself as the "Consortium of Canadian Adult Education Professors." This meeting led to the publication of a directory of Canadian professors.[96]

The next major step was the decision to hold a conference in 1980 on research in adult education in Canada, which met in Vancouver, again just prior to the Adult Education Research Conference. From the outset, the planning for the Vancouver meeting was based on the idea that those present would make a decision concerning whether to establish a Canadian research organization for the field. The decision was to proceed. A Vancouver-based committee was assigned the task of drafting a constitution for the new organization and organizing a founding conference, to be held in Montreal in 1981. At that conference, in addition to the delivery of reports on research, the constitution of the new organization was approved and the life of a new, Canadian research organization for the field began.

The new organization, the Canadian Association for the Study of Adult Education/Association canadienne pour l'étude de l'éducation des adultes (CASAE/ACEEA) was to be bilingual in its operation (the first president was Giselle Painchaud of the University of Montreal) and was deliberately constituted with a minimum of structure and organizational apparatus.

CASAE/ACEEA has been a relatively active organization since its formation in 1981. It has actively fostered research in the field in a variety of ways. Perhaps most important, it has sponsored an annual research conference and published a version of the papers delivered at each such meeting. The papers of the 1988 conference held in Calgary, for instance, resulted in a bound volume of 337 pages, containing summaries of some sixty research presentations.[97] In the spring of 1987, the association launched *The Canadian Journal for the Study of Adult Education*, two issues appearing each year thereafter.[98] It is a bilingual, juried publication and carries research on various dimensions of the field.

There have been several other significant periodicals over the years which have published research and other material about adult education in Canada

---

[96] R. Boshier & B. Thiesfeld, *Professors of Adult Education in Canada* (Vancouver: University of British Columbia/Adult Education Research Center, 1978).

[97] CASAE/ACEEA, *CASAE/ACEEA 1988: Proceedings/Actes* (Calgary, CASAE/ACEEA, 1988).

[98] See *1*, 1 (May 1987).

(the reference here is to material in English, in the main). The journals of the Canadian Association for Adult Education go back to 1936, including *Adult Learning* (1936-1939), *Food for Thought* (1940-1960), *Continuous Learning* (1961-1972) and *Learning* (1976-lapsed). Publications of the federal work-force training authorities under several titles, *Manpower Review, B.T.S.D. Review* and *Adult Training*, were active in the 1960s and 1970s and carried many articles about the field, as did the journal of the Canadian Vocational Association, which also received federal government support. The longest-running juried journal in the field is that published by the Canadian Association for University Continuing Education. Known at first as *Dialogue*, it began publication as a research journal in May of 1973, changing its name the following year to the *Canadian Journal of University Continuing Education*. Other scholarly journals interested in dimensions of the field appeared during the 1980s, such as the *TESL Canada Journal* and the *Journal* of the Canadian Association for Distance Education. The encouragement for engaging in research in adult education and the opportunities to publish the results have grown substantially.

So far in this discussion attention has been focussed on the opportunities within Canada for Canadians to publish their research. There has as well been a long history of Canadians publishing in other countries and in international publications, such as those of UNESCO, the International Labour Organization, and the International Council for Adult Education. However the avenues most frequently turned to have been those in the United States, especially the periodicals produced by their professional associations.

What is now called the *Adult Education Quarterly*, the research journal of the American Association for Adult and Continuing Education, has been seen as the most high profile, prestige publication in which to publish and has been the focus of much attention in Canada. To a lesser extent, Canadian researchers have looked to journals in Great Britain (and other European countries), Australia, New Zealand and some other countries for opportunities to publish their work.

Canadians and Canadian-based scholars have at times gained considerable prominence in the American research journal. An analysis published in 1974 of the articles carried by the research journal between 1964 and 1973 indicated that the University of British Columbia stood second among all North American universities and the only non-American institution in the top eleven. Among individual authors, Gary Dickinson of the University of British Columbia stood first and Coolie Verner ninth, all others in the top eleven being Americans.[99] A study of the frequency of citations in *Adult Education*

---

[99] H.B. Long & S.K. Agyekum, "Adult Education 1964-1973: Reflections of a Changing Discipline," *Adult Education, 14,* 2 (1974) pp.99-120.

between 1968 and 1977 indicated that a Canadian, Roger Boshier, stood first on the list and that two other Canadians were in the top eight—Coolie Verner (4th) and Gary Dickinson (8th).[100] A study published in 1983 of papers delivered at the Adult Education Research Conference, a basically American organization, between 1971 and 1980, determined that if presenters were sorted according to their home institutions, three of the top seven universities were from Canada—the University of British Columbia (4th), the University of Saskatchewan (6th) and OISE (7th).[101] The foregoing is significant evidence not only of the fact that Canadians sought opportunities to publish in American journals and present research at research conferences in that country, but also that some Canadian individuals and institutions were extremely prominent in this activity.

There have been several Canadians in recent decades who have acquired international prominence for their research and scholarly work in the field of adult education. Roby Kidd's text book, *How Adults Learn*, which appeared in 1959 and which emphasized the application of learning theory to the field has had worldwide use. And his writing about the relationship between education and national development has been influential. His colleague, Alan Thomas, had formative influence in the 1960s on the field's thinking about lifelong learning, and in recent years has been doing pioneering work on the impact of legislation, public policy and judicial interpretation in adult education. Allen Tough, also based at OISE, has had widespread international influence through his studies of self-directed learning.

The names of Coolie Verner, Gary Dickinson and Roger Boshier, all of the University of British Columbia, have been referred to in the previous paragraphs. Verner, before he moved to Canada in 1961, was one of the group of American professors who were influential in defining the field of adult education in the 1950s and 1960s. After he came to Canada, he continued important work in several areas, perhaps most notably in his analysis of the concepts used in the field, and also his insistence on the importance of social indicators and other sociological tools in identifying community needs for adult education. Dickinson, while he remained a professor in the field, was a prolific researcher in the Verner sociological tradition and produced a widely used book on teaching techniques for use with adults. Boshier has carried out research in several dimensions of the field, but is best known for his work on the motivation of adult learners.

---

[100] R. Boshier & L. Pickard, "Citation Patterns of Articles Published in *Adult Education* 1968-1977," *Adult Education*, *30*, 1 (1979) pp.34-51.

[101] H.B. Long, "Characteristics of Adult Education Research Reported at the Adult Education Research Conference 1971-1980," *Adult Education*, *33*, 2 (1983) pp.79-96.

A third group of prominent researchers and scholars in Canada relates itself particularly to rural and agricultural interests—in Canada and abroad—and is divided between two institutions particularly, the University of Saskatchewan and the University of Guelph. Brock Whale and Harold Baker, based at Saskatoon, had a very substantial impact through their writings and consultations on the development of their region and the field. At Guelph, there have been several outstanding figures whose impact has been considerable both in Canada and abroad. The two representative figures who will be mentioned are Donald Blackburn, who has edited two books on agricultural extension,[102] and John Cairns, who was based at Guelph in the years following his service with UNESCO and who has had considerable influence internationally in development planning and literacy activity.

It remains to point out that there have been a number of significant contributions to our knowledge of and thinking about the field which have appeared in books which have been published in Canada over the last several decades. Only a few—aside from those already mentioned—will be noted here. Draper's book on community development and Brooke's on adult basic education, which appeared in the early 1970s, contain the work of many others and had widespread influence at the time, when both fields were developing rapidly.[103] Allen Tough's *The Adult's Learning Projects* first appeared at the same time and was of widespread interest internationally, as well as in Canada.[104] To Kidd's two earlier volumes which reflect the development of the field in Canada was added a third, covering mainly the 1960s.[105] Several books have appeared which provide information about key figures in the field (Coady, England, Kidd, Grierson) and important projects (Antigonish Movement, National Film Board, Citizens' Forum, the Banff School, Chautauqua, the CAAE). New lines of inquiry and critical points of view were developed by such works as Faris's book about the CAAE and the Forum projects;[106] Lotz on community development in Canada;[107] Roberts' comparative study of the field in Quebec and Alberta;[108] Welton's volume of historical essays;[109] and

[102] D. Blackburn (Ed.), *Extension Handbook*, 2nd ed. (Toronto: Thompson Educational, 1994); D. Blackburn (Ed.), *Foundations and Changing Practices in Extension* (Guelph, University of Guelph, 1989).

[103] J. Draper (Ed.), *Citizen Participation: Canada* (Toronto: New Press, 1971); M. Brooke (Ed.) *Adult Basic Education* (Toronto: New Press, 1972).

[104] A. Tough, *The Adult's Learning Projects* (Toronto: OISE, 1971).

[105] J.R. Kidd & G. Selman (Eds.), *Coming of Age* (Toronto: Canadian Association for Adult Education, 1978).

[106] R. Faris, *The Passionate Educators*.

[107] J. Lotz, *Understanding Canada* (Toronto: NC Press, 1977).

[108] H. Roberts, *Culture and Adult Education* (Edmonton: University of Alberta, 1982).

[109] M.R. Welton (Ed.), *Knowledge for the People* (Toronto: OISE, 1987).

Thomas' volume examining the concepts of learning and education.[110] Other professional concerns were addressed by Campbell's volumes on professional training and university policies;[111] several works on aspects of instruction;[112] Blackburn's two compendia about agricultural extension;[113] and three works by Selman.[114]

In the span of fifty years, the literature of the field in Canada has developed from next to nothing to a promising and rapidly evolving area of scholarly concern. Commercial and institutional publishers were by the 1980s prepared to look seriously at proposals in this field. Several hundred persons had become involved in carrying out research and publishing material concerning the education of adults.

What Kind of Profession?

In this chapter considerable information has been provided which relates to a growing sense of professionalism in the field of adult education. An increasing number of workers in this field have sought formal or non-formal training in adult education and identify themselves and their careers with the field. At least fifteen universities and many other organizations are providing specialized training in aspects of adult education. The adult education literature contains increasing reference to professional issues, and to the issue of professionalism.

In fifty years we have gone in Canada from an almost total lack of attention to professional aspects of the field to the point where some adult educators are concerned about the possible harmful effects of what is seen by some as "creeping professionalism." There is virtually unanimous support for the idea that those engaged in performing roles in the field—as teacher, program organizer, curriculum developer, counsellor, administrator, and so on—should acquire the knowledge and skills which enable them to carry out these tasks effectively. But there are a number of concerns which relate to the development of a more professional corps of leadership.

---

[110] A.M. Thomas, *Beyond Education* (San Francisco: Jossey-Bass, 1991).

[111] D.D. Campbell, *Adult Education as a Field of Study and Practice*; *The New Majority* (Edmonton: University of Alberta, 1984).

[112] G. Dickinson, *Teaching Adults* (Toronto: New Press, 1973); T. Barer-Stein & J. Draper (Eds.), *The Craft of Teaching Adults* (Toronto: Culture Concepts Inc., 1988); I. Mugridge & D. Kaufman, *Distance Education in Canada* (London: Croom Helm, 1986); M. Taylor & J. Draper (Ed.), *Adult Literacy Perspectives* (Toronto: Culture Concepts, 1989).

[113] D. Blackburn (Ed.), *Foundations and Changing Practices in Extension*; D. Blackburn (Ed.), *Extension Handbook, 2nd ed.*

[114] G. Selman, *Citizenship and the Adult Education Movement in Canada* (Vancouver: University of British Columbia/Centre for Continuing Education, 1991); with Paul Dampier, *The Foundations of Adult Education in Canada* (Toronto: Thompson Educational, 1991); G. Selman, in *Adult Education in Canada: Historical Essays*.

One of the points most frequently made in this connection is the concern that leadership in the field might be controlled by those who have a particular type of training. This matter came to official notice at UNESCO's Third World Conference on Adult Education in 1972 in Tokyo, where it was agreed that

> the need for professionals in adult education should not, however, lead to the establishment of a closed profession. It [is] necessary both to preserve mobility between adult educators and the general field of education and to ensure a close rapport between professional adult educators and non-specialists.[115]

Lowe comments: "How ironic it would be if those who have railed against the insularity of the teaching profession should themselves set up a closed shop."[116] This matter is particularly keenly felt by those persons in adult education who see it ideally as a democratic movement and one which should consciously play a part in the critique and transformation of the society within which it functions.

There is concern in some quarters that along with increased professionalism in adult education will come an attempt to create a "system" of lifelong education. The fear is that one of what is considered to be the "glories" of adult education, namely that participation is voluntary, will increasingly be eroded. Authors such as John Ohliger and Robert Carlson have warned that an inevitable consequence of professionalism will be a tendency for educators to promote more and more circumstances in which adults will be required to use their professional services—be it mandatory continuing education in various professions, mandatory training programs dictated by the courts, or artificially high formal education requirements for workers.[117]

There are as well those who are fearful that a particular type of professional training or qualification will become the only key to enter the charmed leadership circle. There is a view that present training or degree programs in adult education are based on the notion of producing the "generic" adult educator, one who knows a little bit about various things—adult instruction, program planning, administration, research methodologies, and so on—and not enough about any of them. This point of view holds that we should be training experts in all these areas rather than generic adult educators, and further, that by pursuing the present course we are tending to reinforce the barriers between adult education and the rest of the field of education, rather than building bridges with other educators.

---

[115] Quoted in J. Lowe, *The Education of Adults*, p.144.

[116] J. Lowe, *The Education of Adults*, p.141.

[117] R. Carlson, "Professionalization of Adult Education," *Adult Education*, 28, 1 (1977); J. Ohliger, "Is Lifelong Education a Guarantee of Permanent Inadequacy?", *Convergence*, 12, 2 (1974).

Many adult educators agree with the view that what is desirable for the field is perhaps "a profession with a difference." Those making a career of adult education need by one or various means to acquire as much competence as possible with respect to the roles they are performing. But at the same time the field needs to retain flexibility and imagination with respect to utilizing the special talents and knowledge of any who have something of benefit to offer to other learners.

It is also difficult to see the way in which a field as disparate and decentralized as is adult education could become dominated by a "closed" profession. It is true that for instance a provincial department of education, or a federal work-force training department, if they took a narrow view of who could carry out certain functions within their system or sphere of influence, could have the effect of creating a relatively restricted field of operations, but much of the field would still lie outside their influence. The issue does, however, raise the spectre of a deeply divided field of adult education, with an establishment-regulated and dominated system of adult education on the one hand and a counter or alternative system on the other. This has, for different reasons, produced a "Popular Education" movement in a number of Latin American countries, a coalition of organizations and social forces which is in large measure in opposition to, or at least consciously at arm's length from, the constituted authority. It is hoped by most adult educators, we believe, that the field will continue to be many-faceted, with many ideologies and points of view co-existing. Likely no single model of professional training will ever fully meet the needs of the field. Adult education will, we hope, continue to welcome skilled and committed people from many backgrounds, holding many different points of view.

Dr. Moses Coady with a group of students from various countries in the old Extension Department library, about 1950. Courtesy of the Archives, St. Francis Xavier University.

10

Philosophical Considerations

A dult educators do not usually think of their day-to-day decision making as proceeding from philosophical premises. Commonly, like people working in other fields, they act in ways that seem appropriate or natural, and in many cases, according to standards of accepted practice within their place of employment. But if we think about it, we realize that when educators do make decisions about how to act, their decisions are based on their values and their fundamental beliefs about the way things are. By examining philosophical issues that lie behind some of these decisions, we become more aware of the implications and consequences of particular ways of thinking and acting.

After a few introductory remarks to explain the purposes of discussing philosophical issues in this context, this chapter begins by describing how philosophers distinguish the kinds of claims or statements made about issues that might be raised in an ordinary classroom situation. The distinctions they have developed are based on the sorts of evidence or support needed to establish the acceptability of those statements. Next, some of the assumptions held by adult educators and theorists are examined, including fundamentally different views about the nature of society, the role of adult education within society and the basis of our knowledge of the world. In each case, a connection is made between these general positions and the views of adult educators. Some of these ideas are applied to an examination of the concept of autonomy and other matters involved in what Malcolm Knowles calls andragogy, or "the science and art of helping adults learn."[1] The chapter concludes by recognizing some of the ways in which philosophy is changing and how these changes might relate to changes in disciplines and fields of practice such as adult education.

---

[1] M.S. Knowles, *The Modern Practice of Adult Education* (Chicago: Association Press, 1980) p.43.

As Robert Blakely succinctly puts it, "We can—and usually do—refrain from asking philosophical questions, but we cannot avoid acting according to philosophical assumptions."[2] Given that our assumptions may be a result of all sorts of accidents of upbringing and experience, and that they may well be based on little evidence or ill-founded inference or may even be in contradiction with one another, some questioning of them is in order. In fact, it might be argued that relatively self-conscious reflection on one's fundamental beliefs and values is part of what makes an individual more than a simple product of environmental pressures, part of what accounts for a person's ability to be autonomous or self-determining.

In addition to this general reason for examining one's assumptions, educators have particular reasons to reflect on their views. Insofar as learning implies change, educators are involved in the activity of changing people, or at least of helping people change themselves. This carries with it certain responsibilities—among them a responsibility to have examined the beliefs and values that may be conveyed through their words and actions.

Further, educators are constantly faced with the task of trying to understand how other people make sense of whatever is being studied. This task is obstructed if educators are not aware of their own basic assumptions, which make certain conclusions seem obvious to them, but which may not be shared by others.

Without suggesting that such reflection should in any way be restricted to the early, formative stages of a professional career, it is worth noting that reflection on fundamental assumptions may inform or help shape one's outlook and aspirations. It could influence, for example, one's choice of education or employment. Also, it may well become more difficult to find the time, or sufficient detachment from day-to-day pressures, to think through philosophical issues as one becomes involved in a career. So there are good reasons for reflecting on these issues at a relatively early stage of professional practice, as well as during one's subsequent career as a practitioner.

It may be helpful to distinguish between at least two of the many ways in which the word philosophy is used. Sometimes it is used to refer to a discipline or field of study. Most frequently, at least in Canada, "philosophy" in this sense is taken to refer to the Western tradition of philosophy, beginning with Greek philosophers, including Plato and Aristotle, and also emphasizing modern European philosophical thought, from Descartes (writing in the 1600s) to the present. As such, "philosophical" refers to a certain set of issues in epistemology (the study of knowledge), metaphysics (questions which exceed in some way the scope of science), ethics (the study of good or right human conduct), and aesthetics (the study of art and beauty), as well as logic,

---

[2] R. Blakely, "The Path and the Goal," *Adult Education*, 7, 2 (1957) pp.93-98.

language and thought. But "philosophy" is also used to refer more generally to people's most fundamental beliefs and values. The phrase "philosophy of life," for example, usually expresses this latter sense.

For the most part, this chapter is devoted to exploring philosophical considerations in the former sense, that is, issues that commonly arise for adult educators about which philosophers have had something important to say. As can be seen, such examinations can have starting points from the direct experience of adult educators, from examinations of the ideas of those who theorize about adult education or from the works of philosophers that bear on issues involved in adult education. The sections that follow include all of these.

Philosophical Distinctions

To examine our fundamental beliefs and values, and those of theorists and practitioners in adult education, it will be helpful to have some conceptual tools. A few distinctions will therefore be introduced and explained. In order to establish the relevance of these distinctions, they will be discussed in the context of an adult educator who is trying to make practical decisions about how best to conduct her class.

Imagine, for this purpose, that an educator is teaching a class for nurses who are interested in learning how to orient and instruct new and inexperienced nurses being hired in a particular jurisdiction. One of the issues raised by a member of her class is that the experienced nurses feel that something should be done to help the new nurses think more critically about situations, rather than following instructions rigidly and being at a loss when even relatively minor obstacles interfere with standard procedures. The instructor (let's call her Sharon) has looked at a couple of articles about critical thinking but feels ill-equipped to address some of the issues raised by her class. They want to learn how to teach critical thinking but, through class discussion, Sharon realizes that none of them, herself included, has a very clear idea about what critical thinking really is, or how they could promote critical thinking in this context. Some of the issues raised in the discussion include:

1. What does critical thinking mean, or what does it mean to be a critical thinker?

2. Do you have to be an expert to teach critical thinking or can any teacher learn to do it?

3. Are general courses of instruction in critical thinking worthwhile or should they develop a specialized program of their own?

Each of these questions raises different kinds of issues, calling for different sorts of answers that require different types of supporting arguments. Philosophers categorize different kinds of issues or claims according to the grounds that serve to support or undermine them. *Conceptual claims*, for instance, are claims that are true or false depending exclusively on the meaning of words. That is, the truth of a conceptual claim is evident to anyone who has a relatively complete understanding of what the words in it mean. While this might seem to indicate that conceptual claims are relatively straightforward, it will be recalled that many of the central concepts in adult education (see Chapter 1) are sometimes used in confusing and contradictory ways. The language used both to think about the world and to communicate with others affects what we can see and what we can say, and so conceptual issues have fundamental importance to the enterprise of education. In fact, many of the enduring issues in philosophy and education turn out to be conceptual ones.

The first question raised by Sharon and her class, about what critical thinking means, is a conceptual issue. Sometimes people speak and write as if it is quite clear what even complex terms mean, as if the meaning should be clear to any competent person with a dictionary. This is certainly not the case for terms such as "critical thinking," which are used by different people for different purposes. Often such words are used as theoretic terms, in which case they may take on a special meaning. "Learning" is another example of such a term. If it is used by a behaviourist psychologist to mean "a change in behaviour," we must be careful not to extend any conclusions drawn using the particular definition of learning to the more general and varied uses of the term. It may be very relevant to learning to duck when passing under a low doorway but have little application to learning in the sense that one learns to care about one's workmates. Different senses, uses or ways of understanding a concept are called "conceptions."

Philosophers have developed various strategies to clarify the meaning of terms. Although there isn't space here for any serious examination of these strategies, one thing to note is that conceptual questions cannot be settled by more research, at least not research in the traditional sense of conducting experiments and observing the results. If Sharon and her class want to find out what critical thinking means, there will be no point in looking to see what research has "proven" or in conducting their own experiments. It isn't a question of facts that can be established so much as a question of meaning. Instead, the class might look closely at what people who are teaching or writing about critical thinking are trying to achieve, or they might examine the philosophical debate over the nature of critical thinking.

A second type of issue is called *empirical*. Empirical issues are those which are determined on the basis of evidence supplied by our senses, either directly or indirectly. Claims about observable states of affairs in the world are the most obvious examples of empirical claims but other claims for which only supporting evidence is available are also included. Examples of this latter category include claims about past events, claims about unobservable events such as sub-atomic collisions, or conditional claims, that is, claims about what would happen if such and such were the case.

For Sharon's class to answer their second question, about whether special expertise is required or whether they could themselves teach their students to think more critically on the job, they would be considering an empirical issue of this latter sort. This is the sort of issue for which they might be able to find an answer in the research, although it would require care in evaluating whether or not the cases of published research that they found provided examples close enough to their own situation to be relevant. They would also want to be sure that the indicators of success or failure used in the research studies were a reasonable match for the conception of critical thinking that was relevant to their interests—in this case defined as more independent and constructive thought on the part of their students while on the job.

In order to establish the soundness of an empirical claim, we do not usually employ reflection or philosophical methods of inquiry, but are more likely to rely on the standards and practices developed in the sciences, or in the study of history. In education, however, it has often proven extremely difficult to sort out whether one method works better than another for accomplishing a given objective. This does not seem solely a matter of complexity, but also arises from the fact that education involves human intentions and feelings. Thus in certain areas of human endeavour, empirical issues are inextricably connected to other sorts of issues.

Value judgments form a third category. While many value judgments are not generally referred to as being either true or false, reasons can be offered for or against accepting them, and some judgments are more justifiable than others. If, for instance, a particular taxation policy can be shown to be producing undesirable social consequences, such as drastically increasing unemployment, or if it could be shown to be in conflict with some fundamental principle of human justice, we would have reasons for accepting the value judgment that it is a bad taxation policy.

Thus, while value-related issues are often thought of as contentious and irresolvable, it is not the case, as some have thought, that value judgments are simply expressions of opinion that lack a rational or cognitive basis. On the contrary, trying to establish a relatively stable, consistent and coherent set of values is no less a rational enterprise than is the project of establishing a stable, consistent and coherent system of beliefs. Indeed, it seems to be the case that the two are closely related and are jointly involved in our coming to be a mature person. As the issue of what constitutes maturity is of central importance to defining the field of adult education, it is one to which we will return.

When Sharon and her class were considering their third question, whether general instruction is "worthwhile" or whether they "should" consider developing a more specialized program for their own purposes, they were considering value issues. Value judgments are often identifiable because they employ value terms such as worthwhile or good, or because they express judgments about what should or ought to be done. It is of particular importance in a practical field such as education to realize that practical judgments, such as those employing should and ought, are value judgments. As such, their acceptability is not determined by empirical research alone. Whether they are acceptable is also a matter of meeting other sets of standards. Which standards are relevant will depend on the sort of judgments being expressed.

Two broad categories of standards that are relevant for present purposes are those judgments that express *epistemological* and *ethical claims*. The first of these express judgments according to the adequacy of the methods and validations used in claims to knowledge. Such standards of adequacy are of obvious significance to the educational enterprise. Whether one is preparing a lecture, evaluating a textbook, reacting to a comment made in discussion, or judging an assignment, an important issue will be to judge the adequacy of statements as assertions of knowledge. This will involve assessing whether they are true, whether there is evidence in support of claims that are made, and whether the claims are significant or relevant to the points under discussion. If Sharon's class wanted to know whether improved results on a certain kind of standard test were good evidence for the quality of a critical thinking program, they would be raising an epistemological issue.

Ethical judgments are those made about the adequacy of a person's (or a group's) conduct, especially as it relates to the interests of others. Two types of ethical issues that commonly arise in educational settings are issues involving the distribution of educational resources and those involving the treatment of individual students with (or without) respect. If, for instance, one of Sharon's students pointed out that the reason they ought to assist the new nurses to think independently was because that was the only approach consistent with treating them as mature persons, he or she would be making an ethical argument.

One fact worth noting about ethical disputes in particular, is that there is often agreement at an abstract level about the value to be realized in a given situation (for example, respect for persons, fairness, solidarity) but disagreement at the level of practice about what counts in a particular context as acting according to these values, or about how to balance conflicting values. This can be seen from the example of Sharon's student who raised the issue of encouraging independent thought. It is comparatively easy to get people to agree that adult students ought to be treated as mature persons, but rather more difficult to reach agreement about what that means in terms of teaching methods.

Some Fundamental Assumptions in Adult Education

Having now a shared understanding of these distinctions, we will turn our attention to some of the ways in which adult educators differ over fundamental assumptions. It is important to recognize that no simple set of categories can do justice to the range of differences that exist between educators on such matters. As we will see, thinkers who share many assumptions can disagree sharply over others.

Functionalism and Conflict Theory

One important area in which educators disagree about fundamental issues is in their views of society and its relation to individuals. Only some aspects of this disagreement are, strictly speaking, philosophical, but it bears examination here because the different viewpoints have significant consequences for how the role of the educator is conceptualized. While this section may seem rather far removed from the familiar and practical situation of a class initiating new nurses into the workplace, which helped to ground our discussion of certain philosophical issues and claims, the wider perspective it offers can create a background for more familiar educational issues. For instance, thinking about critical thought from the perspective of Paulo Freire, discussed below, can only be done in a political context we might not otherwise consider.

The disagreement between educators can perhaps be captured most succinctly by means of two contrasting metaphors: one portraying society as an organism, the other as a scene of conflict or struggle. The former is derived from a theory called *functionalism*, and is commonly associated with liberal thought; the latter, called *conflict theory*, is more common among Marxist and other more radical critics of existing Western social structures. It should be stressed, before exploring what is at stake in the acceptance of these metaphors, that theorists may vary greatly in how they make use of them—that while the metaphors may be used to point out general areas of disagreement, some liberals may have more in common with some more radical thinkers than they do with some other liberals, and vice versa.

According to those who see society as an organism, the various parts of society contribute to its overall efficient functioning in the same way that the organs of a body each fulfill a necessary role. Schools, labour unions, the courts, businesses and other segments of society, each function as required for the operation of society as a whole. Under changing circumstances, the system adapts by making adjustments in the relations between the various segments of society or in the roles of its institutions.

Usually associated with this view is the belief that society rewards most highly those roles that are most important. Thus, the ablest individuals are attracted to those positions that are critical to the welfare of the society as a whole. For educators who hold these sorts of beliefs about the way society works, the role of adult education is likely to be seen as facilitating the adjustment or improvement of society, particularly by increasing the number of qualified people for positions that are in social demand. Individual students will, it is thought, be able to improve their position by equipping themselves to take on more important functions, ones that are more highly valued and rewarded. In addition, society as a whole will benefit by having more capable people in important positions.

Conflict theorists have a very different view of the way society works. They see it as being composed of groups with fundamentally different and often incompatible interests. Relations between different groups are not based on mutual adaptation for the overall smooth functioning of society, but rather on constant struggle, with some groups trying to maintain positions of entrenched wealth and power over those without. For those who take this view, the belief that individuals succeed by equipping themselves better to fulfill roles important to society is seen as a myth, moreover as a myth that is useful for those in power as it tends to promote satisfaction with the status quo.

Educators who subscribe to this second view tend to see their role in one of three ways. The first suggests that most educational efforts are merely window dressing, that real change in societal relations can proceed only on the basis of a different economic structure. Educational reform, in this view, is likely to be seen as a distraction from the real problems, which are economic and political, or at best as treating the symptoms rather than the root causes of social inequality.

Other conflict theorists, however, have seen a more positive role for educators, believing that education can at least help to create the conditions necessary for the amelioration of political and economic inequities. In the field of adult education, Paulo Freire is one important writer who has taken this position. Based primarily on the experience of literacy work in Brazilian villages, Freire and his colleagues developed what he called a "pedagogy of the oppressed." In his book by that title, Freire argues that education is by its nature a political activity in that it either promotes the assumptions of the existing political and economic structures or it brings people to question them. In either case, it serves a political function.[3] In the context of the very poor villages in which Freire worked, the very fact of increased literacy among the villagers did indeed have significant political consequences. By becoming literate, they gained access to information about a range of possibilities unknown in the circumscribed world of their villages. They were no longer so completely dependent on their employers, the landowners, as they found out

---

[3] P. Freire, *Pedagogy of the Oppressed* (New York: Herder & Herder, 1970).

about alternative social arrangements. They could begin to question the apparent inevitability of existing states of affairs and social relations.

Freire describes this as a first step in the process of "conscientization," the process of becoming aware of contradictions in one's situation and becoming capable of acting to resolve them. Notice that for Freire meaningful or authentic education is not simply the passing on of facts, or even a deeper initiation into the cultural traditions of a society, but necessarily involves the fostering of critical thought regarding the socio-political context in which the learners are situated. Quite naturally, Freire's ideas have had the most influence in situations that resemble those in which his ideas were developed. In Canada, this has tended to be in working with groups facing the most severe obstacles to economic well-being and political autonomy, such groups as Native Indians, immigrant labourers, illiterate adults, and prisoners.

The third conception of the role of educators is illustrated by the Italian Marxist, Antonio Gramsci. In contrast to Freire, Gramsci offers a rather traditional, even conservative, account of school age education. His primary concern was that children of lower-class families were prevented from obtaining the best education available, and not that the education they obtained was ideologically biased.[4] It is only in adulthood, when people have started to work, that education should be focussed on specifically political objectives, primarily under the auspices of worker-controlled organizations such as labour unions and community-based groups.

Subject-Centred and Learner-Centred Approaches

The general distinction between the views of Freire and Gramsci are roughly paralleled by differences among liberal educators. On the one hand, educators who adopt a progressivist approach, usually derived in some way from the thought of John Dewey, tend to emphasize the active role of the learner in creating and defining the value of what is learned. Often this results in what is referred to as a "learner-centred" curriculum. On the other hand are those who, often drawing on the work of R.S. Peters, emphasize the importance of initiation into our cultural traditions and the intrinsic value of what is commonly called a liberal education. This approach tends to result in what is called a "subject-centred" curriculum.

Peters has associated this view with the idea that education is to be valued for its own sake, not primarily or essentially because of its utility or its value as a means towards achieving other goals. This is in contrast, of course, to those who see education's value as residing in its contribution towards individual advancement or social reform.

---

[4] H. Entwistle, *Antonio Gramsci* (London: Routledge & Keegan Paul, 1979).

Many of these positions have entered into debates in adult education. The notion that educational planning should be driven by the interests of the participants is evident in a common saying from thirty years ago—that "adult education has no curriculum." In 1966, the Canadian Association for Adult Education issued *A White Paper*, in which it was stated, "Whatever a citizen chooses to learn is important simply because he chooses to learn it."[5] On the other hand, Colin Griffin has argued that "the primary conceptual framework for adult education ... has been constructed in terms of needs, access and provision rather than in terms of knowledge, culture and power." We need, he says, "a curriculum theory of adult education; one which is primarily concerned with the social and political definition, distribution and evaluation of knowledge."[6]

The view that education is to be valued for its own sake is evident in the 1936 statement of H.F. Munro, President of the Canadian Association for Adult Education, who wrote of "the enterprise of turning an individual into a genuinely competent and wise adult" and of "the love of learning for its own sake, with the consequent enlargement of our philosophical frontiers and the wisdom that knowledge, rightly pursued, brings in its train."[7] George Grant, the well-known Canadian political philosopher, who once worked for the same association, wrote in the association's journal in 1953 that adult education stands for "no limited social ends, but for the highest end, the self-liberation of the human soul by the systematic examination of its own activities."[8] Northrop Frye, the eminent literary critic and educator, went so far as to say, in his book *On Education*, that attempts to be "relevant" are inimical to the realization of the most important values of education.[9]

On the other hand, Canada in particular has a long tradition of adult education projects undertaken with specific political, economic and social ends in mind. One of the most famous of these is the Antigonish Movement in the Maritimes, using adult education as a focus for the organization of co-operative ventures among exploited fishermen and their families. The leading figure in the Antigonish Movement, the Rev. Moses Coady, believed, according to his biographer, that "the adult educator worth his salt was an aggressive agent of change and adult education a mass movement of reform."[10] In 1941, E.A. Corbett, in his Director's Report to the Canadian Association for Adult Educa-

---

[5] Canadian Association for Adult Education, *A White Paper on the Education of Adults in Canada* (Toronto, CAAE, n.d., 1966) p.1.

[6] C. Griffen, *Curriculum Theory in Adult and Lifelong Education* (London: Croom Helm, 1983) pp.38, 68.

[7] H.F. Munro, "Editorial," *Adult Learning, 1,* 2 (1936) pp.2-3.

[8] G. Grant, "Philosophy and Adult Education," *Food for Thought, 14,* 1 (1953) pp.3-8.

[9] N. Frye, *On Education* (Markham, Ontario: Fitzhenry & Whiteside, 1988).

[10] A.F. Laidlaw (Ed.), *The Man from Margaree* (Toronto: McClelland & Stewart, 1971) p.83.

tion, said, "That's our job, to show people what a living, shining thing democ-racy can be."[11] It is interesting to consider our more everyday classroom concerns under the umbrella of the various ideals expressed above.

Three Philosophical Orientations

To gain an appreciation of the issues that lie behind these different posi-tions, one must understand something of the place of epistemological con-cerns in the development of Western philosophical thought. Perhaps the most central project of Western philosophy has been to identify the grounds on which our knowledge is based; that is, on what basis can we identify the differences between those of our beliefs that are true and justified and those that are false or merely speculative? Philosophers such as Descartes have believed that it is possible to derive a foundation for our knowledge of reality from reason alone. This is referred to as *rationalism*. In contrast, British philosophers John Locke, Bishop Berkeley and David Hume believed that our knowledge of reality is based entirely on impressions of the world received through our sensory organs. Because, as mentioned above, claims that are based on information that can be verified through our senses are called em-pirical, this position is referred to as *empiricist*.

Since the end of the eighteenth century, this argument has been modified somewhat, largely because of internal contradictions in each of the major positions. Rather than searching for a foundation on which all knowledge could be grounded, philosophers have turned more to the problem of identify-ing those areas of knowledge or kinds of claims that can be said to be held on the basis of good reasons. One of the most celebrated moves in this direction was Kant's argument that human knowledge and understanding is restricted to the world as it appears to us, that we have no access to any ultimate or unconditioned reality. One of the implications of this argument is that many of the positions taken by earlier philosophers attempting to determine the true nature of reality, which were quite apart from how the world appears to human beings, are meaningless as they are based on a confusion about how language can properly be used.

In this century, several major streams of philosophy have emerged as re-sponses to these historical positions. In the English-speaking world, three have been particularly influential and each of these has had significant influ-ence on educational theorizing. These three strains are positivism, pragmatism and analytic philosophy.

---

[11] E.A. Corbett, "Director's Report to Annual Meeting of Canadian Association for Adult Education 1941," in G. Selman, *Adult Education in Canada: Historical Essays* (Toronto: Thompson Educa-tional, 1995) p.124.

Positivism

The project of *positivists* generally has been to develop a scientific language that is more precise than our ordinary way of speaking, one that includes only claims that are logically true (analytic) and those that can be verified unambiguously by reference to observable states of affairs (empirical). While this has been an extremely influential philosophical doctrine, attempts to apply these notions in understanding human behaviour and social interactions have been quite contentious. One of the most dramatic of these attempts has been the psychological theory of *behaviourism*. Behaviourism is worth considering in detail both because of its historical influence on educational practice, and as an example of a practical theory based on this philosophical doctrine.

Behaviourists have argued that a scientific understanding of human action is desirable and is possible only if the concepts by means of which we understand how people act and react are operationalized in terms of their observable behaviours. In practical terms, this has been interpreted to mean that educators ought to state their aims in terms of the behaviours that they wish their students to exhibit. Thus, educators can develop clear, unambiguous criteria for the achievement of an educational objective, and can eventually establish what means of education are effective in bringing about different objectives.

Simple as this program sounds when described in a few sentences, it is fraught with conceptual difficulties. Chief among these has been that many of the concepts by which we ordinarily make sense of educational activities do not entail any obvious set of behaviours. The fact that someone has learned something, understands something, or has developed an interest in something, implies normally that he or she has developed some new capacity or inclination, but not necessarily that these changes will be manifest in any observable change in behaviour. How could one characterize, for example, the differences that Sharon and her class would expect to find in the physical behaviour of new nurses if their program was successful at fostering critical thinking? How could one intelligibly capture such differences without reference to what the nurses were "trying to do" or some other terms that made reference to their intentions?

Many of the words that are most central to understanding what other people are doing depend for their meaning as much on inferences about purposes and intentions as they do on observable behaviour. Because purposes and intentions are, however, not observable states, they are excluded from behaviouristic analysis. Behaviourists are faced with an unattractive choice: either they accept that much of what we want to understand under the description of educational activity and achievement cannot be captured within their theoretical structure (because the concepts cannot be operationalized adequately) or they conclude that their strictures on what counts as scientific are too rigid.

Either many of the questions we most want to understand cannot be addressed or some of the basic premises of behaviourism must be given up.

As a result of these and other problems, behaviourism has fallen from being one of the most dominant psychological theories, especially in the field of education, to having a rather restricted role in explaining learning in which understanding or cognition is thought to play a limited role. Examples would include learning that is limited to rote memorization, repetitive drill aimed at the development of physical skills or the training of those with very limited mental capacity. Nonetheless, behaviourist language and assumptions remain common enough in educational writing that sensitivity to these issues is required if one is not to adopt them unwittingly.

The history of behaviourism is typical of many of the more positivistic theories, especially in the human or social sciences. Most current philosophers and theorists hold that there is no clear way of separating logical and empirical claims from questions of intention and value. Thus, there is no way to establish a completely neutral, value-free method for establishing the truth. This kind of realization, however, can give rise to concerns that there is no such thing as knowledge in general. This is commonly referred to as relativism. It suggests that all claims to knowledge or truth are relative to the purposes, interests, and intentions of whoever is making the claim. But this suggestion seems to raise possibilities that run strongly against some basic intuitions, intuitions that many people do not want to give up. For instance, some have taken it to mean that there is no reality, only versions of it as viewed by different individuals or different social groups. Further, it has been taken to imply that agreement or shared understanding between people with different backgrounds and purposes is unlikely, or even impossible, as they live in essentially different realities. Claims to truth by one individual or group would then have no more force than statements of preferences or opinions.

Pragmatism and Analytic Philosophy

Philosophers and others have differed greatly over how seriously to take this problem and its apparent consequences for communication between individuals and social groups. One very important tradition in philosophy, especially in American philosophy, is called *pragmatism*. Pragmatists, as the name implies, treat this and other philosophical issues as practical problems to be worked out in experience. Thus, a pragmatist would be inclined to ignore the problem about the nature of reality, and discuss the issue of relativism in terms of its practical consequences in human communication. If, in fact, it turns out that we can successfully communicate with others with very different interests and experiences, if we can translate from language to language and obtain reasonably coherent reactions on the basis of our translations, then the worst fears raised by the issue of relativism can be put to rest.

John Dewey, mentioned earlier in the discussion of learner-centred curriculum, was little troubled by the issue. Dewey was one of the most important of the pragmatists, especially for those in the field of education, with a strong faith in human nature, in democracy and in science. He believed that if human beings were given the freedom to pursue their own interests within a supportive environment, human knowledge and understanding would flourish. A dominant metaphor in his work is the notion of education as growth. This metaphor has great merit in some respects, especially when contrasted to metaphors of production and consumerism that have come to dominate much educational discussion. However, a common objection to this idea is that people's mental lives, unlike plants and other things that grow, have no natural or predetermined shape. Allowing the uneducated person's own interests to guide the educational process is, according to this objection, an abrogation of the educator's responsibility.

One of the sources of this objection is the *analytic* school of philosophy of education. These philosophers believe that many educational theories and programs are based on misunderstandings of the concepts with which we make sense of educational activities and achievements. But, rather than arguing for the development of a new, more scientific language in which to formulate educational theories, as the positivists did, analytic philosophers have argued that we should pay very close attention to the structure of ordinary language and the way we ordinarily use certain concepts. They point out, for example, that the notion of a person's interests, which is central to Dewey's arguments, is ambiguous in an important way. People's "interests" may refer either to that which they are interested in or to what is in their best interests. It is obvious that people should be educated in a way that advances their best interests, but this is quite different, they claim, from using what they are interested in as the determining factor in what they will study.

R.S. Peters, introduced in the section on subject-centred curriculum, and Paul Hirst, two of the most influential analytic philosophers of education, go on to argue that, on the basis of an analysis of the way that the concept of education is employed, only some of the achievements and some of the activities of educational institutions are truly educational. By being careful with the way we use the term, they argue, we could avoid confusing activities that are indoctrinatory, for instance, with those that are genuinely educational. They also argue that "being educated" implies a certain breadth and depth of knowledge, typically taken to mean that an educated person has some acquaintance with each of the traditional disciplines of knowledge. Thus, according to these philosophers, it is the traditions of the academic disciplines, rather than the interests of students, that provide the most significant guide to planning educational activities.

This point returns us to the issue of whether program planning or curriculum development ought to proceed primarily on the basis of the structure of the academic disciplines and other fields of study, or whether it ought to be determined primarily by the interests of those studying. It may be that individual educators will need to determine the most satisfactory way of dealing with this issue on a situation-by-situation basis. Nonetheless, it seems important that educators do consider some of these issues because whether or not philosophers come to agreement about which of the possible positions is most reasonable, educators will end up making judgments and decisions that presuppose some position, at least, for a given context. Sharon, for instance, may want to consider some of the ideas of the analytic philosophers in her quest for an understanding of critical thinking. The educational goal of becoming truly knowledgeable, and of being very clear about what is indoctrination and not education, could be related to the goal of teaching critical thought, although traditional academic disciplines seem far removed from the concerns of new nurses and the practical subjects that need to be dealt with in her classroom.

Autonomy as an Example of an Educational Ideal

Presumably none of us would like to have our professional practice based on ideas that are in fundamental conflict with other of our deeply held beliefs about reality, human nature and so on. To provide an example of how an educator's basic beliefs and values might be connected with, or be in conflict with, some of these positions, we will consider the related concepts of *maturity* and *autonomy*. Most of us are committed to the idea that autonomy is an important character trait, one that we ought to foster in ourselves and enhance in others. Maturity is a particularly important notion for adult educators in that it is one of the characteristics that is typically thought to distinguish adults from children. It is on the basis of a presumption of greater autonomy (in the sense of independence of judgment) that adults are entitled and expected to take an active role in legal and democratic processes, for example.

The issue of autonomy is relevant to an evaluation of each of the major positions discussed. It can be argued that behaviourism, for example, obscures our sensitivity to the issue of students' autonomy, focussing as it does simply on observable inputs and responses. In fact, it tends to treat human beings simply as objects of study who react in this way or that, without regard for their purposes and intentions, which are inextricably related to the issue of autonomy. Notice, for instance, that fostering autonomy is not a legitimate educational objective according to the principles of behaviourism, as it cannot be operationalized in terms of any specific set of behaviours. Thus, unless there is reason to doubt one or more of these descriptions of behaviourism, an approach based on behaviourist theory is inappropriate if we agree that issues involving autonomy are critical to the responsible practice of education.

The dispute between philosophers inspired by pragmatist Dewey and the analytic philosophers can also be understood as crucially involved with the issue of autonomy. Dewey inclines us to think that it is through the practice of autonomy in choosing their educational pursuits that students both express and develop their autonomy. Peters and other analytic philosophers argue that autonomy in its richest sense is closely connected with the ideal of an educated person and that without a relatively broad and deep understanding of our cultural and academic traditions, the freedom to pursue one's interests is of limited value. It is perhaps like the freedom to vote in an election without any real understanding of the issues at stake.

The fact that there can be such fundamental differences between sincere and intelligent people concerned with issues in education, people who are equally concerned about virtues of character such as autonomy, is an indication that this is an area in which human judgment plays a significant role. This issue is not likely to be settled by some scientific discovery or by some startling new argument that no one has ever thought of before. More likely, through reflection and study of others' work, we can each develop a deeper appreciation of the connection between our ideals, such as maturity and autonomy, and our various practices. By considering the importance of autonomy, we become more sensitive to the ways in which common educational practices may pre-empt students' autonomy and encourage them to be dependent on the reasoning or intellectual/political authority of others. It could be helpful for Sharon to consider how the apparently straightforward goal of teaching critical thinking might be better understood when issues of autonomy have first been explored with her class.

Many kinds of study can enhance our understanding of these issues. Historical and literary texts often provide insight into the ways that other individuals and groups have made sense of them. Another source that is not often included in the study of issues in adult education is the writing of philosophers themselves. Consider these comments by Immanual Kant, one of the greatest of Western philosophers, about the nature of *enlightenment*. Kant understands enlightenment as both an individual and a socio-political ideal:

> Enlightenment is man's release from his self-imposed immaturity. This immaturity is man's inability to make use of his understanding without direction from another. It is self-imposed in that its cause lies not in lack of reason but in lack of resolution and courage to use it without direction from another. Laziness and cowardice are the reasons why so great a portion of mankind, long after nature has discharged them from external direction, nevertheless remains in a state of immaturity, and why it is so easy for others to set themselves up as their guardians and kindly assume superintendence over them. It is not easy to be of age. If I have a book which understands for me, a pastor who has a conscience

for me, a physician who decides my diet, and so forth, I need not trouble myself.[12]

Even this short passage raises some critical issues for adult educators. Kant links enlightenment and maturity with ideas we have considered under the notion of autonomy. Notice that he thinks that the most crucial factors that interfere with autonomy are "lack of resolution and courage," not the lack of a development of reason or discipline-based knowledge, as suggested by the analytic philosophers. If Kant is right, it may be that educators should devote far more of their attention to fostering these virtues on the part of their students. It may be that these virtues are best fostered in a situation that emphasizes the shared nature of intellectual inquiry, and de-emphasizes the traditional disciplines as established bodies of knowledge. (Given the changing content of knowledge in the disciplines, many philosophers have come to regard them more as traditions of practice that are modified over time, in part through the use of critical practices that form part of a discipline's structure.)

Another crucial point in this excerpt from Kant is the notion that people are apt to slide into a position of either dependence or superintendence. This is a constant danger in the practice of adult education. Many students and educators find it easier to think according to the book or to act on the basis of some theory they are taught, rather than to use their own judgment and take responsibility for their own decisions. Many others may, quite without malicious intent, assume superintendence of them by taking the place of the book, the pastor or the physician in Kant's examples. This draws attention to the danger of adult educators trying to emphasize the place of their professional expertise to the extent of interfering with the autonomy of their students.

Obviously, this is not an argument against the development of knowledge in the field of adult education, any more than Kant's is an argument against books, pastors or doctors. What it does point out is that there is a dangerous link between the development of knowledge, especially in the fields that involve knowledge of people (the human and social sciences), and conditions in which people's autonomy is limited or discouraged. As adult educators, involved with the education of those who are at least presumed to be in a state of relative maturity, we might be expected to be particularly cautious about acting in ways that might discourage maturity and autonomy in Kant's rather rich sense.

Philosophy and the Language of Adult Education

The above was an example of a way in which philosophical writing, like literary and historical writing, can help us to reflect on the practice of adult

---

[12] Version adapted from I. Kant, *Foundations of the Metaphysics of Morals* (New York: The Liberal Arts Press, 1959 [1784]) p.85.

education. Another way in which philosophical inquiry may contribute to an understanding of this field is in providing what might be called "perspicuous accounts" of central ideas and terms. What is meant by this is that philosophical inquiry may be useful in clarifying conceptual confusions, in showing how certain word uses are related to each other or by providing a more overarching perspective than that obtained by a more specific or narrowly focussed theory.

In order to see what this might mean in a particular case, we will consider one of the most influential concepts in the field, the notion of *andragogy*. This is a particularly useful example, both because of its impact on the field and because of its relation to the concepts of autonomy and maturity, which were discussed in the previous section. By seeing how this concept is applied and by seeing its relation to the more general concepts of adulthood, maturity, and autonomy, we will get a sense of the relation between theoretic and more broadly philosophical understanding.

The andragogical perspective, suggests Malcolm Knowles, is significantly different from at least the traditional approach to teaching children, or pedagogy.[13] It is different because adults are more mature than children, and so their experience is more extensive and plays a more significant role in defining their self-concept. Adults are more likely to be self-directed rather than dependent on others for direction. Unlike children, they expect whatever they learn to have quite a direct and immediate application to their daily lives.

This characterization is based broadly on theories of humanistic psychology, and the criteria that are used to differentiate adult learning from children's learning are psychological characteristics of the learners.[14] But the psychological characteristics are only one of the many criteria by means of which we differentiate the activities of adults from those of children in ways that are relevant to understanding education. Thus, it is to be expected that the phrase "adult learning," when employed by Knowles and others who have adopted his criteria, may be applied more specifically than the same phrase would be by other competent language users. Similarly, the "Knowlsian" use would fail to recognize some of the other, non-psychological criteria implied in the ordinary, non-theoretic use; for instance, it will fail to incorporate the distinctive rights and entitlements normally associated with adulthood. But this "value-laden" feature of concepts such as adulthood is also relevant to the

---

[13] M.S. Knowles, *The Modern Practice of Adult Education* (Chicago: Association Press, 1980) p.43.

[14] As Sharan Merriam has pointed out, this is one of three types of criteria used in the field to make this differentiation. The other two are "the adult's learning situation" and "changes in consciousness." None of these approaches, as characterized by Merriam, identify adult learning as distinctive according to socio/political and legal criteria although the "change in consciousness" approach is a part of explicitly political approaches to education, such as Freire's. S.B. Merriam, "Adult Learning: A Review with Suggestions for the Direction of Future Research" in R.A. Fellenz & G. J. Conti (Eds.), *Building Tomorrow's Research Agenda of Lifelong Learning* (Montana: Kellogg Centre for Adult learning Research: Montana State University, 1989) p.9.

practices of education, even if it is not part of the formalized, "operational-ized" concepts of a psychological theory.

It is, for instance, important to note that adults are considered to be autono-mous agents for legal, political and contractual purposes. Philosophers have pointed out that what it means to act autonomously is that the act is commit-ted freely, in the sense that it is not the result of coercion or compulsion; that it is informed, in the sense that the individual has some idea what is at stake in possible alternative courses of action; and that the individual has a relatively stable set of values or purposes. In our society, barring special circumstances, it is presumed that adults' actions, including those aimed at educational goals, are made under these conditions. In the case of children, it is presumed that these decisions are made under conditions of reduced autonomy.[15] But to make this claim is not only, or even primarily, to point out a set of empirical differences between children and adults, or even about differences in the way they are treated. Adults are entitled to be treated as self-determining agents and only in unusual cases is it acceptable to interfere with this right. It is on the basis of this right that adults are treated differently from children in law, and in many other contexts. Surely educational contexts are one of these.

These considerations are not raised in order to criticize or cast doubt on the utility of Knowles' concept of andragogy. Rather they are used to point out that a concept that is defined in relation to a theoretical framework such as humanistic psychology is necessarily applied according to a narrower and more specific set of criteria than our ordinary language concepts are. This is part of what makes a theoretic concept useful in making claims that can be tested through empirical research. But the price to be paid for this increased precision is the loss of some of the richness of our ordinary, non-theoretic language. Philosophical inquiry may be useful as a means to retain normative or value-laden dimensions of ordinary language and also as a way to clarify the relationship between theoretic concepts and that ordinary language.

Changing Disciplines, Changing World

It has become commonplace to recognize that technological, environmental and economic changes are fundamentally altering people's lives. These changes are difficult to characterize briefly, involving as they do many cur-rents and cross-currents. Some of the most critical trends have been discussed intelligently in Steven A. Rosell's *Changing Maps: Governing in a World of Rapid Change*, a report of a roundtable of Canadian federal government offi-cials.[16] Prominent among the changes they discuss are the effects of global

---

[15] For a more detailed argument of this point, see Mark Selman, "Learning and Philosophy of Mind," *The Canadian Journal for the Study of Adult Education, 2*, 2 (1988) p.39.

[16] S.A. Rosell, *Changing Maps: Governing in a World of Rapid Change* (Ottawa: Carleton University

information networks that not only increase the sheer volume of information available but also alter the way in which information is framed and selected. At the same time, there is increased social fragmentation, with more people holding more strongly to specific affiliations connected with race, ethnicity, gender, sexual orientation or political and religious views than to nation states or other larger and more heterogeneous groupings of people.

Concurrently, academic disciplines are being restructured and rearranged. Philosophy, which at one time was regarded as the "queen of the sciences," and often understood to have a role in determining the relations of the disciplines to each other and to knowledge in general, has tended towards one of two poles. Some philosophers, most notably those interested in issues of language, logic, and cognitive science, have tended to create a new, highly specialized discipline, focussed on technical issues that are, for the most part, outside of common interests and areas of knowledge. Other philosophers, most notably continental European philosophers (such as Michael Foucault and Hans Georg Gadamer), American pragmatist philosophers (such as Richard Rorty) and feminist philosophers (such as Nancy Fraser) have tended to overturn and undermine traditional modern philosophy.[17] While again such movements are difficult to characterize in general terms, the broad tendency of these latter groups of philosophers has been to discount or mock the pretentions of earlier philosophers who claim to have established any kind of objective validity or universality for their views and theories. Rather, they have pointed out that in many ways, the most abstract and purportedly timeless claims to knowledge are closely related to the cultures in which they were developed, the male gender of almost all well-known philosophers, and other contingent and arbitrary facts about the conditions under which such philosophizing has been done.

This approach to philosophical issues has struck a responsive chord among many adult educators who are interested in the field as a way of redressing social and economic imbalances of power. Emphasizing as it does the extent to which power is exercised arbitrarily, or in the interests of the strongest, and attempting to undermine all efforts to legitimize the use of such power according to standards such as reason or justice, it is seen as supporting the interests of those who have been disadvantaged by existing social and institutional relations. To more traditional philosophers, such a stance is problematic. They are inclined to argue that the undermining of categories that are as fundamental as reason and justice must necessarily undermine charges of inequality or

---

Press, 1995).

[17] There are also modernist European philosophers (such as Jurgen Habermas), American pragmatists (such as Hilary Putnam) and feminist philosophers (such as Onora O'Neil and Sabina Lovibond).

unfairness as well, thus weakening arguments against injustices committed by the powerful against those who are weaker.

As is the case in a serious intellectual dispute, there are sophisticated and thoughtful arguments on both sides of this issue. There is also trivial posturing or adoption of style without the depth of thought of more significant writers. There is an unfortunate tendency on the part of those who see themselves as partisans in this debate to advance their own position simply by trivializing the arguments of those who believe otherwise. Defenders of modernism cast postmodern thinkers as being totally relativistic and therefore incoherent. Critics of modernism fail to do justice to the extent to which the best enlightenment philosophers were aware of the limits of reason and other central concepts.

While there is no doubt that postmodern critiques of modern philosophy have raised important challenges to what had become, at least in some cases, dogmatically held beliefs, it is far from clear that we can or would want to do without some of the central insights that have made possible our relatively open and humane society. Perhaps Michel Foucault has made this point best. In his response to Kant's essay "What is Enlightenment?", Foucault suggests that we "must free ourselves from the intellectual blackmail of 'being for or against the Enlightenment'."[18] In other words, we should not determine our own views by either accepting or rejecting everything that enlightenment thinkers have to say. As with other elements of our historical heritage, we must sort through and find what speaks to us now and which ideas are irrelevant or even dangerous. This leaves each of us with the difficult and potentially exciting task of sorting through the complex and important ideas that make up our philosophical assumptions and form the background against which we make many of our day-to-day decisions.

---

[18] Michel Foucault, "What is Enlightenment?" in Paul Rabinow (Ed.), *The Foucault Reader* (New York: Pantheon Books, 1984) p.45.

Kay Desjardins and Ellen Arsenault; March 1956.
Courtesy of the Archives, St. Francis Xavier University.

11

Women and Adult Education: A Postmodern Perspective

By Tammy Dewar

*The pain and poetry of life, the emotional, intuitive, essentially relational na-
ture of our struggles is traditionally excluded from and bracketed out of academic discourse ... We acknowledge the complex and multiple realities we all
experience, the realities of difference; and abandon the positivist claims to
objectivity and truth.*[1]

My intuitive sense is that I must write about women in adult education in Canada as I have experienced it—in a personal a voice,[2] in
context, in community with others, in the narratives that inform our
lives, and with authenticity and passion. To do so is to acknowledge the
contradictions that I (and other women) have experienced during our careers
as adult learners and educators—isolation and community; silence and voice;
oppression and liberation; separateness and connection; official knowledge
and people's knowledge; authenticity and duplicity; bureaucratic structures
and grassroots movements; disappointment and celebration; disregard and
affirmation; power and powerlessness; risk and safety; anger and love.

---

[1] C. Brooks, Z. Dharsey, M. Francis, T. Mitchell, "Working Across our Differences—Perspectives on
Oppression," *Convergence*, *XXVI*, 2 (1993) p.21.

[2] Sight has usually been the metaphor used for knowledge as in "my eyes were opened and I saw the
light." In contrast, the work of C. Gilligan, *In A Different Voice: Psychological Theory and Women's
Development* (Cambridge: Harvard University Press, 1982) and M. Belenky et al. suggest that voice
is a metaphor for understanding women's experience and development. They also point out the
difference between the private (or personal) and public voice (as do other feminists). The private,
subjective voice has usually been viewed as inappropriate to describe the more public aspects of
work. Feminists assert that the personal is the public (or political).

One of the research participants in my doctoral work (an adult educator and doctoral candidate herself in an adult education program) shared a story about researchers which captures my dilemma in writing this chapter:

> "Well, I flew to Edmonton last week for a work related project which involved the rural population in Alberta," Helen began her story, "and just after we took off from the Calgary airport, I looked down at the land and saw this blanket of snow that covered it. Then I looked over at the mountains and was struck by the coldness of the scene, the mountains in the background and this white, cold, uniform blanket of snow that disguised everything that lay beneath it.
>
> "It occurred to me that that's what being a researcher can be like, looking down at things from above, only seeing the uniform white snow, the snow which disguises everyone's beauty, voices, lives. If a farmer or artist or poet looked down, though, they might see something different because they know the beauty and diversity is there. So the challenge as a researcher is to wait for the snow to melt, to see what's really there."[3]

Women's experiences in adult education in Canada have been covered by a blanket of snow. We do not appear in the sanctioned histories to the extent we all know we've been there and continue to be there. The roles we've played in the field itself—learner, tutor, advisor, facilitator, co-ordinator, assistant, professor, collaborator and so on—are often devalued, overlooked and/or underpaid. Our experiences as women adult learners have often been characterized by silence and alienation. Our collaborative and relational approaches to learning and leading have been seen as deficient when compared to the competitive and hierarchical models still prevalent in most institutions. As academics in the field, we bump up against the scientific method which tells us to stuff away our voices and associations with our research "subjects," in order to attain objectivity.

But that is not the whole picture. We also see women in adult education in Canada engaging in and facilitating transformative and empowering learning for themselves and others. We see them creating community and leading in participatory ways. We see them taking risks, and making a difference. We see them working collaboratively and positively with men. We see them supporting and celebrating the accomplishments of others. We see them carrying on the day to day challenges and joys that form the very landscape of adult education in Canada.[4]

There is much under the snow, and it is beginning to melt.

* * * * *

---

[3] Cited in T. Dewar, *Women and Graduate Adult Education: A Feminist Poststructuralist Story of Transformation,* Doctoral Thesis (Calgary: University of Calgary, 1996) p.123.

[4] See T. Dewar, *Women and Graduate Adult Education,* 1996, for a discussion of the themes identified in the previous two paragraphs, as they apply to women in graduate adult education.

At the risk of being "totally relativistic and therefore incoherent,"[5] both the style and content of this chapter is in keeping with a postmodern perspective. It is in the work of postmodern writers that I found answers to troubling issues, the most disconcerting perhaps being my discomfort with some feminist writing and my unease about the proper way to represent knowledge.[6]

While I certainly have experienced the marginalization and oppression[7] that is well documented about women's experiences in adult education, that has not been my total experience. I agree with Jennifer Gore who suggests that

> the grand, broad theories of Marxism, Critical Theory, and Feminism, in their fundamental acknowledgment of structured inequalities and oppressions, in their pedagogical enterprise, arrive at the need to theorize the contradictory moments ... there is something about the lives of those in classrooms, as well as the lives of (social) "classes," about activities that deal with people as thinking, feeling individuals, that requires the phenomenological, personal accounts of multiplicity and contradiction that are beginning to emerge in the works of feminist poststructuralists in education.[8]

The work of feminists in education overall, is in tremendous transition. How postmodernism is influencing educational thought is significant.[9]

In my conversations with many women in adult education, I hear stories of both oppression and empowerment. Community, connection and affirmation are used to describe women's experiences as learners and educators. Oppres-

---

[5] See the discussion of postmodern perspective in the previous chapter.

[6] Defining postmodernism is a challenge (and, some would say, a contradiction in itself)—entire books are written on the subject. Laurel Richardson ("Writing: A Method of Inquiry" in Norman Denzin and Yvonna Lincoln, eds., *Handbook of Qualitative Research*. London, Sage, 1994) provides the most concise explanation I've read: The core of postmodernism is the *doubt* that any method or theory, discourse or genre, tradition or novelty, has a universal and general claim as the "right" or the privileged form of authoritative knowledge. Postmodernism *suspects* all truth claims of masking and serving particular interests in local, cultural, and political struggles." So, for example, postmodernism would question the assumption that researchers are to take an objective stance toward their research, or that the proper way to write a textbook chapter (or research paper) is in an objective, third person voice. Feminist poststructuralism is one outgrowth of the postmodern movement. In this approach, one is "persistently self-conscious about her or his personal biography and social positionality and the positive and negative effects those might have on the research process and the published report of the research" (J. Schuerich, "Methodological Implications of Feminist and Poststructuralist Views of Science" in *NCSTL Monograph Series No 4, ERIC Doc# ED 364 421* (1992) p.8).

[7] See, for example, J. Hugo, "Adult Education History and the Issue of Gender: Toward a Different History of Adult Education in America," *Adult Education Quarterly 41*, 1 (1990) pp.1-16 for a discussion of historical perspectives; E. Hayes and L. Smith, "Women in Adult Education: An Analysis of Perspectives in Major Journals," *Adult Education Quarterly 44*, 4 (1995) pp.201-217 for perspectives on women in adult education publications; and S. Collard and J. Stalker, "Women's Trouble: Women, Gender, and the Learning Environment," *New Directions for Adult and Continuing Education, No 50* (1991) for women in educational environments.

[8] J. Gore, *The Struggle for Pedagogies* (New York: Routledge, 1993) p.49.

[9] For an excellent overview, see K. Pritchard Hughes, "Feminist pedagogy and feminist epistemology: an overview," *International Journal of Lifelong Education 14*, 3 (1995) pp.214-230. For an in-depth treatment of the subject, see J. Gore, *The Struggle for Pedagogies* (New York: Routledge, 1993).

sion and silencing are also used. Two women participating in the same class will describe it differently. Poststructuralism offers an explanation for these differences. As Davies suggests, such a perspective

> ... involves a recognition of the inevitability of contradiction in a world made up of contradictory discourses, and provides a fundamental shift in the definition of self such that the contradictions are not experienced as a personal flaw but as ways of constituting the social world which are themselves amenable to change. I speak myself into existence through the discourses available to me, I know myself through the stories I live and the stories I tell (each of these deeply imbricated in the other) and so I can choose, with others, to change the stories and to develop new ways of talking about them. Equally I can refuse discourses that speak me into existence in ways I no longer wish. That refusal is dependent on my ability to see the way in which my identity is discursively constituted.[10]

My goal is to illuminate many perspectives of women in adult education in Canada, realizing that I see things from my perspective as a white, middle class, heterosexual, educated western woman. To accomplish that end, I contextualize the chapter by referring to a series of e-mail conversations (some of the personal portions of the e-mail have been excluded) which unfolded between myself and the colleagues I called upon to help me with the writing of this chapter.[11] Interspersed between these e-mail excerpts are perspectives from writers in the field. Indented italics are used to fill in the story with my thoughts as I was writing the chapter.[12]

---

[10] Bronwyn Davies and Rom Harre, "Contradiction in Lived and Told Narratives" *Research on Language and Social Interaction 25* (1991/2) pp.8-9. The notion of competing and contradictory discourses comes out of the work of feminist poststructuralists such as C. Weedon, *Feminist Practice and Poststructuralist Theory* (New York: Basil Blackwell, 1987); B. Davies and R. Harre, "Contradiction in Lived and Told Narratives" *Research on Lived Experience* (Newbury Park: Sage, 1991/92); and P. Lather, *Getting Smart: Feminist Research and Pedagogy with/in the Postmodern* (New York: Routledge, 1991). Discourse refers to the common sense beliefs a particular group of people have and the language they use to express it. The language they then use (especially in regards to self), can influence their own power within a particular context. Of contradictory discourses, Weedon suggests, "How we live our lives as conscious thinking subjects, and how we give meaning to the material social relations under which we live and which structure our everyday lives, depends on the range and social power of existing discourses, our access to them and the political strength of the interests which they represent" (p.26). Examples include any of the professional discourses (ie. legal, medical, educational). Very often, the average person can be powerless because they do not have access to the language of the discourse—they must rely on the lawyer, the doctor, the educator to interpret and represent their interests.

[11] Private e-mail, Carley, November 3, 1996. While the protocol of quoting from various types of electronic means is still in transition, some distinction has been made between public discussion lists on the internet and private communication between people. Public lists are those that can be accessed by anyone over the internet, and standard practice is that one can quote from those, provided full reference is used. E-mail communication between people is considered private and, therefore, permission must be gained from individual authors before quoting. Permission has been granted by all e-mail authors referenced in this chapter.

[12] Laurel Richardson's work is seminal in challenging the notion that knowledge must be represented in an objective, distanced manner, usually characterized by an absent narrator and passive voice. She points out that using these conventions "increases the probability of one's work being accepted into core social science journals, but they are not prima facie evidence of greater—or lesser—truth value or significance than social science writing using other conventions" (1990, p.17). See the following sources: *Writing Strategies: Reaching Diverse Audiences* (Newbury Park: Sage, 1990);

* * * * *

From: Lynn

To: Tammy Dewar

Subject: Chapter on Women in Adult Education

As you noted, life is really busy right now—term papers coming due! Much and all as I would like to be really helpful with this project ... and also feeling guilty because I don't have the time ... here are some thoughts that come to me over the weekend, for what they are worth:

1. The whole area of health teaching done by public health nurses and the Victorian Order of Nurses. Prevention is one of their main mandates so a great deal of their work involves teaching patients, families, and workers in the community—they have a long history in Canada. The VON is a Canadian organization. I remember one woman who ran the well-baby clinic at the Montreal Settlement (an outreach program run by McGill, I believe) who used education of low income pregnant women plus supplements to their diets to produce what she called "Blue-Ribbon Babies"—these were babies with normal birth weights because the mothers were properly nourished, and as a result had a lower incidence of birth defects and learning disabilities. This was a research project of the '60s.

2. Also related to nursing is the work of Helen Mussalem—she was very involved in nursing education and was also a high profile Canadian with the World Health Organization and the UN.

3. What about all the work of Christian education workers, nuns, and deaconesses? Women weren't allowed into the ministry in many denominations but they often did a great deal of work in educating their congregations for leadership and missions. Some as port workers were likely the first to do organized ESL while others went to the mission fields and developed schools and hospitals. As a child I remember most of these missionaries being women, often in remote communities here at home and in developing countries where educating/training the indigenous populations was again their main mandate.

4. Another group of women who have a great impact are journalists like Doris Anderson (Chatelaine magazine editor & Status of Women Committee): June Callwood (tried to create awareness by writing and speaking about issues long before it was socially acceptable—she was a founder of Nellie's (abused women in Toronto.) and Casey House (AIDS victims, also in Toronto); Barbara Frum, Jeanne Sauve, Laura Sabia, Anne Francis, Dian Francis, Judy Rebick, Judy LaMarsh (she had a show like Peter Gzowski's in the years between "This Country in the Morning" and "Morningside"), etc. Also there are French women and women of colour who have been educators and leaders in Quebec and the Maritimes particularly. Another is

---

"The Consequences of Poetic Representation," in *Investigating Subjectivity: Research on Lived Experience*, eds. C. Ellis and M Flaherty (Newbury Park: Sage, 1992); "Poetic Representation, Ethnographic Presentation and Transgressive Validity: The Case of the Skipped Line," *The Sociological Quarterly, 34*, 4 (1993); "Writing: A Method of Inquiry," in Norman Denzin and Yvonna Lincoln, eds., *Handbook of Qualitative Research* (London: Sage, 1994). See my dissertation for an example of a multi-genre approach (individual/collaborative autobiography, real/imaginary dialogue, circles of learning, narrative, fictional representation, stories, deconstruction and poetry) to the representation of a research project.

Judith Plant (and friends), an American who lives and publishes in Canada: "Healing the Wound" which deals with ecofeminism issues is one that I am familiar with.

When I look at the other topics you listed I can see that keeping this to one chapter will be your major challenge—you could indeed write a book about each of them and still not exhaust their potential! I'd love to see you write a chapter on "a feminist/women's critique of the behaviour of the field" or "the contradictory discourses in the field that impact women!!!"!13•

Lynn's e-mail reminded me of the opening to an article I'd just read:

Where are the women role models in adult education? When I as a graduate student of adult education asked this question I was repeatedly referred to the same one or two names. It wasn't until I was able to work directly with the adult education historical documents myself in the 1990s that I discovered information about the kind of woman— energetic, visionary—that I was looking for.!14•

At the end of my master's program, I could not name one Canadian woman adult educator from our history of adult education in Canada, but I could name men—Roby Kidd, E.A. Corbett, Moses Coady. It is only recently that I have come to realize this is not because I was not paying attention in my master's classes; it is because the documentation of women in adult education in Canada is sadly lacking.!15•

I went searching for an explanation.

Writing about women in adult education history in the United States, Jane Hugo suggests that

Looking beyond the histories to evidence generated by the adult education field itself, it is clear that historians' choices gradually excluded female adult educators from the historical narrative and precluded the inclusion of still other women by viewing their work as outside the boundaries of the field.!16•

Hugo suggests that there are three main reasons for the exclusion and marginalization of women. One, that the entire adult education enterprise has been concerned with establishing its credibility overall. Such a focus has led to looking at organizational concerns and to those in leadership positions within them. As she says, "The roles of women in these areas are

---

[13] Private e-mail, Lynn, November 4, 1996.

[14] L. Karlovic, "Jessie Allen Charters," *Adult Learning* May/June, 1993, p.13.

[15] A valuable resource, however, for adult educators who would like to address this lack in their own classrooms is the *Herstory, The Canadian Women's Calendar* series. Published annually (with the exception of 1983 and 1984) since 1974 by the Saskatoon Women's Calendar Collective, these calendars profile women and women's organizations of our past and present. I was amazed by the number of women I read about who played significant roles in adult education in Canada. Michael Welton has written of women in adult education. See, for example, M. Welton, ed. *Educating for a Brighter New Day: Women's Organizations as Learning Sites* (Halifax: Dalhousie University, 1995) or M. Welton "Amateurs Out to Change the World: A Retrospective on Community Development" *Convergence 28*, 2 (1995) pp.49-61. Convergence, while concerned with international issues overall, is also an excellent resource. See their subject index for a wealth of articles about women in adult education. Refer also to Chapter 4 by Shauna Butterwick in this book.

[16] J. Hugo, "Adult Education History," p.2.

often obscured by historians' focus on first, the organizations themselves as educational agents as opposed to the men and women who staffed those organizations and second, their focus on the upper levels of institutions where women were more likely to be structurally excluded."[17]

Second, men have held the power in defining the field and, therefore, their perspectives tend to be reflected in the literature. This, together with gender roles that have excluded women from leadership positions, has created an "historical narrative in which women were absent because the circle effect [men attending to what men said] mechanism acted as a barrier."[18]

Third, the discontinuous nature and the types of roles held by women adult educators has made it difficult for historians to trace. Many women practitioners at the grassroots level may have considered writing for adult education journals, but spent their time writing program materials for the learners whom they served instead.

Hugo suggests that a more inclusive history could be achieved through compensatory approaches to women's marginalization (writing women into the history of adult education), but suggests that a critical approach may be more fruitful:

> ... adult education historians need to make socially constructed and maintained sex roles problematic by asking what relationships exist between gender constructs and aspects of adult education like programming, leadership positions, professionalization, or the formulation of theory and its translation into practice.[19]

Hugo's comments certainly seem to be applicable to women in Canada, and challenge me to think deeper about why I may not know about women in adult education history. While a good majority of classmates in my graduate work in adult education (at least 80 percent) were women, the majority of our professors were men. Except for a Women in Education course that I took, gender issues were not raised in the core courses in my program. As Walker suggests, "In most adult education curricula, there is an absence of women, women's concerns, and feminist literature that might provide a basis from which women learners could begin to articulate, present, and theorize about their experiences."[20]

I wonder, though, how this might range across individual experience. Are there courses in adult education (either at the certificate, bachelor's or graduate levels) that do include a more balanced historical perspective? Perhaps the literature is out there and I haven't been made aware of it. It would depend upon the institution, the program and the individual instructor and participants within the course.[21]

[17] Ibid., p.7.

[18] Ibid., p.8.

[19] Ibid., p.12.

[20] G. Walker as paraphrased in S. Collard and J. Stalker "Women's Trouble: Women, Gender, and the Learning Environment," *New Directions for Adult and Continuing Education, No 50* (1991) p.76.

[21] While the context of this discussion is historical perspectives on women and how an individual professor's perspective might influence curriculum choices, how women are portrayed overall in the literature (and how that then informs adult education curricula) is important. E. Hayes and L. Smith, "Women in Adult Eduation: An Analysis of Perspectives in Major Journals," *Adult Education*

* * * * *

Subject: Re: Chapter on Women in Adult Education

To: Tammy

From: Mary

I don't have much time to reflect on it yet but off the top I would say PLEASE say something about the role of women as important informal educators in the world—the transmission of culture, spirituality, practicalities, etc. You could do a continuum of contribution from the most informal but integral (sharing of info on child-rearing, domestic duty, gardening, etc.) to the most formal, prestigious (researchers in the field of adult education, professors, community leaders). If you like this idea let me know and we can talk further.[22]

From: Helen

To: Tammy

Subject: Women in Ad Ed

I like your idea of looking at women's participation in the field as learners because I think the whole issue boils down first of all to women's discovery of self (of course I'm speaking personally) and then extending that to other women (women's ways of knowing).[23]

Because of their learning and participatory styles women always seem to be in conflict with the academic establishment, the historical male model and that then causes us stress because we are seldom recognized for who we are. That's why you don't hear (historically) about the women in adult education except for the few who have made it their "mission."

With respect to women as adult education practitioners, we have an entirely different approach. I'm thinking about my course—Creating Programs in Adult Education—and something I want to get into a little more in the

---

Quarterly 44, 4 (1994), pp.201-217 used qualitative content analysis to examine 112 articles in four major North American and British adult education journals for their perspectives on women. Five dominant perspectives emerged—women as adult learners, women as deficient, women as coping with new social roles, women as marginalized, and women as collaborative learners. A sixth perspective (only identified in one article), women as feminist, was noted by the authors as holding more promise in that it "provides the opportunity to identify and understand feminists' proactive efforts to create positive change for themselves and other women. In addition, it becomes possible to clarify the values and political agendas that underlie alternative feminist approaches" (p.213). The literature chosen by individual professors for inclusion in the adult education curriculum could portray a multitude of perspectives of women. As Hayes and Smith point out, adult education has the potential to make valuable contributions to general feminist scholarship on women and gender. As an expanding and diverse educational arena, with women as its most rapidly growing student population, adult education represents a societal factor with a potentially significant relationship to both the maintenance and change of gender-related roles and norms (p.214).

[22] Personal e-mail, Mary, November 2, 1996.

[23] The phrase "ways of knowing" has come to be associated with the work of M. Belenky, B. Clinchy, N. Goldberger and J. Mattuck Tarule, *Women's Ways of Knowing: The Development of Self, Voice, and Mind* (New York: Basic Books, 1986). Their work suggests that women experience truth, knowledge and development in five "ways of knowing." Their main finding suggests the importance of relationships, caring, and a sense of community to women's experiences as learners/knowers. While they also suggest that these ways of knowing could be found in men's thinking, they did not claim that their findings did represent men's experiences.

near future. Women's planning processes are very different, I think, and no one has really addressed gender issues in the field of program planning. This is one of the things that accounts for a reaction to the traditional or classic model of program planning versus participatory approaches. Also, women are far more sensitive to (and experienced in) negotiating power and interests—something Cervero and Wilson don't touch upon. I must keep these thoughts to come back to.

Coming back to my first point and one of your last, influential women in adult education. I think we have difficulty finding them because they don't stand out the way male models do. Women's influence is far, far more subtle. We have learned to do that because it's the only power we hold. Some may interpret that as devious or manipulative, but I would think of it as survival. We influence in very intuitive and subtle ways far more, I think, than our male counterparts. And often more powerfully and significantly. That's why it's more difficult to "pick out" historically significant women in adult ed. There are far more women making an influence in ways that do not draw the spotlight and in ways that are more enduring.

Holy smoke! Did I get on a roll or what? Where did all that come from? In any case I'm glad I sat down to do this. It's been the bright spot in a weekend that has just seen me write myself out of my research so that I'm looking at an incredibly sanitized version of what is supposed to be me. To quote my advisor "Stay with the objective—I do believe it will have a stronger impact on the academic community." And this was from a woman. Interestingly enough, women and I have seldom got along and in key times they have always betrayed me ... I do have to question whether this is really an academic community I want to belong to.[24]

Mary's and Helen's e-mails illuminate the relationships between gender constructs and certain aspects of adult education which Hugo suggests we examine. They both allude to the informal, but influential roles that women have played in adult education, but which may not have been suitably recognized historically or present day. Helen also identifies the importance of discovering self, an approach to learning not often attended to in educational settings. Her final discussion of women as educators and academics points to a number of competing and contradictory discourses in which women find themselves.

Rethinking "influential" seems particularly relevant in looking at the role that women have played overall in adult education. While influential typically brings to mind one's ranking in an organization, one's publication record, or one's authority and sanctioned power within an organization, some of the more informal roles "influence" in subtle ways. Program associates or assistants (usually women) are often the first contact for adult learners wishing to return to an educational setting. Their support and encouragement, together

---

[24] Personal e-mail, Helen, November 24, 1996.

with helping new learners navigate the educational bureaucracy, is over-looked. One only has to review course and program evaluations for proof of their importance and influence.[25]

Similarly, the roles played by the secretaries of adult education associations in Canada—the Canadian Association for Adult Education (CAAE), Canadian Association for the Study of Adult Education (CASAE), the Canadian Association for University Continuing Education (CAUCE)—are not adequately recognized. The behind the scenes work of these people (again, usually women) has far reaching influence.

The same can be said for the multitude of women in part-time instructional or co-ordinating roles in a variety of community/volunteer organizations, parent groups, churches, and continuing education groups. While organizations are coming to recognize that these women are the front-line ambassadors of the organization, they still tend to be underpaid and undervalued. As Helen says, "There are far more women making an influence in ways that do not draw the spotlight and in ways that are more enduring." One just needs to take a look around.

Helen's observation that women's learning "boils down first of all to women's discovery of self" reflects the growing recognition that many women have felt alienated and silenced[26] in traditional educational environments that have valued competition and argument over collaboration and dialogue. Very often, a return to adult education (no matter what the particular context) can spark a process of discovery of self for women.[27] Adult education methods are held up as participatory, collaborative, and supportive of relationships. With the guidance of a facilitator, learners come to construct their knowledge within a supportive and safe environment.[28] This is very much in keeping with feminist approaches to learning.

Herein lies the contradiction, however. Adult education methods, overall, are said to be about participation and collaboration. That is not always so and is especially not so in graduate adult education programs. When Helen says, "I do have to question whether this is really an academic community I want to belong to." she is referring to the contradictory discourses in graduate adult

---

[25] In a recent conversation with Lynn, she pointed out that associates and assistants outside the adult education field also play an educational role overall. Consider the informal educating they do in their daily interactions with supervisors and colleagues, because they are the central information source for the activities of an office. This certainly challenges our definition of an adult educator.

[26] See Belenkey et al., *Women's Ways of Knowing*; R. Hall et al. "The Classroom Climate: A Chilly One for Women?" (Washington: Association of American Colleges, n.d.); and M. Lewis and R. Simon "A Discourse Intended for Her: Learning and Teaching within Patriarchy," in J. Gaskell and A. McLaren, eds., *Women and Education* (Calgary: Detselig Enterprises, 1991).

[27] Belenkey et al., *Women's Ways of Knowing*, 1986.

[28] The adult education literature is full of such examples, too numerous to mention here.

education that place both women and men in challenging positions. As one participant in my research noted:

> The other thing that I found very contradictory is that here were all these people teaching me adult education who never used any practices of adult education. It's like you get into a university setting and you do things a certain way regardless of what you know. I mean here they're talking about needs assessments and being interactive and I thought so," Elizabeth laughed, "let's see some of it and I saw nothing."[29]

S. Benson et al. make an even stronger criticism of their experiences in a graduate adult education program when they say, "As women and as a woman from another culture, we have found that we are discouraged, or at least not encouraged, to participate in the academic discourse. The many "rules" of the discourse within the traditional institution, rules about power and knowledge, favour the participation of others."[30] The adult education field has yet to grapple with an institutional academic discourse that does not support the very values upon which the entire adult education enterprise is built. Adult educators who espouse and want to live feminist practices and/or adult education practices must find a way to work with these contradictions.[31]

It is no wonder that women graduate students question how they will fit into adult education overall. People have asked me how many times I thought of quitting my Ph.D. program. Every day, I replied. Now that I am involved in teaching graduate courses in adult education, the tension has heightened. I find it incredibly difficult to remain true to what adult education and feminism have taught me over the years, and maintain my credibility as a professor caught in a system that still insists on specific ways to represent knowledge and specific grades to assess that knowledge.

Helen's comment that "women and I have seldom got along and in key times they have always betrayed me" also reminds me of an interesting con-

---

[29] As cited in Dewar, *Women and Graduate Adult Education*, p.98.

[30] S. Benson, J. Fretz, S. Jiao, and K. Kennett "When Silence Isn't Golden: Four Female Graduate Students' Experiences of Academic Discourse," *Proceedings of the Annual Conference of the Canadian Association for the Study of Adult Education* (Vancouver: Simon Fraser University at Harbour Center, 1994, p.37). For yet another perspective on women's learning in higher education, see E. Hayes and D. Flannery, "Narratives of Adult Women's Learning in Higher Education: Insights from Dissertation Research," Paper presented at the Annual Meeting of the American Educational Research Association (New York: 1996). They identify four concerns—lack of any coherent line of research on women's learning, little incorporation of a gendered analysis, need for research that involves a more diverse group of adult women, and adult women's experiences of being "outsiders" in higher education. While their research confirms many of the themes mentioned in this chapter, they also found some intriguing challenges and contradictions to popular beliefs. For example, a popular assertion is that women tend to be "silent" in classroom discussions due to self-doubts and low confidence. In contrast, as we described above, the women in Furst's (1994) study described themselves as outspoken (p.7).

[31] See G. Payeur "Women as Adult Educators," *Adult Learning* (1993) p.12-14, for a personal account of this "integration."

versation that took place among the women in my research. One of them suggested that there appears to be a need for women professors to push their women students, to be more demanding than their male counterparts, and, in some cases, to oppress and silence women. The suggestion was that women professors had a challenging time themselves as graduate students and so, thus, they pass this on to their own students. There was really no consensus on the issue, as some of the other women in the study felt that the women professors they had were excellent adult education role models. To me, it is a very troubling contradictory discourse in academic adult education that can alienate women from each other.

* * * * *

The experiences of women in adult education mirror those of women in many other disciplines and fields of study. While the feminist movement has done much to address women's marginalization and oppression, its relevance to all women in all contexts at all times is being questioned. Tetreault suggests there are five phases a discipline moves through in its increasing inclusion of gender issues.[32]

Phase one, male scholarship, assumes that male experience is the norm. Phase two, compensatory scholarship, considers women as deficient and the emphasis is to bring them up to the male standard. Phase three, bifocal scholarship, views the human experience as dual, male and female, and strong roles are expected of each gender. Phase four, feminist scholarship, views women multidimensionally. Phase five, multifocal/relational scholarship is gender balanced. There is a realization that experiences are the same and different across genders.[33]

Linda Sattem's research suggests that much of adult education research is reflective of phases two and three. As she says of the scholarship in adult education at these levels, "valuable information is learned about women and their experiences. This information was and is missing from our knowledge base. The danger would be that adult education stays in these early phases."[34] Collard and Law echo this sentiment by suggesting that

> However, to our knowledge, adult education has yet to consider the impact of postmodern thought on its foundational bases and on the normative social and political goals it draws from these.[35]

---

[32] M. Tetreault "Feminist Phase Theory: An Experienced-Derived Evaluation Model," *Journal of Higher Learning* 56, 4 (1985) pp.363-384.

[33] Paraphrased from L. Sattem, *Adult Education and Feminist Phase Theory: Practicing What we Teach* (Ohio State University: Proceedings of the Annual Midwest Research to Practice Conference, 1993).

[34] L. Sattem, *Adult Education and Feminist Phase Theory*, p.95.

[35] S. Collard and M. Law, "Universal Abandon: Postmodernity, Politics and Adult Education," in

It is my hope that this chapter has raised questions about the role of women in adult education. There is much I did not address adequately—women in instructional roles, women as planners, and women in administration being only a few examples. As women recover their history and voices through the scholarship we have already seen, I hope we move on to embrace a multifocal practice and scholarship that transcends universal categories and labels such as gender, class or race, to acknowledge the sameness and difference in all of us.

Annual Adult Education Research Conference Proceedings (Athens: Georgia University, 1990) p.54.

Community newspapers, radio stations, welfare rights groups, women's centres ... popular education happens in many non-traditional ways. Photo courtesy of Vincent Greason.

12

The Contemporary Scene

I
t is the intention in this chapter to focus on adult education in Canada in the most recent three decades, since approximately 1970. This will involve pulling together some material which has already been presented in previous chapters. There are two main reasons for doing this. The first is to describe the main features of the field in Canada at the present time. The other is to identify current trends in adult education, ones which represent forces or directions which appear to be shaping the future of the field.

Why 1970 as a Starting Point?

Neither 1970 nor any other date holds any particular magic to mark the beginning of a new era, but the beginning of the 1970s is in some respects a reasonable starting point. The impact of the increasing rate of technological and social change was being brought home at that time by such books as Alvin Toffler's *Future Shock*, which appeared in 1970.[1] Some of the social movements spawned in the turbulent 1960s were taking form and settling in for the long run. In the case of the women's movement, for instance, government had by this time been persuaded to take their concerns seriously, and the landmark report on the Royal Commission on the Status of Women was issued in 1970. A dramatic devolution of powers from the federal to the provincial governments had gathered pace during the 1960s and by the early 1970s scholarly books were appearing under such titles as *Canada in Question*, which expressed concern about the degree of decentralization within Confederation.[2]

In the field of education, the community college systems in the various provinces, which began to develop in the mid- and late-1960s, were rapidly

---

[1] A. Toffler, *Future Shock* (London: Bodley Head, 1970).

[2] D.V. Smiley, *Canada in Question: Federalism in the Seventies* (Toronto: McGraw-Hill Ryerson, 1972).

changing the nature of educational opportunities open to adults. The creation of TV Ontario in 1970 was a harbinger of many related educational innovations to follow. The field of adult education itself was rapidly moving towards professionalism, with the first two books dealing with specialized areas of practice, *Citizen Participation: Canada* and *Adult Basic Education* appearing early in the decade.[3] Allen Tough's influential study of "self-directed" adult learning, *The Adult's Learning Projects*, appeared in 1971.[4] Community development seemed to be taking a new lease on life in Canada with the emergence of the National Film Board's Challenge for Change project, Frontier College's entry into that field, and the launching in Canada of the "community school" movement, all in or around 1970.

The international community of ideas also seemed to be signalling a new era of development in the field. In 1970, two influential books appeared, Ivan Illich's *Deschooling Society* and Paulo Freire's *Pedagogy of the Oppressed*,[5] both of which were to have substantial impact on adult education in this country, as elsewhere. In Europe, new concepts and practices were emerging which were to have widespread influence: the efforts of the Council of Europe to promote the idea of *education permanente*; the work of the Organization for Economic Co-operation and Development in connection with the policy of recurrent education; and the promotion by UNESCO of the concept of lifelong education, particularly by means of its highly publicized report, *Learning To Be*, which appeared in 1972.[6] In that same year, UNESCO held in Tokyo its Third World Conference on Adult Education. The proceedings of that intergovernmental conference indicated a widespread acceptance among governments in all parts of the world of the place of adult education in educational planning, and also focussed attention particularly on the need to increase the effectiveness of adult education in serving the more educationally disadvantaged.[7] Two important royal commissions on education in Canada, the Worth Commission in Alberta and the Wright Commission in Ontario, reported in 1972 and both were clearly influenced by these European and international developments.[8] There are therefore reasons to see the early 1970s as the beginning of significant trends in the field of adult education.

---

[3] J. Draper (Ed.), *Citizen Participation: Canada* (Toronto: New Press, 1971); M. Brooke, *Adult Basic Education* (Toronto: New Press, 1972).

[4] A. Tough, *The Adult's Learning Projects* (Toronto: OISE, 1971).

[5] I. Illich, *Deschooling Society* (New York: Harper & Row, 1970); P. Freire, *Pedagogy of the Oppressed* (New York: Herder & Herder, 1970).

[6] UNESCO, *Learning To Be* (Paris: UNESCO, 1972).

[7] J. Lowe, *The Education of Adults: A World Perspective* (Toronto: OISE, 1975).

[8] *A Choice of Futures*, Report of the Commission [Alberta] on Educational Planning (Edmonton: Queen's Printer, 1972); *The Learning Society*, Report of the Commission on Post-Secondary Education in Ontario (Toronto: Ontario Ministry of Public Services, 1972).

The nearly thirty years under review in this chapter were ones of triumph and tragedy for mankind. Conditions such as the extent of famine in Africa, the widespread denial of human rights, the arms race, the increasing numbers of illiterates in the world, the challenge of AIDS, and environmental disasters were all serious in themselves and evoked the spectre of future difficulties. The period also brought the first landing on the moon and, twenty years later, the recovery of pictures of Neptune from a spacecraft which had travelled for twelve years and was about to pass beyond the earth's solar system. It was a time which included the oil crisis of 1973 and its aftermath, the Iranian revolution of 1978 and the upsurge of fundamentalist religion, the more developed world's problems of unemployment, and increasing awareness of the aging of their population. The dismantling of apartheid in South Africa, the release of Nelson Mandela and his subsequent election to the presidency were causes for celebration, as was the tearing down of the Berlin wall, but the terrible events of Tiananmen Square, Somalia, the former Yugoslavia and Rwanda were among the harsh reminders of deep problems facing the world. In Canada, although we were a favoured nation in many respects, these years have been ones of stress and frustration. Among the events of the period were: the imposition of price controls; continued relatively high levels of unemployment and the spread of poverty in Canadian society; the upsurge of separatism in Quebec leading to two referenda and many stresses and strains on the fabric of the country; the continuing struggle over constitutional amendment, the repatriation of the constitution and the creation of the Charter of Rights and Freedoms, but also including the failures of the Meech and Charlottetown Accords; and the deeply felt political struggles over the Free Trade agreements. The women's movement has continued to progress and gained particularly widespread attention in the struggle over the Charter. Relations between the First Nations people and Canadian governments, both federal and provincial, have been troubled at times, most notably over the Charter, the Oka crisis of 1990, the negotiations over Meech Lake and the failure of the Charlottetown Accord.

Such were some of the events which affected the kind of society and psychological climate in which Canadians, and Canadian adult education, functioned in these three tumultuous decades. There was wealth—or at least prosperity—for many who could function effectively in an increasingly high-tech world. There was extended or chronic poverty and unemployment for many who did not find a place in that world. In Canada, as in the international community, the gap between the rich and the poor, the "haves" and the "have-nots", widened.

There were also important events which affected what might be termed the "intellectual climate" within which Canadian adult education was functioning. There were, first of all, a number of significant reports and other publications which reinforced the sense of importance of the field. The landmark report of UNESCO's International Commission on the Development of Education, *Learning To Be*,[9] which appeared in 1972, was in many respects the most eloquent of them all. Modern conditions demanded the development of what they termed "a learning society" if man were to remain in control of events, and not the other way around. Change was taking place so rapidly in contemporary society, nothing less than lifelong learning—and much of the emphasis was on learning rather than education—would enable men and women to cope. Another influential document of the period was *No Limits to Learning*, a report written in 1979 by J. W. Botkin and others for the prestigious international "think tank," the Club of Rome. They argued that if humanity was to save itself from environmental and other follies which were being perpetrated, it would have to call on its "untapped resources of vision and creativity" in order to "bail humankind out of its predicament."[10] The Organization for Economic Co-operation and Development, a body representing the most highly developed and wealthiest nations in the world, embraced the concept of "recurrent education" in the early 1970s.[11] It was argued that such an approach—an integration or alternation of work and education throughout adult life—would have both social and economic benefits. These three approaches, all of which accorded new prominence to adult education and adult learning, were perhaps the most important among many of the period, which during these three decades brought adult education into prominence among economic and social planners as never before.

At the same time that adult education was gaining this new prominence, it—and the field of education as a whole—was the subject of vigorous criticism from various quarters. The 1960s had been a turbulent time for the field of education, with much of the leadership in this process coming from the students or learners themselves. By late in the decade, the crisis of confidence with respect to the educational strategies being employed, what Philip Coombs termed "the linear expansion of existing or inherited educational systems,"[12] was being taken seriously by educational and development planners. Two eloquent critics of current educational practice, Ivan Illich and Paulo Freire, published powerful statements of their points of view in 1970. Illich's *Deschooling Society* identified what he saw to be the "institutionalizing" effect that educational systems were having on students—creating dependence on the teaching profession—and he also condemned the attempt,

---

[9] UNESCO, *Learning To Be*.

[10] J. Botkin, M. Elmandjra & M. Malitza, *No Limits to Learning* (Oxford: Pergamon, 1979) p.xiii.

[11] Organization for Economic Co-operation and Development, *Recurrent Education: Trends and Issues* (Paris: OECD, 1975).

[12] P. Coombs, *The World Crisis in Education: View from the Eighties* (New York: Oxford, 1985) p.7.

through such institutions, to impose a middle-class set of values on all students. He was no less critical of a lifelong education policy, if it was to produce the same effects.[13] Paulo Freire's critique had much in common with that of Illich, and was firmly rooted in adult education practice. His *Pedagogy of the Oppressed* advanced the view, as Illich did, that existing educational systems were based on a largely unconscious assumption that its role was to develop people to "fit" into the society, more or less as it was presently constituted; it was an education for "domestication," whereas what was needed was an education for freedom. In his view, educators were deluding themselves if they thought they were being—or even could be—neutral in their influence with respect to the future of society; they must, in Freire's view, be forces for change, or forces which reinforced the status quo.[14]

These and other critiques of education have had considerable impact on the field of education, including adult education, since they appeared. They have made all educators who were willing to listen more sensitive to the implications of their policies and practices. They have also provided great encouragement to those sectors of the field of adult education which sought to use education as an instrument, or at least a handmaiden of social change. More specifically, many of those in the field of literacy or basic education, about which Freire spoke in considerable detail (having developed his ideas while working in such situations himself), have drawn inspiration and methodological assistance from his writings. The result has been a more polarized field than was the case in earlier decades. Much of the field has taken part or at least fallen in with the move towards professionalism, a "needs meeting" and market orientation model, which have been the dominant trends of the period. On the other hand, the adult educators who have been concerned with linking their efforts with attempts to bring about social change have been strengthened in their views by the radical critiques such as those referred to above. In addition, the national organization representing the field, the Canadian Association for Adult Education, directed its energies for some years to allying itself with several social movements—the women's movement, literacy, peace and environmental organizations and so on—a further source of encouragement to adult educators who were involved in education for social change.

---

[13] I. Illich, *Deschooling Society*.

[14] P. Freire, *Pedagogy of the Oppressed*.

The Development of the Field of Adult Education

Participation

The last three decades have seen spectacular growth in participation in adult education on the part of Canadians. This has been a period during which some parts of the educational system have experienced slowed rates of growth, but adult education has seemingly not been affected in that way. The simplest way to document this growth is to compare three reports issued by Statistics Canada, in 1963, 1984 and 1993.[15] The first of these indicated that "one in twenty-five" adult Canadians had taken part in adult education during the year studied (1959-60) and the second announced in its title, *One in Every Five*, how drastically the picture had changed. The latest such report found that by 1992, approximately one-third of all adults were taking part in adult education annually. These were, of course, percentages of a growing total population. The number of adult learners had increased at a much more rapid rate of growth than that of the adult population as a whole. As was pointed out in Chapter 5, the numbers of persons actively engaged in learning was clearly a much higher number.

Providers

Accompanying the rapid growth of the field—and perhaps in part explaining it—has been the proliferation of agencies which provide adult educational opportunities. The three most notable new developments in the case of the providing agencies have been the community college, the considerable expansion of the private sector, and the increased prominence of the social movement.

The single most important development in the field during this period has undoubtedly been the creation, beginning in the 1960s, of community college systems in most of the provinces. As documented by Dennison and Gallagher[16] in their study, although the functions of the colleges have differed from one jurisdiction to another, they have all seen as one of their main tasks the provision of opportunities for part-time study for adults in their communities. The importance of their activities in this field was revealed in the participation study, *One in Every Five*, just referred to, in which the colleges

---

[15] Dominion Bureau of Statistics, *Participants in Further Education in Canada* (Ottawa: D.B.S., 1963); Mary Sue Devereau, *One in Every Five: A Survey of Adult Education in Canada* (Ottawa: Statistics Canada & Dept. of Secretary of State, 1984); Statistics Canada, *Adult Education and Training Survey*, 1993.

[16] J. Dennison & P. Gallagher, *Canada's Community Colleges* (Vancouver: University of British Columbia, 1986).

(including the Quebec CEGEPs) were shown to be the largest provider of adult education of all the educational institutions.[17]

The expansion of the private sector of the field takes several different forms. First of all, particularly since the early 1980s, the federal work-force authorities as a matter of policy sought to purchase an increasing proportion of the training for their trainees from the private sector and correspondingly less from the public educational institutions. This policy was particularly emphasized under the terms of the National Training Act of 1982 and the Canadian Job Strategy program of 1985. This has led to the offering of training at the job site, by arrangement with private sector employers, and also to the creation of many private sector educational agencies, established in order to be able to take advantage of the federal government's policies in this area. Quite apart from the impact of federal policies, there has been a rapid growth in the number of proprietary educational and training institutions in the private sector, and the expansion of many previously established firms. Continuing or adult education having become a more widely accepted phenomenon in our society, expanded opportunities have presented themselves for the sale of services in this area—everything from learning about deep sea or scuba diving, to learning how to operate a computer. A further dimension of this trend has been a considerable increase in the extent of private consulting in the area of adult education and training. But by far the most significant dimension of the private sector was the training conducted by business and industry for its own employees (and in some cases, for the employees of other corporations as well). The national study published in 1985 revealed that education provided by "employers" was the largest single category of "course provider," accounting for 18 percent of the total. And employers provided 42 percent of "job related" courses. The figures for 1992 are approximately the same.[18]

Two further, somewhat conjectural points might be made with respect to who provides adult education. The statistics available relate in the main to formal and non-formal education; the reports refer to numbers of "enrollments" and "courses." Education takes place in other ways as well. Social movements such as the environmental movements, for instance, have seen that "media events" and other forms of influence over people's attitudes, ones which are not educational programs in the traditional sense of the term, nevertheless can be effective in informing (and perhaps persuading) people with respect to the issues being dealt with. There seems at this time no dependable way of quantifying such activity, much less attempting to evaluate its educational effectiveness, but it does appear to be the case that such approaches to

---

[17] Mary Sue Devereau, *One in Every Five.*

[18] Statistics Canada, *Adult Education and Training Survey.*

alerting people to issues and providing information about them has greatly gained in usage in these most recent decades.

The second point perhaps does not logically fall under the heading of "providers," but it is closely related to it. We refer to the increased awareness in recent years of what is referred to as "self-directed learning." This phenomenon is of particular interest to Canadian students of adult education because the leading figure in research into this area is a Canadian, Allen Tough.[19] The point of view taken in this work is that most of the education engaged in by adults does not take the form of enrolling in a course or a program, but is directed by the learner himself or herself. Research has revealed that virtually everyone undertakes such self-directed learning projects in the course of a year. Tough was the main figure in launching investigation into this form of learning effort, but it has had wide influence and has been picked up by many other investigators.[20] This research is controversial: some question the soundness of the research; others, for ideological reasons, prefer not to take self-directed learning seriously as part of what Philip Coombs has termed the educational "network,"[21] perhaps because it is slippery to define and not easily directly controlled by policy. A new kind of "provider" of adult education—the learner himself or herself—has come into our ken.

Distance Education and Educational Technology[22]

Distance education—the provision of instruction to learners who are at a distance from the instructor or instructing institution—has grown dramatically in these recent decades, and it has taken a variety of forms. The creation of the Open University in Britain, which began taking students in 1971, has been instrumental in encouraging the growth of similar institutions elsewhere, including Canada. The Open University took the long-established practice of "correspondence study" and embellished it in a variety of ways—supplementary broadcasts, local tutoring and counselling centres, audio and other augmentation of the traditional print materials in the course packages, and brief residential periods of instruction. The three most prominent institutions in Canada of a somewhat similar nature are the Télé-Université in Quebec (part of the University of Quebec), Athabasca University in Alberta, and the Open Learning Agency in British Columbia, all created in the 1970s.[23]

---

[19] A. Tough, *The Adult's Learning Projects*.

[20] See for instance A. Tough, "Major Learning Efforts: Recent Research and Future Directions," *Adult Education*, *28*, 4 (1978) pp.250-63.

[21] P. Coombs, *The World Crisis in Education*.

[22] The principal authors acknowledge the assistance of Bill Fallis, Professor at George Brown College in Toronto, in writing this section.

[23] J. Wilson, B. Bell & W. Powell, *The Provincial Educational Communications Organizations in*

In addition to these new special purpose institutions, many already existing ones took a fresh interest in the possibilities of this "new generation" of distance education techniques and have greatly expanded their offerings by these means.[24] A leading example of this has been the University of Waterloo, which by the mid-1980s had approximately three hundred courses available, in their case with heavy reliance on audiocassettes containing versions of on-campus lectures.[25] Teleconferencing and other communications techniques through which an instructor can be in touch with individual students or groups of students at remote locations are also being widely used. Computer-managed or computer-assisted instruction is being employed in many settings. In the last few years there has been rapid expansion of the provision of "on-line" instruction, which provides a variety of instructional resources for the learner, all accessed through the personal computer (and available to be downloaded and printed at the learner's discretion at his or her home base). Those taking courses on-line are frequently also able to communicate with other students taking the same course through the use of electronic or e-mail "coffee rooms" or "student lounges."

A third major sector of distance education is that of provincial educational communications organizations, particularly TV Ontario, Radio-Québec, ACCESS Alberta, and the Knowledge Network (part of the Open Learning Agency) in British Columbia, all established in the 1970s.[26] Generally, these organizations broadcast both general educational programs (just as general viewing, not as courses of instruction) and also credit and non-credit courses for which people may register. Any "credit" which students gain by means of these courses is normally awarded by other institutions (colleges, universities and so on) in the provincial system rather than by the broadcasting agency itself. The four organizations differ somewhat in their activities, but are also involved in closed-circuit broadcasting, videotape services and computer-related applications. At the time of writing, conservative policies and budget restrictions have brought about the privatization of ACCESS Alberta and the Ontario government has announced it is considering the privatization of TV Ontario.

Technological innovations and new instructional technologies have had substantial impact on the offerings of educational institutions in Canada in the last few decades. Much of this activity has focussed on the delivery of credit

---

Canada (Toronto: Ontario Educational Communications Authority, 1984).

[24] See I. Mugridge & D. Kaufman (Ed.), *Distance Education in Canada* (London: Croom Helm, 1986).

[25] E. Burge et al., *Communications and Information Technologies and Distance Education in Canada* (Toronto: Ontario Educational Communications Authority, 1984).

[26] J. Wilson et al., *The Provincial Educational Communications Organizations.*

or formal courses, both on the campus and at a distance. From the learner's point of view, the "world" of available instruction has become just that; it has become possible through the personal computer for someone in Canada to gain access to courses of instruction originating in other centres, other countries or even other continents. Although there are clearly many benefits which can flow from the application of these technologies to the field of education, there are at the same time aspects of the introduction of these innovations which are of concern to many in the field. These may be summarized under two headings, learner issues and social issues.

Learner Issues. The issue of control over the content of courses becomes more complex. In face-to-face instructional settings, the content can be adjusted by the instructor to take into account the characteristics of the learner, the local context and current issues. With more technological applications, the content is more likely to be controlled centrally and more difficult to adjust, thus providing less opportunity for the student to have an influence on the content of the course. The same may be true with respect to the processes employed in the course. A third issue has to do with the possible impact of distance and technology on the emotional commitment of the student to the course, a factor which as Holmberg reminds us depends to a considerable extent on the relationship which is established between teacher and learner.[27] Not only do such factors limit the learner's commitment to the course, but may also limit the type of learnings which are derived from it. The typical setting or circumstances of the distance education learner may be more conducive to learning in the "rational" realm, than in others, such as the relational, the emotional or the "metaphoric."[28] Such issues for the learner may in part be dealt with by further elaboration of distance education techniques, but remain a challenge for those working in this aspect of the field.

Societal Issues. The first of these may be seen in terms of the important distinction between information and knowledge. As Garrison and others have pointed out, there is more to acquiring knowledge than receiving information; information must be shared, be critically analyzed and be applied in order to become knowledge.[29] If society's expectations of and investment in distance education are to be realized, such issues must be adequately dealt with. There is as well the issue of what sectors of society are in a position to take advantage of the application of advanced technologies to educational opportunities. How widely available in our society are the means of accessing the newer technologies, and what is the impact of this state of affairs on the phenome-

---

[27] B. Holmberg, *Theory and Practice of Distance Education* (London: Croom Helm, 1989).

[28] Griffin in D. Boud & V. Griffin, *Appreciating Adults Learning* (London: Kogan Page, 1987).

[29] D.R. Garrison, "An Analysis and Evaluation of Audio Teleconferencing to Facilitate Education at a Distance," *The American Journal of Distance Education*, *4*, 3 (1990) pp.13-24.

non of the "haves" and the "have-nots" in Canada? Finally, there is the issue of goals and content from society's point of view. What contribution will distance education instruction make to what might be termed social or citizenship education? Will adequate attention be paid only to the conveying of information, or will the new technologies also be applied to the fostering of participational skills and other aspects of the development of citizens of democratic society? The foregoing is not to suggest that such important challenges are not understood by those in the field of distance education, but rather as a summary of some issues which it is widely appreciated must be addressed.

Program Areas

It is a safe assumption that all program or content areas of adult education have grown significantly in these past two decades. In what follows the emphasis will be given to a number of areas which have, for various reasons, grown especially rapidly.

In Canada, as in many other countries, vocational and technical training have received priority treatment in recent years. The conservative governments which have been in power in many Western countries for much of this period have had a particular interest in promoting the industrial sector and in providing the skilled labour force necessary for such economic development. The great interest shown in vocational training and in such concepts as "recurrent education," which links further education and worker proficiency, have been manifestations of such priorities.[30] The emphasis on vocational education has become so pronounced in this period that some international experts in the field of education have expressed concern about the extent of its dominance in public policy over other areas of adult learning.[31]

Both senior levels of government in Canada have been giving strong emphasis to vocational training. The stage was set at the federal level by two developments, the vast expansion of funding for this field initiated by the Technical and Vocational Training Assistance Act of 1960, and the decision by the federal authorities in the mid-1960s to assume authority in the field of vocational and technical education. The federal government drew a line between education, which was clearly a provincial responsibility, and training, which it now claimed to be within its powers, arising out of its constitutional responsibility for the economic development of the country. The Occupational Training Act of 1967, the National Training Act of 1982 and subsequent measures have been based on this interpretation and have radically altered the

---

[30] J. Bengtsson in T. Schuller & J. Megarry (Eds.), *Recurrent Education and Lifelong Learning* (London: Nichols Publishing, 1979).

[31] See, for instance, J. Lowe, *The Education of Adults*.

basis of public policy towards this aspect of adult education in Canada. At the same time the various provinces pursued their own policies in this area, generally lending the same emphasis to the vocational/technical sector. Federal initiatives to explore a comprehensive "paid educational leave" policy for Canada, have produced two major reports on the subject[32] but were not successful in securing the active support of the three major interested parties, management, labour and government.

A further major development in federal and provincial policies towards vocational and technical education has arisen from federal initiatives in just the last few years. Two basic decisions were made; the first was to institutionalize the participation of certain "stakeholders" in the determination of policy through the creation of Labour Force Development Boards at the federal and provincial levels (and in the case of Ontario, regional as well) on which management and organized labour had the dominant voices; the second was to transfer to the provinces increasingly in coming years some financial resources and responsibility for the carrying out of vocational and technical training. (At the time of writing, a number of the provincial boards, so recently created, have been disbanded or are in serious disarray.) The decision by federal authorities to delegate vocational training to the provinces represents a reversal of the policies introduced in 1967, when the federal authorities assumed responsibility for such activity. In 1996 the federal and Alberta governments signed the first of what will presumably be a series of federalprovincial agreements under which funds (in this case $344 million over three years) will be transferred to the provinces, which will assume responsibility for job training, counselling and placement for the unemployed. The federal authorities have indicated their willingness to enter into such arrangements with all provinces and territories.

An area of adult education which has grown spectacularly since 1970 is that of continuing professional education. It is almost in the nature of professions that practitioners must keep up to date with new knowledge and conditions affecting their fields of practice, in order to be able to perform at the expected level. Professional people have traditionally continued their education through reading, professional conferences, study groups and the like. In the 1960s and early 1970s, professional groups, responding to a realization that they were facing a severe problem in keeping up with an accelerated rate of change, and as well to a new level of scrutiny from the "consumer," stepped up their educational efforts. Typically, the professional body and the pre-service training institution (universities, institutes of technology and so

---

[32] R.J. Adams, *Education and Working Canadians*, Report of the Commission of Inquiry on Educational Leave and Productivity (Ottawa: Labour Canada, 1979); National Advisory Panel on Skill Development Leave, *Learning for Life*, Report of the Panel to the Minister of Employment and Immigration, 1984).

on) co-operatively established continuing education programs through which needed information and education could be provided for practitioners. In some cases professions have established regulations which make the continuation or renewal of licenses to practice conditional upon the practitioners being able to show evidence of efforts to update their knowledge and skills. Continuing professional education has in many instances been at the growing and innovative frontier of methodologies in adult education. While it is not possible to quantify the growth or extent of continuing professional education in Canada, it is clear to anyone at all knowledgeable about the field as a whole that this has been one of the areas of most rapid growth in the last two decades.

One of the areas of the field which has been developing most quickly is that of full- and part-time study towards academic credentials. For present purposes, this will be examined in two sections, post-secondary education and adult basic education. Growth in the post-secondary field has been the most spectacular. The creation of the systems of community colleges and institutes in the various provinces has undoubtedly been the most important single factor. These institutions, which began their spectacular growth in the 1960s, have by their very existence encouraged many to continue their education, have brought many new programs and fields of training into being, and have made post-secondary education much more accessible, both geographically and financially. Furthermore, the colleges generally have from the outset seen the adult and part-time student as one of the main clientele they intend to serve, so they have designed services of many kinds for this group.[33] As has already been mentioned, as of the Statistics Canada study published in 1984, the community colleges served more adult students than any other sector of the educational system.[34] In recent years these institutions have been seriously affected, however, by financial restrictions and by the loss of many seat purchases by federal authorities.

The universities of the country greatly expanded their services to adult part-time students in this period. Although it is not possible to state all the reasons with assurance, it would appear that demographic trends which resulted in decreased demand for university services in the traditional eighteen-to-twenty-four-year age groups encouraged the universities of the country to become more interested in older, part-time students. New, special purpose units within certain universities, such as Atkinson College at York University and Woodsworth College at the University of Toronto, have been established to serve the part-time student. New distance education institutions such as Athabasca University (Alberta), Tele-Université (Quebec) and the Open

---

[33] J. Dennison & P. Gallagher, *Canada's Community Colleges*.

[34] Mary Sue Devereau, *One in Every Five*.

Learning Agency (British Columbia), and other distance education programs have made many post-secondary educational opportunities more accessible. The statistics available indicate that in the period between 1970 and the present, part-time credit course enrollments at Canadian universities increased enormously, reaching 279,850 by 1985-86.[35] This represented approximately 38 percent of all credit enrollments. Of the part-time enrollees, approximately three-quarters of these persons were twenty-five years or older.[36] In his study of the matter, Campbell indicates that in 1974-75, the number of part-time students in Canadian universities (credit and non-credit) exceeded the number of full-time students for the first time.[37]

Another area of rapid development during the 1970s and 1980s was the field of adult basic education (ABE), which is here meant to include everything from literacy education through to high school completion for adults, and beyond the literacy level, at least, is normally closely related to formal educational credentials. Two developments during the 1960s laid the foundations for this rapid expansion. The census of 1961 revealed as never before the extent of under-education in the Canadian population.[38] Secondly, with the rapid expansion of vocational and technical education made possible by the Technical and Vocational Training Assistance Act of 1960, it soon became clear that many of the persons who were most in need of such training did not have a sufficient level of basic education to enable them to cope with the training which was being made available. As a result, the federal Manpower authorities were drawn into financing a great deal of basic education for adults.[39] These efforts, and those of the provincial authorities (where the record was very uneven) led to a dramatic expansion of adult basic education programs across the country. In 1982, the federal authorities cut back their support for ABE activities and the initiative began to shift increasingly to provincially and privately sponsored programs. In addition to the various work-force related programs, the provinces have in most cases developed alternative curricula and programs through which adults can gain formal qualifications at the high school level—through the General Educational Development (GED) examination system and by other means. It is not clear as yet how budget restrictions and "user-pay" fee policies have affected the character and extent of ABE in Canada but the negative effects have been substantial.

---

[35] *University Affairs* (May 1986).

[36] Ibid.

[37] D.D. Campbell, *The New Majority* (Edmonton: University of Alberta, 1984).

[38] M. Brooke, *Adult Basic Education* (Toronto: New Press, 1972).

[39] M. Taylor & J. Draper (Eds.), *Adult Literacy Perspectives* (Toronto: Culture Concepts Inc., 1989).

The field of literacy education has been a prominent concern in the Third World for several decades. Canadian activity in this area began to take shape in the 1960s and came into prominence in the mid-1970s.[40] Although federal authorities cut back on their commitment to the full range of ABE activities in the 1970s, they have in recent years provided leadership in the field of literacy education. In this case, literacy was seen to be an essential element of citizenship in contemporary society, and the federal initiatives have come through the Secretary of State's Department (National Literacy Secretariat) rather than through work-force training. Federal funds were provided on a larger scale than previously for this work, beginning in 1988, in support of work by the non-governmental and voluntary sector, and through joint initiatives with the provinces. Literacy education has been a rapidly expanding part of adult education in Canada but is suffering from a shortage of funding.

Reference must be made as well to the emergence in the past two decades of adult education programs and services intended for, and in many cases under the sponsorship of, the Native people of Canada. In keeping with the proclamation by the Native Indian Brotherhood (since 1982, the Assembly of First Nations) in 1972 of the intention of the Native people to develop educational services under their own control, and with the support in many respects of the federal government, there has been a dramatic expansion of adult education activities, much of it under the direction of Native organizations.[41] This educational activity has been of various kinds, perhaps most notably in three areas: education related to the aspirations of the Native people in such areas as human rights, cultural and political development, and land claims; general educational development, largely in the area of adult basic education; and increased access to post-secondary education and professional training. This activity has been developed both on the reserves and in the cities of the South, where many special purpose organizations and institutions have been established. The release in 1996 of the report of the Royal Commission on Aboriginal Peoples will no doubt lead to a re-examination of this whole policy area.

The women's movement, in its contemporary form, was a product of social forces during the 1960s and by 1970, when the Royal Commission on the Status of Women reported, was very much a going concern. From the very beginning there was a strong educational dimension to the movement, at first aimed largely at "consciousness raising" among women, but increasingly as time went on concerned as well with assisting women to gain the confidence

---

[40] Ibid.

[41] See for instance, *Affiliation and Accreditation: Research Study Report for the First Nations Federation of Adult Educators* (Vancouver: The Merritt Group, 1988). See also C. Haig-Brown, *Taking Control: Power and Contradiciton in First Nations Adult Education* (Unpublished Ph.D. Thesis, University of B.C., 1991).

and qualifications needed as they altered their goals and moved into new roles in Canadian society. Some of the longer-established women's organizations, such as the Y.W.C.A., took a leading role in the new women's movement, but the most prominent women's groups of the recent decades have been newly-established ones. The Voice of Women organization was prominent in the early years, especially in the area of political and social action. Other bodies, most notably the National Action Committee on the Status of Women, an umbrella organization which speaks for 230 women's organizations, became more prominent in the 1980s. In the field of education, many important developments have taken place. A new organization which emerged in the 1970s, the Canadian Congress on Learning Opportunities for Women, has taken a vigorous lead in promoting educational opportunities for women, through the creation of new programs and promoting satisfactory access for women to existing ones. Many educational institutions in Canada have created new programs of interest to women, such as "women's studies," and have provided support services for women students, particularly by means of peer support groups and counselling services of various kinds. Particular attention has been paid by the women's movement to the vocational training programs provided by the two senior levels of government, to the end that access (and benefits) be fairly available to women, including those programs related to occupations which have not traditionally been women's fields of work. These and other matters related to this subject are dealt with in greater detail in Chapter 4.

An important phenomenon of these decades has been the educational activities undertaken by the various social movements already referred to. The peace movement, groups representing the interests of Native people, those concerned with aspects of the environment, the women's movement, and those concerned with the welfare of the growing number of older persons—to name only some—have engaged in a great range of informational and educational endeavours which have reached and influenced many Canadians. Much of the activity of these movements has not taken the form of traditional types of adult education—courses, classes and so on—but none would question their educational impact in the broad sense of the term. The women's movement has utilized perhaps the broadest range of educational activities of any of these groups and as well has pioneered many approaches to the field of educational counselling.

There has been a significant increase of interest and activity in Canada in the latter part of this period in "popular education." Drawing inspiration from Latin America and other parts of the Third World, those engaging in this work have brought to bear highly participational educational methods in efforts to bring about social change. The heightened tensions in Canadian society resulting from the neo-conservative political agenda—the increase in poverty and in the gap between the "haves" and "have-nots," the decrease in social services, high levels of unemployment—have led to a psychological climate conducive to controversial and adversarial approaches of various kinds. It is not surprising that such a trend has become evident in educational circles as well. A number of Canadian educators have been active in the recently formed North American Alliance for Popular and Adult Education, and Canadian organizations have been conducting programs which have been consciously developed in keeping with popular education theories and methodologies.[42]

The Canadian Association for Adult Education, the national organization for the field in English-speaking Canada, which has cultivated links with the voluntary sector throughout its history, resolved during the celebration of its fiftieth anniversary in 1985 to strengthen its co-operative working relationships with six social movements—adult literacy, the peace movement, cultural sovereignty, environmental citizenship, local economical development and the women's movement. In each case, the commitment of the CAAE was to co-operative endeavours in connection with the educational, as distinct from the social or political action of these groups. For the CAAE, this represented a re-focussing on a theme which has run through its history. During the 1950s and the following decade, the CAAE was prominent as well in the profession building aspects of the field, but since that time, and especially since the mid-1980s, the organization has returned to a more dominant commitment to the social movement roots of the field. With the recent termination of federal grants to the organization, there is uncertainty with respect to its future.

Many other aspects of the rapidly growing field of adult education could be mentioned here, but those discussed above represent a number which have developed most remarkably during these decades. There is a concern on the part of many adult educators that a combination of conservative government policies and trends towards professionalism in the field of practice are producing an adult education enterprise—especially in the public sector—which is increasingly concerned with vocational and academic aspects and correspondingly less interested in the social and citizenship dimensions of adult learning in this country.

The Budget Crunch

As we have seen in Chapter 8, the 1990s can be characterized as a time when educational policies have been highly determined by the needs of the job market and by the over-riding concern for deficit reduction. Policy making and financing for adult education has been largely driven by the short-term economic goals of our federal and provincial governments. In addition to this fiscal determinant, the other prominent driving force in directing policy devel-

---

[42] See, for instance, D. Clover, "Theoretical Foundations and Practice of Critical Environmental Adult Education in Canada," *Convergence, 28*, 2, pp.44-53.

opment and funding for adult education has been the promotion of new technologies in expanding and diversifying distance education.

Generally speaking, the broader goals of adult education as an instrument in building a just and participatory society have had little influence on policy development and program funding in this decade. While considerable lip-service has been paid to the concepts of lifelong learning and healthy communities, overall funding for adult education has declined and funding programs have concentrated on job training and innovations in distance education. As this approach to adult education has been implemented across the country, common trends in program policy and funding have emerged. While there are notable exceptions and some variation in degree or packaging, it is possible to identify the following common characteristics and impacts:

- *Decline in funding: Getting more for less*—Federal and provincial funding for adult education has declined steadily since 1990. Federal grants to national groups like the CAAE and the ICEA have been eliminated. Federal support for apprenticeship training, block purchase of seats and labour-force development boards has been cut dramatically. In most jurisdictions, provincial transfer payments to colleges and universities have declined by 20 percent or more. Voluntary agencies which have long been leaders in adult education work have seen their funding plummet since 1990. As a result, educational institutions are trying to increase enrollments, class sizes and tuition fees while lowering delivery hours and total number of faculty. Voluntary agencies have curtailed major elements of their educational programming. The adult learner finds herself or himself in bigger classes, with fewer options for community-based learning.

- *Priority to user-pay programs and revenue-generating programs*— The most common response to the decline in funding is to eliminate programs that "lose money." The decision to cut programs is often based solely on economic criteria rather than on a more nuanced analysis of the contribution of the program to the development of our society. On the other hand, priority is given to programs where users can pay the full cost and generate revenues for other activities. This trend puts increasing downward pressure on access and raises important questions about how we finance lifelong learning.

- *Continuing education as an instrument for revenue generation*—Traditionally, continuing education programs have been offered by colleges, universities and school boards as a vehicle for opening these institutions to the community and supporting the learning goals of individuals and groups. The current funding crisis has caused institutions to cut continuing education programs unless they are making money. Little or no investment is made in community outreach or the development of new continuing education capacity. The tables have been turned, so that the main function of continuing education is to raise funds for the sponsoring institutions.

- *Increased priority for public-private partnerships and contract training*—Under the labels of "cost-sharing" and "partnerships," governments are reducing their contributions and devolving more responsibility for financing education to the private sector, to students and to educational institutions themselves. As a result, educational institutions are adopting more of an entrepreneurial attitude. They are actively seeking partnerships with the private sector and setting up units that sell training services. This has led to some innovative and mutually beneficial ventures in the educational field. It also tends to tie new program development to the needs and interests of the private sector rather than society at large.

- *Increased emphasis on marketing and on education as a product*— Given the heightened competition among educational institutions, marketing has become a high priority. On the one hand, this has helped institutions be more self-critical about their relative strengths and weaknesses. But it also leads them to redirect significant resources from program development to advertising and marketing campaigns.

- *Increased investment in fund raising*—Universities have long been good fund raisers. Increasingly, we see community colleges and other institutions developing their own fund-raising capacity. Like the initiatives above, this is a two-edged sword. On the one hand, it gives institutions greater flexibility and independence. However, on the other hand, it may introduce new disparities between institutions and divert resources away from learners.

- *Increased funding for job-related training*—Public educational institutions are tailoring their activities in order to attract job-related and labour-adjustment funding to their institutions. Programs that are not eligible for such funding are being shrunk or eliminated altogether. Such programs may include general education programs, theatre and other creative arts, or programs like nursing where the job market appears to be saturated in the short term. At the same time, private educational institutions are competing for the lucrative job-training dollars and can often win contracts because they are not constrained by collective agreements or public education policies.

- *Withdrawal of federal government from the funding and policy development arena*—As part of its strategy in addressing federal-provincial tensions, the federal government has decided to transfer most of its role in policy and funding for labour-force development and training to the provinces. In areas where the federal government retains responsibility, such as citizenship and culture, it is making dramatic cuts to program funding. Instead of using its influence to shape a common vision of adult education and lifelong learning for Canada, the federal government is jumping ship.

- *Decline in financial support for voluntary activity*—A strong voluntary sector is an essential component of a democratic society. It plays a vital role in nurturing citizenship, in lobbying for innovative policies and in creating new structures to improve the quality of life in communities. The role of voluntary agencies in adult education is crucial and yet they have been the hardest hit by the wave of funding cuts in the 1990s. Fortunately, we know from history that the voluntary sector is incredibly resourceful and resilient. While the funding crisis may cause some temporary setbacks in the work of these groups, we can remain confident that they will find new ways of continuing their work in adult education.

Taken together, these characteristics signal an important and potentially dangerous shift in the funding system for adult education in Canada. Clearly, it would be folly to underestimate the need to manage the short-term difficulties caused by government deficits and the vagaries of international money markets. At the same time, it is equally foolish to concentrate the bulk of our resources on solving the most immediate problems. Like good investment managers, we should have a mixed portfolio of strategies and funding programs. In his book *The Good Society,* Robert Bellah writes:

> The idea of education for citizenship in a complex world is not some quaint leftover from a nineteenth century curriculum. It is an essential task for a free society in the modern world.[43]

The current approach to funding fails to recognize the essential nature and breadth of the adult education endeavour. Our current investments in the area of citizenship education, community building, and cultural and social development are paltry in comparison with the dimensions of the task. Ultimately, the current cost-cutting measures are likely to cost us more in the long run.

---

[43] R. Bellah, *The Good Society* (New York: Knopf, 1991) p.177.

Adult Education in the Labour Movement

By D'Arcy Martin[44]

Myles Horton, who founded the Highlander Center in Tennessee and gave his long and productive life to grassroots education in the labour and civil rights movements, said, "Our job as a gardener or as an educator is to know that the potential is there or will unfold. People have a potential for growth; it's inside, it's in the seeds."[45]

That is part of the faith of most adult educators. Faith is what built the labour movement. Nobody would start a union based on a feasibility study. For that faith to be rekindled in a new generation requires careful attention to the union culture. Mike Newman of Australia emphasizes the differences among unions, but draws out five factors that are common:

1. Unionists own their union, and feel a right to control it.

2. Unionists unite, especially against management.

3. Unionists care beyond their immediate interests.

4. Unions deal with wages, which make them important to members, employers and governments.

5. Unionists often feel beleaguered, or under attack.[46]

Union culture doesn't just vary across unions, it changes over time. And it needs to change significantly in the years ahead. A key issue to be addressed again among labour educators is the balance among the three main political traditions: ideological, social and business unionism. Each current should be assessed critically, to see what it still has to offer workers in the future.

In ideological unionism, a broad social reform movement, such as social democracy or Marxism or Catholic social action, establishes a working-class wing. The function of this wing, a union structure, is to anchor the wider social vision in a working-class constituency. While viable in some countries like Nicaragua, such unionism in Canada has proven slow to respond to changes in the economic and social environment, and of limited value to members in their daily battles for dignity and fairness on the job.

In business unionism, a broad social consensus is assumed. Here, the union fixes problems and keeps its membership ahead of the game in wages and benefits. While still strong culturally, particularly in the construction trades,

---

[44] This is the last of three sections on adult education in the labour movement written by D'Arcy Martin for this edition of the book. See also Chapters 2 and 6.

[45] Myles Horton, *The Long Haul: An Autobiography*. With Judith Kohl and Herbert Kohl (New York: Doubleday, 1990) p.133.

[46] Michael Newman, *The Third Contract: Theory and Practice in Trade Union Training* (Sydney, Australia: Stewart Victor Publishing, 1993) p.16-20.

this perspective is eroded by the downsizing and re-engineering of the secure, high-waged jobs on which it is based.

In social unionism, a balance is struck between the social passion of the ideological current and the opportunistic ethos of the business current. Yet, as co-ordinated bargaining is attacked by the employers and unions are pressed to defend their members, social unionism risks being ambivalent and failing to inspire and mobilize its members in the face of a new employer offensive.

These approaches, then, need to be re-examined in the light of new conditions. For many union activists, the approach of popular education, with its participatory and creative power, is very attractive. Implied in it is a commitment to organize the unionized, to revive the social vision that launched the movement in the first place. Such a revival will oblige some truth telling about the ways that racist, anti-democratic and cowardly behaviour are still rewarded in parts of labour life. And it will mean re-committing to inclusion, to internal democracy, to celebration and to outreach.

Inclusion. Unions are being called on to include women, young people and people of colour to an unprecedented degree. Since the latter two are not dominant in numbers of votes in most unions, this requires some vision, some sense of where the movement's future lies. The combination of layoffs by seniority, political reaction and economic fear works against such vision.

A perspective of inclusion means the full menu of employment equity, such as hiring and promotion in the workplace and the informal practices of the union. But the front line of such battles is harassment and abusive behaviour among members. With the escalation of stress in many workplaces,[47] incidents of tension and violence are on the increase. A union commitment to address these issues up-front is needed. But an active commitment to unlearning past habits of dominance and exclusion is also required, and the pain and delicacy of this process needs to be more carefully and compassionately shared.[48]

Internal Democracy. Within labour itself, the skills of participatory decision making, of democratic communication, of productive problem solving, of simple good listening, are spread thin. These are process politics, not the kind of positional and electoral politics traditionally valued by the "players" in the labour leadership. Bad processes result in bad treatment of staff, in dodging creative ideas because of overload and in treating challenges as attacks.

This is particularly important given the rapidly changing nature of work. With new technologies that de-skill, with re-engineering processes that provoke anxiety and use it as a tool, the labour movement must put its own house

---

[47] Robert Karasek and Tores Theorell, *Healthy Work: Stress, Productivity and the Reconstruction of Working Life* (New York: Basic Books, 1990).

[48] See Bell Hooks, *Teaching to Transgress: Education as the Practice of Freedom* (New York: Routledge, 1994) esp. Chapter 4.

in order. Genuine unity is needed to negotiate funding from employers for the educational programs labour promotes. As public funding for education declines, and dues dollars shrink, bargaining for a form of paid educational leave from the employers becomes increasingly important.

Celebration. Workers need to create, as well as to fight. In fact, it is in celebration that people recover their hope, without which struggle is pointless. Union members engage in community building outside the union. And they know that apparently closed doors are not a barrier when there is a window open somewhere. As educator and artist dian marino used to say, "Look for the cracks in consent." Unevenly across the country, unionists have developed arts, heritage and media initiatives that blow our own horn and use the power of laughter to open doors or go around them.

Outreach. Labour educators need to link up with others who share a vision of adult education for democracy. Here there are opportunities to share tools, to learn from the experience of other social sectors, and to draw nourishment for dealing with the large number of vocal adversaries. In this way, the profile of genuine, problem-posing adult education can also be increased. Networks are needed that are capable of sharing lessons across sectors and helping both individuals and organizations to keep balance in stormy weather. As the organizational core of the social resistance to fragmented, top-down, corporate-style education, the labour movement has a responsibility here.

In these areas, labour educators face very practical choices. It takes time in courses to help people learn to listen critically; it takes nerve to argue that it isn't just for quantifiable goals that people are attracted to union life but because it gives them a taste of a better way of being together; it takes imagination to value the creative streak in course participants and the commitment of labour-positive artists by building both into our educational events. And it takes stamina to keep seeking common ground with people whose reflexes are different.

Marge Piercy speaks to the beauty of work, including the work of the labour educator in the title poem of her collection "To Be of Use":

> The work of the world is common as mud.
> Botched, it smears the hands, crumbles to dust.
> But the thing worth doing well done
> has a shape that satisfies, clean and evident.
> Greek amphoras for wine or oil,
> Hopi vases that held corn, are put in museums
> but you know they were made to be used.
> The pitcher cries for water to carry
> and a person for work that is real.

May union courses have a shape that satisfies, and may all Canadians have work that is real.

Canadian Adult Education and the International Community

No account of the concerns and character of Canadian adult education in recent decades would be complete without reference to the active part played by Canadians and Canadian institutions in the world community. Many Canadian organizations—churches, voluntary organizations, co-operatives, labour unions, professional associations and so on—have sent personnel or in some way have contributed to international aid efforts. Some of these organizations took advantage of funds which were at one time available from the Canadian International Development Agency (CIDA) on a matching basis for such work. There have been several organizations—CIDA, the World University Service of Canada, the Canadian University Service Overseas—which have specialized in such activities and have sent and maintained large numbers of Canadians abroad, many of them involved in organizing adult education work or teaching adults. CIDA has also financed projects which have been carried out by others, for instance, the Association of Universities and Colleges of Canada, the Association of Canadian Community Colleges, the Canadian Association for Adult Education, and many individual institutions. Individual Canadians have been recruited by international organizations such as UNESCO, the World Health Organization, the International Labour Organization and others, to work at headquarters or in Third World countries carrying out educational work. Some Canadians have occupied key positions in international bodies—Eugene Bussiere and John Cairns at UNESCO, Paul Belanger at the UNESCO Institute at Hamburg, Kalman Kaplansky and John Whitehouse at the International Labour Organization and so on—and organized work in many countries.[49]

In addition, successful and innovative adult education projects in Canada which were seen by other countries as having something to offer to their development processes were invited to share their experience. The Antigonish Movement in Nova Scotia and other Canadian co-operative organizations were active in this work in recent decades, as they had been earlier.[50] National Farm Radio Forum was also adapted for use in other countries. The Challenge for Change projects of the National Film Board, which made use of film and videotape as part of the community development process, was of great interest in other countries, and persons connected with it were asked to go abroad and share their expertise.[51]

---

[49] For an account of government-financed aid programs, with emphasis on "human resource development" aspects, see J. McNie & D. Audreae in B.B. Cassara (Ed.), *Adult Education through World Collaboration* (Malabar, FA: Krieger, 1995).

[50] E. Stabler, *Founders* (Edmonton: University of Alberta, 1987); P. Milner (Ed.), *Human Development Through Social Change* (Antigonish: Nova Scotia, Formac Publishing, 1979).

[51] D.B. Jones, *Movies and Memoranda* (Ottawa: Canadian Film Institute, 1981); The John Grierson Project, *John Grierson and the NFB* (Montreal: ECW Press, 1984).

A particularly important Canadian contribution during this period was the creation of the International Council for Adult Education (ICAE), largely as a result of leadership provided by a Canadian, Dr. Roby Kidd. International co-operation in the field of adult education at the inter-governmental level had been encouraged and facilitated since World War II by the relevant United Nations specialized agency, UNESCO. Roby Kidd played a leading role in UNESCO activities in the latter part of the 1950s, and it was partly in recognition of this fact that UNESCO accepted Canada's invitation to hold its Second World Conference on Adult Education in Montreal, in 1960. Kidd was elected president of that conference and by means of resourceful leadership brought the conference to a successful conclusion, in spite of it being a time of heightened Cold War tensions. As a result he emerged from the conference as one of the best-known adult education leaders in the world.

It was recognized in the field that an organization such as UNESCO could accomplish only so much. The resources it could devote to any one of its enormous range of interests were limited, and such an inter-governmental organization was of necessity somewhat unwieldy and slow to act. There had been a non-governmental international body in the field between the wars, the World Association for Adult Education, but it was disbanded during World War II. There was some discussion at the Montreal Conference in 1960 of establishing a new organization, but the time and conditions were judged not to be appropriate. Kidd was committed to the idea of creating such a body and as the time for the Third UNESCO World Conference approached, which was to be held in Tokyo in 1972, he began to encourage leaders in the field in various parts of the world to think in those terms. At Tokyo, he "lobbied" on behalf of the idea and arranged for a meeting of interested delegates (outside the formal agenda) to discuss the idea. From this meeting he received strong support and in the ensuing months he sought out persons and organizations willing to support such a new body. In the following year, 1973, the ICAE was formally established with its headquarters in Toronto. Kidd thereafter served for six years as secretary-general of the organization, with early funding coming from CIDA, the Kellogg Foundation, the governments of West Germany, Iran and the United Kingdom, and international organizations such as OECD, UNESCO and the Commonwealth Secretariat. It is generally agreed that Kidd's leadership was the crucial factor in the creation of the Council which, since its formation, has done much important work in the international community with respect to adult education and development concerns.[52] Kidd remained a leading figure in the ICAE until his death in

---

[52] J. Lowe, *The Education of Adults*; N. Cochrane et al., *J.R. Kidd: An International Legacy of Learning* (Vancouver: University of British Columbia/Centre for Continuing Education, 1986).

1982, and the headquarters of the organization continues to be located in Toronto.

In more recent years the ICAE has become increasingly significant to adult education in Canada. Whereas during the 1970s it was of interest to a number of Canadian practitioners simply by virtue of the fact that the headquarters of the organization was located in Toronto, in the subsequent decade, under the leadership of Kidd's successor as secretary-general, Dr. Budd Hall, the work of the organization began to have more impact on adult education in Canada as a field of practice. This arose largely from the fact that the Council established specialized ongoing programs in certain subject matter areas which are just as significant to Canadian society as they are to that of Third World countries. Four examples are: learning in the context of environmental education; the role of women and the contributions of feminist critique and practice; education in relation to the peace and human rights movements; and services in the field of literacy and adult basic education. In all of these areas, Canadian adult educators drew information and inspiration from the activities of the ICAE and from the international sharing of experience by means particularly of the Council's journal, *Convergence*, and by other means of communication. In all of the areas mentioned above, the work of the Council gave encouragement to "popular education" approaches. At the time of writing, the membership of the ICAE includes over one hundred national, regional and sectoral organizations and represents "the worldwide adult education movement of non-governmental organizations working at the grassroots, national and regional levels."[53]

In recent years, Canadians have taken particular interest as well in the work of UNESCO's International Institute for Education in Hamburg. This began in the 1970s, when the Institute did significant work on developing the theoretical basis of the concept of lifelong learning, something to which two Canadians particularly, Roby Kidd and Alan Thomas, had made valuable pioneering contributions in the previous decade. Interest in the Institute was heightened when an outstanding adult educator from Quebec, Paul Belanger, was appointed as its director. The Institute has served the field well in a number of important ways, and has come into prominence particularly in the process leading up to UNESCO's Fifth International Conference on Adult Education, to be held in Hamburg in 1997. In that connection the Institute has organized a complex process which will culminate in a worldwide survey of research in adult education.

---

[53] International Council for Adult Education, *Annual Report 1995*.

Disparate Forces in the Field

Many aspects of the foregoing discussion document the rapid growth of adult education in recent years and indicate something of the extent to which the education of adults has been accepted increasingly as an important social and personal concern. We have been moving towards the ideal stated in the well-known *1919 Report* on adult education in Great Britain, that education should become "both universal and lifelong,"[54] though the limitations as to who is being served and who is not is a matter of widespread concern. There are a number of identifiable groups in our society which are not being served by adult education as well as are those with higher incomes and with higher levels of formal education. These groups are identified in a 1982 publication issued by the two Canadian national adult education organizations, *From the Adult's Point of View*. They were listed as: women, Native people, older adults, the handicapped, immigrants, adults with low educational attainment, and francophones outside Quebec.[55]

Although there is clearly a great deal to be done yet—in Canada as elsewhere—in terms of what has been described as the democratization of adult education, the field has made substantial strides in the last three decades, in terms of the general acceptance and understanding of the idea; its acceptance as a basis for public policy in areas such as work force training, public health, citizenship and economic development; the development of institutional structures, curricula and methodology; and the training of a professional staff for the field.

Reference has already been made to the expansion of government's role in vocational and technical training. In addition, there have been a series of commissions appointed by government in recent years which have in their reports placed emphasis on the importance of adult education. There have of course been reports commissioned specifically on adult education and related policies, and this in itself has been a sign of increased recognition of the field. But what has been more remarkable is the fact that public bodies which were asked to examine other subjects have also chosen to give prominent place to the role of adult education. The Worth Commission in Alberta and the Wright Commission in Ontario, both of which reported in 1972 and gave a prominent place to recommendations concerning adult and lifelong education, have already been mentioned, as have the two government-commissioned studies of paid educational leave. Perhaps typical in some respects of the increased recognition accorded to adult education was the report of the Parliamentary

---

[54] *The 1919 Report*, Report of the Adult Education Committee of the Ministry of Reconstruction of the United Kingdom (Nottingham: University of Nottingham/Department of Adult Education, 1980 [1919]) p.4.

[55] CAAE/ICEA, *From the Adult's Point of View* (Toronto/Montreal: CAAE/ICEA, 1982).

Task Force on Employment Opportunities for the 1980s. Though the mandate of this body was focussed on employment and economic development, ten out of the sixteen recommendations featured in its summary of outstanding recommendations dealt with education and training. Finally, it should be pointed out that in several of the provinces in Canada in the past two decades, ministries of government have been established which have been devoted in large part to the education of adults. The designations have included phrases such as "further education" and "job training."

Another indication of the increasing acceptance of the importance of adult education has been the establishment of institutional structures which have been put in place largely to meet the educational needs of adults. A number of these have already been dealt with in this chapter—provincial broadcasting organizations, distance education agencies, and perhaps most pervasive in their influence, the community college and institute systems in the various provinces.

No figures exist to document this matter, but the "work force" of adult education in this country has clearly expanded enormously in this period. Reference was made in Chapter 9 to Cyril Houle's analysis of those who provide leadership in the adult education enterprise.[56] He saw them falling in three categories: full-time career adult educators; part-time teachers of adults (whose chief livelihood and/or expertise lies elsewhere, such as the business accountant who teaches a night class in his specialty); and the volunteers, who organize, give leadership to, and teach so much of adult education activity. A field which has evolved in Canada over forty years from involving one in twenty-five Canadians (1960) to one in three Canadians (1996) has clearly grown in all those dimensions, but perhaps most noticeably in the career or full-time category. With a great expansion in the number of institutions actively engaged in offering programs, the number of administrators and program organizers alone has clearly increased many fold. The number of full-time teachers of adults, in the new college systems and in the private sector particularly, has also expanded enormously. And a number of more specialized fields within adult education have developed during this period: for instance, curriculum developers, media and computer specialists, counsellors of adults, and consultants in the field. It is not known how many hundreds of thousands of persons are now involved in the field of adult education in one of these capacities, but the number is certainly of that order.

A further indication of the growth of the field is the increase in the number of persons who seek professional education in adult education. Those who engage in such study are mainly those who are in full-time positions in the

---

[56] C.O. Houle in M.S. Knowles (Ed.), *Handbook of Adult Education in the United States* (Chicago: Adult Education Association of the USA, 1960).

field, and predominantly those who are in, or wish to be in, administrative, programming or other specialized roles. University graduate degree programs in the field of adult education, as described in an earlier chapter, have grown from offerings at two institutions in 1960 to fifteen at the present time (with other universities as well offering individual courses, as distinct from degree programs). In the 1990s there has been an expansion of under-graduate degrees in the field as well. Within these programs there are several thousand persons engaged in degree studies in adult education, and most if not all these programs are not able to accept all the qualified persons who apply to enter.

There is extensive training of adult educators in other settings as well. Business and industry typically provide such training for the instructors within their programs. Most of the large educational institutions, public and private, provide opportunities for the persons they employ to teach adults to learn more about teaching. Many of the voluntary organizations, such as the Y.M. and Y.W.C.A., the Red Cross, the St. John's Ambulance Association, the Guide and Scout organizations, and many churches, provide training in the field for their leaders and instructors.

There has as well been a rapid increase in the volume of research and publication in Canada on aspects of adult education. The growth of graduate degree programs has perhaps been the most important factor in the expansion of research activity. The volume of publication about adult education has grown very quickly since the beginning of the 1970s. In 1970, there were no academic journals devoted to publishing in this field, though the Canadian Association for Adult Education was publishing its more "popular" journal, *Continuous Learning*. Since that time, four academic, juried journals have been created, all of which are publishing at the time of writing. As well, commercial publishers and university presses across Canada have taken an increasing interest and have published a number of volumes over the years. In addition, many Canadian researchers publish in journals and books which are produced outside Canada. The most recent survey of material being published by Canadian scholars in adult education revealed that in the six years from 1982 to 1987, there had been 1,483 publications in the field, written by 551 different Canadians.[57] This represented a very substantial change from the situation which existed in 1970.

Further to the matter of research and publication, during recent years there have been some studies published which have moved our view of the field to a different level of analysis. Much examination of the historical development of adult education in this country has been of a traditional type, based on institutional and biographical studies, and generally approached with little evidence of a strong theoretical framework or an informing worldview on the part of

---

[57] J.R.A. Dobson, "Canadian Adult Education Literature," *Caravan, 1*, 2 (1987).

the authors. In the past two decades this has begun to change. One of the earliest book-length studies to appear which involved the application of theory from the social sciences was Faris's *The Passionate Educators*,[58] a study of the CAAE and other voluntary associations and the role of interlocking "elites" in the development of the CAAE and broadcasting policy. Another significant study, of a very different type, was Lotz's book *Understanding Canada*, a somewhat journalistic and strongly revisionist view of Canadian experience with community development. Gregory Baum's *Catholics and Canadian Socialism* was not essentially a book about adult education, but it brought to the field from another quarter an arresting view of the Antigonish Movement. Another important work is the study by Hayden Roberts, entitled *Culture and Adult Education*, which presents a comparative study of adult education as it has developed in two provinces, Quebec and Alberta, and utilizing theoretical models from political science and sociology. Michael Welton edited a book entitled *Knowledge for the People,* which appeared in 1987, and another, *In Defense of the Lifeworld: Critical Perspectives on Adult Learning (1995)* which along with Lotz's work have encouraged a somewhat more radical and revisionist approach to the history of the field.[59] Alan Thomas, in a monograph which was published in 1985 (expanded to book-length treatment in 1990), utilized insights from sociology, political science, cultural and communications theory in a study of the relationship between public policy, learning and education in our society.[60] Gordon Selman related certain aspects of the history of adult education in this century to the social history of Canada in his *Citizenship and the Adult Education Movement in Canada*, which appeared in 1991.[61] These several works, selected as examples of various perspectives and not intended to be a complete list, are representative of analyzes of the field which are based on more theoretical approaches, and in some cases a more strongly revisionist worldview than has been true of much of the literature of the field. They are no doubt as well an indication of some future directions of scholarship in adult education.

As will have become abundantly clear in the foregoing chapter about the "contemporary scene," the picture is remarkably complex. At the time of writing it would appear, on the one hand, that the extent of overall participation in adult education continues to increase. Because of the substantial de-

---

[58] R. Faris, *The Passionate Educators* (Toronto: Peter Martin, 1975).

[59] M. Welton (Ed.), *Knowledge for the People* (Toronto: OISE, 1987); M. Welton, (Ed.), *In Defense of the Lifeworld: Critical Perspectives on Adult Learning* (Albany, NY: State University of New York Press, 1995).

[60] A.M. Thomas in M. Hogue & C. Quinn (Eds.), *Learning in Society: Toward a New Paradigm* (Ottawa: Canadian Commission for UNESCO, 1985); and *Beyond Education: New Perspectives on Society's Management of Education* (Toronto: Jossey-Bass/MacMillan, 1990).

[61] G. Selman, *Citizenship and the Adult Education Movement in Canada* (Vancouver: University of British Columbia/Center for Continuing Education, 1991).

mand for learning opportunities, and because of government policies, there has recently been an enormous expansion in the number and variety of private sector providers in the field. Although the overall enterprise has continued to expand, there have been significant shifts or dislocations within the field. The "user-pay" policies which have been forced upon many providers have resulted in sharp fee increases in many sectors of the field and have led to the curtailment or complete elimination of many services to disadvantaged persons. The latter have been adversely affected as well by cuts in social service and work force development programs which are designed to meet the training and educational needs of the disadvantaged. These and related developments have contributed to an expansion of provision within the voluntary sector and to an expansion as well of "popular education" approaches which link learning and education with efforts to bring about social change. Distance education in its many forms has been one of the major areas of expansion in recent years. The work force of adult education has grown enormously and the opportunities for professional training in the field have expanded and become more varied. It is reasonable to state that adult and lifelong education have been ever more widely accepted in society as a whole and in government policies. In terms of public policy, the emphasis has been placed on further academic or formal education and on vocational and technical training. Adult education continues to be a highly decentralized enterprise in Canadian society, with many sponsors, public and private, many success stories and many problems. In many respects it reflects the nature of the society as a whole, and as such is subject to the same range of critiques and points of view as to its nature and with respect to how well or otherwise it is meeting the needs of the Canadian people.

Lumber camp workers in class (location not known).
Courtesy of Frontier College.

13
Future Prospects

In the previous chapter we examined some characteristics of the Canadian scene in the past thirty years and some trends in the development of adult education in that period. Our concern in this final chapter is some thoughts about the future—though it will be no surprise to the reader to know that the authors have no magical powers to foresee the future. We look to the future in somewhat the same spirit as did St. Augustine, who stated in his Confessions: "Nor is it fitly said, there are three times, past, present and future; ... it might more fitly be said, there are three times; a present of things past, a present of things present, and a present of things future." We, like others, have questions and concerns. Many of them are based on the experience of the last few decades and on what we perceive to be trends at the present time.

The first and most obvious is the anticipation of continued rapid growth of participation in adult education. We have already noted the remarkable growth of the field, especially in the last forty years, when participation by adults in Canada has grown from less than 5 percent a year to approximately 33 percent. From everything we know about the forces that have prompted this dramatic growth—technological and social change, changing employment patterns, the rising expectations and desire for change on the part of various social groups and so on—it seems safe to predict a continuation of growth in the participation rate. There may be change in terms of the nature of the providers of learning opportunities and the organization and methodology of the field, but the phenomenon of adult learning will presumably continue to grow, and at a dramatic rate.

In the last three decades there have been at least three sets of forces which have had major impact on what might be termed the "foundations" of adult education. The first has flowed from the increasing acceptance in society of the necessity of adult and lifelong learning and has had the effect of strengthening adult educators' sense of the identity and importance of their work. The second group of forces has somewhat the opposite effect, reinforcing divisions within the field of practice and raising vexing questions. Finally, there have been the effects in the most recent fifteen or twenty years of fiscal austerity, neo-conservative attitudes and a "user-pay" approach to social services. A new context has been created, raising problems for some parts of the field which have required new—and not always satisfactory—approaches.

On the one hand, educators who are engaged in working with adults and who take an interest and feel a stake in the field as a whole have many reasons to believe that much progress has been made. As has just been mentioned, the growth in the field has been phenomenal. Government support of adult education, particularly in the vocational and academic areas, has increased enormously. A whole new institutional system has emerged in Canada—the community colleges—which has from its inception attached considerable importance to meeting a wide variety of adult learning needs. Royal commissions and other major studies, many of a type which in past decades tended to ignore or make only passing reference to adult education, have given major emphasis to the importance of the field. Government and other planners at the national and international levels are according an important place in development planning to the education of adults. Some figures such as Freire, Illich and Coombs, reports of the Club of Rome, the comprehensive UNESCO reports of 1972 and 1996, and those of other international bodies, which have attracted the attention of the educational, economic and social planning sectors throughout the world, have attached importance to adult education as part of their proposals. An increasing number of the priorities that are espoused by governments—clearly in the belief that they will find favour with the voting public—such as vocational training, literacy training, environmental, public health and multi-cultural education, are ones which consist of, or rely heavily upon, forms of adult learning. There are many grounds for adult educators to feel that the field has gained enormously in recognition as well as participation.

At the same time, there are a variety of forces which are preventing, or at least working against, a sense of cohesion and common cause among adult educators. It should be said at the outset that there has never really been a time when those involved in the panorama of activities that constitute the broad field of adult education have in any real sense felt that they were part of a common endeavour. Few of those working in training programs in business and industry, or in professional continuing education, for instance, have ever had a sense of common cause with community development workers or those within social movements who were part of the search for social change. Few of those who have adopted a professional and "service ethic" approach to adult education in recent decades feel they have a great deal in common with those who seek to use it as an instrument of social change. Few of those who work with adults, but whose primary personal identification is with their institution or with their subject matter specialty, have any sense of being part of the adult education "movement" as it has developed historically.

Our constitutional arrangements in Canada are a further factor working against a sense of cohesion in the field. The fact that public education in this country is not one system but at least thirteen (ten provinces, two [soon to be three] territories, and the federal government) means that most educators have a "compartmentalized" view of the field. Federal policies at the time of writing, involving as they do the further devolution of powers in the field of vocational training to the provinces, simply accentuate the sectionalism which exists. To the extent that the Canadian Association for Adult Education and its French language counterpart, the ICEA, represented an effort to span these gulfs, their current tribulations are perhaps symbolic of the increasing lack of cohesion.

A second, and perhaps more important, factor preventing a cohesive view is the effect of specialization of role and the wide dispersal of adult education in society. The enormous variety of organizations and institutions which sponsor adult education—chess clubs, churches, colleges, unions, private sector schools, the women's movement, educational institutions, government departments, the military and so on—in itself poses a challenge. As well, there is an increasing specialization of function within the field. To the long-familiar roles of administrator, teacher and programme have now been added many others—curriculum developer, counsellor, computer and media specialist, and consultant, to name only some. What do a course designer in a distance education institution, a specialist in multi-cultural programs in a local Y.W.C.A. and a teacher of bread making in a local school board night class feel they have in common professionally?

A third barrier to a sense of cohesion in adult education is the effects of institutionalization. As some of the providing institutions in the field have become large systems in themselves, such as university-based continuing education, large training units within industry, educational units within the labour movement, or training groups within government, such areas easily come to be felt by their constituents to be worlds of their own. More and more teachers of adults are employed on a full-time basis, but such persons typically come to this work on the basis of their competence in their subject matter fields and do not necessarily identify themselves with adult education as a field of activity.

Finally, and perhaps most basic, there are profound philosophical and ideological differences within the field. For instance, adult educators in social movements, popular education or in community development projects may feel they have little in common with those in the public institutional systems, much less with those in business and industry. The former see adult education as one of the instruments of bringing about change in society, and they tend to see the other segments of the field as devoted to adjusting people to the system, rather than helping people to examine the system and, if they see fit, to change it. Many who work as educators on behalf of disadvantaged people in our society find that they cannot or do not choose to separate their educational activities from more general efforts to improve the lot of the groups in which they are working. On the other hand, many of those in institutional settings have never appreciated the connection between adult education and social change, or reject as inappropriate the harnessing of adult education, as they understand it, to the promotion of social change.

The balance of the forces of cohesion and of division in adult education may be placed in the historical context of recent decades. As has been suggested earlier, in the discussion of the emergence of professional training in the field, there was for many decades an assumption that the various branches of adult education—for instance in such areas as agricultural extension, the educational institutions and the world of voluntary organizations—were essentially worlds unto themselves. The emergence of organizations of adult educators and of academic professional training which spanned the various jurisdictions were phenomena that began to build a sense of common interests, if not common cause. In Canada, for instance, a national organization devoted to the promotion of adult education, the Canadian Association for Adult Education, was formed in 1935. The CAAE came to represent some elements in the field, but in the 1960s, when adult education activity expanded enormously, the organization consciously attempted to interest some of those in other major areas of growth such as vocational training, the emerging college sector, counselling and human relations training, in linking themselves with the rest of the field through the CAAE. This was a difficult process to manage, however, as the traditional sense of being a "social movement," which had inspired some of the leaders of the CAAE, came into conflict with an emerging professionalism of those in other sectors. A short-lived experiment during the 1960s of trying to consolidate the emerging professional organizations in the provinces with the national organization came unglued late in the decade—"the center would not hold."[1] The 1970s and since have seen the further development of the provincial organizations, but many of them, in their turn, could not command the loyalty and support of an increasingly diversified field of practice and other more specialized bodies attracted practitioners. We have seen the emergence of specialized organizations such as the Canadian Association for Distance Education, the Movement for Canadian Literacy and the Canadian Association for the Study of Adult Education, to name only three, each representing the emergence of a field within a field.

The 1980s and since have brought further challenges. Adult education has continued to grow vigourously during these two decades and practice in the

---

[1] G. Selman, "Alan Thomas and the Canadian Association for Adult Education 1961-1970" in *Adult Education in Canada: Historical Essays* (Toronto: Thompson Educational, 1995).

field has become more specialized and segmented. To the somewhat natural effects of these forces, however, have been added those which have flowed from the neo-conservative social philosophy which has influenced public policy in these years. The effects of the latter have been such as to drive an even deeper wedge between different elements of adult education in Canada. For one thing, the policies of downsizing and privatization of many government services (in adult education terms, particularly in vocational and technical education) have reduced the scale of the public sector's role in adult education and spawned a major expansion of private sector providers. Further, with the restriction of budgetary support for public educational institutions, these bodies have been forced to become more self-supporting financially. The pressure has been particularly hard on those institutional activities, including adult or continuing education, which are seen by many to be of low priority among institutional functions. The adult education activities carried out by public school boards, colleges and universities have thus come under severe financial pressures. They have had to become more self-supporting out of student fees and in many cases are required to return a net profit to the parent institution every year. This in turn has in many cases forced the adult or continuing education units of the institutions to put increased emphasis on those parts of their program which can operate on the basis of increasingly high student fees and to curtail or eliminate those services—typically services to more disadvantaged persons—which cannot "pay their way." In many cases, programs in adult basic education, English (or French) as a second language, literacy education and special services to special needs learners have been reduced or eliminated. Whereas at an earlier time, the adult educator who was employed by a college or a university might well be involved in a wide range of types of educational programming (credit courses, professional in-service development, general interest programs and courses about contentious public issues), the person's role may in more recent years, because of institutional policies, be very limited with respect to general interest programs and exclude the community issue or public affairs type of course entirely. In this way, cleavages in the field have been further accentuated.

There has been another phenomenon at work that has tended to divide adult educators. As life has become more difficult for various kinds of institutions and organizations in these years of restricted budgets, adult education and some other functions that tend to be low priority in the institutions have had to look to their political base of support within their parent agencies. The adult education units, rather than stressing the fact that they "represent" the interest of the community in its claim for a share of institutional attention and resources, are increasingly forced into a position of being "institutional people." Many adult education units of public educational institutions have increasingly "faded into the woodwork" of their parent body and are less interested than they once were in maintaining common cause, or even contact, with other elements of adult education outside their own institutional system.

* * *

In fact, the question must be raised—and will, if anything, be even more relevant in the future—as to whether it is sensible to think in terms of "adult education" any longer as a single field. There is ample confusion at the present time about the boundaries or limits of the field. Reference was made in the first chapter to the forty-year-old woman who returns to her education. If she attends college or university full time, or even part time in the daytime, she will not show up in the adult education statistics. But if she took the same program by part-time evening study, she likely would. Under any of these circumstances she would fit into the definition of adult education that has been produced by UNESCO, but she does not, if a daytime student, fall within most Canadian definitions. That there are deep cleavages among adult education practitioners at the present time is attested to by the fact that in most provinces there are now ten or twelve separate organizations of adult educators. Some of the reasons for these cleavages have already been described.

But the picture is rapidly becoming much more complicated than this. What has been referred to above is a lack of cohesion among adult education practitioners who function in the world of education and training. As was described in the previous chapter, there is also at the present time an emerging realization of ways in which adult and lifelong learning can be incorporated as a strategy within other fields of professional activity, such as organizational development, management training, social group work and community organization, community planning and community development. Present indications are that educational specialists in these other worlds of practice will likely be trained and employed for the most part with little contact with the field of adult education as it has grown up over the decades.[2]

Some practitioners, perhaps especially some who have been in the field for many years, may see virtue in attempting to maintain the idea of a widely inclusive field of adult education. It is undoubtedly the case that most others do not feel this way, and in fact do not see that there is anything important at stake in maintaining a sense of cohesion among those in the various specialized fields of practice.

With reference to the world of adult education practice, as we look towards the future, it is possible to discern several main clusters or groupings of adult education services. They are not discreet or mutually exclusive categories, and some providing agencies may be operating in more than one area.

---

[2] See, for instance, S.A. Rosell et al., *Changing Maps: Governing in a World of Rapid Change* (Ottawa: Carleton University, 1995).

1. *Academic, credential and vocational.* This category includes much of the work done by the formal educational systems (public and private), business and industry, professional associations, and vocational and technical education in the public and private sectors. Much of this activity is publicly mandated and subsidized, much is provided by employers, but an appreciable amount is simply purchased by individuals in the marketplace. In the neo-conservative 1980s and 1990s, it has been this sector of the field which has been the predominant focus of government support.

2. *Personal interest and development.* This includes much of what has been termed "general interest" or, in some settings, "community education," and relates to hobbies and the expanding of personal skills, understanding or horizons. It includes the arts, humanities, hobby-related and cultural matters generally, as well as other areas of personal development and inter-personal skills. Some such activities are provided by the public educational system, but where that is the case, there is a growing tendency for such work to be required to be financially self-supporting, if not profit making. A great, perhaps growing, portion of this kind of adult education is being provided by the private sector, including membership organizations and local community and neighbourhood agencies of various kinds.

3. *Social action and social change.* This includes various kinds of educational activity which are dedicated to, or "harnessed" to active efforts to critique and change society in some way. (Note that it is meant to include education in relation to these matters, not propaganda, though the line is sometimes difficult to draw, partly because the sponsoring organization is frequently not interested in drawing it.) While the public education system is mandated to be active in type 1, above, and on a fee-for-service basis provides some of type 2, it has of late done little in this third area, and the trend is perhaps in the direction of complete withdrawal. The sponsors of activity in this third area tend to be groups and organizations whose purpose is to seek social change—social movements (environment, women's movements, peace and disarmament and so on), groups which are broadly humanitarian in purpose (human rights, United Nations groups, some churches and so on), or groups which are working on behalf of parts of the population who are suffering under a sense of grievance (First Nations people, older persons, some labour groups, the poor, handicapped persons and so on). In some other societies, this third category has for some time been described as "popular education," and the term is coming into more widespread use in Canada as well.

To these divisions, which are based on a combination of content and general programming approaches, can be added others which arise from the specializations of delivery modes and the rapidly developing technology of education.

* * *

To the extent that the foregoing represents a fair picture of some of the forces at work in the field of adult education, many questions present themselves concerning the future.

The first has to do with the organization of the field. If we perceive the division of the field into something like the three major sections described above, what are to be the relationships among providers within and among these sectors? In the first category, that of formal or credit study and vocational/technical and in-service continuing education, there are already some strong organizational structures in place. In the public sector, these include the machinery and policy structures of government, as well as strong sectional organizations such as the Association of Universities and Colleges of Canada, the Association of Community Colleges of Canada and the like. In the area of adult education, there are also some reasonably strong national associations, such as the Canadian Association for University Continuing Education. While these sectors of the field have shown little inclination to co-operate on a broad front across institutional boundaries, there is a great deal of consultation and co-operative effort within specific programs. There are articulation agreements between colleges and universities, partnerships between universities and/or colleges and professional bodies concerning continuing professional education, and working relationships established between some sectors of business and industry and the institutional providers of educational and training programs, public and private. This sector of adult education is made up to a large extent of the "big battalions" of educational providers—big government, big policy strength, big institutions, big systems and big budgets. Although they typically have many strengths on which to draw, to the extent that adult or continuing education is still a marginal activity in some of these organizations, their paths may be far from smooth. There are signs in some jurisdictions of provincial ministries of education (under their various names) taking an increased interest in the co-ordination of such work—most often in the name of budget efficiencies.

In the second cluster, that of general interest and self-development activities, which represents a major part of the field overall, we tend to have the "patternless mosaic" of services and providers that has historically been typical of the field of adult education. A great deal of this work is done within membership organizations on behalf of their members, but much is provided for the general public as well, by public institutions—universities, colleges, school boards, community centers, neighbourhood houses and the like. There are as well a large number of voluntary, non-profit, church and proprietary agencies which provide programs of this kind. As a general rule, there has been no attempt to co-ordinate or bring order into this field of offerings. The outstanding exception is that of the Province of Alberta and its Further Education Council policy, which channels public funds into the support of adult education activities offered by community organizations if they are co-ordinated through local planning councils. The Alberta experience is generally seen to be an enlightened one and as well to be largely responsible for the fact that Alberta has the highest participation rates in adult education of any jurisdiction in Canada. But under present austerity budget conditions, it seems unlikely that other provinces/territories will follow Alberta's example, at least in the near future.

The third sector, that part of adult education linked closely with efforts to bring about social change, is developing rapidly in Canadian society. Much of it is sponsored by social movements, such as the environmental, human rights, peace and disarmament groups, and by groups suffering under grievances or disadvantages, such as the women's movement, First Nations groups, the poor, and some cultural and ethnic groups. Their efforts are almost by definition separate from each other because they are based in the particular characteristics of the conditions being faced by the different groups. In perhaps most instances, the adult education involved is maintained and managed by the group or movement itself, but in some cases "outside" sources—social work agencies, independent consultants—are playing an active role. It is likely that somewhat more communication among and perhaps co-ordination of providers in this sector will develop in the coming years.

A second major question which arises from the present circumstances has to do with the future of what may be generally termed citizenship education. By this is meant everything from conveying knowledge about government and how it works (what has traditionally been termed "civics") through to active involvement in the community change processes. It has to do with the participation of citizens in the workings of democratic society and to community economic development. There has been a trend in recent years which has involved the diminution of the role of the public educational institutions in citizenship education for adults.[3] Under their altered financial situation and perhaps for other reasons as well, the continuing education units of these institutions have retreated from much, in many instances all, of their work of this kind. The social movements and other interested parties are active in this area, and much useful work is being done. But the question does arise as to whether our citizens are adequately served when their knowledge about social change and particular public affairs issues is based on the partisan views of the movements and the episodic and sometimes slanted views of the mass media. There is widespread concern on the part of experts from various fields and from many in the general public that our democratic practices are being

---

[3] G. Selman, *Citizenship and the Adult Education Movement in Canada* (Vancouver: University of British Columbia/Centre for Continuing Education, 1991).

dangerously weakened and that executive and administrative decision making is coming to dominate public life.[4]

Many adult educators are concerned about this question. How can we strengthen the voice of the public interest, as distinct from private interest in Canadian life? How can we reinforce what Roselle, Coleman, Putnam and others have termed our "social capital"—the "network of civic engagement" in our society?[5] Part of the answer may lie with the creation of independent research and educational organizations devoted to the study of public questions. We have some of those now, but there is widespread dismay, or at least concern, about the socio-political biases that appear to guide their actions. Can we create such agencies which are more democratically based and which could be of greater assistance to our citizens in the examination of public questions? The device of the Royal Commission has in many instances served Canadian society well, but what is being looked for now is a more sustained and broadly based approach, one which can operate over a range of questions, as different concerns appear on the public agenda. The search goes on.

The Scandinavian countries, most notably Sweden and Denmark, have for many decades approached this matter through the use of public funds to support and strengthen the educational work of recognized associations in their countries that are engaged in the examination of public questions and citizenship education generally.[6] It is no accident that Sweden has the highest participation rates in adult education of any country in the world. One important characteristic of the Swedish system is that although the state grants funds to these educational associations in support of their work there is no attempt to control the content or point of view taken in the work. It is apparently believed that what is most important is not the particular point of view taken in the educational endeavours but that people are thereby engaged in the consideration of public affairs questions. Somewhat the same assumptions presumably lay behind the small grants provided annually by the Canadian government to our two national adult education associations, the CAAE and the ICEA, but even these have been terminated recently. One question that presents itself, therefore, as we look to the future of adult education and its relationship to our society, is how as a people we should provide for learning related to the citizen's role in Canadian life. Are we content to leave this

---

[4] See J.R. Saul, *The Unconscious Civilization* (Concord, Ontario: Anansi, 1995); R. Gwyn, *Nationalism without Walls* (Toronto: McClelland & Stewart, 1995); P.C. Newman, *The Canadian Revolution* (Toronto: Viking, 1995).

[5] R.D. Putnam, *Making Democracy Work* (Princeton: Princeton University Press, 1993); J.S. Coleman, *Foundations of Social Theory* (Cambridge: Harvard University Press, 1990); S.A. Rosell et al., *Changing Maps.*

[6] See G. Selman, *Citizenship and the Adult Education Movement in Canada.*

crucial adult education task to the efforts of interested parties and the mass media, or must something further be considered?

A further dimension of the task of engaging citizens in the democratic process and in the process of social change, however, is represented by the popular education movement. Popular education has taken various forms in the present century. The term has been applied to work in Scandinavia, such as that referred to above. But the more prominent form of such work in recent decades is that which has developed in the Third World, most notably in Latin America. In many of these settings, popular education has been an instrument of forces in society that tend to be critical of constituted authority and the established order of things and to be working actively for social change. Popular education "involves a high degree of participation, recognizes mutual learning, stresses the creation of new knowledge and is directed towards social, economic or other forms of justice and democracy. It is political in its intent and has as its goal structural change."[7] Popular education "attempts to change people's attitudes and behaviours" and to equip them "to become effective in the struggle for change."[8] The popular education movement, in this latter sense, has taken various forms in Canada over the decades, most strongly, perhaps in some of the social movements which emerged in the 1960s. It is likely that the increasingly "rights-conscious" nature of Canadian society which followed from passage of the Charter and Rights and Freedoms in 1982 has also contributed to the growth of popular education.[9] The Adult Education Department and the Transformative Learning Center of the Ontario Institute for Studies in Education, in close association with the International Council for Adult Education, have been active in exploring the theoretical basis and application of popular education in Canadian society. They have been active partners as well in the North American Alliance for Popular and Adult Education, which was formed in the early 1990s.

A third major issue for adult education arising from our present situation has to do with the future of professional and other training for the "work force" of adult education. This is a most complex question in that the field is so varied, both in the nature of the setting in which the educational activities take place and also in the variety of roles performed by the educators. Some aspects of this complexity were examined in Chapter 9. Even without any expectation of things changing substantially in the future (a dubious assumption, at best), the question deserves a prominent place on the field's agenda.

---

[7] D. Clover, "Gender Transformative Learning and Environmental Action," *Gender and Education*, 7, 3 (1995) p.246.

[8] R. Arnold and B. Burke cited in D. Clover, "Gender Transformative Learning."

[9] See P. Newman, *The Canadian Revolution*; R. Gwyn, *Nationalism without Walls*.

For one thing, adult education activities are conducted by many agencies in society in addition to the traditional educational institutions. These include unions and professional associations, business and industry, large voluntary and non-profit organizations, the churches and the military, to name just a few examples. In fact, the wide variety of work situations is what led the creators of university-based professional development programs to adopt two general policies. The first was to operate degree programs in the field mainly at the graduate level, on the assumption that those wishing the training would come from other fields of activity in which they would frequently have an under-graduate qualification already. The second characteristic was that, because the students would come from such a variety of backgrounds and work situations, the curriculum would have to be a generic one. It would be impossible to create a program which was suited to the particular work situations of all comers, so the alternative was to try to determine those needs which were common to most, if not all practitioners—such things as the nature of adult learning, the program planning process, research methodologies and so on. This strategy has worked reasonably well in meeting the needs of educators, in advancing relevant research and in contributing to the enhancement of a professionalism in the field. But in the view of many it has suffered—and will do so increasingly as time goes by—from the fact that it tends to produce generalists, when what is required as the field becomes more complex are more specialists—media experts, curriculum developers, specialists in human resource development, counsellors, community and group process experts and so on. Where will these specialists come from? From other academic fields? From a co-operative effort between adult education specialists and those in these other fields of expertise? Will the training of adult educators in the future occur increasingly within the context of other fields of specialty?

A second major issue facing the field of professional training in adult education is that of the philosophical basis or context of the work. Many settings in which adult education takes place in our society are in situations where there is a strong political or philosophical basis for the work. Educators working in the labour movement, social movements of various kinds, the churches, organizations representing the interests of disadvantaged persons and other such venues, frequently have a profound commitment to the cause or purpose which they are serving. Although professional training programs tend to pay some attention to such issues, usually in "foundations" courses, it is of necessity a rapid survey of the ideological and philosophical issues and of historical examples. There are increasing signs that this is not meeting the needs of students. What can be done about this? Again, does it call for co-operative arrangements between university/college professional training departments and other sectors? Or does it point to an increasing tendency for the training of adult educators to take place "on the job" or in other departments of the educational institutions?

Finally, on the subject of training, more attention must be given to the wide variety of training needs. For many who intend to make a career in the field, the graduate degree appears to be a satisfactory qualification. But for the vast majority of those in the field, this is not the case. For most, some brief, in-service, highly relevant and applied training is what suits the situation best (and is often all that the person concerned will agree to participate in). This is frequently supplied by the employing institution, utilizing its own staff or consultants as instructors. A most encouraging and important development in the field in recent years is the increased availability of bachelor's level degree programs for adult educators. Some such programs have been with us for some decades, but there is currently a significant expansion of such work, as described in Chapter 9, and this is an important trend which presumably will continue. There is also the need for a variety of applied types of adult education training at the college level, of the one- or two-year variety. In short, with the whole field of adult education expanding in terms of its size and variety, there is, and will increasingly be, a need for a great range of training opportunities for those working in the field. Due attention must be given to the development of these various kinds of programs and to the inter-relationship among them—the co-ordination of offerings, the laddering of programs, suitable prior learning assessment and related features.

* * *

Much could be said about future prospects in the area of the methodologies of the field. This is not a major pre-occupation of the present volume, but the methodologies by their very nature are grounded in the nature of the field and have an impact on its character. Only two main points will be made briefly.

One of the most obvious trends in adult education is the increased utilization of distance education in its various forms. Most of our educational institutions and many of the ministries of education across the country are engaged in distance education, in some cases as the chief means of delivering instruction, in others as supplementary to face-to-face instruction. The technology of communication is developing at an enormous rate and has had correspondingly substantial impact on the means employed for distance education. One of the concerns about distance education is that of the isolation of the student or learner. Against the background of a society which many observers feel is also suffering from a breakdown in a sense of community and common cause, the isolating tendency of distance education methods takes on additional significance. At the time of writing, there are encouraging signs that the technology is now being utilized in such a way as to offset to some degree the isolation of the student. As on-line instruction via the home computer is growing at an astonishing pace, it is encouraging to see the ways in which the technology is being used by educators to provide a means of communication between student and teacher and among students. It may safely be predicted that this is a trend that will develop rapidly in the years ahead, in both extent and variety.

The other comment on the subject of methodology has to do with the re-emergence of the community-based small group as a setting for adult learning. The small group has always been with us, of course, since the earliest times of the modern adult education movement. There appears to have been a somewhat cyclical interest in the small group over the decades, against the background of the field which has been mainly concerned with larger groups and classes, led by a teacher in the traditional sense. In the 1930s, for instance, in the work of such projects as the Antigonish Movement and Farm and Citizens' Forum and in the widespread study group activities in the churches, we saw an upsurge of interest in the small group as a setting for adult learning. Moses Coady and Ned Corbett, in their well-known statements about the field, put particular stress on the small group as the most effective setting for learning.[10] It is probably fair to say that in the years since World War II, the small group has gone into relative decline in the overall picture of the field, the liberal arts discussions group movement and the human relations training movements notwithstanding. We may be on the brink of something of a resurgence of interest in the group, however. The "popular education" movement, which continues to grow in spite of financial and other difficulties, attaches particular importance to the small group as part of its "participatory" approach to attracting members and carrying out its educational work. And those who are looking to learning as the basis of a revival of a more meaningful democratic citizenship in our society are focussing on the local community and the small group as a setting for learning.

* * *

Adult learning and adult education have never been the "property" of adult educators or even of the broader field of education. Adult education has been a means to a great variety of ends in our society and as such has been utilized by many agencies and in many causes. One of the most interesting phenomena that have emerged since the publication of the first edition of this book, however, is the "adoption" of adult and lifelong learning by an increasing number of other fields of specialty as a necessary strategy in their work. The "language" of adult and lifelong learning has been taken up, to a degree never

---

[10] See M.M. Coady, *Masters of Their Own Destiny* (New York: Harper and Bros, 1939) & E.A. Corbett, *We Have With Us Tonight* (Toronto: Ryerson, 1957).

before experienced, by those in the fields of work force development, citizenship and social development, organizational strategies and management training.[11]

This trend raises serious and complex questions for adult educators. What is to be the relationship between the field of adult education, as we have known it, and these other fields? Will we expect those wishing expertise in fostering adult learning to "come to us"? It seems likely that something much more forthcoming and imaginative is required on the part of adult educators.

In conclusion, we point out that increasingly in recent years the focus of attention, both within Canada and internationally, has shifted from adult and lifelong "education" to adult and lifelong "learning." This is, of course, an enormously important transformation in the conceptualization of society's resources for the promotion of learning. The adult educator, in the sense we have understood the term, has an important role to play in the world of lifelong learning, but will be one of many specialists who have contributions to make.

Symptomatic of the shift to thinking in terms of learning instead of focussing on education are the documents issued by UNESCO in preparation for the Fifth International Conference on Adult Education, held in Hamburg, Germany in 1997. Although the title of the conference contained the term "adult education," the language of the documentation used the term adult and lifelong "learning." In the document entitled "Agenda for the Future," the conference organizers relied on the term "learning" almost exclusively and took some pains to explain what they referred to as an "enlarged vision of adult learning." They stated:

> Adult learning encompasses the different dimensions of life and human agency: at the workplace, in the community and in the individual sphere, for the benefit of society and for individual enrichment andgrowth. Learning throughout life cannot be uni-dimensional: a balance has to be found between work, social and community life and personal development, so that people can learn to know, to do, to live together, to be, to become and to create a synergy between all these experiences.[12]

As Jacques Delors has pointed out in his introductory essay to the recent UNESCO report, *Learning: The Treasure Within*, education is not a panacea for the world's ills, but it is "one of the principal means available to foster a deeper and more harmonious form of human development."[13]

---

[11] R.D. Putnam, *Making Democracy Work*; P.M. Senge, *The Fifth Discipline* (New York: Doubleday, 1990); S.A. Rosell et al., *Changing Maps*; D.P. Keating in Rosell, *Changing Maps*.

[12] UNESCO, "Draft of 'Agenda for the Future,'" issued by conference organizers "to start an open dialogue" leading up to the Fifth International Conference on Adult Education, 1996.

[13] UNESCO, *Learning: The Treasure* Within, Report of the International Commission on Education for the Twenty-First Century (Paris: UNESCO, 1996) p.13.

Index